THE IMPACT OF EC ENVIRONMENTAL LAW IN THE UNITED KINGDOM

Edited by

Jane Holder

Lecturer in Law, University College London

CENTRE FOR THE LAW OF THE EUROPEAN UNION

JOHN WILEY & SONS

Chichester · New York · Weinheim · Brisbane · Singapore · Toronto

Copyright © 1997 by John Wiley & Sons Ltd,
Baffins Lane, Chichester,
West Sussex PO19 1UD, England

National 01243 779777
International (+44) 1243 779777
e-mail (for orders and customer service enquiries):
cs-books@wiley.co.uk
Visit our Home Page on http://www.wiley.co.uk
or http://www.wiley.com

Other Wiley Editorial Offices

John Wiley & Sons, Inc., 605 Third Avenue,
New York, NY 10158–0012, USA

WILEY-VCH Verlag GmbH, Pappelallee 3,
D-69469 Weinheim, Germany

Jacaranda Wiley Ltd, 33 Park Road, Milton,
Queensland 4064, Australia

John Wiley & Sons (Asia) Pte Ltd, 2 Clementi Loop #02–01,
Jin Xing Distripark, Singapore 129809

John Wiley & Sons (Canada) Ltd, 22 Worcester Road,
Rexdale, Ontario M9W 1L1, Canada

Library of Congress Cataloging-in-Publication Data

The impact of EC environmental law in the United Kingdom/edited by
Jane Holder
     p. cm.
   "Centre for the Law of the European Union."
   Includes bibliographical references and index.
   ISBN 0–471–97535–4 (cloth)
   1. Environmental law – European Union countries. 2. European
Union – Great Britain. I. Holder, Jane. II. University College,
London. Centre for the Law of the European Union.
   KJE6242.I48   1997
   341.7′62′094–dc21   97–9286
                                                                            CIP

British Library Cataloguing in Publication Data

A catalogue record for this book is available from the British Library

ISBN 0–471–97535–4

Phototypeset in 10/12 pt Baskerville by Intype London Ltd
Printed and bound in Great Britain by Bookcraft (Bath) Ltd, Midsomer Norton,
Somerset

This book is printed on acid-free paper responsibly manufactured from sustainable
forestation, for which at least two trees are planted for each one used for paper
production.

THE IMPACT OF EC ENVIRONMENTAL LAW IN THE UNITED KINGDOM

Wiley Series in
EUROPEAN LAW

Barnard/EC Employment Law, Revised Edition
0–471–93917–X 500 Pages

Burrows/European Social Law
0–471–96537–5 480 Pages

Emiliou/The European Union and World Trade Law
0–471–95552–3 390 Pages

Caiger/1996 Onwards: Lowering the Barriers Further
0–471–95768–2 300 Pages

Cross/Electric Utility Regulation in the European Union
0–471–95793–3 350 Pages

Ehlermann/Proceedings of the European Competition Forum
0–471–96668–1 248 Pages

Farr/Harmonisation of Technical Standards, Second Edition
0–471–95926–X 400 Pages

Goyder/EC Distribution Law, Second Edition
0–471–96122–1 350 Pages

Hervey/Sex Equality Law in the European Union
0–471–96436–0 400 Pages

Yaqub/European Travel Law
0–471–94354–1 800 Pages

Forthcoming titles

Kaye/European Case Law on the Judgments Convention
0–471–94089–5 512 Pages

IN MEMORY OF SIMON BALL

This book is dedicated to the memory of Simon Ball. Simon's work in environmental law drew the discipline together and gave it a much needed identity. His clear exposition, insights, and appreciation of the broader picture will be very much missed by academics, practitioners, and students alike.

Simon set a very high standard for teaching and researching environmental law. He also made time for supporting projects and conferences, and, as an encouraging and precise external examiner for the University of London, made an invaluable contribution to its LLM course on United Kingdom environmental law and policy.

Simon had substantially completed his chapter, 'Has the UK government implemented the Habitats Directive properly?', at the time of his death. We thank Simon's partner, Frances Wells, and Colin Reid for their help in ensuring that Simon's chapter is published.

CONTENTS

CONTRIBUTORS

Ian Bache, Department of Politics, University of Sheffield, Elmfield, Northumberland Road, Sheffield S10 2TU

Simon Ball, formerly Senior Lecturer in Law, Law School, University of Sheffield

Tom Burns, Lecturer in Law, School of Law, University of Strathclyde, Stenhouse Building, 173 Cathedral St, Glasgow G4 0RG

Judge David Edward, Court of Justice of the European Communities, L-2925 Luxembourg

Sue Elworthy, Research Associate, School of Public Administration and Law, The Robert Gordon University, Kings Street, Aberdeen

David Freestone, Legal Advisor, Environmental Affairs, The World Bank, 1818 H Street NW, Washington DC 20433, USA

Laurence Gormley, Professor of Law, Department of European and Economic Law, Rijks Universiteit Groningen, Postbus 716, 9700 Groningen, Netherlands.

Chris Hilson, Lecturer in Law, Department of Law, Old Whiteknights House University of Reading, PO Box 217, Whiteknights, Reading RG6 2AH

Jane Holder, Lecturer in Law, Centre for the Law of the European Union, Faculty of Laws, University College London, Bentham House, Endsleigh Gardens, London WCIH OEG

Ludwig Krämer, Head of Legal Services, European Commission, DGXI.E.3—BU 2/167, 200 rue de la Loi, B-1049 Brussels, Belgium

Donald McGillivray, Lecturer in Law, School of Law, University of Kent, Canterbury CT2 7NP

Owen McIntyre, Lecturer in Law, Faculty of Law, Mansfield Cooper Building, University of Manchester, Oxford Road, Manchester M13 9PL

Francis McManus, Lecturer in Law, Department of Law, Napier University, Sighthill Court, Edinburgh EH11 4BN

Richard Macrory, Professor of Environmental Law, Denton Hall Environment Law and Management Group, Imperial College, 48 Prince's Gardens, London SW7 2PE

Karen Morrow, Lecturer in Law, Faculty and School of Law, Queen's University, Belfast BT7 1NN

Michael Purdue, Professor of Law, School of Law, City University, Northampton Square, London EC1V 0HB

Ray Purdy, Research Associate, Denton Hall Environment Law and Management Group, Imperial College, 48 Prince's Gardens, London SW7 2PE

Colin Reid, Professor of Law, Department of Law, University of Dundee, Dundee DD1 4HN

Joanne Scott, Lecturer in Law, School of Law, Queen Mary and Westfield College, Mile End Road, London E1 4NS

William Sheate, Research Associate, Denton Hall Environment Law and Management Group, Imperial College, 48 Prince's Gardens, London SW7 2PE

Han Somsen, Lecturer in Law, Faculty of Law, Catholic University of Nijmegan, PO Box 9049, 6500 KK Nijmegan, Netherlands

Sharon Turner, Lecturer in Law, Faculty and School of Law, Queen's University, Belfast BT7 1NN

Lynda M Warren, Professor of Law, Department of Law, The University of Wales, Hugh Owen Building, Penglais, Aberystwyth SY23 3DY

John Zetter, Divisional Manager International Planning and Research 4/E1 Eland House, Bressenden Place, London SW1E 5DU

FOREWORD

The protection of the environment by EC law has thrown up a range of new legal problems. Initially, they stemmed from the absence of any express provision in the founding Treaties for environmental policy or legislation. This reflected the relative unimportance, from a political point of view, of environmental issues at the time when those Treaties were drafted. In the absence of a text, it fell to the European Court of Justice to resolve questions as to the appropriate legal base for legislative measures and the extent to which environmental considerations could override one of the fundamental principles of the European Economic Community Treaty, the free movement of goods.

Following amendment of the Treaty by the Single European Act and the Treaty on European Union, the debate has now moved on considerably. Now, the principles of subsidiarity, preventive action and sustainable development and the precautionary principle all provide scope for litigation and will, no doubt, create further novel legal problems.

One continuing concern is the effectiveness of judicial protection. Before national courts, the issue is focused particularly on the 'direct effect' of environmental legislation. Before the Court of First Instance and the European Court of Justice, the problem is frequently one of the *locus standi* of private litigants to bring actions at all.

The effectiveness of environmental legislation before national courts may be called into question in two respects. First, the Member States have a poor record of implementation of environmental directives. The European Court of Justice has already handed down 60 judgments regarding the failure of Member States to fulfil environmental obligations, and a further 15 cases are currently pending. Secondly, the Court's jurisprudence on direct effect is not readily transposable to the general and sometimes vague concepts used in environmental legislation. So direct effect has not, to date, been the formidable weapon to litigants in the implementation of environmental legislation that it has in other fields such as competition and social law.

This has been due, in particular, to the fact that many environmental directives are designed to protect the environment generally rather than to 'create individual rights which national courts must protect' (the terminology of *Van*

Gend en Loos). Advocate General Elmer recently suggested that the Court should adopt a wide and purposive interpretation of the Environmental Assessment Directive (Council Directive 85/33/EEC) in order to find the requisite nexus for direct effect (Opinion of 26 March 1996 in Case C-72/95, *Kraaijeveld*, judgment of 26 October 1996, not yet reported). The Court did not follow this approach. However, it held that, even while the Directive gives Member States a degree of discretion in setting thresholds for environmental impact assessments, the courts can set aside national legislation that goes beyond the limits of that discretion. This is not 'direct effect' in the traditional sense and it would perhaps be as well to find another formula in order to avoid confusion.

Before the Community Courts, natural and legal persons may institute proceedings only against Community acts which affect them directly and individually. Although the rigour of the European Court of Justice's test of *locus standi* has been mitigated to a limited degree in recent jurisprudence, particularly in relation to competition, dumping and state aids, the test remains restrictive and Article 173 is far from offering an *actio popularis* for the protection of the environment. This has been demonstrated very recently by two Orders of the Court of First Instance.

In Case T-583/93, *Greenpeace and Others* v. *Commission* [1995] ECR II-2205 (currently under appeal to the Court of Justice as Case C-321/95P *Greenpeace*, OJ C 315 25.11.95, p. 12), three environmental associations and 16 local residents sought to annul a Commission grant of financial assistance from the European Regional Development Fund to the Kingdom of Spain for the building of two power stations in the Canary Islands. The invitation to the Court of First Instance to adopt a liberal approach and to recognise their interest in the protection of the environment was rejected. The Court held that the factual situation of the 16 individuals was not substantially distinct from those of all the people who live or pursue an economic activity in the areas concerned. Similarly, the three environmental associations could not rely on the standing of their individual members and, since they had not participated in any Commission procedure prior to the decision, there were no 'special circumstances' to give them *locus standi*. This reasoning was followed in the *French Polynesia* case (T-219/95R *Danielsson and Others* v. *Commission* [1995] ECR II-3051), where three residents of Tahiti sought, in essence, to suspend the French nuclear tests on the atoll of Mururoa in 1995 for breach of Article 34 of the Euratom Treaty, which requires additional health and safety measures for particularly dangerous nuclear experiments.

The problem of enforcing environmental legislation before the courts is, of course, already well known in the legal systems of the Member States, and the cross-fertilisation of ideas and principles between the national and Community legal orders is rarely more marked than in this field. But it is important to recognise that, underlying these legal debates, there is a permanent tension between the political, social and economic advantages of, on the one hand, projects that provide employment, energy and amenities for the present generation and, on the other hand, protection of the environment for future generations.

Judges cannot, and should not, be expected to make political, social and economic choices. But legal rules and procedures can at least help to ensure that such choices are made in an objective, transparent and unemotional way. Books such as this help, in their turn, to promote a greater understanding of the advantages and limitations of existing and proposed rules and procedures and, consequently, a more informed debate.

Judge David Edward
CMG, QC, LLB, FRSE
Court of Justice of the European Communities

ACKNOWLEDGEMENTS

I would like to thank David O'Keeffe and Margot Horspool at the Centre for the Law of the European Union, University College London, for their continued support and inspiration. Eva Evans made the conference, and therefore this book, possible, and my greatest thanks go to her. Thanks also to Chris Loweth and Paul Osborne who worked so hard to make sure that the references are as accurate as possible.

The contributors to this book have made the editing process a joy: I have learnt much and made important links with colleagues working on European Community environmental law in other academic institutions, policy research groups and government. Above all, considerable thanks are due to those contributors who submitted their papers on time, and even early. Several chapters were written early in 1996. As far as possible, these contributors have taken into account changes to the law since. At times, however, the law has proved to be a moving target, which suggests that there is still much valuable work to do in the future.

Jane Holder
February 1997

TABLES

Cases by Country

Cases before the European Court

Acts by Country

Statutory Instruments (UK)

European Treaties and Annexed Acts

EC Decisions

EC Directives

EC Regulations

EC Recommendations and Resolutions

EC Documents

EC Proposed Legislation

International Agreements and Conventions

Part I

CURRENT ISSUES

Chapter 1

INTRODUCTION

Jane Holder

Articles 130r, s, and t of the EC Treaty represent the engagement of two major legal and political projects of the second half of the twentieth century: European integration and environmental protection. The aim of this book is to assess the impact of these movements in the United Kingdom. It also offers an opportunity to consider the extent of cross-fertilisation of principles, ideas, and legal arguments between different areas of EC law. The 'impact' of EC law is treated as one part of a wider scheme of its effectiveness, embracing also implementation, enforcement, and compliance,[1] although some authors have contributed their own interpretation of its meaning. What is meant by *environmental* law is more open to discussion, particularly in the light of the concerted effort of some contributors to expand the boundaries of the discipline to take in aspects of public health, and animal welfare.

The book originated in a conference on the impact of EC environmental law in the United Kingdom, held at the Centre for the Law of the European Union, University College London in November 1995, and chaired by Judge David Edward of the Court of Justice of the European Communities. The consensus of the conference was that the influence of EC environmental law may be seen in most areas of environmental policy and law in the United Kingdom and that national law and policy making on the environment takes place within parameters set by the European Union. From this perspective, EC environmental law begins to look less like a *sui generis*, legal category and more like a constituent part of the legal foundation of the European Union. This accords also with the sense that the nature of environmental problems means that environmental protection must form part of a wider range of policies and law. Nevertheless, there was also agreement that the enforcement of EC environmental law remains problematic, at least when viewed from a European perspective. The gap between the process of Europeanisation of environmental law on the one hand,

---

[1] Following Snyder, 'The Effectiveness of European Community Law: Institutions, Processes, Tools and Techniques' (1993) 56 MLR 19–54, at 19.

and the laggardly implementation of the law on the other, is taken up and explored by many of the contributors.

Environmental law highlights particularly well the integration of what have become Community norms with national law, policy, and legal culture. We find from a number of contributions that the process of influence is not one-way; EC environmental law, particularly that on nature conservation, has been influenced by British environmental law because of the latter's long history and the strength of administrative practice and culture. Of importance is whether EC environmental law has been accommodated in existing United Kingdom legal regimes without being fundamentally compromised. A common finding is that EC law often has quite different effects from those anticipated or aimed for. This contraflow of norms and legal influences makes the process of implementation all the more fascinating. Added to this is the significance of international environmental law on EC and national environmental law. Discussion on the influences and impacts which bear on United Kingdom environmental law therefore inevitably extends beyond the scope of the Euro-pean Union.

The book is divided into six parts. Part I on the development and current state of EC environmental law provides a framework. Ludwig Krämer reviews recent developments, giving an insider's view of the workings of the European Commission. He cites the increased use of voluntary and economic mechanisms in EC environmental law as giving credence to a view of environmental law as shaped by a modernist, or reformist, agenda. Richard Macrory and Ray Purdy address the pervasive problem of enforcement, their main concerns being the relative effectiveness of formal and informal enforcement mechanisms available to the European Commission, and the discretion granted to Member States by environmental directives. They present valuable research on the enforcement of EC environmental law against the Member States which reveals more sketchy enforcement than is usually portrayed. This reality of enforcement is counter-poised with the rhetoric of rights in Chris Hilson's chapter on the legal status and enforceability of Community environmental rights. The place of policy (and politics) in law is in the background throughout Part I, but this is seen particularly in Karen Morrow and Sharon Turner's chapter on the state and process of implementation of EC environmental law in Northern Ireland. As this and subsequent chapters show, the process of implementation varies con-siderably between England, Wales, Scotland, and Northern Ireland.

Part II comprises chapters on the impact on UK environmental law and policy of a triumvirate of principles of EC environmental law—subsidiarity, precaution, and proportionality. It is by such principles that certain social values (including environmental protection) are absorbed into law.[2] In the case of the principle of subsidiarity, political expediency also plays a part. Notwithstanding the apparent wholesale acceptance of the principles in policy statements, their legal status

---

[2] Smith, 'How Law Hides Risk', in Teubner, *Environmental Law and Ecological Responsibility* (Chichester: Wiley, 1994), p. 135.

remains uncertain. With regard to subsidiarity, David Freestone and Han Somsen assess the likely future structure of EC environmental law in the light of some of the new 'subsidiarity directives': the proposed directive on the ecological quality of water[3], a proposed directive on ambient air quality[4] and Directive 96/61/EC on integrated pollution prevention and control[5]. Owen McIntyre examines the case law relating to the principle of proportionality which, similarly to subsidiarity, has wider application than environmental law. He concludes that the principle is a central consideration for decision-makers at Community and national level and for any party contemplating a challenge to environmental measures which they view as onerous or burdensome. In my chapter on the precautionary principle, I ask whether its legal effect is to impose an obligation on Member States so that activities of the Member States may be judged in its light. The answer currently given by the British courts, and also the European Court of Justice, is a resounding 'no'. Acceptance of the precautionary principle therefore remains at the level of policy statements which are not enforceable by individuals and may be given such weight as a decision-maker thinks appropriate. Discussion in this Part raises the possibility of the judicial creation of a workable hierarchy of these principles with, perhaps, the prospect of subsidiarity trumping the others.

The integrated nature of pollutants and environmental problems is reflected in the cross-sectoral nature of much EC law on the environment; this, for example, is the defining characteristic of Directive 85/337/EEC[6] on environmental assessment and Directive 90/313/EEC[7] on freedom of access to environmental information. In recognition of this, the book does not offer a comprehensive assessment of legal impacts on different environmental media but rather, in Parts III, IV and V, discusses the development of different regulatory techniques to achieve environmental protection, directed by European law and policy, in particular areas of interest—pollution control, nature conservation, and land use and development. The boundaries between these different areas of environmental law are now so fluid that there is considerable cross-referencing between the chapters in these Parts.

Disciplinary boundaries similarly hinder research on the environment. The benefits to be gained from collaboration with colleagues from disciplines other than law become clear on reading Ian Bache and Donald McGillivray's chapter in which they measure a political theory of legal implementation against the practice of implementing Directive 778/80/EEC[8] on the quality of drinking water. This approach leads to a broad assessment of the impacts of the Directive, including the arrangement of policy networks, the empowerment of cam-

---

[3] OJ 1994 C 22, p. 6.
[4] OJ 1995 C 238, p. 10.
[5] Directive 96/61 EC integrated pollution prevention and control (IPPC) OJ 1996 L 257, 10.8.1996.
[6] Directive 85/337/EEC on the assessment of the effects of certain public and private projects on the environment, OJ 1985 L 175, p. 40.
[7] Directive 90/313/EEC on freedom of access to environmental information, OJ 1990 L 158, p. 5.
[8] Directive 778/80/EEC on the quality of drinking water, OJ 1980 L 229, p. 11.

paigning groups, and media attention in the form of a moral panic on drinking water quality. Last, but not least, is the changing constitutional-legal role of the European Commission. In Part III, two hitherto neglected areas of environmental law—marine and coastal water protection, and noise pollution—are brought into the fold. In examining the state of implementation and practical effects of the Bathing Water, Urban Waste Water, and Habitats Directives, Lynda Warren broadens the scope of water pollution and conservation law and examines also the highly topical issue of the environmental impact of shipping. In their chapter on noise law, Francis McManus and Tom Burns assess the impact of a 'people-centred' approach to noise pollution and highlight the nature of a predominantly urban environmental problem.

Nature conservation is the subject of Part IV. Colin Reid provides a panorama of EC conservation law and its implementation in the United Kingdom in a manner which puts the recent implementation of Directive 92/43/EEC on the conservation of natural habitats and of wild fauna and flora perfectly into perspective. Simon Ball focuses on the implementation of this Directive, concluding that its absorption into the existing regime of protection for Sites of Special Scientific Interest represents a minimalist approach to achieving the Directive's aims. The standard of protection given by the Directive has been translated into a lesser standard because of the philosophy of voluntariness which underpins the Sites of Special Scientific Interest system. Both chapters underline the economic imperatives of EC environmental law. This is seen particularly clearly in the *Lappel Bank*[9] litigation concerning the application of Directive 79/409/EEC on the conservation of wild birds[10] in which there were different legal responses to economic considerations in British courts and the European Court of Justice.

The broad theme of Part V is land use. Michael Purdue proves that, although the Community has only recently been granted a mandate of sorts in matters of town and country planning, the impact of EC law in this area has been considerable, ranging over waste law, pollution control, nature conservation, freedom of access to environmental information, and, of course, environmental assessment. With regard to the last, John Zetter continues the discussion by posing the question (provocatively, given his position in the Department of the Environment) 'Has Directive 85/337 had an impact?'. In responding to this he traces the slow filling in of gaps in the original implementing legislation and stresses that the process of amending UK legislation to accord with the Directive continues. He brings the saga of implementation up to date with news of negotiations leading to the Directive's amendment and assesses the prospects of UK law conforming with these. William Sheate takes a step further by looking at the likelihood of environmental assessment being expanded to encompass the assessment of policies. Having reviewed the failure of proposals for strategic

---

[9] Case C-44/95, *R* v. *Secretary of State for the Environment, ex parte the Royal Society for the Protection of Birds* [1997] 2 WLR 123.
[10] Directive 79/409/EEC on the conservation of wild birds OJ 1979 L 103, p. 79.

environmental assessment in the past he predicts that advances in environmental policy appraisal will take place ouside the Community's legislative framework.

The tension between various Community policy aims becomes clear when an environmental perspective is adopted; nowhere more so than in the case of the BSE crisis, and free movement of goods law (including live animals), discussed in Part VI in chapters by Laurence Gormley, and Sue Elworthy, and in the case of the environmental impacts of the Community's regional development policy, examined by Joanne Scott. The two last chapters take the reader on 'legal trips' from Brussels to South Uist in the Outer Hebrides, and from Rio de Janeiro to Inverness and the Cairn Gorms. The chapters in this Part also locate the principles of subsidiarity, precaution, and proportionality in a practical framework of risk assessment, trans-European trade, and financial assistance.

As we await the first successful case on direct effect of an environmental directive, the next tranche of enforcement actions brought by the European Commission for infringement of EC environmental directives, and the first round of legislation amended to accord with the dictates of subsidiarity, it is hoped that this book will provide a forum for collective reflection and assessment on the progress and influence so far of EC environmental law in the United Kingdom.

Chapter 2

RECENT DEVELOPMENTS IN EC ENVIRONMENTAL LAW

Ludwig Krämer

The notion of 'recent developments' is not very precise. For the purposes of this chapter it will be taken to cover the years 1991 to 1995–96, a period which is marked by considerable changes in legal trends at EC level: the Maastricht Treaty on European Union was adopted and entered into effect; there was extensive discussion on subsidiarity—practically, on the question whether there should be more areas left to national environmental legislation and decision-making; the Fifth EC Environmental Action Programme was approved and put into operation; Austria, Sweden and Finland joined the Community; and unemployment within the EC reached peak figures, which made, in numerous cases, environmental concerns of subordinate importance.

Since 1 January 1991 the EC adopted, in the environmental sector, 30 pieces of legislation (regulations or directives). This figure is in marked contrast with figures quoted in particular by some legal writers, such as, for instance Haigh,[1] which are sometimes used to illustrate—and criticise—the amount of legislative activity of the EC. The main reasons for this difference are:

- The present chapter does not include regulations or directives which amend existing regulations or directives, or which adapt them to technical progress; the reason for this is that such legislation normally is of limited importance.
- It is always arguable what is 'environmental' legislation; Haigh is very broad in his approach and includes numerous measures in the area of worker protection, internal market and nuclear safety. The approach in this chapter is considerably narrower and is limited to measures which have an environmental content.

---

[1] N. Haigh, *Manual of Environmental Policy: The EC and Britain*, 3rd release (London: Longman, 1996), Appendix I.

- Haigh mentions every measure, such as for instance the criteria for the award of an eco-label for paper tissues. Such a decision is considered here as part of the monitoring of the Eco-labelling Regulation.
- The decisions to ratify international environmental conventions are not mentioned in this chapter. Indeed, these conventions, when ratified, are neither monitored nor enforced by Community institutions.

As regards proposed legislation, there have been, since 1991, 13 proposals for directives and regulations. Furthermore, eight communications or Green Papers have been made in the environmental sector.

Since 1993, the Commission announces and publishes its annual legislative programme. Reference to announced legislation is therefore made to the years 1993 to 1996. In contrast to that, the announcements made in the Fifth Environmental Action Programme have not been systematically examined, since they are of a less precise nature and do not constitute a formal commitment to submit draft legislation to the Council and the European Parliament. It is obvious that trends in environmental law are not limited to legislative activities or to communications. Thus, for instance, the Court of Justice has issued, between 1991 and 1995, some judgments which have had, overall, a very considerable influence on EC legislation, policy makers, individuals and economic operators.[2] Also, national and international events, such as the Rio-Conference on the environment, the Chernobyl accident, the Brent Spar incident, and national environmental legislation may have considerable influence on EC environmental law. However, these latter elements will not be examined here.

General trends

Deregulation

The most striking feature of EC environmental legislation over the last five years is the significant decrease of the legislative activity at EC level. The following table shows an obvious trend:

---

[2] See for instance Court of Justice, Case C-157/89, *Commission* v. *Italy* [1991] ECR 57; Case C-131/88, *Commission* v. *Germany* [1991] ECR I-825; Case C-57/89, *Commission* v. *Germany* [1991] ECR I-883; Case C-300/89, *Commission* v. *Council* [1991] ECR I-2867; Case C-70/88, *European Parliament* v. *Council* [1991] ECR I-4529; Case C-190/90, *Commission* v. *Netherlands* [1992] ECR I-3265; Case C-2/90, *Commission* v. *Belgium* [1992] I-4431; Case C-337/89, *Commission* v. *United Kingdom* [1992] ECR I-6103; Case C-155/91, *Commission* v. *Council* [1993] ECR I-939; Case C-56/90, *Commission* v. *United Kingdom* [1993] ECR I-4109; Case C-355/90, *Commission* v. *Spain* [1993] ECR I-4221; Case C-41/93, *France* v. *Commission* [1994] ECR I-1829; Case C-187/93, *European Parliament* v. *Council* [1994] ECR I-2857; Case C-422/92, *Commission* v. *Germany* [1995] ECR I-1097; Case C-431/92, *Commission* v. *Germany* [1995] ECR I-2189.

	Adopted directives/ regulations	Proposed directives/ regulations	Announced directives/ regulations
1991	10	1	
1992	8	2 (1 amendment)	
1993	6	3 (1 amendment)	
1994	5	4 (2 amendments)	
1995	1	3 (2 amendments)	
1996 (30 April)	—	—	

a marked reduction of environmental legislation and proposals. It will be seen in the discussion below of the EC's different legal measures that the reduction in quantity went in parallel with a reduction in intensity of environmental measures.

In contrast to that, the number of communications has reached levels which were never reached before. Communications—sometimes in the form of a green paper—present a specific problem to the Council and the European Parliament, without committing the Commission to submit concrete proposals. Sometimes, they announce future proposals; sometimes they seem to replace proposals. Legally, Commission communications have no value; they are of a political nature and are therefore mentioned here only in order to illustrate the substitution of legislative action by (political) declarations. Indeed, it cannot be seen that the communications published so far significantly influenced the legal reality. Even their informative character and effect is limited.

The evolution of adopted and proposed legislation and of communications is all the more 'surprising' as Council's Resolution on the Fifth Environmental Action Programme had stated that profound modifications of production, consumption and behaviour patterns were necessary; that many forms of the (then) present economic activity were not sustainable; and that more ambitious policies and strategies were necessary at Community level.[3]

In its progress report on the Fifth Environmental Action Programme, the Commission stated:

Until the Fifth Programme, environmental policy was overwhelmingly a matter of attacking a problem with legislation. Whilst the approach satisfied some, it was not fully effective and there is a recognition of the need to simplify regulations and make them more coherent. Regulations helped resolve some problems but it brought about the realisation that there were issues which could not be successfully treated in this way and which therefore needed other instruments to complement the command and control approach.[4]

Other instruments are thus seen to 'complement' regulations. The Fifth Environmental Action Programme identified as such instruments:

---

[3] Council Resolution of 1 February 1993, OJ 1993 C 138, p. 1.
[4] European Commission, *Progress Report on the Implementation of the Fifth Action Programme*, COM(95) 624 final, 10 January 1996.

- taxes and levies;
- fiscal measures of encouragement;
- state aids;
- environmental audits;
- environmental civil liability.

As regards taxes and levies, the proposal on a carbon dioxide–energy tax[5] met fundamental criticism by the United Kingdom and is therefore politically dead; at best there will be an EC measure which invites or recommends Member States to introduce such a tax—if they so wish. That is the situation at the time of writing: one can hardly talk of a 'new' instrument. No other tax and levy measures have been proposed or are in preparation. However, in 1996 the Commission sent a communication to the other institutions on national taxes and levies.[6]

As regards fiscal measures of encouragement, no measures have been taken or suggested. The Commission has pointed out 'that the business community has shown resistance arguing, inter alia, about the need to concentrate on real environmental objectives, to guarantee fiscal neutrality and to ensure a level playing field with competitors within and outside the European Union'.[7] On state aids, the Commission adopted, in 1993, guidelines on 'state aids for environmental protection', which replaced earlier guidelines.[8] It is not apparent that the practice of Member States, existing until then, has significantly been influenced by these new guidelines. In particular, state aids are used by some Member States only and are fixed according to national preferences, priorities or needs, which often are more of an economic than ecological character.[9]

Environmental audits are regulated by Regulation 1836/93/EEC[10] which makes the participation of industrial companies to such a system voluntary. Until now, such eco-audits seemed slowly to find acceptance with larger companies in Northern Europe, while France and the southern Member States remain rather distrustful of this new instrument.

Environmental civil liability measures have not been suggested. There is a Green Paper on this question[11] and an announcement that there would be, in 1995, a communication on a framework system for environmental liability.[12]

Furthermore, no negotiated agreements—contracts between economic operators and public authorities, whereby economic operators oblige themselves to

---

[5] Proposal for a directive on a carbon dioxide–energy tax, OJ 1992 C 196, p. 1.
[6] European Commission, Environmental taxes and charges in the single market COM (97) 9 of 29.1.1997.
[7] *Ibid.*
[8] European Commission, Guidelines on state aids for environmental protection, OJ 1994 C 72, p. 3.
[9] See Krämer, 'Die Integrierung umweltpolitischer Erfordernisse in die gemeinschaftliche Wettbewerbspolitik', in Rengeling, *Umweltschutz und andere Politiken der Europäischen Gemeinschaft* (Köln-Berlin-Bonn-München: 1993), pp. 47 *et seq.*
[10] Regulation 1836/93 allowing voluntary participation by companies in the industrial sector in a Community eco-management and audit scheme, OJ 1993 L 168, p. 1.
[11] European Commission, Green Paper on remedying environmental damage, OJ 1993 C 149, p. 12.
[12] European Commission, work programme 1995, OJ 1995 C 225, at p. 26.

adopt this or that attitude or to take or omit this or that measure—have been fully developed at EC level, although a communication on this subject was made in 1996.[13]

In conclusion, it can be stated that the diminution of the number of directives or regulations adopted or proposed has not had as a consequence an increase of the number of other instruments. There are simply fewer environmental measures suggested, discussed and adopted at EC level. In contrast, more discussion papers have been published or announced.

Departure from the level playing field

What is striking about the adopted and announced legislation is the marked tendency not to fix any more common environmental standards. This trend has developed over a number of years, but has certainly become more marked during the last five years. Its most remarkable expression is the Directive on integrated pollution prevention and control (IPPC).[14] This provides that for industrial installations the emission limit values are, as a rule, fixed at the level of individual installations and that best available technologies must be used, though economic circumstances—probably those of the company in question—are to be taken into consideration.

Practically, this approach will lead to the fixing of emission values no longer at EC level or national level—though Member States could do this—but at local level. One might anticipate attempts to fix such levels as low as possible, in order to create competitive advantages for the individual company.

This approach is in marked contrast to the approaches which Directive 76/464/EEC[15] had chosen for discharges of toxic, persistent, or bioaccumulable contaminants into waters; it also contrasts markedly to the approach of Directive 84/360/EEC[16] which provided, for air contaminants and specific industrial installations, the fixing of EC-wide emission standards.

At present, the IPPC approach is generally praised as the model for future legislation. This is to some extent based on a linguistic confusion: indeed, the 'integrated' approach only means that a specific piece of regulation deals with all emissions into the environment, thus air emissions, water discharges, waste generation, noise emissions etc. This approach has been followed since the 1980s and found its expression for instance in Directive 87/217/EEC on asbestos.[17] However, it does not say anything about whether emission values are fixed at local or at EC level.

The departure from fixing values at EC level can be observed everywhere.

---

[13] European Commission, Environmental Agreements COM (96) 561 final, of 27 November 1966.
[14] Directive 96/61/EC on integrated pollution prevention and control (OJ L 257 10.8.96).
[15] Directive 76/464/EEC on pollution caused by certain dangerous substances discharged into the aquatic environment of the Community, OJ 1976 L 129, p. 23.
[16] Directive 84/360/EEC on the combating of air pollution from industrial plants, OJ 1984 L 188, p. 20.
[17] Directive 87/217/EEC on the prevention and reduction of environmental pollution by asbestos, OJ 1987 L 85, p. 40.

The proposal on the ecological quality of water[18] invites Member States to fix quality objectives, without giving any value—emission limit or quality objective—itself. The announced framework proposal for water[19] is to follow the same pattern. The proposal for a directive on ambient air quality[20] also omits to fix values. Directive 91/156/EEC[21] obliges Member States to establish waste management plans 'as soon as possible', no longer—as under Directive 75/442/EEC[22]—within two years, etc.

Of course, product-related directives, which are based on Article 100a of the EC Treaty, continue to fix numeric values; the best example are the different directives on car emissions.[23] However, this rather confirms the above-made assertion, since these product-related directives are made to establish and organise the internal market. Where environmental aspects play a more dominant role, even product-related directives based on Article 100a become less precise. Examples are Directive 94/62/EEC on packaging:[24] Member States must fix targets for the recovery of packaging waste, which are between 15% and 60%; however, where they find recovery possibilities in other Member States or in third countries, they may go beyond these fixed targets; or Directive 92/112/EEC[25] which fixes targets for banning discharges to the sea from the titanium dioxide industry within specific time-limits, but allows Member States to anticipate these dates.

Other trends in environmental legislation

Increase in transparency

A number of EC measures undertake to increase transparency on environmental issues. Access to environmental information was generally made possible through Directive 90/313/EEC;[26] as regards the EC level, this directive was completed, in 1993/94, by a Council and a Commission decision to give access to Community documents.[27] Directive 91/692/EEC[28] intends to rationalise and

---

[18] Proposal for a directive on the ecological quality of water, OJ 1994 C 222, p. 6.
[19] European Commission, Communication on a European Community water policy, COM(96) 59 final of 21 February 1996, p. 17.
[20] Proposal for a directive on the quality of air, OJ 1994 C 216, p. 4; amended OJ 1995 C 238, p. 10.
[21] Directive 91/156/EEC amending Directive 75/442/EEC on waste, OJ 1991 L 78, p. 32.
[22] Directive 75/442/EEC on waste, OJ 1975 L 194, p. 39.
[23] See Directives 91/441/EEC, OJ 1991 L 242, p. 1; 93/59/EEC, OJ 1993 L 186, p. 21; 94/12/EEC, OJ 1994 L 100, p. 42.
[24] Directive 94/62/EEC on packaging and packaging waste, OJ 1994 L 365, p. 10.
[25] Directive 92/112/EEC on waste from the titanium dioxide industry, OJ 1992 L 409, p. 11.
[26] Directive 90/313/EEC on the freedom of access to environmental information, OJ 1990 L 158, p. 56.
[27] Council Decision 93/731/EEC on access to Council documents, OJ 1993 L 340, p. 43; Commission Decision 94/90/ECSC/EC/Euratom on access to Commission documents, OJ 1994 L 46, p. 58.
[28] Directive 91/692/EEC on the standardisation and rationalisation of implementation reports, OJ 1992 L 377, p. 48.

standardise Member States' reports on the implementation of environmental directives.

Another way of increasing transparency is the improvement of information on products and on companies' performance. As regards products, an eco-label was set up at EC level[29] which intends to inform consumers on environmental performances of products in order to allow them to choose environmentally friendly products. Regulation 2092/91/EEC[30] follows a similar idea, since it fixes conditions for organic agriculture and allows products which come from such a production to bear the indication 'organic'.

Directive 92/32/EEC[31] introduces an EC symbol 'dangerous for the environment' for chemical substances; for chemical preparations, a similar directive is in preparation. Directive 91/157/EEC[32] introduces a label for batteries which contain certain dangerous substances, thus informing the consumer of the necessity to dispose of the battery separately. Finally, Regulation 1836/93/EEC[33] is to be mentioned which creates an EC system of eco-management and eco-audit and allows companies which decide to join in with this system to mention their successful participation in their business papers.

All these texts demonstrate the effort to increase access to environmental information. The trend seems set to continue. One might expect, in the foreseeable future, a label on tropical wood which comes from sustainable production or on spray gases which do not affect the ozone layer. Of course, it could also be that information, for instance on genetically modified food or food which is treated with ionizing rays, will not be given to consumers. Generally, however, even the events surrounding the BSE (Bovine Spongiform Encephalopathy) disease indicate that consumers more and more require precise information on environmental and health aspects of products.

It is clear, though, that all the mentioned texts rather contain promises for *future* transparency and information than actual realisations. Indeed, information on the environment is at present far from complete, useful, transparent, and easily accessible. Past measures have not yet had the result of allowing us to have a clear picture of the state of the environment within the EC. And we are still far away from having sufficient transparency of discharges and emissions of the individual polluter.[34]

To the efforts of increasing transparency might also be counted the increased efforts of data reporting. Only some examples are given: Directive 92/72/EEC[35] fixes concentration values for ozone. Where these values are exceeded, Member

---

[29] Regulation 880/92/EEC on a Community eco-label award scheme, OJ 1992 L 99, p. 1.
[30] Regulation 2092/91/EEC on organic production of agricultural products and indications referring thereto on agricultural products and foodstuffs, OJ 1991 L 198, p. 1.
[31] Directive 92/32/EEC amending for the seventh time Directive 67/548/EEC on the classification, packaging and labelling of dangerous substances, OJ 1992 L 154, p. 1.
[32] Directive 91/157/EEC on batteries and accumulators containing certain dangerous substances, OJ 1991 L 78, p. 38.
[33] Regulation 1836/93/EEC, see note 10 above.
[34] See Directive 96/61/EC on IPPC, see note 14 above.
[35] Directive 92/72/EEC on air pollution by ozone, OJ 1992 L 297, p. 1.

States do not have to take measures to bring the values down, but rather—to inform the population! Protection is thus replaced by information and considerations of prevention or precaution do not play a prominent role in such an approach.

Directive 96/61/EC on IPPC[36] provides, as a rule, for the fixing of emission limit values at plant, local or regional level. In order to avoid too uneven a playing field, Member States shall have to report every three years on the values which have been fixed on their territory; on the basis of these reports, the EC is possibly to draw up common standards.

Reporting requirements are also an essential element of the proposals on the ecological quality of water[37] and ambient air quality.[38]

In all these cases, one might argue that the abandoning of fixed, binding values goes hand in hand with increased reporting and informing and, as will be seen below, with an increased planning requirement.

Financial support for the environment

The 'polluter pays' principle, laid down in Article 130r(2) of the EC Treaty,[39] means that it should not be the taxpayer but the polluter who pays for environmental impairment or damage or for the precautionary or preventive measures.[40] Despite this principle, which has been discussed at Community level for more than 20 years, there is a marked tendency to make public funds available for environmental purposes.

In primary law, Article 130d provides for the setting up of an EC cohesion fund, destined to co-finance transport and environmental projects in poorer Member States—at present in Greece, Portugal, Spain, and Ireland. This fund was set up in 1994[41] and equipped with 14.4 billion ECU until 1999.

Article 130s(5) provides that, where an EC measure, adopted by majority decision in Council, is considered disproportionately expensive for public authorities of a Member State, the Council may provide for a financial support for that Member State. As regards secondary law, Directive 92/43/EEC[42] contains a similar clause. Regulation 1973/92/EEC[43] set up an environmental fund, LIFE, equipped with 400 million ECU for four years, destined to co-finance

---

[36] See note 14 above.

[37] See note 18 above.

[38] See note 20 above.

[39] Article 130r(2):'Community policy on the environment shall aim at a high level of protection . . . It shall be based on the precautionary principle and on the principles that preventive action should be taken, that environmental damage should as a priority be rectified at source and that the polluter should pay.'

[40] Recommendation 75/436 on cost allocation and action by public authorities on environmental matters, OJ 1975 L 194, p. 1.

[41] Regulation 1164/94/EEC establishing a Cohesion Fund, OJ 1994 L 130, p. 1.

[42] Directive 92/43/EEC on the conservation of natural habitats and of wild fauna and flora, OJ 1992 L 206, p. 7.

[43] Regulation 1973/92/EEC establishing a financial instrument for the environment (LIFE), OJ 1992 L 206, p. 1.

pilot and demonstration projects in the area of environmental policy. Other EC financial means for environmental measures are made available through the structural funds, research programmes, technology, energy and transport programmes—amongst others the programmes SPRINT, SAVE, THERMIE, ALTENER, EURET, and the European Investment Bank. As regards the national level, the EC has issued guidelines for state aids in environmental matters.[44] It is difficult to estimate whether, in general, national public support for environmental measures increases. With respect to the EC level, the overall availability of public funds for the environment has undoubtedly increased.

It is not possible to examine in this contribution whether such a development is to be welcome and what consequences it will have on environmental law (cf. Chapter 19 by Joanne Scott below). Only two ideas may be launched: on the one hand, every ECU which is spent to protect, preserve, and improve the quality of the environment is well spent. And on the other, the equality of legal obligations of Member States, polluters, and economic operators, might be affected by some measures being financed out of the common pot, and others not.

Clean-up and management plans

Article 130s(3), inserted into the EC Treaty by the Maastricht Treaty on European Union, provides for the adoption of general environmental action programmes. There might be doubts, whether the EC would be legally obliged to provide for such action programmes; politically, however, the practice of environmental action programmes, which have been existing at EC level for more than 20 years,[45] is not put into question, all the more since the European Parliament has acquired a co-decision right for such programmes.

The inclusion of Article 130s(3) into the EC Treaty clearly demonstrates the importance which EC law and policy attach to clean-up and management plans in environmental matters.[46] There are numerous provisions in secondary EC law, where Member States are obliged to provide for the drawing up and implementation of such plans—and their number seems rather to increase in recent texts.

Leaving aside the different directives of the 1970s and 1980s, we find such planning requirements in Directive 91/271/EEC for municipal waste water,[47] Directive 91/676/EEC on water pollution through nitrates,[48] in the proposal

---

[44] See note 8 above.

[45] First Environmental Action Programme OJ 1973 C 112, p. 1; Second Environmental Action Programme OJ 1977 C 139, p. 1; Third Environmental Action Programme OJ 1983 C 46, p. 1; Fourth Environmental Action Programme OJ 1987 C 328, p. 1; Fifth Environmental Action Programme OJ 1993 C 138, p. 1.

[46] See Commission proposal, based on Article 130s(3) of the EC Treaty, to amend the Fifth Environmental Action Programme, COM(95) 432, p. 6 February 1996.

[47] Directive 91/271/EEC on urban waste water treatment, OJ 1991 L 135, p. 40.

[48] Directive 91/676/EEC on the protection of waters against pollution caused by nitrates from agricultural sources, OJ 1991 L 375, p. 1.

on the ecological quality of water,[49] and of ambient air quality,[50] in the Directives 91/156/EEC on waste[51] and 91/689/EEC on hazardous waste,[52] Directive 94/62/EEC on packaging and packaging waste,[53] and Directive 92/43/EEC on the conservation of natural habitats and of wild fauna and flora[54] etc. Regulation 793/93/EEC on existing chemicals[55] contains planning elements and Regulation 1836/93/EEC[56] even provides for planning requirements for companies which participate in the eco-audit system which is established by that regulation.

Past experience shows that these legal obligations are only very partially complied with by numerous Member States, to an extent that one could seriously doubt, under the existing enforcement mechanisms, of the usefulness of fixing binding clean-up plans (cf. Chapter 3 by Richard Macrory and Ray Purdy below). This observation rather leads to a request for better enforcement of existing rules, but does not put into question the tendency in EC law to ask local, regional, or national authorities to draw up plans.

Hardly any systematic research exists of number and content of such plans and the progress in environmental clean-up which they achieved. Despite this, it is likely that the planning idea will continue to be promoted in EC environmental law.

Trends in the different sectors

Water

Since 1991, two directives were adopted, on municipal waste water[57] and on the protection of waters against pollution through nitrates from agricultural sources.[58] The Commission proposed a directive on the ecological quality of water,[59] which will, however, be withdrawn again.[60] Furthermore, the Commission proposed to amend the directives on the quality of bathing water[61] and on drinking water.[62] It announced an amendment of the directive on discharges of dangerous substances into waters[63] and a general framework directive on

---

[49] See note 18 above.
[50] See note 20 above.
[51] See note 21 above.
[52] Directive 91/689/EEC on hazardous waste, OJ 1991 L 377, p. 20.
[53] See note 24 above.
[54] See note 42 above.
[55] Regulation 793/93/EEC on the evaluation and control of the risks of existing substances, OJ 1993 L 84, p. 1.
[56] See note 10 above.
[57] Directive 91/271/EEC, see note 47 above.
[58] Directive 91/676/EEC, see note 48 above.
[59] See note 18 above.
[60] European Commission, Communication on a European Community water policy, COM(96) 59 final of 21 February 1996, p. 18.
[61] Proposal for a directive on bathing water, OJ 1994 C 112, p. 3.
[62] Proposal for a directive on the quality of drinking water, COM(93) 680 final.
[63] European Commission, work programme 1994, COM(93) 588 final of 24 November 1993, p. 18.

water.[64] The most striking feature in this list is the fact that since 1990, there is no further activity on fixing limit values and quality objectives for discharges of dangerous substances into waters.[65] Work on Directive 76/464/EEC has thus practically come to a standstill—despite the request of the EC ministerial water seminar of 1988 to speed work up,[66] despite several corresponding requests from the European Parliament,[67] despite the fact that the Commission itself indicated that it would submit, in 1994, a proposal for an amendment of that Directive,[68] and despite the fact that the Council had agreed, in 1983 to a list of 129 substances, which were to be regulated with priority at EC level.[69]

Overall, the EC has, between 1976 and 1996, managed to fix emission values and quality objectives for 17 substances—less than one substance per year! No revision of the standards have ever been suggested, not one single substance of the less dangerous substances—the 'list II-substances', which include such problematic substances as chromium, nickel, lead, biocides, nitrites etc.—has been regulated at EC level. It is not an exaggeration to state that the added value of this directive to reducing water pollution has been rather limited.

This EC activity must undoubtedly be seen together with the above-mentioned trend for deregulation. *De facto*, the EC is progressively giving up attempts to regulate—i.e. to fix common standards for industrial installations. Responsibility for such standards is left or transferred to Member States. It must be feared that this will not lead to competition for the best or most stringent standards. Rather, there will be continuous pressure on national regulators not to fix too stringent standards in order not to affect the economic operators' competitiveness with regard to competitors from other Member States or, indeed, from third countries.

Both the adopted and proposed directives rely heavily on clean-up plans in order to implement the different legal requirements that are foreseen in the directives. And one might imagine how important sound financial, ecological, administrative, and economical planning is, if one realises that the overall costs of implementing the directive on municipal waste water until the year 2005— in particular the building of waste water treatment plants and municipal canalisation—are estimated to be between 60 and 100 billion ECU. Also early planning is of primary importance if the delays which Member States unanimously had agreed are to be respected.

As regards the Nitrates Directive,[70] it should be observed that the Fifth Environmental Action Programme announced that the usefulness of proposing a directive on protecting waters against phosphates would be examined.[71] No

---

[64] See note 60 above.
[65] Directives 82/176/EEC, OJ 1982 L 81, p. 29; 83/513/EEC, OJ 1983 L 291, p. 1; 84/156/EEC, OJ 1984 L 74, p. 49; 84/491/EEC, OJ 1984 L 274, p. 11; 86/280/EEC, OJ 1986 L 181, p. 16.
[66] European Commission, EC Bull. No 6 (1988), 2.1.1975.
[67] Resolution European Parliament, on Directive 76/464/EEC, OJ 1990 C284, 12.11.1990, p. 191.
[68] See note 63 above.
[69] Council Resolution of 7 February 1983, OJ 1983 C 46, p. 17.
[70] Directive 91/676/EEC, see note 48 above.
[71] OJ 1993 C 138 p. 1.

mention, however, on the question whether there should be a directive on protecting waters against pesticides. Seen in this context, the Nitrates Directive does not seem to be part of a coherent strategy.

Air pollution

Since 1991, nine directives and regulations were adopted. Two of them concern substances which destroy the ozone layer,[72] which shows the ongoing concern at international level and within the Community about the continuous threat to the ozone layer. A number of other directives deal with the ongoing pollution from cars, where it is more and more clear to everybody that the problems of air pollution and damage to the environment are not significantly improved by the different texts. Directives 91/441/EEC,[73] 93/59/EEC[74] and 94/12/EEC[75] deal with emissions from vehicles, Directive 93/12/EEC[76] on the sulphur content of gas oil and Directive 94/63/EEC[77] on the control of volatile organic compound (VOC) emissions from the storage and distribution of petrol. Directive 92/72/EEC[78] deals with air pollution by ozone and Directive 94/67/EEC[79] with emissions to air—as well as to water and to soil—of the incineration of hazardous waste.

Proposals were made for a directive on a tax on carbon dioxide emissions and on energy,[80] as well as a directive on the framework on ambient air quality.[81] The announcement of a proposal on reducing carbon dioxide emissions from cars[82] and a proposal for reducing VOC emissions from several industrial sectors[83] have not yet been submitted. Overall, the development of these different texts illustrates well the general trends in environmental policy. There is a concern about the ozone layer, which pushes for quick action at EC level. The threat of climate change has not helped to overcome the fundamental objection, in particular of the United Kingdom, to any tax provision fixed at EC level. The delegation of a carbon tax to the Member States, which is at present considered, is of little use, since Member States may introduce such a tax at present anyway; furthermore, the invitation to introduce such a tax originates from the United Nations Conference on Environment and Development ('the Earth Summit') in Rio de Janeiro in 1992.

---

[72] Regulations 594/91/EEC on ozone-depleting substances, OJ 1991 L 67, p. 1; 3093/94/EEC on ozone-depleting substances, OJ 1994 L 333, p. 1.
[73] Directive 91/441/EEC on emissions from motor vehicles, OJ 1991 L 242, p. 1.
[74] Directive 93/59/EEC amending Directive 70/220/EEC on motor vehicle emissions, OJ 1970 L 186, p. 21.
[75] Directive 94/12/EEC on motor vehicle emissions, OJ 1994 L 100, p. 42.
[76] Directive 93/12/EEC on sulphur content of certain liquid fuels, OJ 1993 L 74, p. 81.
[77] Directive 94/63/EEC on the control of volatile organic compound emissions resulting from the storage of petrol and its distribution from terminals to service stations, OJ 1994 L 365, p. 24.
[78] Directive 92/72/EEC, see note 35 above.
[79] Directive 94/67/EEC on the incineration of hazardous waste, OJ 1994 L 365, p. 34.
[80] See note 5 above.
[81] See note 20 above.
[82] European Commission, work programme 1994, COM(93) 588 final of 24 November 1993, p. 18.
[83] *Ibid.*

The problems linked to Directive 92/72/EEC[84] on air pollution by ozone—no impositions of sanctions, only a requirement to inform the population in the case of limits that have been exceeded—have been mentioned above. The approach in the proposal for a directive on ambient air quality[85] follows the same pattern: data shall be collected, in order to obtain more information on the state and the evolution of air contamination, but no limit values are foreseen and thus no sanctions in the case of high concentrations. In its intensity of regulation, the proposal is even less far-reaching than Directive 84/360/EEC on air pollution,[86] which fixes at least general requirements of new and existing industrial installations. Product-related measures continue to be adopted by the Community. The establishment and the functioning of the internal market require such measures; also, there is the underlying apprehension that in the absence of EC measures, there would be legislative activity at national level which could affect the free flow of goods.

Chemicals

This sector is product-related. Therefore, it is not surprising to see that legislation in this area is particularly numerous. Thus, Directive 67/548/EEC on chemical substances was amended once by the Council[87] and ten times adapted to technical progress; these adaptations provided for classification, labelling and packaging requirements of further hazardous substances, which were added to the EC list. Directive 88/379/EEC on dangerous preparations[88] was amended four times; Directive 76/769/EEC on the restriction on marketing and use of dangerous chemicals[89] was amended eight times, which added new restrictions to the existing ones.

Apart from these basic directives, a number of other measures have been adopted in order to set up the internal market for chemicals. Directive 91/414/EEC[90] provided for the marketing of pesticides; the Directive was adopted 15 years after the Commission's proposal! Regulation 2455/92/EEC[91] fine tuned earlier provisions on the export and import of chemicals, with a view to contributing to further worldwide approximated standards in this area. Regulation 793/93/EEC[92] introduces an EC-wide evaluation procedure for existing chemicals,

---

[84] See note 35 above.
[85] See note 20 above.
[86] Directive 84/360/EEC, see note 16 above.
[87] Directive 92/32/EEC, see note 31 above.
[88] Directive 88/379/EEC on the classification, packaging, and labelling of dangerous preparations, OJ 1988 L 187, p. 14.
[89] Directive 76/769/EEC on restrictions on the marketing and use of certain dangerous substances and preparations, OJ 1976 L 262, p. 201.
[90] Directive 91/414/EEC on placing of plant protection products on the market, OJ 1991 L 230, p. 1.
[91] Regulation 2455/92/EEC on the export and import of certain dangerous chemicals, OJ 1992 L 251, p. 13.
[92] Regulation 793/93/EEC, see note 55 above.

without, though, introducing itself a system for EC-wide conclusions of such risk assessment results.

A proposal to amend Directive 82/501/EEC on accident prevention of chemical installations was submitted in 1993[93] and adopted in 1996. A proposal to harmonise national legislation on biocides was submitted in the same year.[94] There are no further announcements for legislative measures in the legislative programmes since 1993.

Overall, the chemical sector, which is strongly marked by the necessity to establish and monitor an internal market for chemicals, based on a high level of environmental protection, shows the signs of consolidating existing, product-related legislation and cautiously extending the provisions on sectors such as biocides and pesticides.

Waste

Seven pieces of legislation have been adopted since 1991: directives on waste[95] and on hazardous waste,[96] a regulation on the shipment of waste;[97] furthermore, directives on more specific items such as waste from the titanium dioxide industry,[98] batteries,[99] packaging and packaging waste,[100] and on the incineration of hazardous waste.[101] Two further proposals, on landfills—proposed in 1991[102]—and on PCB-PCT (Polychlorinated Bi-phenols and Polychlorinated Tri-phenols) wastes[103]—proposed in 1988, are likely to be adopted during 1996. Furthermore, two Commission proposals on regulating the export of waste to third countries[104] are being discussed in Council.

For 1996 the Commission announced a proposal for a directive on end-of-life vehicles[105] and a proposal on the marking of packs,[106] which is requested under Directive 94/62/EC.

The borderline character of waste regulation between free circulation of goods and environmental concerns is well mirrored by the fact that of the adopted texts, three are based on Article 100a—Directives 91/157/EEC, 92/

---

[93] Proposal for an amendment of Directive 82/501/EEC, OJ 1994 C 106, p. 4; amended OJ 1995 C 238, p. 4. Adopted as Directive 96/82/EC, OJ 1997, L 10, p. 13.
[94] Proposal for a directive on biocides, OJ 1993 C 239, p. 3; amended OJ 1995 C 261, p. 5.
[95] Directive 91/156/EEC, see note 21 above.
[96] Directive 91/689/EEC, see note 52 above.
[97] Regulation 259/93/EEC on the supervision and control of shipments within, into and out of the European Community, OJ 1993 L 30, p. 1.
[98] Directive 92/112/EEC, see note 25 above.
[99] Directive 91/157/EEC, see note 32 above.
[100] Directive 94/62/EEC, see note 24 above.
[101] Directive 94/67/EEC, see note 79 above.
[102] Proposal for a directive on landfills, OJ 1991 C 190, p. 1.
[103] Proposal for a directive on PCB/PCT, OJ 1988 C 319, p. 57; amended OJ 1991 C 299, p. 9. The proposal is now adopted, see Directive 96/59/EC, OJ 1996, L 243, p. 31.
[104] Proposal to amend Regulation 259/93/EEC, OJ 1995 C 164, p. 8; the proposal is now adopted, see Regulation 120/97/EC, OJ 1997 L 22, p. 14; proposal to amend Regulation 259/93/EEC, COM(94) 678 final, 8.2.95.
[105] European Commission, work programme 1996, EU Bull, Suppl. 1/96 p. 28.
[106] COM (96) 191, final of 25 November 1996.

112/EEC and 94/62/EC—while four are based on the environmental provision of Article 130s. It should be mentioned the Court of Justice declared, in 1993, that wastes are, in the sense of Article 30 of the EC Treaty, goods, though with special characteristics.[107] Since then, the general policy of the Council may be described as going back to Article 130s, where general waste aspects are in question, but to use Article 100a as a legal basis where waste from a specific economic sector is regulated. Though this might create difficulties for border-line cases, this seems no longer to be in dispute.

Standard-setting at EC level is influenced by the fact that there is an inter-national convention on the shipment of hazardous waste, to which the EC adhered in 1993[108] and that also the OECD is actively busy in dealing with international aspects of wastes. Thus, it is not yet altogether clear in which way a ban of exports of hazardous wastes to all non-OECD countries, decided in 1995 in the context of the Basel Convention, will effectively be put into operation by the EC.

As regards the EC level, continuous efforts are made to reach a harmonised definition of waste, a problem that has existed for more than 20 years. The concept, to complete the legal definition of waste and of hazardous waste by corresponding lists, will yet have to find general acceptance within the EC. The ongoing controversy as to what type of actions Member States may take in the area of waste and what is to be regulated at EC level—taxes, recycling quota, take-back schemes, specific waste streams etc.—produces considerable uncer-tainty as to the coming years. A review of the EC waste strategy of 1989,[109] which aims at contributing to this discussion, was submitted in 1996.[110]

Noise

During the last five years, only one directive was adopted, on noise from aero-planes;[111] this directive transposed international standards into EC law. One further directive was amended.[112]

In 1996, the Commission announced a communication on a noise policy at EC level,[113] which is, until now, not yet made public. Such a noise policy has already been announced in several previous EC environmental action pro-grammes.[114] Until now, EC legislation on noise only dealt with product-related noise limit values, in particular noise levels from cars, motorcycles, and aero-planes on the one hand, from construction equipment and household

---

[107] Case C-2/90, *Commission* v. *Belgium (Wallonian Waste)* [1992] ECR 4431, ECJ.
[108] Decision 93/98/EEC to conclude the Basel Convention on the control of transboundary move-ment of hazardous wastes and their disposal, OJ 1993 L 39, p. 1.
[109] Council Resolution of 7 May 1990, OJ 1990 C 122, p. 2.
[110] European Commission, COM (96) final of 30 June 1996 and Council Resolution of 24 February 1997, OJ 1997 C 76 p. 1.
[111] Directive 92/14/EEC on the limitation of noise from aeroplanes, OJ 1992 L 76, p. 21.
[112] Directive 95/27/EEC amending Directive 86/662/EEC on noise from construction machines, OJ 1995 L 168, p. 14.
[113] European Commission, see note 105 above, p. 29.
[114] See for instance Second Environmental Action Programme, OJ 1977 C 139, para. 67.

machinery on the other. These levels refer to new products and aim principally at ensuring the free circulation of (new) goods.

Nature protection

The Community adopted one directive, Directive 92/43/EEC on the conservation of natural habitats and of wild fauna and flora.[115] Furthermore, in 1991, the Council adopted Regulation 3254/91/EEC[116] on leg-hold traps and on the prohibition of import of skins from certain animals of countries which continue to allow cruel—'inhumane'—capturing methods. Due to political pressure from some third countries which would have been affected by this import ban, the Regulation had not yet come into effect at the time of writing (mid-1996). Regulation 3626/82/EEC[117] on trade in endangered species was, between 1991 and 1995, amended five times.

In 1991, Regulation 2092/91/EEC[118] on organic production of agricultural products was adopted; Regulation 2078/92/EEC[119] deals with agricultural production methods compatible with the requirement of the protection of the environment and the maintenance of the countryside.

The Commission proposed to the Council to substitute Regulation 3626/82/EEC with a new one[120] and proposed an amendment of Directive 79/409/EEC on the conservation of wild birds.[121] New specific legislation on nature protection was not proposed or announced.

The most important of all this legislation is Directive 92/43/EEC which tries to establish, by the year 2000, a coherent European network of habitats for a number of endangered fauna and flora species. The Directive will require a considerable number of actions by Member States in order to set up the network; past experience from the development of habitat protection for birds does not really inspire too much optimism that the target of the year 2000 will be reached. Furthermore, it is obvious that the designation of habitats is but a first step in order to ensure the survival of endangered species.

Regulation 3254/91/EEC raises problems, because it tries to ensure worldwide the use of 'humane' killing methods for animals; indeed, the animals with which the regulation is concerned are not endangered species. This raises the

---

[115] Directive 92/43/EEC, see note 42 above.
[116] Regulation 3254/91/EEC on the ban of leg-hold traps and of imports of certain animals captured by inhumane methods, OJ 1991 L 308, p. 1.
[117] Regulation 3626/82/EEC on international trade in endangered species of wild fauna and flora, OJ 1982 L 384, p. 1; amended by Regulations 3675/91/EEC, OJ 1991 L 349, p. 13; 1970/92, OJ 1992 L 201, p. 1; 1534/93/EEC, OJ 1993 L 151, p. 22; 558/95, OJ 1995 L 57, p. 1.
[118] Regulation 2092/91/EEC, see note 30 above.
[119] Regulation 2078/92/EEC on agricultural production methods compatible with the requirements of the protection of the environment and the maintenance of the countryside, OJ 1992 L 215, p. 85.
[120] Proposal for a regulation amending Regulation 3626/82/EEC, see note 117 above, OJ 1992 C 26, p. 1; the proposal is now adopted, see Regulation 338/97/EC, OJ 1997 L 61, p. 1.
[121] Proposal for a directive amending Directive 79/409/EEC on the conservation of wild birds, OJ 1994 C 100, p. 12.

question, whether GATT rules—or the new rules of the World Trade Organisation (WTO)—allow measures to be taken with the aim of protecting the environment outside the territory of a contracting state (or, in this case, the EC); in considering this question, it should be noted that the regulation in effect provides for an import ban because of the production methods in some states. In the author's opinion it is legally possible to provide for the protection of the environment outside one's own territory.[122] However, the subject is very controversial among states, legal authors, and international organisations.

Horizontal measures

The Council adopted Directive 91/692/EEC[123] on standardisation and rationalisation of implementation reports for environmental directives, and Regulation 880/92/EEC[124] on an eco-label, Regulation 1973/92/EEC[125] on a financial instrument for the environment (LIFE), and Regulation 1836/93/EEC[126] on an eco-management and audit scheme. Directive 96/61/EEC on the integrated pollution prevention and control of industrial installations was also adopted.[127]

In the 1996 programme the Commission announced discussion papers (communications) on negotiated agreements with industry, on environmental levies, and on the implementation of EC environmental policy.[128] These papers were all submitted; however, no legislative proposals of a horizontal nature were announced.

The different adopted and proposed texts are all of considerable weight. They all follow the approach which was described above, i.e. providing mainly procedural provisions, but abandoning the fixing of standards or criteria which are designed to reduce emissions to the environment. Making environmental impact assessments, authorising installations by looking at their emissions in an integrated way, increasing transparency or information, or auditing performances are useful mechanisms. However, as such they do not reduce the quantity of pollutants which enter the environment. This remains, from the environmental point of view, the primary task and, although the procedures to take the environment into consideration are important, they are not really an end in themselves.

This observation is confirmed by the fact that the participation of undertakings in the eco-audit scheme is voluntary, and that also the application for obtaining an eco-label for a product is voluntary. Industry seems rather reluctant

---

[122] See as the most recent example the EC decision to ban the export of British cows and products from such cows, because of 'mad cow' disease. As far as the export to third countries is concerned, this decision can only be explained by the will to protect the health of persons in non-EC countries.

[123] Directive 91/692/EEC, see note 28 above.

[124] Regulation 880/92/EEC, see note 29 above.

[125] Regulation 1973/92/EEC, see note 43 above.

[126] Regulation 1836/93/EEC, see note 10 above.

[127] See note 14 above.

[128] European Commission, work programme 1996, EU Bull., Suppl. 1/96, pp. 28 *et seq.*

to accept the eco-labelling scheme fully and the eco-audit system is likely to encounter some acceptance problems in Member States with a Roman law tradition.

Conclusion

Community environmental law evolves. It has undergone considerable changes during the last five years, marked particularly by greater recurrence to general measures and by the abandoning of numerical reductions of emissions.

The recent Dobris report on Europe's state of the environment,[129] published by the European Environmental Agency, shows that the European environment is not too well off. Protecting this environment with the means of the law is the objective of environmental law. This author will not try to answer the question whether the evolution of EC environmental law of the last five years has successfully managed to improve the state of the environment.

---

[129] European Environment Agency, *Europe's Environment: The Dobris Assessment* (Copenhagen: EEA 1995).

Chapter 3

THE ENFORCEMENT OF EC ENVIRONMENTAL LAW AGAINST MEMBER STATES

Richard Macrory and Ray Purdy

The context of EC law enforcement

The main focus of this chapter concerns the institutional and legal machinery contained within the EC Treaty and designed to ensure that Member States implement their environmental obligations under EC law. Modern international environmental treaties have increasingly built in what are often quite elaborate mechanisms to improve compliance by parties. It is clear, however, that the Community system goes beyond anything yet devised at international level, and from one perspective can be regarded as a laboratory for arrangements for supra-national governance. As with any experimental system, all is by no means perfect with present arrangements, and we will suggest some reforms to existing procedures to improve their effectiveness. Member States themselves have endorsed the importance that should be given to the issue of implementation and in one of the Declarations attached to the Maastricht Treaty the conference noted that it ' . . . considers it essential for the proper functioning of the Community that the measures taken by the different Member States should result in Community law being applied with the same effectiveness and rigour as in the application of their national law'.[1] The question of implementation is likely to be on the agenda of the current Inter-Governmental Conference, and the DGXI of the European Commission is in the process of preparing its own discussion paper on the subject as it relates to the environment.

One of the four central functions given the European Commission under the Treaty is to 'ensure that the provisions of this Treaty and measures taken by the institutions pursuant thereto are applied'.[2] Again, the Maastricht Declaration

---

[1] Declaration 19.1, Treaty on European Union, 7 February 1992.
[2] Article 155. The other three functions are to formulate recommendations or deliver opinions; have its own power of decision and participate in the shaping of Community measures; exercise powers conferred upon it by the Council.

on Implementation endorsed this role,[3] and our main concern will be with the Commission's functions and powers. But to put the issue in a broader context it is worth remembering that there are a range of general principles designed to ensure that Community obligations are better integrated into national systems of law.

Regulations or directives?

The initial choice of legal instrument is critical. Adopting a regulation as opposed to the directive in theory means that one can rely upon national legal systems to ensure that its provisions are implemented since a regulation is 'binding in its entirety and directly applicable in all Member States'.[4] The whole issue of the nature of the current hierarchy of Community legal instruments is to be addressed by the Inter-Governmental Conference,[5] and in various suggestions for reform that have been made since the 1980s, notably by the European Parliament, the directive has been signally absent.[6] Some have argued for the wholesale replacement of directives by regulations,[7] but such a move would not necessarily provide the panacea it might imply. Not all regulations are truly self-executory in that they may still require Member States to establish competent bodies or develop other detailed requirements to ensure their implementation. In the environmental field examples of what Adam and Winter describe as 'framework regulations'[8] include the Eco-labelling Regulation 880/92/EEC which requires Member States to establish competent national bodies for the award of eco-labels and the Eco-Audit Regulation 1836/93/EEC under which Member States must establish a system for the accreditation of independent environmental verifiers. Another example is Regulation 259/93/EEC on the Supervision and Control of Shipments of Waste which similarly required detailed action by Member States before it could be implemented, and significantly did not apply until 15 months after publication giving Member States time to introduce the required national measures.[9]

---

[3] 'The Conference calls upon the Commission to ensure in exercising its powers under Article 155 of this Treaty that Member States fulfil their obligations'. Declaration 19.2, see note 1 above.

[4] EC Treaty, Article 189.

[5] Declaration 16, Treaty on European Union: 'The Conference agrees that the Intergovernmental Conference to be convened in 1996 will examine to what extent it might be possible to review the classification of Community acts with a view to establishing an appropriate hierarchy between the different categories of act.'

[6] Diedrichsen, 'The System of Legal Acts in the History of Drafts and Proposals of the EC Treaty', in Winter (ed), *Sources and Categories of European Union Law* (Baden Baden: Nomos Verlagsgesellschaft, 1996).

[7] Sutherland Report *Internal Market after 1992: Report of the High-Ranking Expert-Group to the Commission of the European Communities* (Brussels, CEC, 1992).

[8] Adam and Winter, 'Framework Element Regulations', in Winter, *op. cit.* note 6.

[9] Jans, *European Environmental Law* (The Hague: Kluwer Law International, 1995), p. 42. Article 44 provides that the Regulation entered into force three days after publication in the Official Journal, but did not apply until the end of the later period.

In practice, the vast majority of legal instruments in the environmental field to date have taken the form of directives. When the House of Lords Select Committee on the European Communities examined the issue of implementation and enforcement of EC environmental law, it concluded that directives should continue to be used in the environmental field.[10] By prescribing goals but leaving the means to achieve them to the choice of Member States, directives recognise the varied legal and administrative cultures within different countries, an issue which may be even more important should there be further substantial enlargement of the Community. As Winter notes, 'The directive is not a tool for finally reaching uniformity but a tool which tolerates diversity continuously.'[11] Nevertheless, it has to be admitted that many directives have contained considerable detail,[12] and while the legal effect of directives and regulations remains distinct,[13] when it comes to substantive content the borderline between regulations requiring national implementing measures and directives that appear to go beyond the prescription of goals is fine. The House of Lords Committee felt that too little had been developed by way of systematic principle concerning the choice of instrument, and it called on the Council of Ministers to develop more elaborate guidelines. It is not an issue which the European Court of Justice has yet considered, nor is it clear that it would have jurisdiction to do so.[14] In practice, regulations have been used in the environmental field especially where a uniform regime was needed to deal with trade with third countries.[15] Cross-border trade may represent another example, and regulations have been justified where the relevant policy is intended to impose rights and obligations directly on industry.[16] But, unless they are replaced as a form of Community instrument following the Inter-Governmental Conference and any subsequent Treaty changes, directives are likely to remain dominant in the environmental field. This is reinforced by the subsidiarity principles now contained in Article 3b of the Treaty, the third paragraph of which provides that, 'Any action by the Community shall not go beyond what is necessary to achieve the objectives of this Treaty.' According to the Edinburgh Guidelines[17] produced by the European

---

[10] House of Lords Select Committee on the European Communities, *Report on the Implementation and Enforcement of Environmental Legislation*, Session 1991–92, Ninth Report, HL Paper 53–1, (London: HMSO, 1992).

[11] Winter, 'The Directive: Problems of Construction and Directions for Reform', in Winter, *op. cit.* note 6.

[12] See Prechal, *Directives in European Community Law* (Oxford: Clarendon Press, 1995) pp. 44–60.

[13] In particular, the European Court of Justice has confirmed that directives cannot in themselves impose obligation on individuals, and thus do not have horizontal effect: Case C-91/92, *Faccini Dori* v. *Recreb Srl* [1995] 72 CMLR 665.

[14] But it might be called upon to rule on the choice of a regulation or directive in the context of Article 3b of the Treaty (subsidiarity), quoted below.

[15] E.g. Regulation 3626/82/EEC on international trade in endangered species of wild flora and fauna.

[16] For example, Regulation 793/93/EEC on the evaluation and control of the risks of existing substances states in its Preamble that a regulation is an appropriate instrument since it imposes directly on manufacturers and importers precise requirements to be implemented at the same time and in the same manner throughout the Community. Quoted in Jans, *op. cit.* note 9.

[17] Conclusions of the Presidency, Edinburgh, European Council; EC Bull. No. 12 (1992).

Council in 1992, and which elaborated the principles of subsidiarity, this implied that directives were generally to be preferred to regulations, and that where appropriate framework directives were preferable to those containing detailed measures.

The internalising doctrines of the Court of Justice: Is there still a need for the Commission?

The past 15 years or so has seen the development of three key doctrines by the European Court of Justice whose effect is to give far greater bite to provisions of Community directives within national systems where Member States have failed to transpose directives or have done so insufficiently. First, the direct effect doctrine under which provisions of directives which are unconditional and sufficiently precise may be relied upon against the state or emanations of the state. Secondly, the principle of sympathetic interpretation[18] which requires national courts when applying national law whether passed before or after the relevant directive to interpret the national law so far as possible in the light of the wording and purpose of the directive. And finally, the principle that Member States must compensate for damage caused to individuals by the failure to transpose a directive properly.[19] These doctrines have essentially derived from the Court's interpretation of the general principle of cooperation under Article 5, but from another perspective they can be seen as a criticism of the failure of the Commission to use the existing institutional machinery under the Treaty to ensure that directives are fully implemented within national systems. Certainly if these procedures were working effectively, and directives were properly implemented within the time-limits specified, the rationale for these doctrines would be diminished.

Given the current developments in case law, it could be argued that the principles now developed by the European Court are potentially so powerful that we need worry less about the inadequacies of the Commission's enforcement procedures; in essence the courts can now fill in the implementation gaps that remain. This would, however, be a mistaken view. As a matter of general principle the European Court has recognised that the question whether individuals can, for example, rely upon the direct effect doctrine is quite separate from the question of whether Member States have complied with their obligations to implement a directive.[20] Furthermore, each of the doctrines has limitations which mean that they could never totally replace the responsibility of the Commission. The direct effect doctrine does not apply to all provisions of directives, in that there will be many obligations under environmental directives

[18] Case C-106/89, *Marleasing* v. *La Comercial Internacional de Alimentación* [1990] I-ECR 4135.
[19] Joined Cases C-6/90 and C-9/90, *Francovich and Bonifaci* v. *Italy* [1991] I-ECR 5357; and Cases C-46/83, *Brasserie du Pêcheur SA* v. *Germany* and C-48/93, *R* v. *Secretary of State for Transport, ex parte Factortame Ltd (Factortame III)* [1996] 1 CMLR 889.
[20] Case C-431/92, *Commission* v. *Germany (Grosskrotzenburg)* [1992] ECR I-2189.

which are insufficiently precise and clear to have direct effect.[21] This was confirmed in the *Lombardia Waste* case[22] where the European Court of Justice held
that Article 4 of the Waste Directive 75/442 EEC (since replaced) which
required that Member States take all necessary measures to ensure that waste
is disposed of without endangering human health and without harming the
environment was ' . . . neither unconditional nor sufficiently precise and thus
is not capable of conferring rights on which individuals may rely as against the
State'. It is also now clear that the direct effect doctrine cannot be claimed
against private parties but remains limited to the state or emanations of the
state.[23] There may, however, be situations where the direct effect doctrine can
be said to have 'indirect' horizontal effect[24] in that private parties can be legally
affected by the invocation of the principle—for example, where the grant of a
planning permission by a local authority is successfully challenged under the
direct effect doctrine—but this does not detract from the basic constraints on
its application. As for the doctrine of sympathetic interpretation, we have yet
to see its application in the environmental field, and although the principle is
potentially more far-reaching than the direct effect doctrine since the status of
the parties before the national court is not relevant, the court's interpretive
duty can only be applied 'as far as possible'. It is clear that the doctrine is in
any event subject to certain limitations; it must respect general Community
principles of legal certainty and non-retroactivity, and the application of the
doctrine cannot be used to impose criminal liability on an individual unless
such liabilities have already been imposed by the national law.[25] Furthermore,
the doctrine cannot be readily invoked in the absence of at least some framework
of national law to interpret. To take an example in the environmental field, the
United Kingdom still does not possess national laws introducing a prior consent
system for afforestation required under the Environmental Assessment Directive.[26] If afforestation were to take place in the absence of environmental

---

[21] See Holder, 'A Dead End for Direct Effect? Prospects for Enforcement of European Community
Environmental Law by Individuals: *Comitato di Coordinamento per la Difesa della Cava and others* v.
Regione Lombardia and others' (1996) JEL Vol. 8, No. 2, 313; Krämer, 'The Implementation of
Community Environmental Directives within Member States: Some Implications of the Direct
Effect Doctrine' (1991) JEL Vol. 3, No. 1, 39.
[22] Case C-236/92, *Comitato di Coordinamento per la Difesa della Cava* v. *Regione Lombardia* [1994] ECR
I-483.
[23] Case C-91/92, *Faccini Dori* v. *Recreb Srl* [1995] 72 CMLR 665.
[24] Jans, *op. cit.* note 9, pp. 171–173.
[25] See Opinion of Advocate General Van Gerven in Case C-106/89, *Marleasing op. cit.* note 18. The
same limitation probably also applies to the imposition of civil penalties.
[26] Directive 85/337/EEC on the assessment of the effects of certain public and private projects on
the environment, OJ 1985 L 175, p. 40. In connection with afforestation, the British regulations, the Environmental Assessment (Afforestation) Regulations 1988 were tied to the grant
system. Since no requirements for assessment were applicable where no grant was applied for
(and afforestation remains outside the development control system) the Commission did not
accept that this represented proper implementation of the Directive. The UK government
appeared to accept this position, though no legislative changes have yet been made: Commission
of the European Communities, Press Release 31 July 1992: 'United Kingdom Infringements—
The Commission terminates five procedures and sends two reasoned opinions'. See Haigh,
Manual of Environmental Policy (London: Sweet and Maxwell), paras. 11.2–14—11.2–21.

assessment procedures, it is difficult to see how a third party could raise the issue before a national court. The provisions of the Directive as they relate to afforestation projects have been held not to have direct effect[27] and it would take a bold judge to interpret sympathetically the provisions of the Town and Country Planning Act 1990 to override expressly the exclusion of afforestation from the definition of development. The third major doctrine, the principle that individuals may claim damages from Member States for losses caused by breach of Community law including the failure to implement directives is still under development[28] and is itself hedged with limitations, though it is now clear that it can apply whether or not a directive has direct effect.[29] But the doctrine is essentially a principle of compensation and does not ensure that directives are fully implemented, though its very existence—and this must surely be one of the motivations behind its development—will do much to concentrate the minds of Member State governments to ensure effective implementation. The European Court has also stated that the doctrine only applies to provisions of directives which are interpreted as intending 'to confer rights upon individuals'.[30] It is arguable from previous case law that when it comes to environmental directives the Court of Justice has been fairly liberal in assuming that they confer rights upon individuals,[31] but there are bound to be provisions of directives and indeed perhaps whole directives themselves which can be considered to be concerned purely with the protection of the environment *per se* rather than the creation of individual rights.

These comments are not intended to belittle the legal importance of these doctrines and their potential for profound impact on national systems where Member States have failed to implement directives. But despite their development the role of the European Commission in ensuring implementation will remain of significance, and in certain instances is the only legal method to deal with recalcitrant Member States.

The structure of EC environmental legislation

The European Commission's ability to ensure effective implementation and enforcement of EC environmental law is strongly influenced by the differing structural character of much of the legislation that has been agreed. For those Community laws dealing explicitly with environmental standards for tradeable products (e.g. emissions from motor vehicles, lead content of paint), the pres-

---

[27] In the Petition of the Kincardine and Deeside District Council Court of Session, Edinburgh, 8 March 1991. See Macrory, 'Environmental Assessment and EC Law' (1992) JEL Vol. 4, No. 2, 273.
[28] See cases referred to in note 19 above.
[29] *Factortame III, op.cit.* note 19, paras. 18–22.
[30] *Ibid.* para. 51.
[31] Pernice, 'Kriterien der normativen Umsetzung von Umweltrichtlinien der EG im Lichte der Rechtsprechung des EuGH', (1994) *Europarecht* 325–341. See also Geddes, *Protection of Individual Rights Under EC Law* (London: Butterworths, 1995).

sures of the market and the more visible means of verifying compliance mean that implementation does not appear to be a major issue. This may not be true of all sectors, especially, say, where product manufacture is dominated by a large number of small and medium-sized enterprises, or where opportunities and the economic incentives for avoidance are powerful. But the presence of industrial competitors with a strong interest in ensuring compliance is a significant factor.

The main difficulty occurs with those Community policies which are dependent largely on national action taken within the confines of Member States, and do not involve products or services which are sold or traded across national boundaries. Examples would include the protection of groundwaters, the carrying out of environmental assessment procedures in connection with a construction project, or the prohibition of hunting of protected species of birds—nor is there necessarily an economic imperative or interest which will necessarily guard against non-implementation. Even within this class of directives, there are considerable differences in the nature of obligations placed on Member States which compound the problem of monitoring and securing implementation. Some directives prescribe explicit and precise goals that must be achieved in a given sector, which *in theory* are at least more readily susceptible to monitoring and enforcement.[32] Another class contains similarly precise goals in specific sectors or areas but the relevant articles leave a large element of discretion to Member States in determining where they are to apply—examples would include the designation of specific waters or habitats.[33] Depending on the precise provisions of the legislation in question, the discretion involved may by no means be wholly unfettered and in a number of cases the European Court of Justice appears to have adopted what is essentially an objective approach towards review—the bathing water case[34] being a clear example. Examples of more recent legislation cut across conventional administrative boundaries and sectors, and their requirements reach deep into national decision-making at many levels. This type of 'horizontal' directive, exemplified by the 1985 Environmental Assessment Directive (85/337/EEC) and the Access to Environmental Information Directive (90/313/EEC), raises acute difficulties for both Member States and the Community institutions when it comes to ensuring full implementation.

If we feel that implementation of Community environmental problems remains a problem, one approach is to attack the substantive content of policies contained in Community environmental laws. If Community laws were less

---

[32] For example, Directive 80/779/EEC on air quality limit values and guide values for sulphur dioxide and suspended particulate; Directive 80/778/EEC relating to the quality of water intended for human consumption.

[33] E.g. the designation of shellfish waters under Directive 79/923/EEC. Under the Habitats Directive (Directive 92/43/EEC), there are more elaborate procedures for the Commission to check the designation by Member States of Sites of Community Importance, but there remain ambiguities; see World Wide Fund for Nature, *Spotlight on the Habitats Directive* (Brussels: World Wide Fund for Nature, 1996).

[34] Case C-56/90, *Commission of the European Communities* v. *United Kingdom of Great Britain and Northern Ireland* (1993) JEL Vol. 6, No. 1, 125; [1993] *Water Law* 168.

ambitious, if some of the scientific basis was more rational, if more reliance was made on market-based instruments and voluntary mechanisms, then, so the argument goes, questions of non-implementation would diminish. Furthermore the pressure of the subsidiarity concept may result in the substantive obligations under directives granting more discretion to Member States, making the legal review and enforcement of their obligations less straightforward.[35] Despite these tendencies, the prospect of both self-executing, market-based instruments or instruments drafted in such loose language as to be effectively unenforceable by legal means will, in our view, in most areas of environmental concern largely remain the exception rather than the rule. Given the limitations of what can be described as the internalising doctrines of the European Court (direct effect, sympathetic interpretation, and the right to damages), there will still remain a powerful and important role for the Commission to ensure that Member States comply with the obligations they accept. Now that qualified majority voting at Council level applies to most environmental proposals,[36] we may see measures which some Member States have to accept legally even if they are in fundamental disagreement, or have been unable to force compromises.[37] This may cause greater problems of implementation within national systems, making the Commission's role all the more significant.

Article 169 procedures

Although the Commission has a clear duty under the EC Treaty to ensure that Community obligations are properly implemented by Member States, it was not until the early 1980s, a decade after the initiation of explicit Community environmental policies, and stung by criticisms of the European Parliament following the Seveso incident,[38] that the Commission began to take its role more seriously. Since that date, the Commission, largely through its legal unit within DGXI, concentrated on improving its enforcement efforts, using both conventional legal processes available under Community law, and less formal methods. The formal legal procedures available to the Commission in persuading a Member State to comply with Community obligations derive from Article 169 of the Treaty, and as such are common to all areas of Community

---

[35] Some evidence for this can be seen in the proposed Directive on the Ecological Quality of Water (OJ 1994 C 222, p. 6 (see also COM (93) 680 final)) where the obligations of Member States are often expressed in such vague terms as to make enforcement near impossible.

[36] EC Treaty Article 130s as amended at Maastricht.

[37] By contrast Directive 85/337/EEC on environmental assessment took almost 13 years to agree with the final text differing completely from the original draft, mainly because unanimous voting was required with Member States, and especially Britain, pressing for amendments to make the directive more consistent with their existing systems. See Sheate and Macrory, 'Agriculture and the EC Environmental Assessment Directive: Lessons for Community Policy Making' (1989) JCMS Vol. 28, No. 1, 68–81.

[38] See Resolution of the European Parliament, OJ 1984 C 127, p. 67, and Haigh, 'Background Paper: Challenges to Environmental Protection' (Brussels: Joint Public Hearing of European Parliament and European Commission, 30 May 1996).

policy. The terms of Article 169 are interpreted to divide into three separate stages: (a) the sending of a formal Article 169 letter to the Member State; (b) the sending of a reasoned opinion; and finally (c) referral to the European Court. Under the Commission's own rules of procedure, each of these decisions requires a collective decision of the whole Commission, giving each stage considerable institutional authority but also making it an elaborate process. The procedures are also susceptible to blocking by Commissioners responsible for portfolios other than the environment, but although this is known to happen in practice, and sometimes for fairly crude political and even nationalistic reasons, it is near impossible to secure hard evidence as to the significance of such internal political pressures.

The first two stages often end in a settlement and the majority of proceedings started do not end up before the European Court. Either the Member State complies with the Commission's requirements, or a mutually acceptable agreement is reached without the need for judicial intervention. As might be expected with any quasi-administrative system of enforcement, the formal stages are usually surrounded by less formal procedures. The service of an initial Article 169 letter, for example, does not normally take place without some considerable forewarning and correspondence between the Member State concerned and the Commission,[39] and in recent years the Commission has developed the use of further informal methods such as regular meetings (known as 'reunions-paquet') with individual Member States to discuss infringement cases and to provide a forum for resolving disputes by persuasion rather than legal action. Delays in reaching the Court are a significant weakness in the current framework. In environmental actions the average time span under the first Commission decision to initiate proceedings under Article 169 and the judgment by the Court, is currently 56 months,[40] while some environmental actions taken by the Commission have taken up to five years for the Court to give a ruling.[41]

The Treaty does not define what is meant by non-implementation but the Commission has generally identified three broad categories of infringement which are used for statistical purposes.

1. Non-notification implies a failure by a Member State to communicate to the Commission national laws and other national measures implementing the Community instruments in question; each directive prescribes a time-limit (normally two or three years) by which date Member States must notify their national laws used or passed to implement the directive. In reality this represents the most mechanistic aspect of the Commission's enforcement

---

[39] Though in cases of non-notification, the Commission now generally moves direct to Article 169 proceedings, having given Member States a formal reminder of the deadline contained in the relevant directive some six months earlier. It has also been agreed under internal rules that a full decision of all Commissioners is not required for this first stage.

[40] Krämer, 'Public Interest Litigation in Environmental Matters Before European Courts' (1996) JEL Vol. 8, No. 1, 1.

[41] Case C-45/91, *Commission* v. *Greece* [1992] ECR I-2509.

work since either notification has taken place or it has not. The Commission's main discretion is judging whether a Member State's argument that the communication of national legislation has been delayed but will be forthcoming is sufficient to justify withholding Article 169 proceedings. For its part the Court of Justice has consistently refused to permit Member States to raise defences concerning internal political or legal problems as justifying a delay in notification,[42] and it is sometimes surprising that cases still reach the European Court where such arguments are raised. The rise in the volume of legal proceedings for non-communication has been dramatic with just 15 proceedings begun for non-communication in the environmental sector in 1982 rising to 131 in 1990, but trailing back to 42 in 1994. In part this reflects the body of environmental legislation agreed at any particular period, but overall, the Commission's latest report on implementation records a general fall in all areas for non-notification representing in its view an improvement in the attitude of Member States.

2.   The second type of infringement concerns incomplete or incorrect transposition of Community obligations into national law. A Member State has communicated the text of national implementing measures but these are considered to fail to reflect fully the obligations under the relevant directive. This is legally more complex, requiring the Commission both to understand fully the meaning of the obligations under the relevant directive and to compare these with what are often highly complex national laws.

In the case of directives such as Directive 85/337/EEC on environmental assessment many items of national legislation may be sent, and transposition of directives within countries such as Belgium, Spain or Germany with a federated structure will often require different items of state legislation. In some cases, a Member State may have passed new, dedicated laws to implement a directive, but it may equally decide to rely upon pre-existing legislation as reflecting the directive's obligations, making the Commission's task all the more complex because the relationships between the old national legislation and the new directive will be less clear. The Commission's task is made more demanding because few Member States provide the Commission with clear and detailed guides to their national legislation and how it relates to provisions of the relevant directive. Despite the difficulties involved, ensuring correct transposal into national law is perhaps the most critical stage of the process, and much could be done to improve the effectiveness of the procedures in this respect. Ensuring that national law fully reflects Community directives cannot in itself guarantee implementation of Community obligations since one is then largely dependent on the effectiveness and capacity of national systems, both legal and administrative, to respect the rule of law. But the basic substantive content of the

---

[42] See, for example, Case 77/69, *Commission* v. *Belgium* [1970] ECR 237; Case 280/83, *Commission* v. *Italy* [1984] ECR 2361.

law would at least be in place at national level, and that must be the crucial starting point.

3. The third category involves the failure to apply the Community obligations in practice, whatever the state of the national law. Infringement proceedings of this type often represent the most controversial and politically sensitive element of the Commission's enforcement work, but have grown in importance and numbers in recent years. In certain cases, there is an uncomfortable overlap between a particular case that is treated as a failure to apply in practice but is in reality caused by the failure of the Member State to transpose correctly,[43] as illustrated by cases concerning the failure to consider an environmental assessment for particular projects where the national legislation has provided no reflection of those project classes. In a recent case concerning environmental assessment, the German government went so far as to argue that Article 169 proceedings should be used only in respect of the failure to notify or transpose provisions of directives correctly into national law, and that the Commission should have no interest in pursuing issues further if the appropriate national law was in place.[44] Although the Commission lost the case on the facts, the Court nevertheless confirmed that the Commission was fully entitled to bring Article 169 proceedings alleging that a Member State had failed to fulfil its Community obligations in that it has not achieved the results required by a directive in a particular case.

Complaints procedure

Given the small size of the legal unit within DGXI which has the lead internal responsibility for carrying out the Commission's implementation tasks (less than 20 individuals), it is in many ways remarkable what has been achieved in recent years in bringing home to Member States the nature of their responsibilities. But the Commission has a heavy burden. It is faced now with 15 Member States, each with distinct administrative and legal cultures, and with many more jurisdictions at regional and local level. There are some 70 major items of Community environmental legislation,[45] together with the increasing relevance of the requirement under the Treaty that environmental policies are integrated into other areas of Community policy.[46] In contrast to competition policy and some other areas of Community policy the Commission has no powers of

---

[43] See Macrory, 'The Enforcement of Community Laws: Some Critical Issues' (1992) 29 CML Rev 347–369.

[44] Case C-431/92, *Commission v. Federal Republic of Germany* [1995] ECR I-2189. See Macrory, 'In Court' (1995) *ENDS Report*, Vol. 251, 41.

[45] Haigh identifies 485 different items of Community environmental legislation though many of these are minor or amending pieces: *Manual of Environmental Policy: the EC and Britain* (London: Longman, 1996).

[46] Article 130r(2).

inspection on the ground, and initially is heavily dependent on the quality of information supplied by Member States. Against this background, it is hardly surprising that the Commission has felt the need to look to other sources of information to assist in its task of monitoring the state of implementation.

The complaints procedure has perhaps been the most visible symbol of this need for external assistance. Initially developed in the context of market rules in the late 1960s, the procedures have been extended by the Commission as a means of alerting it to potential breaches of any area of EC law. Once the Commission decided to make more vigorous efforts in the environmental field following the Seveso incident, the complaints procedure was vigorously pro-moted and publicised as a key element of the Commission's strategy.[47] The numbers of complaints in the environmental sector rose rapidly from just 10 in 1982 to 480 in 1990[48] dropping to 265 in 1995,[49] and every year the environ-mental field has made up a higher proportion of the total complaints received (from under 3% in 1982 to almost 40% in 1990). For individuals or non-govern-mental organisations the process has obvious attractions. No legal costs are involved nor is there any risk of a financial penalty should the allegation prove unfounded. The procedures provided an opportunity for direct access to a level of administration with potentially superior powers to that of the Member State, and can generate valuable national publicity, for local campaigns. Perhaps rather rashly the Commission offered to investigate every single complaint to the extent that it could, though since the majority concerned have concerned allegations of failure to apply EC law in practice, the Commission's powers of inquiry have largely been confined to seeking elaborative comments from the Member State.

From the Commission's perspective the procedures provided both evidence of infringements but also a means of bringing the Commission closer in touch with individual citizens. As the Commission's 1992 Annual Report on Monitoring noted on the complaint's mechanism, '[T]he Commission has tried to encourage its use with the aim of improving the application of Community law and at the same time fostering a real people's Europe. The success of the campaign has surpassed expectations, in particular on the environmental front.'[50] But there have also been drawbacks. The numbers of complaints received annually from each Member State vary tremendously with the United Kingdom and Spain consistently producing the highest numbers, but the figures reveal less about the comparative state of compliance and rather more about the vigour of non-governmental organisations and the accessibility of national dispute mechanisms. In many ways the Commission's approach appeared reac-tive and lacking in strategy; although it clearly has limited resources, and is under a general duty to consider but not necessarily investigate every com-

---

[47] See generally Krämer, 'Rights of Complaint and Access to Information at the Commission of the EC', in Deimann and Dyssli (eds) *Environmental Rights* (London: Cameron May, 1996).
[48] *Ibid.*
[49] Speech of Environment Commissioner, Brussels, 30 May 1996.
[50] European Commission (1992), *Tenth Annual Report to the European Parliament on Commission Moni-toring of the Application of Community Law*, OJ 1993 C 233, at p. 7.

plaint,[51] it has given no clear indication of any sense of priorities.[52] Expectations have exceeded the Commission's capacity to deliver, which may account for the recent fall-back in the number of complaints. Complainants may also feel that they have a particular interest in the allegation raised (although it is clear that no legal interest need be shown), and can be frustrated in finding that from a legal perspective they have no role beyond that of an informant. The Commission essentially has complete discretion to decide whether or not to commence enforcement proceedings, and third parties, including complainants, are not entitled to challenge its decision in court.[53] The names of complainants are kept confidential should they wish, as is documentation relating to infringement proceedings. In 1996, however, the World Wide Fund for Nature challenged the Commission's decision not to release to the organisation internal documents concerning the alleged infringement of structural fund regulations in connection with the Mulaghmore visitor's centre in Ireland. The organisation argued that this was in breach of the 1994 Code of Conduct on the public access to Council and Commission documents[54] and the Commission decision concerning access to Commission documents.[55] The United Kingdom intervened in support of the Commission arguing that all documentation held by the Commission relating to infringement proceedings should never be disclosed to the public, irrespective of conduct. But in 1997 the Court of Justice disagreed with the Commission's argument and held that the Code of Conduct did create rights invocable by third parties.[56] Certainly, the House of Lords Select Committee in its 1990 review of enforcement concluded ' . . . the complaints procedure remains a vital means for individual citizens to bring pressure on regulatory authorities to comply with Community law. The sheer numbers of complaints made and of consequent referral to the Court of Justice are sufficient testament to the need for such a mechanism.'[57]

The Twelfth Report on Implementation—a critical analysis

Each year the European Commission draws up a report on the monitoring of the application of EC law. At the time of writing, the most recent report

---

[51] Case 210/81, *Demo-Studio Schmidt* [1984] 1 CMLR 63.
[52] In contrast, in the competition field, the Commission has indicated that it will only investigate cases which have 'particular political, economic or legal significance for the Community', European Commission (1993), Notice of Cooperation between National Courts and the Commission in Applying Articles 85 and 86 of the EEC Treaty, OJ 1993 C 39, p. 6.
[53] Case C-247/87, *Star Fruit Company SA* v. *Commission* [1989] ECR 291; Case 246/81, *Bethell* v. *Commission* [1982] ECR 2277. See also Snyder (1993) 'The Effectiveness of European Community Law: Institutions, Processes, Tools and Techniques' (1993) 56 MLR 19.
[54] OJ 1993 L 340, p. 41.
[55] Commission Decision 94/90/EC, OJ 1994 L 46, p. 58.
[56] Case T–105/95 *WWF (UK)* v. *Commission*, 5 March 1997. Although the code of conduct permits refusal on the grounds of investigation, the decision implies that the commission cannot give blanket refusals without justification.
[57] House of Lords, *op. cit.* note 10.

published was the twelfth report, released in June 1995,[58] and consisting of a sector by sector breakdown and six detailed annexes of all EC law as at 31 December 1994. The report is therefore not solely confined to reporting on the environment and analyses the legal situation in other areas of Community policy. As the report allows Member States and their citizens to gauge their own and other Member States' progress, it has caused a certain degree of controversy due to its politically sensitive nature. Consequently, there has been a trend in recent years to minimise the information contained in the reports, with the noticeable omission in the 1995 report of statistics for the number of complaints made to the Commission. The Commission has also placed greater emphasis on the notification of national implementing measures, whilst omitting tables on the conformity of national implementing measures and the application of directives. The implications of this will be examined in greater depth at a later stage in this section.

On a general note, the report is not very 'reader friendly', and there is considerable difficulty in attempting to analyse the accuracy of the figures contained in it. The Commission gives the full list of environmental directives at point 2.8, and the progress in implementing them is summed up at Annex IV. Although it lists 136 environmental directives applicable to the environment these are integrated with the 1238 directives presented in chronological order in Annex IV and it is a very time-consuming process examining each one individually. The report is also very selective in its analysis of EC environmental law and its conclusions do not always appear to match the figures. It appears that it was probably compiled in a short space of time and it is likely that the environment section and the annex were completed by two different depart-ments. The report contains mistakes such as placing Directive 81/1051/EEC under noise in the list of environmental directives,[59] although this directive in fact concerns acquired rights for doctors, nurses, dentists and veterinary sur-geons. There are also many other areas of the report that are potentially confusing. The Commission comments that 'nature protection is another wide-spread problem area (protection of wild birds in Germany, France, Ireland, Italy, the Netherlands and Spain)' in the incorrect application of directives section. There have been no actions brought against France or Ireland for incorrect application of these directives (although France has not properly implemented the wild birds Directive). The report also claims that the Spanish legislation concerning access to environmental information conflicts with Direc-tive 90/313/EEC.[60] This may be correct but they have not had any proceedings brought against them according to figures contained in the annex.

The Commission in the twelfth report concludes that *action taken on cases of failure to notify* in 1994 breaks down as follows:

---

[58] Commission of the European Communities, *Twelfth Annual Report on Monitoring the Application of Community Law (1994)*, COM(95) 500 final.

[59] *Ibid.* p. 72, point 2.8.

[60] *Ibid.* p. 60, point 1.3.

- 42 Article 169 letters (90 in 1993)
- 46 reasoned opinions (26 in 1993)
- 3 referrals to the European Court of Justice (3 in 1993).

From this breakdown on cases of failure to notify it might be inferred that during the period covered by the twelfth report the results achieved by the Member States have been satisfactory. However, the breakdown of all the directives in Annex IV of the report showed considerable disparities with the Commission's figures. We concluded that the breakdown of action taken on cases of failure to notify was:

- 62 Article 169 letters
- 53 reasoned opinions
- 3 referrals to the European Court of Justice.

The full breakdown of our figures is contained in Appendix 1 of this book. It is clear to see that the difference in the Commission's conclusion and the figures contained in Annex IV is quite extensive and suggests that the Commission has seriously miscalculated or presented the data in a misleading fashion. In a number of respects the report also presents figures which on the surface improve the overall picture, though in overall numbers these are not immensely significant.[61]

What is most noticeable, after analysis of the report, is that the Commission only includes actions for the particular given year (in this instance—1994). Whilst this is a perfectly reasonable way of presenting the report, it does not provide a full picture of the true state of compliance with EC environmental law. To gain a more accurate picture of this dark side of non-compliance we compiled the results for all the infringement procedures for failing to notify which had not been terminated (i.e. 1994 and before). We discovered that the figures were far higher than could have been expected, even though we have presented the figures in exactly the same manner that the Commission has done in the report. On this analysis the position is:

- 90 Article 169 letters
- 67 reasoned opinions
- 6 referrals to the European Court of Justice.

On p. 72 of the report, the Commission has produced a table which illustrates the progress of Member States in implementing directives applicable to the

---

[61] 1. The results include measures to be terminated in 1995, but do not include enforcement measures to be taken in 1995, which improves the position of Member States.

2. If a country persistently fails to notify measures for a directive, then this is not included in the statistics, which simply concentrate on the directive, not the action taken. Therefore, if one Member State has two actions brought against it for not notifying any measures for a particular directive and another has had only one action taken against it, no distinction appears in the report.

3. The Commission has joined actions, so although a Member State may have two separate actions brought against it under two different directives at the reasoned opinion stage, if they are referred to the Court of Justice the actions may be classed and reported as one.

Member State	Directives applicable on 31 December 1994	Directives for which measures have been notified	%
Denmark	125	125	100
Netherlands	125	123	98
Ireland	125	121	97
France	125	118	94
Luxembourg	125	116	93
Germany	127	116	91
Spain	129	111	86
Belgium	125	106	85
Greece	130	110	85
Portugal	129	106	82
United Kingdom	125	102	82
Italy	125	95	76

Source: Table 2.8, Twelfth Report of Commission, Environment (1995).

environment (see table 2.8). Again this is exclusively devoted to directives for which measures have been notified—and again there is considerable difficulty in analysing these figures. There is no explanation concerning which directives are applicable to each Member State. It is difficult to comprehend from the Annex (IV) why the United Kingdom has 125 directives which are applicable to it, whereas Greece has 130. In some instances the annex did state that the directive was addressed to a particular Member State,[62] but this was not consistent with the numbers contained in the table.

After the figures in the report were released, ENDS commented that 'the UK has a poor record in transposing EC environmental legislation into its laws on time'.[63] But on closer analysis of the figures contained in the table it was obvious that the statistics representing the United Kingdom were incorrect if Annex IV was to be relied upon, and indeed it is the only country where the figures do not match. In the table the Commission had recorded the number of directives that have not been notified as 23, whereas the annex recorded only 15 directives that the United Kingdom had not notified.[64] If the annex is correct then the United Kingdom would have notified implementing measures for 88% of the directives, which would place them significantly higher in the 'league table'—from second from bottom to seventh. Tables such as these are very politically sensitive because at the end of the day figures appear to represent hard facts and are difficult to play down.

There is also a written section (para 1.3) dedicated to the *conformity of national*

---

[62] E.g. Directive 90/656/EEC—Transitional measures—protection of the environment (addressed Germany); Directive 90/660/EEC—Transitional measures—protection of the environment (addressed Germany); Directive 81/857/EEC—Air quality (addressed Greece).

[63] See 'Greater Citizen's Rights Mooted to Spur Compliance with EC Laws' (1995) *ENDS Report*, Vol. 249, 37.

[64] Directives: 91/156/EEC, 91/157/EEC, 92/112/EEC, 93/86/EEC, 91/271/EEC, 92/72/EEC, 92/43/EEC, 91/325/EEC, 91/410/EEC, 91/632/EEC, 92/37/EEC, 93/67/EEC, 93/90/EEC, 93/105/EEC, 94/15/EC.

implementing measures, where the Commission comments that there were only two reasoned opinions and one referral to the Court of Justice in 1994. It appears from the figures contained in Annex IV that this is correct. As was mentioned earlier, the Commission has neglected to give figures for the conformity of national implementing measures in the environment section of the twelfth report. The stages of proceedings were probably placed in the annex and not included in the section dedicated to the environment, because there were no Article 169 proceedings initiated in 1994 by the Commission. This is quite controversial, especially in light of the Commission's boast that 'the number of infringement proceedings for incorrect transposal fell in 1994'.[65]

It is extremely difficult to present the figures for directives that are not properly implemented in any logical way, so the full breakdown of the figures is contained in Appendix 2 of this book. It was noticeable that there has been a considerable number of judgments which have not been complied with. A judgment of the Court can only be given in the form of a simple declaration that by the act or omission specified the Member State has failed to fulfil an obligation under the Treaty. If the Member State continues not to fulfil its obligations it will violate Article 171 of the EC Treaty, but will not receive any further sanctions other than the Commission issuing a reasoned opinion and the case possibly going back before the Court of Justice if the judgment has not been complied with within a reasonable time-limit. The report lists eight actions that have been commenced/terminated under Article 171 for conformity of national implementing measures. Germany is to receive a supplementary reasoned opinion in 1995 after failing to comply with a 171 referral in 1993. This demonstrates the potential ineffectiveness of EC law— even though the Maastricht Treaty inserted a provision where the Court of Justice could issue penalties against Member States for failure to comply with its judgments, this has still to be used. There are also Member States that have still not complied with actions brought against them as long ago as 1988.[66]

It is apparent that there have been 45 actions taken by the Commission against Member States for non-conformity of national implementing measures, which are included in the report (whether they are to be sent or are terminated). It was noticeable that out of this number there was only problems implementing 17 directives. Further, out of this figure, there were 26 actions brought under just four directives.[67] This could mean that Member States have had problems implementing certain laws either because of their legal or administrative cultures, or due to a problem with the directive itself. Alternatively, it could also show that the Commission may strictly enforce certain areas of law and check them more rigorously (e.g. radiation protection); or if it finds one Member

---

[65] *Op. cit.* note 58, p. 59, point 1.3.
[66] Directive 80/778/EEC on the quality of drinking water; Italy: C-87/363—reasoned opinion 1988.
[67] The four are: Directive 85/337/EEC—Assessment of the effects of projects on the environment; Directive 70/409/EEC—Conservation of wild birds; Directive 84/466/EEC—Radiation protection; and Directive 80/68/EEC—Protection of groundwater.

State in breach of a particular directive, it checks all the other Members States for possible breaches for the same one.

There is also a section (para 1.4) dedicated to the *incorrect application of environmental directives*, where the Commission comments that it sent six reasoned opinions to Member States during the year. There were also no Article 169 letters sent in 1994 for directives that were not properly applied. It appears that the Commission has put far more of its enforcement efforts into the notification of implementing measures by Member States and has placed less emphasis on the application and actual implementing side of Community environmental law.

Again, as we did for notification, it is necessary to compile the results for all the infringement procedures for incorrect application of directives which had not been terminated or issued yet. This provides a more objective idea of the level of control and application of EC environmental law. The full breakdown of our figures is contained in Appendix 3 of this book.

- 0 Article 169 letters
- 22 reasoned Opinions
- 12 referrals to the European Court of Justice

Close analysis reveals that the Commission is having many problems terminating existing actions and this is affecting its ability to initiate new proceedings. At the date the report was compiled the Commission had only made plans to initiate two new proceedings in 1995, and these were to be taken under Article 171.

There were 43 actions recorded in the report as being brought for incorrect application in practice (a similar amount as failure to implement). There were similarly only 16 problem directives, and 22 of the actions brought were for the misapplication of only four directives.[68] The directives that have created the most significant problems have been those concerned with water. It is obvious that there is a large backlog of outstanding cases where the Member States are still having difficulty applying the law. There are still four actions from 1989 where Member States are applying the law incorrectly.[69] There have also been four instances of 'dual' actions brought against Member States who have had two separate actions brought against them under the same directive.[70] Many of the actions brought for breach of directives under the applying heading were also

---

[68] The four are: Directive 85/339/EEC—Containers for liquids for human consumption; Directive 76/464/EEC—Dangerous substances in the sea; Directive 80/778/EEC—Quality of drinking water; Directive 79/409/EEC—Conservation of wild birds.

[69] Directive 85/339/EEC—Containers for human consumption—Belgium: C-89/330/EEC (referral); Directive 79/409/EEC—Conservation of wild birds—Germany: C-89/57 (referral); Directive 79/409/EEC–Conservation of wild birds—Italy: C-87/327 (referral); Directive 80/68/EEC—Protection of groundwater—United Kingdom: C-85/354 (reasoned opinion).

[70] Germany—Directive 80/778/EEC—Quality of drinking water; Italy—Directive 76/464/EEC—Dangerous substances in the sea; Italy—Directive 79/409/EEC—Conservation of wild birds; United Kingdom—Directive 80/778/EEC—Quality of drinking water.

the same directives which Member States failed to implement properly (e.g. conservation of wild birds).

Close analysis also reveals the inconsistencies shown by the different Member States in implementing directives. Although Denmark and Italy were consistently at either end of the scale, it was noticeable that many countries that had very good records for notifying measures had very poor ones for conformity of implementing measures and application of directives. The Netherlands and Ireland had very impressive records of notifying laws and were rated second and third respectively, in the European 'league table' (table 2.8). However, the Netherlands had difficulty in the conformity of national implementing measures for seven directives, and Ireland, five. In comparison, some countries that were poor at notifying laws had far fewer cases brought against them for poor implementation. In the European league table for notification, Greece were positioned ninth and Portugal tenth, but Greece did not have any actions brought against it for non-implementation, and Portugal only had one. Similarly, Belgium was poor at notifying and implementing the law but had only one action brought against it for applying it incorrectly. Germany had the biggest problems implementing and applying the law, and had difficulty implementing nine directives, and applying seven directives. For the record, the United Kingdom is recorded as having problems implementing three directives and applying three directives. Close analysis of the figures also reveals that the Commission appears to be having considerable difficulties in clearing up the backlog of cases.

In September 1995, the European Parliament issued its response to the twelfth report.[71] This was quite critical of the report and the Commission, and although it contended that its own power base was being undermined and that the Commission ignored its previous recommendations, it does contain some interesting observations and conclusions. It is quite critical of the lack of information contained in the report and suggests that the Commission should list: terminated cases, complaints—broken down by sector, and a detailed comprehensive list of all the oral and written questions which led it to initiate infringement proceedings, the Member States concerned, and results obtained through action by or *vis-à-vis* the Member States. The Parliament also suggested that the power of enforcement is the only way to monitor the application of EC law. It suggests the establishment of a body of Community environmental inspectors, an instrument to facilitate public involvement in the application of EC environmental law via direct access to justice, increasing the staff complement of the relevant Directorate General, and the setting up of closer cooperation between administrative departments when drafting measures and then monitoring them.

---

[71] European Parliament—Committee on the Environment, Public Health and Consumer Protection, 'Draft Opinion for the Committee on Legal Affairs and Citizens' Rights on the Twelfth Annual Report on Monitoring the Application of Community Law' (COM(95) 0500 final—C4-0233/95) 28 September 1995.

Proposals for reform

In this final section we make a number of proposals for improving the Community mechanisms for dealing with the implementation and enforcement of EC law. These are based on the assumption that the Commission's basic responsibilities in this area will not be fundamentally altered as a consequence of the Inter-Governmental Conference, nor do we expect that the new European Environment Agency will take a lead role in enforcement, despite pressures from the European Parliament for it to do so when its constituent powers are reviewed by the Council of Ministers.[72] And in making such proposals, we recognise they form only one element in the search for improved implementation, though one that we would argue is of central importance.

1. The Inter-Governmental Conference will be required to consider the whole question of the classification and hierarchy of Community legal instruments.[73] Our own view is that directives will continue to play an important role, but nevertheless the rationale for the choice between regulations and directives needs addressing, rather than leaving in the rather haphazard fashion that appears to exist at present.

2. The quality of draftsmen of Community instruments is a constant complaint, though not all the blame can be put on the Commission; Member States still make last minute late night compromises in Council with apparent little thought for the ambiguities created. Nevertheless the tradition of specialised legal draftsmen as opposed to legal translators has never been strong within the Community, and greater attention can be paid to improving the process. Equally significantly, it is important that lessons learnt from past mistakes are effectively fed back into the development of new legislation and internally within the Commission, the relationship between the legal unit and policy departments who usually have the responsibility for initial drafting is especially significant and in this context it would be valuable to understand why this should be the case. The twelfth report indicates that a small number of directives have caused the most problems, especially in the conformity of national implementing measures and incorrect application of directives; the European Parliament has also made the point that 'in each environmental sector there are delays in the application of directives—always the same ones—and, apart from rare exceptions, the Commission is still waiting or is pursuing discussions'.[74]

3. There should be a general requirement that draft implementing national

---

[72] Regulation 1210/90/EEC, Article 20 requires the Council to consider extending the Agency's tasks including, *inter alia*, being associated in the monitoring of the implementation of legislation.

[73] 'The Conference agrees that the Intergovernmental Conference to be convened in 1996 will examine to what extent it might be possible to review the classification of Community Acts with a view to establishing an appropriate hierarchy between the differing categories of Act.'

[74] European Parliament, *op. cit.* note 71.

legislation be sent to the Commission at least six months before a directive comes into force. All institutions are reluctant to lose face, and once national laws have been passed, Member States will naturally resist change if the Commission queries their consistency with a directive. The Commission cannot, of course, guarantee authoritative interpretation of the directive and there will still be room for argument, but dealing with a draft is much less problematical and early changes may avoid future problems. In practice this happens from time to time[75] but at present there is no systematic and consistent procedure. Directive 94/62/EEC on packaging appears to be the first environmental instrument which does contain such a requirement,[76] although the ambiguous language (no timescales are specified, for example) leaves room for avoidance and few Member States have yet complied with the obligation.[77] Nevertheless, it may provide a model for a requirement that should generally be included in future directives, and even if this results in the timescales for bringing into force being extended from the normal period of two years to, say, three, this may well be worth the price if the result is greatly improved transposition.

4. In providing details of national legislation implementing a directive, Member States should provide a systematic analysis which provides an article by article guide to the relevant implementing provisions in national law. Again this rarely happens in practice at present,[78] and such a requirement would both sharpen thinking at Member State level and improve the quality of the Commission's own analysis. Such documentation should be available to the public.

5. There should be a fast track procedure for going to the European Court of Justice in cases of non-notification. At present the Commission moves automatically into sending an Article 169 letter once the deadline period has passed, but given the clear-cut nature of the breach there seems little point in requiring a reasoned opinion stage which leads to further delay.

6. There has also been abuse of the Article 171 procedure by many Member States. The length of time that it takes to go to the Court is already exceptionally high because it is overburdened with actions, without having to place further sanctions against Member States under Article 171 proceedings. During the time between these proceedings breaches of law will continue to occur, much to the detriment of the environment. The sooner that the Community clarifies what the penalties under the Maastricht provision are, the less likely will actions progress to the Article 171 stage.

7. The Commission should be more prepared to publish informal guides to

---

[75] It is well known, for example, that the UK government and Commission officials had considerable discussions concerning the provisions of the Water Act 1989 when it was still at Bill stage, leading to changes in the final version.

[76] Article 12 of Directive 94/62/EEC on packaging and packaging waste.

[77] European Commission, pers. comm. 29 May 1996.

[78] Krämer, 'Public Interest Litigation in Environmental Matters Before European Courts' (1996) JEL Vol. 8, No. 1, 1.

its understanding of new directives and their implications, in the manner of administrative circulars. Such material would assist both Member States and other interests such as industry who may be affected by the implementation of new legislation. Again such guidance could never be the final legal interpretation on EC legislation since that responsibility rests with the Court, but such a limitation is a familiar feature of national government advisory material. Since the Council remains the final decision-maker on new EC legislation, in an ideal world such guidance would in fact be jointly issued by the Commission and Council, but this may be too optimistic to consider as a realistic possibility. Since the Commission is also responsible for enforcement actions against Member States, it may well be reluctant to issue advance opinions on its interpretation for fear that this might inhibit or prevent it taking enforcement proceedings at a later stage should its views on the law change. It seems, however, unlikely that the Commission would be legally barred from commencing proceedings which were inconsistent with previous advice issued by it, providing it was taking an objective view of the legal position, though the issue might well be relevant to any claim for damages under *Francovich* principles,[79] against a Member State which had *bona fide* relied upon the Commission's interpretative advice.

8. While the complaints procedure should remain in place, the Commission should be prepared to develop and publish a more coherent strategy on its priorities for investigation. Under current staffing arrangements it is simply unrealistic for the Commission to commit itself to give the same attention to all alleged cases of infringement. At the same time there is a case for some form of filtering process. One model would be, along the lines of the UK Ombudsman procedure, for all complaints to be made initially to Members of the European Parliament who would then decide which ones to pass on to the Commission for investigation. Our own preference, however, would be for the establishment of Commission officials within each Member State to act as the first point of referral. It may be that their role would be confined to the preparation of an initial dossier (including observations from national or local government) for later referral to the relevant Directorate General, but this would be preferable to the current cumbersome procedure under which Commission officials deal with national representatives in Brussels who act as a sort of distant postbox with national governments, even at the stage of acquiring a relatively straightforward factual background to a complaint.

9. For those countries with highly devolved systems of government, such as Belgium, Spain, or Germany, the implementation of directives can present real problems. To what extent can a central government claim it has no responsibility for failure to implement because of lack of constitutional

---

[79] See para. 56, Judgment of the ECJ, Joined Cases C-46 and C-48/93, *Brasserie du Pêcheur SA* v. *Germany* and *R* v. *Secretary of State for Transport, ex parte Factortame (Factortame III)* [1996] 1 CMLR 889.

powers? The legal answer of course is that it is the Member State that fails, and the European Court of Justice has consistently refused to acknowledge that internal constitutional arrangements can provide any justification for failure to implement Community obligations.[80] One solution is to ensure that where EC law is concerned, central or federal government possesses the legal power to pass national laws implementing a Community obligation overriding where necessary a reluctant devolved administration. Yet this centralising effect of EC law[81] runs counter to concepts of federalism that invoke genuine decentralised powers as well as centralisation. It may be that in a more mature system of Community law, we need to move beyond traditional concepts of the Member State—with central government traditionally representing the Member State on the analogy of foreign policy powers. In practice this is beginning to happen in some cases with representatives of regional administrations taking part in the development of Community legislation. In the context of enforcement, this would imply that the Commission should be able to bring Article 169 proceedings directly against a regional body where in accordance with national constitutional arrangements it has the real powers to implement. This suggestion raises complex political and administrative questions but it is one that should be addressed.

10. Detailed and quality information concerning the state of implementation is important. It alerts Member States to the position in other countries and may encourage them to bring peer pressure to bear on recalcitrant countries. It informs citizens of Member States of the position in their country so that they in turn may pressurise their own countries where necessary. And it can act as a significant monitor and check on the way that the Commission is carrying out its own enforcement responsibilities. As we have illustrated, the present structure and contents of the Commission's annual reports is defective and open to criticism. The Commission has not included full statistics in the main text of its report for conformity of national implementing measures and incorrect application of directives, and is in essence painting half a picture by only including statistics and tables on notification.

There is a compelling case for the Commission producing an annual implementation report devoted solely to environmental matters, similar to that produced in the competition field. The proportion of annual complaints concerning the environment compared to other areas of Community policy demonstrates the public significance of Community environmental policy, and such a report would provide a necessary and appropriate counterpart to the more sophisticated reports on the physical

---

[80] Case C-96/81, *Commission v. Netherlands* [1982] ECR 1791.
[81] See Haigh, 'Devolved Responsibility and Centralization: Effects of EEC Environmental Policy' (1986) 64 *Public Administration* 197.

state of the Community's environment which are likely to emerge from the activities of the European Environment Agency.

There is no single solution to the problem of ensuring more effective implementation of Community environmental legislation. It requires positive and consistent input at all levels of administration, at Community, national and local level, and a conscious appreciation of the importance of the issue from the design of new legislation to the monitoring of its impact in practice. The Inter-Governmental Conference and the prospect of new Member States from Central and Eastern Europe provide an opportunity for a re-evaluation of the adequacy of current arrangements, and there are welcome signals that the subject is now being treated with more seriousness. Within this complex web the role of the European Commission is both distinctive and critical, but the current arrangements are by no means satisfactory. Far from aiming to diminish the Commission's role, Member States will need to appreciate that in the long term it is in their own interests and that of its citizens that the Commission is able to carry out its enforcement responsibilities in an effective and consistent manner.

See Addendum on p. 335.

Chapter 4

COMMUNITY RIGHTS IN ENVIRONMENTAL LAW: RHETORIC OR REALITY?

Chris Hilson

Do citizens of the Union enjoy a right to clean water under the Drinking Water Directive 80/778/EEC? Or a right to clean air under directives on ambient air quality such as Directive 80/779/EEC on smoke and sulphur dioxide, or Directive 85/203/EEC on nitrogen oxide?[1] According to recent European Court of Justice case law, the answer in relation to these particular directives is 'yes', because they are intended to protect human health. However, other environmental directives which are not so intended, apparently do not confer rights on citizens. In other words the rights which citizens enjoy under environmental directives are very narrowly drawn and anthropocentric in their focus; the Court of Justice is, as yet, far from creating proper environmental rights as such. What is more, it is one thing to speak the language of rights and something quite different to create effective enforcement mechanisms to protect those rights: rights without effective remedies are hardly worth having. The most obvious fora for citizens to enforce their Community rights under environmental directives is in their national courts. However, an examination of UK experience in rights cases reveals a depressing picture and the prospects for *Francovich*[2] enforcement of rights in the environmental area are, it is submitted, no more uplifting.

The context of rights

There are three principal means of privately enforcing EC law, environmental

---

[1] At the outset, it should be noted that the term 'rights' here is being used in the sense of rights enjoyed under directives (or, often the Treaty in non-environmental cases), and not in the sense of fundamental human rights. There is a clear distinction between the two: human rights act as a trump card over executive or legislative action, whereas rights in the straightforward Community sense are actually contained in Community legislative action. However, as will be seen later in the text (e.g. in relation to standing in national law), that is not to say that Community rights might not act as a form of trump over national law remedial obstacles.

[2] Cases C-6 and 9/90, *Francovich* v. *Italian State* [1993] 2 CMLR 66.

or otherwise: the principle of direct effect; the principle of indirect effect or sympathetic interpretation; and liability of the Member State under *Francovich*. Beginning with the principle of direct effect, briefly stated, a Member State must implement a directive by a given date. If proper implementation has not taken place by that date, then citizens are, in certain circumstances, able to rely on the terms of the directive directly as against the Member State or emanations of the Member State[3] in an action in their national courts.[4] Those circumstances are that the relevant terms of the directive must be sufficiently clear, precise and unconditional.[5] Directives are only directly effective 'vertically' against the Member State or emanations of the Member State; they are not directly effective 'horizontally' against private individuals. Nevertheless, the principle of indirect effect or sympathetic interpretation may come into play in an action against a private individual.[6] Under this principle, national courts are obliged, as far as possible, to interpret provisions of national law, whether adopted before or after a directive, in the light of the wording and purpose of the directive. After *Francovich*, citizens may also be able to sue their Member State for damages for non-implementation of a directive and now also for faulty implementation (and possibly for practical breaches of a directive, though the latter is not yet clear).[7] However, certain conditions must be satisfied before such an action can be brought: first, the directive must confer rights on individuals; secondly, it must be possible to determine the content of those rights from the provisions of the directive; and finally, there must be a causal link between the breach of

---

[3] See Case C-188/89, *Foster* v. *British Gas plc* [1990] 3 All ER 897; in an employment case, our national courts have decided that a privatised water company counts as an emanation of the state—see *Griffin* v. *South West Water Services Ltd* [1995] IRLR 15; [1995] *Water Law* 5.

[4] An important point to note is that not all actions which raise the direct effect principle are concerned with 'reading' the terms of the directive directly in place of the faulty or non-existent domestic implementing legislation. This is particularly true where the directive has been properly implemented but where there is a practical breach of national quality standards which derive from the directive. The recent case of *R* v. *Secretary of State for the Environment, ex parte Friends of the Earth Ltd* [1996] 1 CMLR 117 is a good example of this: FOE argued that their directly effective Community rights under the Drinking Water Directive were being threatened, but at no point did they need to 'read' any provisions from the directive directly.

[5] The ECJ has, for example, ruled that Article 4 of the Waste Framework Directive 75/442/EEC is not directly effective because its provisions are neither unconditional nor sufficiently precise (though, as note 45 below makes clear, the Court did not in fact use the language of 'direct effect'): Case C-236/92, *Comitato di Coordinamento per la Difesa della Cava* v. *Regione Lombardia* [1994] ECR I-483.

[6] Although it should be noted that this principle is not limited to actions against private individuals but can also be applied in an action against the state or an emanation of the state—see e.g. *R* v. *Secretary of State for the Environment, ex parte Greenpeace* [1994] 4 All ER 352.

[7] *Francovich* was a case involving an act of non-transposition of a directive by the Italian national legislature. In the recent joined cases of C-46/93 and C-48/93, *Brasserie du Pêcheur SA* v. *Federal Republic of Germany* and *R* v. *Secretary of State for Transport, ex parte Factortame Ltd* (*Factortame IV*) [1996] All ER (EC) 301, the ECJ has confirmed that there is a general principle of liability for breach of Community law. In other words, liability is not limited to non-transposition of directives and may exist e.g. in relation to defective transposition of directives (as in Case C-392/93, *R.* v. *H.M. Treasury, ex parte British Telecommunications Plc* [1996] 2 CMLR 217) and for breaches of Treaty provisions (as in the above *Brasserie* and *Factortame* cases).

the Member State's obligation and the damage suffered by the person concerned.[8]

Only with one of these, *Francovich*, has the Court of Justice explicitly referred in its judgment to the need for the directive to confer rights on the individual as a precondition. Nevertheless, it is commonly accepted that the same is true of direct effect and indirect effect—to rely on either of these, the directive must confer a right upon the individual bringing the action.[9]

The next question we need to ask ourselves therefore is under which directives does one enjoy personal or individual rights—the prerequisite of direct effect, indirect effect and *Francovich* enforcement? And who enjoys these personal rights? Because we are concerned with who has rights under a directive, this can be viewed as a question of standing for the purposes of EC law jurisprudence on actions in national courts.[10] After all, *locus standi* or standing is concerned with the question of who is allowed to come before the court.

The ECJ case law on rights

There are essentially two approaches to the issue of standing or who enjoys rights under EC law. First, there is the restrictive view, which holds that rights will only be enjoyed by those who are 'directly affected' (not to be confused with 'direct effect') by an EC law or, in the case of ordinary citizens in relation to environmental directives, where the directive is intended to protect human health. Everybody else possesses simply an *interest* in the application or enforcement of the law rather than a *right* as such. This may be protected by the national

---

[8] The recent ECJ decision in *Brasserie du Pêcheur* and *Factortame* (*Factortame IV*), note 7 above, appears to replace the original *Francovich* conditions with the following: (a) the rule of law infringed must be intended to confer rights on individuals; (b) the breach must be sufficiently serious and (c) there must be a direct causal link between the breach of the obligation by the Member State and the damage sustained by injured parties. This new second condition is designed to impose on Member States the same conditions on liability as those imposed by the ECJ on Community institutions under Article 215 of the EC Treaty. For the moment, we are concerned with rights, which feature in both versions.

[9] See e.g. Van Gerven, 'Bridging the Gap Between Community and National Laws: Towards a Principle of Homogeneity in the Field of Legal Remedies' (1995) 32 CML Rev 679, at 682; Steiner, *Enforcing EC Law* (1995), pp. 42–43. Steiner notes the move away from the expression 'directly effective Community rights' to 'Community rights', which arose because Community rights were also relevant under Community laws which were not directly effective but where the principles of indirect effect or state liability under *Francovich* applied. In relation to indirect effect, one might ask how the relevance of rights is reconcilable with the statement in the *Faccini Dori* case to the effect that a directive cannot, of itself, impose obligations on individuals, the correlative of which is that individuals enjoy no *rights* as against other private individuals (Case C-91/92, *Faccini Dori* v. *Recreb Srl* [1995] All ER (EC) 1, at 20–21). The answer would seem to be that one's *rights* under a directive are still being protected via the principle of sympathetic interpretation—it is simply that one does not enjoy *directly effective* rights against individuals.

[10] This should not be confused with standing in national law, although, as will be seen later, a reference to Community rights (standing) may be used to argue for the grant of standing in national law.

law of particular Member States but EC law does not require it. Secondly, there is a 'citizen action' approach, which would allow any citizen rights under EC law, whether or not the citizen is directly affected, and whether or not the directive is intended to protect human health.

As things stand, the Court of Justice adopts the first approach. The case which emphasises this most clearly is the non-environmental, *Rewe* case.[11] In that case, Advocate General[12] (hereafter AG) Capotorti distinguishes between persons with personal or individual rights under EC law and persons who merely have an interest in the application of the law. Those with personal rights under EC legislation can invoke it in national courts; those who have only a general interest in the enforcement of that legislation cannot invoke it unless national law so provides.[13] On the facts of the case, AG Capotorti distinguishes between: on the one hand importers and exporters, who have a personal right under the Common Customs Tariff because customs duties directly affect them economically; and on the other hand, traders, who merely have an interest in seeing that customs duties are properly applied in relation to imported goods which compete with those produced or distributed by them.[14]

The question for our purposes is who enjoys personal rights in the case of environmental directives? There are some environmental directives which clearly give personal rights to citizens.[15] The Environmental Assessment Directive 85/337/EEC, for example, provides the 'public concerned' by a project covered by the Directive with certain rights in terms of consultation and the provision of information. Similarly, Directive 90/313/EEC on access to environmental information provides all citizens with a right of access to information on the environment. More difficult are those environmental directives which do not *explicitly* provide such rights, as is the case with most of the pollution and nature conservation directives.

There are some interesting *obiter*[16] observations on who enjoys rights under pollution directives, made in a number of Article 169 cases brought by the Commission against Germany. The *ratio* of these Article 169 cases concerns the need to have directives implemented by proper, legislative means rather than by administrative means such as circulars: only if directives

---

[11] Case 158/80, *Rewe* v. *Hauptzollampt Kiel* [1981] ECR 1805—a case cited by Krämer, 'The Implementation of Community Environmental Directives Within Member States: Some Implications of the Direct Effect Doctrine' (1991) JEL Vol. 2, No. 1, 39, at 52.

[12] The opinions given by the Advocate Generals are not as persuasive as the judgment of the Court, but they nevertheless carry considerable weight. See further Vranken, 'Role of the Advocate General in the Law-Making Process of the European Community' (1996) 25(1) *Anglo American Law Review* 39.

[13] Note 11 above, at 1850, para. 6. Capotorti states that 'Any other view would entail allowing a kind of azione popolare [civil action serving as a test case on a matter affecting public interests] on the basis of directly applicable Community provisions.'

[14] The traders, although obviously affected economically, are affected less directly.

[15] See Krämer, note 11 above, at 54.

[16] Although, since the ECJ lacks a doctrine of binding precedent, the distinction between the *ratio decidendi* and *obiter dicta* is not of great significance.

are implemented into national law in a manner that is sufficiently public, binding, specific, clear and precise, can rights be created that are enforceable in national courts.[17] However, the cases also contain some significant *obiter dicta* on who enjoys these rights, and it is these dicta which will be discussed below.

The most restrictive dicta can be found in the Opinion of AG Jacobs in Case C-58/89, *Commission v. Germany*.[18] He argues that the only people with personal rights under Directives 75/440/EEC and 79/869/EEC on surface water for drinking which must be enforceable in national courts, are the water undertakings.[19] In other words, he would limit the scope of personal rights to those who are directly affected economically by the Directives. Despite the fact that the Directives are stated (in the preamble) to be intended for the protection of human health[20] (the significance of this will become apparent below), AG Jacobs thinks that it is going too far to suggest that 'the national measures must be such as to confer rights on third parties to challenge inadequate compliance or implementation. It is true that the public at large, as well as ecologists and environmental pressure groups, have a general interest in water quality, and indeed in the respect for Community law. It does not however automatically follow that enforceable rights must be made available to them in the national courts.'[21]

In contrast to the Opinion of AG Jacobs, the Court in Case C-58/89 ruled that since Directives 75/440/EEC and 79/869/EEC on surface water for drinking are *explicitly* intended to protect human health, it implies that 'whenever non-compliance with the measures required by the directives in question might endanger the health of persons, those concerned should be able to rely on mandatory rules in order to enforce their rights'.[22] Similarly, in Case C-361/88, *Commission v. Germany*, the Court states that since the limit values laid down in Article 2 of Directive 80/779/EEC (sulphur dioxide and suspended particulates in air) are imposed 'in order to protect human health in particular', the implication is 'that whenever the exceeding of the limit values could endanger human health, the persons concerned must be in a position to rely on manda-

---

[17] Note that 'legislative means' connotes a general, legal context that is sufficiently clear, precise, public and binding—express, specific legislation to transpose the directive into national law is not required: Case C-131/88, *Commission v. Germany* [1991] I-ECR 825, at 867, para. 6.

[18] [1991] I-ECR 4983. The *obiter* nature of the remarks is emphasised at 5009, para. 36.

[19] Companies can enjoy a personal or individual right, because individuals include natural or legal persons.

[20] This intention is stated in the preamble of Directive 75/440/EEC, and since 79/869/EEC is merely a supplement, it applies to that too.

[21] Note 18 above, at 5008. Cf. the more recent Case C-237/90, *Commission v. Germany*, not yet reported, annotated Holder and Elworthy, (1994) 31 CML Rev 123, where AG Jacobs states that the Drinking Water Directive 80/778/EEC confers rights on individuals other than water undertakers (at 132). However, this statement is seemingly made in the context of a (*Francovich*) compensation for damage claim, rather than in the context of an individual taking preventive enforcement action.

[22] Note 18 above, at 5023, para. 14. It added that a further reason for establishing the limits in a binding form is to enable the operators of surface water sampling points to know exactly what their obligations are.

tory rules in order to be able to assert their rights'.[23] The Court held that Germany was in breach of EC law because it could not be claimed 'that individuals are in a position to know with certainty the full extent of their rights in order to rely on them, where appropriate, before the national courts or that those whose activities are liable to give rise to nuisances are adequately informed of the extent of their obligations'.[24] In other words, because all of the above directives are intended to protect human health, those whose health may be affected enjoy personal rights under the directives which must be enforceable in national courts.[25] Whether, as a *group* an organisation such as Greenpeace or Friends of the Earth would be regarded by the European Court of Justice as capable of enjoying *personal* or individual rights is open to question, though it must be said that if they decided that such groups could not enjoy rights through their members,[26] the enforcement potential of actions in national courts would be seriously weakened.

What of directives which are not explicitly intended to protect human health (to go by their preambles), such as the Groundwater Directive 80/68/EEC and the Dangerous Substances in Water Directive 76/464/EEC and its daughter directives? The judgment of the Court in Case C-131/88, *Commission* v. *Germany*[27] states only that the Groundwater Directive 80/68/EEC creates individual rights

---

[23] [1991] I-ECR 2567, at 2601, para. 16.

[24] *Ibid.* at 2602, para. 20.

[25] See also Case C-59/89, *Commission* v. *Germany* [1991] I-ECR 2607 which makes similar comments about Directive 82/884/EEC on lead in air (at 2631, para. 19 and at 2632, para. 23) and Case C-298/95, *Commission* v. *Germany*, nyr, in respect of Directives 78/659/EEC and 79/923/EEC on water standards for fish and shellfish.

[26] In terms of our national courts, note that in the Court of Appeal in *Ex parte Friends of the Earth Ltd*, note 4 above, at 141, the Court was prepared to assume that the Drinking Water Directive did confer rights on individuals, 'and that includes the applicants' (i.e. the group FOE as well as an individual, Christine Orengo). See also Fitzpatrick, 'Local Protection of the Environment and European Community Harmonisation Directives: The London Lorries Case' (1992) JEL Vol. 4, No. 1, 121, at 136. He notes that in *R* v. *London Boroughs Transport Committee, ex parte Freight Transport Association Ltd* (*Ibid.* at 121), the fact that the associations were representative bodies acting on behalf of individual members, and might therefore have been said not to enjoy individual rights themselves, was not raised. Fitzpatrick, stating that direct effect is a matter of justiciability rather than individual rights, concludes that the nature of the applicant should make no difference. In terms of the requirements that the provisions of the directive be clear, precise etc., direct effect could be said to be a matter of justiciability. However, the *Rewe* case (note 11 above) tells us, *pace* Fitzpatrick, that direct effect *is* also about individual rights and in that respect, the nature of the applicant is important: a third party who does not enjoy individual rights under a directive cannot rely on direct effect. The question, therefore, is whether an environmental group (or a freight association) can derive an individual right for itself via its members who *are* acknowledged to enjoy individual rights. This link between a group's interests and those of its members is considered in some detail in the context of domestic standing in Hilson and Cram, 'Judicial Review and Environmental Law: Is There a Coherent View of Standing?' (1996) 16(1) *Legal Studies* 1. Of course, if one is to inquire into this link in relation to groups and associations, one might also ask the same question in relation to commercial companies (cf. note 19 above), noting of course that many large environmental groups are themselves limited companies.

[27] See note 17 above.

for companies concerned with the substances referred to in the Directive.[28] While the judgment is silent on the position of ordinary citizens, it probably follows from the cases discussed in the previous paragraph that, since the Groundwater Directive is not *explicitly* intended to protect human health, they would not possess rights under the directive which must be enforceable in national courts. The Opinion of AG Van Gerven in the case does discuss ordinary citizens, but it is hardly clear on the matter. He states that, although Directive 80/68/EEC is designed to create rights for individuals (the companies concerned), '(c)lear and precise implementation of the directive's provisions may also be important for third parties (for instance environmental groups or neighbourhood residents) seeking to have the prohibitions and restrictions contained in the directive *enforced* as against the authorities or other individuals'.[29] There are two ways in which this might be read. The fact that he specifically contrasts those who enjoy individual rights with the position of third parties probably indicates that he thinks third parties enjoy no rights as such. However it could at least be argued that his use of the word 'enforced' implies that they do have rights.[30]

AG Van Gerven's ambiguous Opinion apart, the cases thus evince only two approaches to who enjoys rights under pollution-related directives. AG Jacobs, in Case C-58/89, believes that only regulated companies enjoy personal rights under environmental directives which must be enforceable in national courts. However, the predominant view in Cases C-361/88, C-59/89 and C-58/89, is that where a directive is explicitly intended to protect human health, ordinary citizens whose health may be affected also have personal rights which must be enforceable in national courts.[31] The point to be made though, is that even this predominant view is extremely restrictive in its focus. First, it can be argued that citizens should enjoy rights under, for example, the Groundwater Directive 80/68/EEC and the Dangerous Substances in Water Directive 76/464/EEC and its daughter directives. It seems strange that the existence of rights should rest on whether the directive's preamble explicitly lists the protection of human health as its intention. Whatever their preambles say, most pollution-related directives affect human health. Directives 80/68/EEC and 76/464/EEC are no exception to this: groundwater is the source of much of the UK's drinking water supply; and dangerous substances in surface waters may endanger the health of those who engage in fishing and watersports. It may be thought that these threats to human health should also provide the foundation for rights under EC law.

Even extending rights to cover health interests in this way arguably does not go far enough. Concentrating on the protection of human health is anthropo-

---

[28] [1991] I-ECR 825, at 867, paras. 6–7 of the judgment. Since the time of writing, there is now also a case on dangerous substances – see Case C-262/95, *Commission* v. *Germany* (not yet reported).
[29] *Ibid.* at 850, para. 7 of his Opinion. Emphasis added.
[30] Alternatively, it may indicate the enforcement of an interest or expectation via a non-legal channel of redress.
[31] See also Krämer, note 11 above, at 52–54.

centric.[32] True environmental rights will only arise if rights are also granted to citizens in respect of EC directives which have nothing to do with the protection of human health, such as nature conservation directives. Why does it matter that rights are thus extended? The answer is because, as we have seen, rights are a precondition to enforcement action, whether via direct effect, indirect effect or *Francovich*. If there are no rights enjoyed by citizens under a particular directive, the enforcement armoury is lessened. The Commission is overstretched for the purposes of enforcement under Article 169 proceedings.[33] Granting citizens rights across the whole range of environmental directives may go some way towards providing an effective second enforcement arm in the national courts. Indeed, the House of Lords Select Committee on the European Communities, among others, has come out in favour of allowing 'citizen actions' as an effective, alternative means of ensuring compliance with EC environmental law.[34]

Enforcing Community rights in national courts

So far then, we have seen that the ECJ has recognised that citizens enjoy rights in an environmental context, although it has been suggested that, for the better enforcement of EC environmental law, these rights ought perhaps to be extended beyond their current anthropocentric focus. However, this is only a preliminary matter. There is little point in creating rights unless they can in some meaningful way be enforced in national courts. It is this problem to which we now turn.

Preventive enforcement action

Where a person wishes to enforce a directive where they have suffered no legally recognisable damage, they will typically bring administrative law proceedings (either by way of judicial review or a statutory appeal). Environmental groups, for example, will not normally have suffered any damage but there are now a number of examples where they have sought to protect their Community rights in this way. In essence, an applicant or appellant faces four barriers in adminis-

---

[32] See Miller, 'Environmental Rights: European Fact or English Fiction?' [1995] JLS 374, at 375 and 390.

[33] On the problems associated with Article 169 proceedings in respect of environmental directives, see e.g. Macrory, 'The Enforcement of Community Environmental Laws: Some Critical Issues' (1992) 29 CML Rev 347; Macrory and Purdy, 'The Enforcement of EC Environmental Law Against Member States', Chapter 3 above; and Stuart, 'Combating Non-Compliance with European Community Environmental Directives' (1994) 6 ELM 160.

[34] House of Lords Select Committee on the European Communities, *Report on the Implementation and Enforcement of Environmental Legislation*, Session 1991–92, Ninth Report, HL Paper 53–1, at para. 45; see also HL debates, 21 January 1993, and Geddes, 'Locus Standi and EEC Environmental Measures' (1992) JEL Vol. 4, No. 1, 29, at 39.

trative law proceedings: first, they have to gain access under domestic law (the question of standing); secondly, they have to persuade the court of the substance of their claim; thirdly, even if the court is convinced of the merits, they must persuade the court to grant a remedy; and finally, there is the fact that, unless legally aided, they must pay their own costs and, if they lose, usually[35] those of the other side too.[36] The last of these is likely to put litigants off bringing an action in the first place, and to that extent represents perhaps the greatest hindrance to the effective enforcement of Community rights. There would therefore be some merit in having uniform Community rules to the effect that, in public interest challenges, while the challenger should be able to recover their costs from the respondents on winning, they should not have to pay the respondent's costs on losing.[37] In addition, there should perhaps be a Member State or Community fund to which environmental groups could apply to cover their own costs in worthy cases where they do lose.

In the recent past in England and Wales, the first hurdle on standing was a significant barrier in the way of effective enforcement of Community rights. At the root of this was the restrictive approach adopted by Schiemann J (as he then was) in the *Rose Theatre* decision.[38] Indeed, it was this decision which led Geddes[39] to suggest, on the basis of *Factortame*,[40] that where an applicant had difficulty making a case for standing under national law, they might try arguing that EC law required them to have access to the courts to enable them effectively to protect their Community *rights*.[41] Today, however, the courts have adopted a much more generous approach to standing in judicial review cases,[42] particularly in relation to group applicants,[43] and it now seems unlikely that applicants will

---

[35] Though not always—see e.g. *Ex parte Greenpeace*, note 6 above.

[36] See Purdue, 'A Harpoon for Greenpeace?: Judicial Review of the Regulation of Radioactive Substances' (1994) JEL Vol. 6, No. 2, 337, at 341–342; Grosz, 'When We Can't See the Wood for the Fees', *The Guardian*, 2 March 1993.

[37] Indeed, something similar was suggested in a draft proposal for a directive on access to environmental justice (unpublished) which would have given environmental groups broad rights of standing in national courts. So far, this has not materialised as an official proposal, although in a recent report on the application of EC law, the Commission has stated that it is actively considering the matter (OJ 1995 C 254, p. 47). The draft proposal reflected a concern set out in the Fifth Environmental Action Programme to improve access to justice in environmental law (OJ 1993 C 138, p. 5, at p. 82).

[38] *R v. Secretary of State for the Environment, ex parte Rose Theatre Trust Co Ltd* [1990] 1 QB 504.

[39] Note 34 above. See also Geddes, 'Unlocking the Doors of Judicial Protection' (1993) NLJ 98.

[40] Case C-213/89, *R v. Secretary of State for Transport, ex parte Factortame Ltd (Factortame II)* [1990] 3 CMLR 1.

[41] The so-called doctrine of effectiveness. See also Steiner, note 9 above, at p. 77, and joined Cases C-87, 88 and 89/90, *Verholen v. Sociale Versekeringsbank* [1991] ECR I-3757, at 3790, where the Court stated that: '(w)hile it is, in principle, for national law to determine an individual's standing and legal interest in bringing proceedings, Community law nevertheless requires that the national legislation does not undermine the right to effective judicial protection'.

[42] See e.g. *R v. Her Majesty's Inspectorate of Pollution, ex parte Greenpeace Ltd (No. 2)* [1994] 4 All ER 329; *R v. Secretary of State for Foreign Affairs, ex parte World Development Movement Ltd* [1995] 1 All ER 611; *R v. Secretary of State for the Environment, ex parte Friends of the Earth Ltd* (1994) 2 CML Rev 760. See further Hilson and Cram, note 26 above. However cf. the restrictive High Court decision reported in *The Times*, 25 March 1997.

[43] See Hilson and Cram, note 26 above.

need to resort to this argument.[44] In the event that they do need to do so, it must be remembered that the argument will presumably only be successful in what we have seen are the limited number of cases where *rights* currently exist under environmental directives.

Although domestic standing arguably no longer poses a significant problem to the effective protection of Community rights in environmental cases, there is still a long way to go to convince our national courts of the substance of many claims and to grant remedies. If one looks at recent administrative law cases relating to the environment, the following approaches to Community rights[45] can be seen:

1. In the environmental assessment cases, the courts decide against the chal-
    lengers on the EC law issue without making an Article 177 reference. In
    these cases then, one does not know whether the European Court of Justice
    would agree and hence whether rights are in fact being infringed. In the
    RSPB case[46] for example, Simon Brown J held that the decision as to whether
    a particular development requires an environmental assessment is essen-
    tially a discretionary one for the authority to take, subject only to *Wednesbury*
    challenge. In *Twyford Down*,[47] the Court decided that 'pipeline projects'
    were not covered by the Environmental Assessment Directive. As can be
    seen below, it then proceeded to state reasons why the challengers would
    fail even if it had decided the central EC law issue in their favour.

2. The courts state that the litigant does not possess Community rights. At
    first instance in *Ex parte Friends of the Earth*,[48] Schiemann J thought that the
    applicants probably did not enjoy Community rights under the Drinking
    Water Directive because they had suffered no damage. In *Velcourt*, Tucker J
    held that the applicant council was not an individual for the purposes of

---

[44] Indeed in some cases, our national law on standing is possibly more generous than the position enjoyed under Community law. In the EOC case for example (*Equal Opportunities Commission* v. *Secretary of State for Employment* [1994] 1 All ER 910), the EOC was granted standing as a matter of national law by the House of Lords, but lacking rights itself under the relevant EC law, the EOC may have lacked standing for the purposes of EC law (unless, as a surrogate group acting on behalf of others, it could derive a right from the one enjoyed by the person/s it was representing—cf. note 26 above, which concerned representational groups acting for their own members' interests where the question was whether they could derive a right from those enjoyed by their individual members).

[45] As opposed to statements by our national courts on the other requirements of direct effect or indirect effect, which might be better seen as questions of justiciability—see note 26 above (although cf. the *Lombardia* case, note 5 above, where the ECJ's actual language was that because Article 4 of the Waste Framework Directive was neither unconditional nor sufficiently precise, it did not confer rights on individuals). See e.g. the *Velcourt* case (*Wychavon District Council* v. *Secretary of State for the Environment and Velcourt Ltd* (1994) JEL Vol. 6, No. 2, 351), where Tucker J held that the Environmental Assessment Directive was not directly effective because not all of its provisions were sufficiently clear and precise; he also held that the principle of indirect effect could not apply, because the national implementing legislation was incapable of an interpretation which was consistent with the Directive.

[46] *R* v. *Swale Borough Council and Medway Ports Authority, ex parte The Royal Society for the Protection of Birds* (1991) JEL Vol. 3, No. 1, 135.

[47] *Twyford Parish Council* v. *Secretary of State for Transport* (1992) JEL Vol. 4, No. 2, 273.

[48] Note 42 above.

EC law, but an emanation of the state and hence could not enjoy *individual* rights under EC law.[49]

3. Even if the litigant does possess Community rights, the courts state that these have not been infringed. In *Twyford Down*, McCullough J held that, although the challengers might enjoy Community rights under the Environmental Assessment Directive, these rights had not been infringed because they had suffered no damage. He further stated that the appellants' Community rights had not been infringed because the environmental information was present, albeit in an unofficial form. Next, in the Court of Appeal in *Ex parte Friends of the Earth*,[50] although the Court was prepared to assume that the appellants enjoyed Community rights under the Drinking Water Directive, it stated in effect that these rights had not been infringed because the implementing legislation had been approved by the Commission and the Court of Justice.[51]

4. The courts state that, even if Community rights had been infringed, they would, in their discretion, have refused to grant a remedy, either: because of the expense of protecting any such rights (this was only explicitly given as a reason for denying a remedy in *Ex parte RSPB*, although it seems to be an underlying factor in most of the cases);[52] or because the environmental information was present, albeit in an unofficial form (*Ex parte Beebee*,[53] the

---

[49] The council, in their role as the planning authority (and therefore an emanation of the state for those purposes), had denied planning permission to Velcourt. An Inspector allowed Velcourt's appeal and, in their role as protectors of the public interest under s. 222 of the Local Government Act 1972, the council challenged his decision. However, in stating that the council remained an emanation of the state and could not enjoy individual rights, Tucker J was arguably guilty of ignoring the varied, overlapping roles which councils are inevitably forced to adopt. As Fitzpatrick states (in 'Redressing the Late Implementation of the Environmental Impact Assessment Directive' (1994) JEL Vol. 6, No. 2, 351, at 362), ' . . . it might also be said that the local authority was also acting, not merely as an aggrieved public authority whose decision had been overturned by an appeal process, but was acting to protect the public interest.'

[50] Note 4 above.

[51] See further, annotation by Hilson, 'Ex parte Friends of the Earth: Enforcement of the Drinking Water Directive' (1995) 32 CML Rev 1461, at 1468.

[52] In the more recent RSPB case (*R v. Secretary of State for the Environment, ex parte The Royal Society for the Protection of Birds* (1995) JEL Vol. 7, No. 2, 245), the remedy of an interim declaration was also denied expressly on expense grounds. However, since it involved the classification of special protection areas under the Birds Directive 79/409—a directive not intended to protect human health—on the basis of current ECJ jurisprudence, the case is not one which involves the protection of Community *rights*. It is obviously pertinent to the enforcement of EC law however. In the environmental assessment cases, as we have seen, in ruling against the challengers, our national courts tended to decide on the EC law point themselves, without making an Article 177 reference. That left it to the Commission to bring Article 169 proceedings if it saw fit, but even if it did so, by the time the case reached the ECJ, the sites would have been destroyed because there is no mechanism for taking swift, interim action at that level (a problem discussed by Stuart, note 33 above). The recent RSPB case raises similar problems at a national level where our national courts do make an Article 177 reference: without a cross-undertaking in damages, the House of Lords were not prepared to grant what was effectively an interim injunction, to prevent development until the ECJ had ruled on the point in dispute. Hence, even if the ECJ eventually rules in their favour (as it has done since the time of writing – see case C-44/95, *R v. Secretary of State for the Environment, ex parte The Royal Society for the Protection of Birds* [1996] 3 CMLR 411), the site will have been destroyed.

[53] *R v. Poole Borough Council, ex parte Beebee and Others* (1991) JEL Vol. 3, No. 2, 293.

Velcourt case);[54] or because the appellants had suffered no prejudice (*Twyford Down*).

I would suggest that the above cases can usefully be split into two different categories. First, there are the environmental assessment cases.[55] Whether or not the European Court of Justice would agree with our courts' approach in 1. above on the specific technical questions concerning the Environmental Assessment Directive will not be addressed here. More important are the more general issues raised by 2.–4. In the environmental assessment cases, the language of rights ought to be easily applied. The right under the Environmental Assessment Directive, which is a procedural one,[56] should exist without the need to prove damage, because, as Ward notes,[57] the litigants are seeking a public law remedy; they are not seeking damages for infringement of a private law right. The *personal* right under a directive which litigants must possess to make use of direct effect does not have to be a *private law* right. Next, this right ought to be regarded as infringed if the forms and procedures set out in the directive have not been followed. And finally, in order to provide effective protection for Community rights in line with *Factortame*, this right should be enforced by the granting of a remedy to quash the original decision and to order the process to begin again.[58] Since there is no wording or express derogation in the directive which allows it, the expense and delay to the developers and the taxpayer should not be taken into account here. In exercising their remedial discretion, our courts are accustomed to adopting a pragmatic line, taking economic and practical considerations into account. However, given the conflict with the principle of effective protection of Community rights, it seems unlikely that the European Court of Justice would condone this type of balancing by a national court.

The *Ex parte Friends of the Earth* case is different. Here, in effect, the position was that drinking water should have been brought up to Community standards by a certain date and that had not been done. A similar case might be brought in relation to breaches of EC-based bathing water standards or ambient air quality standards. Unlike environmental assessment, these cases do pose some— albeit possibly not insuperable—problems to the language of rights. If one has a right to drinking water, bathing water or air which meets the relevant standards

---

[54] See also *Ex parte Greenpeace*, note 6 above, where a remedy was denied because the ministers' error of law was deemed to have made no difference—although they had wrongly concluded that the Radioactive Substances Act 1993 did not require a justification exercise before the grant of authorisation to BNFL for the discharge of radioactive waste, the ministers had in fact concluded that the emissions were justified. As Purdue states (note 36 above, at 349), '(i)t would though be interesting to know the views of the European Court as to the approach a national court should take where the error has not affected the outcome'.

[55] *Twyford Down*; *Ex parte Beebee*; *Ex parte RSPB*; *Velcourt*.

[56] I.e. it is a right not to an outcome, but to have a given procedure carried out.

[57] Ward, 'The Right to an Effective Remedy in European Community Law and Environmental Protection: A Case Study of United Kingdom Decisions Concerning the Environmental Assessment Directive' (1993) JEL Vol. 4, No. 2, 221.

[58] Cf. Steiner, note 9 above, at pp. 81–82.

and this right has been infringed because the standards have not been met, what remedy can a national court impose to enforce this right? A simple *one-off* declaration to the effect that the rights have been infringed would be one possibility.[59] Indeed one could argue that the principle of effective protection at least requires that this basic remedy be available in national courts. Neverthe- less, it is hardly a powerful remedy for protecting rights in this context. It only tells us that the state is in breach of its strict[60] primary obligation to achieve the standards. It tells us nothing of the state's secondary obligation to remedy the breach of its primary obligation. There are two possible approaches that national courts could take to enforcing this secondary obligation. First, they could themselves order what *continuing* action the state should take to bring the water or air quality up to standard more quickly.[61] However, the problem facing the courts would be to choose from a wide spectrum of possible action. On the one hand, they could order extremely controversial action to be taken. With drinking water, for example, that might involve the input of considerable government funds to introduce treatment plants more quickly[62] or a ban on pesticide usage in relevant areas.[63] Similarly with bathing water, considerable funds could be spent to bring sewage treatment works on stream very quickly. With air quality, it might involve widespread bans on vehicle use.[64] On the other hand, they could order only a slight increase in pressure, far short of these extremes. In contrast, with the enforcement of a right to equal treatment, or a right to have an environmental assessment carried out, the court is not faced with this spectrum of choice. Protection of both of these rights will come at some cost to society, but that cost is relatively contained.

Should this lead us to the conclusion that it therefore only makes sense to talk of rights where there is only one choice that should or should not have been made (as with equal treatment or environmental assessment)? Where there is a spectrum of choice depending on the amount of financial resources one is prepared to commit, are we in the realm not of rights but of politics?[65] Possibly not. There may be a way of providing rights with protection which falls somewhere between the fairly powerless one-off remedy of a declaration and the position of allowing the courts to become embroiled in a spectrum of political choice. And that would be for the courts to leave the question of the speed of compliance as a *subjective* matter for the state to decide (as opposed to the *objective* approach described earlier where the court decides what action

---

[59] See Hilson, note 51 above, at 1470–1471. This would resemble the ECJ's pronouncement in an Article 169 action and should therefore be unforgiving of excuses in the same way—see e.g. Case C-337/89, *Commission* v. *United Kingdom* [1992] I-ECR 6103.

[60] See Case C-337/89, note 59 above.

[61] See Hilson, note 51 above.

[62] Obviously, the amount of money that could in theory be spent to achieve compliance quickly is virtually limitless.

[63] See Hilson, note 51 above, at 1467.

[64] See Krämer, *European Environmental Law Casebook* (London: Sweet and Maxwell, 1993), p. 369.

[65] See Miller, note 32 above, at 388.

is to be taken), but to make that decision reviewable on *Wednesbury* grounds.[66] If the pace of compliance was proceeding at a *Wednesbury* unreasonable pace, then the court should be prepared to step in and order increased action to be taken. This approach has the advantage of keeping the courts out of politics to a much greater degree than with the objective approach, whilst still providing the citizen with a certain minimum floor of protection for his or her rights.

Where damage has been suffered

National law causes of action

If a citizen suffers damage as a result of drinking water, breathing air, or swimming in bathing water in breach of Community standards, there are two possibilities available in terms of civil liability. First, they may be able to sue the company[67] concerned on the basis of traditional national law causes of action such as trespass, nuisance (public and private), *Rylands* v. *Fletcher*,[68] negligence or, with drinking water, under the Consumer Protection Act 1987 (water being a product), for breach of statutory duty under s. 22(2) of the Water Industry Act 1991, or for breach of contract.[69] Secondly, they may be able to sue the state under *Francovich*. This second possibility will be addressed in the next section. With the first, the High Court's decision in *Ex parte Friends of the Earth* reveals another area where rights may come into play, although only in relation to drinking water. Section 22(2) of the Water Industry Act 1991 only specifically allows an action for damages to be brought where there has been a breach of an enforcement order. The applicants argued that this deprived them (in principle, since they had not in fact suffered any damage) of their Community rights because it meant one could not bring an action for damages for harm suffered as a result of breaches of Community drinking water standards where (as in the case) the Secretary of State had accepted undertakings from the water company rather than serving them with enforcement orders. Schiemann J rejected this, stating that if the person enjoyed any rights under EC law, then he could enforce them despite the wording of s. 22(2). It is not clear exactly what cause of action he had in mind when he said this, but it appears he was

---

[66] See Hilson, note 51 above, at 1466 and 1470. A decision is *Wednesbury* unreasonable if it is one which no reasonable authority could have reached (*Associated Provincial Picture Houses Ltd* v. *Wednesbury Corporation* [1948] 1 KB 223).

[67] With drinking water, this will be the water company; with air, whichever company is thought to be responsible for the air pollution if there is one (it may however be due to e.g. motor vehicle emissions which are produced by millions of individual drivers); with bathing water, it is likely to be the water company with sewage discharges into bathing waters.

[68] (1865) 3 H&C 774; (1868) LR 3 HL; 37 LJ Ex 161; 19 LT 220, HL.

[69] Indeed, virtually all of these causes of action were listed in the Camelford claim arising out of the incident where large quantities of aluminium sulphate were tipped into the drinking water supply (see Ghandi, 'Liability for Water Supply—*Gibbons and Others* v. *South West Water Services Ltd*' [1993] *Water Law* 95). The claim was settled out of court and hence whether they would all have been successful remains a source of academic debate.

suggesting that one could still bring an action for breach of statutory duty. This would appear to be based on *Factortame*[70] reasoning.[71] EC law has traditionally left the question of causes of action up to Member States. However, after *Factortame*, one might argue that the lack of a national law cause of action for breach of statutory duty where an undertaking has been accepted effectively impedes the protection of one's Community rights and therefore that such an action should be available where an undertaking has been accepted.

The significance of this application of rights is, however, rather limited. In any claim arising from drinking water in breach of standards, it will make a considerable difference whether the damage suffered is immediate, resulting from a high-dose exposure, or whether it results from a long-term, low-dose exposure. With the former, it is unlikely that the plaintiff will need to rely on s. 22(2) of the Water Industry Act 1991 in any event, because one or more of the other causes of action is almost certain to be made out.[72] With long-term, low-dose exposure, it may be more useful in so far as the other fault-based causes of action will be difficult to establish and breach of statutory duty here avoids the need to show fault. However, it is not the only one to do so, because of course the plaintiff may be able to rely on strict liability under the Consumer Protection Act 1987.[73] Moreover, for both of these forms of strict liability, proving causation is still likely to be extremely difficult. In other words, having a Community right here may enable you to sue for breach of statutory duty despite the wording of s. 22(2) of the Water Industry Act 1991, but it will not help you to cross the remaining hurdle of causation. As we shall see below, much the same problem arises under *Francovich*.

Enforcing rights under Francovich

After *Francovich*, where damage has been suffered as a result of drinking water, breathing air, or swimming in bathing water in practical breach of Community standards, the person concerned may be able to sue his/her Member State[74] for damages if the *Francovich* conditions outlined earlier are satisfied. All of the relevant directives are intended to protect human health, so the requirement that they should confer rights on the individual will be satisfied. Because all of these directives contain limit values, there will be little problem with the

---

[70] Note 40 above.

[71] See further Hilson, note 51 above, at 1469.

[72] In which case the lack of a cause of action for breach of statutory duty where an undertaking has been accepted does not impede the protection of one's Community rights, since other causes of action are available to protect them.

[73] The same argument as that in note 72 above may also apply here therefore.

[74] Although the doctrine of direct effect applies in relation to actions brought against the state and emanations of the state (see note 3 above), it is not clear whether *Francovich* can be used in an action for damages directly against an emanation of the state rather than the state itself (see Ross, 'Beyond *Francovich*' (1993) 56 MLR 55, at 70). The statement of claim in the Camelford case appears to have assumed that it is possible, because *Francovich* was one of the causes of action listed in the claim brought against the water authority (as it was then, though of course privatised water companies are also classed as emanations of the state—see note 3 above).

requirement that the rights should be ascertainable from the provisions of the directive.[75] However, it is the final requirement—that of proving causation—which produces difficulties.[76] As Miller notes, *Francovich* does at least remove one possible causation problem in that one no longer has to identify the polluter from 'a multiplicity of pollution sources', because the state is the defendant.[77] However, it does not remove the need to prove a causal link between the illness suffered and the breach of Community standards. And in the environmental sphere, it is typically necessary to rely on epidemiological evidence to establish such a link. *Francovich* itself was an employment case where causation was very straightforward.[78] No doubt the European Court of Justice will have to rule at some stage whether epidemiological evidence is permissible as evidence in environmental *Francovich* claims and will also have to decide exactly what the standard of proof must be (does the causal link have to be proved on a balance of probabilities?).[79] In *Reay and Hope* v. *BNFL*[80] (a purely domestic case rather than a *Francovich* one), a UK national court, while it did not rule out reliance on epidemiological studies, laid down quite stringent tests which such studies must satisfy.[81] In terms of the standard of proof, as is the norm in English law, the case appears to state that the plaintiff must prove his or her case on a balance of probabilities.[82]

On the basis of current (often conflicting) epidemiological studies, it seems unlikely that one could prove, on a balance of probabilities, that, for example: breaches of Community air quality standards arising from vehicle emissions had

---

[75] See Holder and Elworthy, note 21 above, at 132–133; Somsen and Bovis, 'Enforcement of EC Environmental Law and the Implications of the Francovich Judgment' [1992] *Water Law* 184, at 188.

[76] It will be recalled that the recent joined cases of *Brasserie du Pêcheur* and *Factortame* (*Factortame IV*), note 7 above, appear to erase the second requirement and to replace it with a condition that the breach should be a sufficiently serious one. The test for whether a breach is sufficiently serious is if 'the Member State . . . manifestly and gravely disregarded the limits on its [legislative] discretion'. The question of the seriousness of the breach is stated to be broadly one of fact for the national courts to decide. If this new condition applies to practical breach cases, it too might cause some difficulty. When does a breach become sufficiently serious in this context? If someone has suffered damage from pollution, should that not, in itself, be regarded as a serious breach?

[77] Which would be a particular advantage in relation to air pollution from motor vehicles for example.

[78] Miller (note 32 above, at 385) states that '(o)nce Signor Francovich had demonstrated his standing, it followed (indeed it was almost tautologous) that he had suffered a financial loss in circumstances which the original directive was designed to mitigate.'

[79] In joined Cases C-46/93 and C-48/93, *Brasserie du Pêcheur* and *Factortame* (*Factortame IV*), note 7 above, the ECJ states that it is for national courts to determine whether there is a direct causal link between the breach of obligation by the state and the damage sustained by the injured parties. However, this simply means that the national court would decide the factual issue—the legal basis on which that factual question is addressed (i.e. permissible evidence, standard of proof) would presumably be a matter for the ECJ.

[80] [1994] Env LR 320; see Holder, 'The Sellafield Litigation and Questions of Causation in Environmental Law' (1994) 47 CLP 287; Wilkinson, '*Reay and Hope* v. *British Nuclear Fuels plc*' [1994] *Water Law* 22.

[81] *Ibid.*

[82] *Ibid.*

caused the onset of asthma,[83] or even emergency asthmatic attacks in those who already have the disease;[84] that swimmers/surfers' illnesses were caused by breaches of Community bathing water standards;[85] or that gastric cancer is caused by ingesting drinking water with nitrate levels in breach of Community standards.[86] However, it is the possibility of this position changing which is likely to make the European Court of Justice think twice about allowing epidemiological evidence (let alone allowing a standard of proof lower than a balance of probabilities). As Miller notes, the problem would be that of a multiplicity of potential claimants[87]—the floodgates issue. This might not arise particularly starkly in the bathing water context,[88] but a moment's thought about the number of children with asthma reveals how acute the problem would be in relation to air pollution.[89] It seems unlikely that the European Court of Justice would leave Member States open to this scale of potential liability.

Francovich is therefore something of a disappointment as far as enforcement of the limited number of Community rights in the environmental field is concerned. As current science stands, in long-term, low-dose exposure cases (e.g. drinking water and nitrates), and in some short-term, high-dose cases (e.g. bathing cases and asthma attacks) there seems to be little hope of satisfying the causation requirement. Even if epidemiology does eventually make a case, the European Court of Justice is likely to close the door on it, including in

---

[83] It has been suggested, for example, that the rise in asthma levels in children may be due to the fact that they spend longer indoors than children did in the past and that, due to increased insulation, houses are now less well ventilated. For studies suggesting alternative causes of asthma, see e.g. (1995) *ENDS Report*, Vol. 249, 9; Omran and Russell, 'Continuing Increase in Respiratory Symptoms and Atopy in Aberdeen Schoolchildren' (1996) 312 *British Medical Journal* 34.

[84] Although epidemiological studies do apparently show a link between air pollution episodes and emergency hospital visits for asthma and other respiratory illness, it has been suggested that these are caused in particular by PM10 levels (a particle of less than 10 microns in size, associated with e.g. vehicle emissions and Orimulsion) for which there are currently no EC standards. Ground level ozone is also thought to be responsible, but although EC standards do exist there, they are simply informational triggers—not the mandatory ones which would be necessary to found a *Francovich* claim. It remains unclear to what extent nitrogen oxide or sulphur dioxide levels (on which there are EC standards) might also be responsible (see Bates, 'Air Pollution: Time for More Clean Air Legislation?' (1996) 312 *British Medical Journal* 649).

[85] Miller (note 32 above, at 387), citing the *ENDS Report*, states that '(r)ecent research appears to suggest that the risk of contracting diarrhoea and sore throats is independent of measured levels of coliforms and enteroviruses, for which limit values are specified in the 1976 Directive, but is related to strains of virus to which the Directive makes no reference'. That may be true of viruses, but there are studies however which suggest that faecal streptococci at levels of between 35–70/100 ml cause gastro-intestinal illness (see (1994) *ENDS Report*, Vol. 239, 29). Nevertheless, there would still remain problems in establishing *Francovich* causation. First, under the 1976 Directive, there are only guide values for faecal streptococci; there are no mandatory limits. Under a recent proposal to amend the Directive (see OJ 1994, C 112, p. 3), a generous mandatory level of 400/100 ml has been put forward. But even if this proposed amendment were to go through, it would presumably be very difficult to prove that one's illness was caused by a breach of the standard, because if the studies above are right, one is quite likely to have caught the illness anyway, even if the waters were within the standard.

[86] Holder and Elworthy, note 21 above, at 133–134.

[87] Miller, note 32 above, at 386.

[88] *Ibid.* at 387.

[89] *Ibid.* at 386.

claims which do not raise large floodgates issues (e.g. bathing), because if they allow it in one case, they would arguably have to allow it in subsequent claims which did raise floodgates problems.

Conclusion

If the European Court of Justice is serious about the creation of rights under environmental directives, it should give greater thought both to the purpose of creating these rights and to the relationship between rights and remedies. If the purpose is conceived of as improving the enforcement of environmental directives, then it seems that the scope of rights should be broadened beyond directives which are explicitly intended to protect human health. As for the relationship between rights and remedies, it has been suggested here that some directives which are essentially programmatic in nature, such as those on drinking water and air quality, create greater problems regarding this relationship than others such as environmental assessment. Nevertheless, even with environmental assessment, where the relationship between rights and remedies ought to be relatively straightforward, our national courts have been unwilling to provide remedial protection. Neither does *Francovich* offer much hope as a means of protecting rights in cases where there is damage. The causation requirement laid down in that case is likely to prove insuperable in all but a few cases. All of this should come as no great surprise. The concept of rights and the principles of direct effect, indirect effect and *Francovich* liability were developed in relation to directives connected with the social sphere and the single market. The environment is quite unlike these areas. We must therefore continue to wait for a European Court of Justice case which can lead us beyond speculation based on a jurisprudence developed for other areas towards a jurisprudence of the environment.

Chapter 5

THE IMPACT OF EC LAW ON THE ENVIRONMENTAL LAW OF NORTHERN IRELAND

Karen Morrow and Sharon Turner

Introduction

While it is true to say that the motive force initiating the process of modernis-ation which has begun in Northern Ireland environmental law in recent years owes much to EC law, the extent of the influence exercised by the latter in the Province has until very recently been (at best) qualified. Despite the swift development of a prodigious body of EC environmental law,[1] its impact in Northern Ireland has, to date, been relatively minor for several reasons—some of these represent general problems with EC law, others are unique to Northern Ireland, and these will form the basis of discussion.

Tardy implementation

It is interesting and relevant to note that the genesis of EC environmental law coincides neatly with the imposition of direct rule from Westminster in Northern Ireland in the early 1970s and in this coincidence lies the heart of the problem of delayed implementation. Most environmental issues were included under the general class of 'transferred matters' which formed the legislative competence of the Northern Ireland Parliament to legislate for the 'peace, order and good government' of its territory under s. 4(1) of the Government of Ireland Act 1920. When direct rule was reinstated, transferred matters (environmental issues among them), instead of being the subject of primary legislation, were under the new constitutional settlement, routinely dealt with by delegated legislation, specifically Orders in Council.[2] Separate laws for Northern Ireland were and are necessary because of the distinctive corpus of law which remained on the

---

[1] See for example Krämer, *The EC Treaty and Environmental Law*, 2nd ed. (London: Sweet and Maxwell, 1995).

[2] For discussion of the constitutional impact of direct rule on the quality of law-making and democracy in Northern Ireland, see Hadfield, *The Constitution of Northern Ireland* (Belfast: SLS Legal Publications, 1989), ch. V.

statute book from the period before partition as well as that which had been built up in the Province under devolved government. Environmental law was accorded low priority (particularly in the early years) under direct rule, when the already overloaded Westminster system had to take on the additional burden of legislating for Northern Ireland.[3] Most environmental law in Great Britain owes its origin in any event to EC law,[4] and the government has made considerable efforts to comply with its demands, at least on the mainland. However, the fact that EC law is in a state of constant evolution and the subject of frequent amendment means that it has been difficult for lost legislative ground to be made up in Northern Ireland.

The Department of the Environment for Northern Ireland (which is virtually omnicompetent in environmental governance in the Province)[5] has a heavy burden thrust upon it in its responsibility to provide draft legislation for Parliament. The DoE(NI), like its counterpart on the mainland, is not responsible for only environmental issues; in Northern Ireland its remit extends, amongst other things, to roads, vehicle and driver testing, public records, and responsibility for the land registry, as well as environmental regulation. The Department has also been historically understaffed and underfunded which has compounded its problems in keeping up to date with its obligations. The making of Orders in Council is itself a lengthy and cumbersome business; it takes a minimum of 64 weeks to adopt such an Order, contributing to the problem of delay.

Tackling the implementation backlog

It is clear then, for a variety of reasons, that the law which is currently applicable in Northern Ireland has fallen far behind the requirements of EC law (and indeed lags substantially behind legal development in this area in the rest of the United Kingdom) and this is particularly the case in pollution control in all environmental media.[6] The chronic problem posed by the habitually tardy implementation of Community environmental Directives in Northern Ireland has been well documented; the House of Commons Environment Committee in its (highly critical) report *Environmental Issues in Northern Ireland*[7] focused attention on the extent of the problem. The Committee concluded:

. . . as a matter of general principle we consider that the government should ensure that environmental legislation is consistent throughout the United Kingdom . . . the

---

[3] The legislative burden of the state had expanded almost beyond recognition between the introduction of devolved government in Northern Ireland in 1922 and the imposition of direct rule.

[4] See for example, Ball and Bell, *Environmental Law*, 3rd ed. (London: Blackstone, 1995), ch. 4.

[5] The Department of Agriculture for Northern Ireland, and the Department of Economic Development also play an important (though subsidiary) role in environmental control in Northern Ireland; the role of local government is however extremely limited.

[6] For an examination of these and other environmental laws applicable to Northern Ireland, see Turner and Morrow, *Northern Ireland Environmental Law* (Dublin: Gill & Macmillan, 1997).

[7] House of Commons Environment Committee, First Report, *Environmental Issues in Northern Ireland* HC 39 (1990–92).

United Kingdom is under a legal obligation to implement the requirements of directives *throughout the country* within the specified time-limits . . .

For future legislation, we recommend the Government review its practices to ensure that implementation in Northern Ireland is carried out simultaneously with the rest of the country.[8]

As a result of this trenchant criticism and, more particularly, successful infringement proceedings before the European Court of Justice concerning non-implementation of the Drinking Water Directive[9] in Northern Ireland, the government committed itself both to dealing with the considerable backlog of law which had built up during the preceding two decades and to preventing future problems by increasing its use of simultaneous legislation. Where simultaneous legislation is not feasible because of Northern Ireland's special circumstances the government has committed itself to make the 'best possible arrangements and at the same time to comply with EC standards and maintain parity with the position in the rest of the United Kingdom'.[10] This commitment has however, as will be demonstrated below, met with only partial success.

The profile of environmental issues was raised by the creation, in November 1990 of the Environment Service within the DoE(NI). The Environment Service[11] has been given extra resources in order to improve the regulatory and legislative regime applicable to the Northern Ireland environment. Under the Environment Service, liaison with the DoE in London has been improved and thus has enabled the DoE(NI) to be better apprised of its responsibilities under EC law, which has been another factor in speeding up the provision of draft legislation. The Environment Service has made considerable progress (though this has been subject to considerable delay).[12] Particular progress has been made in the law governing species and habitat conservation and in environmental impact assessment.[13] New legislation governing pollution control in each of the environmental media has however been particularly prone to delay and is currently running at an average of five years behind parallel provision for England and Wales and Scotland. The situation with regard to updating environmental legislation is however now markedly better than at any time since direct rule was re-imposed, the antiquated primary controls represented by the Water Act (Northern Ireland) 1972, the Alkali &c. Works Regulation Act 1906 and the Pollution Control and Local Government (Northern Ireland) Order 1978[14] each having been the focus of legislative activity since the early 1990s. Pressure to ensure that environmental legislation applicable to Northern Ireland com-

---

[8] *Ibid.* paras. 31–32.

[9] Case C-337/89, *Commission* v. *UK* [1992] I-ECR 6103.

[10] DoE(NI) Memorandum, para. 2.1 in the Minutes of Evidence to the House of Commons Environment Committee, Session 1992–93.

[11] The Environment Service has been given Next Steps agency status as the Environment and Heritage Service from 1 April 1996.

[12] See the DoE(NI) Memorandum contained in the Minutes of Evidence to the House of Commons Environment Committee, note 10 above.

[13] See Turner and Morrow, *op. cit.* note 6.

[14] SI 1978 No. 1049.

plies with the requirements of EC law has also been exerted through more generalised attempts to improve mechanisms promoting the implementation of EC measures throughout the Community. Notable among these has been Directive 91/692/EEC[15] which amends most of the major sectoral environmental directives, adding a requirement that Member States report to the Commission on their implementation every three years. The UK government will thus be placed under enhanced scrutiny in respect of the implementation of EC environmental law generally and further failures to ensure that the appropriate domestic action covers the whole state will be thrown into sharp relief.

This chapter will examine briefly both the current and proposed statutory regimes dealing with controlling pollution of the water, air and land resources.[16]

Water pollution

Up until the early 1990s the legislative framework governing the prevention and control of pollution in Northern Ireland's inland, coastal and groundwaters comprised two pieces of legislation adopted in 1972 and 1973 respectively, neither of which had been subject to any significant amendment during that period. The Water Act (NI) 1972[17] introduced the first controls on discharges of trade and sewage effluent and other polluting substances to such waters, namely, the discharge consent system and the general water pollution offence, while the Water and Sewerage Services (NI) Order 1973[18] introduced a discharge consent system to regulate discharges of trade effluent to DoE(NI) sewers and treatment works. Both of these provisions remain in place today but have been subject to considerable amendment since 1993 to make provision for the implementation of EC directives concerning the prevention and control of water pollution. The DoE(NI)'s Environment Service is responsible for enforcing the provisions of the Water Act (NI) 1972 while the Department's Water Executive is responsible for setting consents for discharges of trade effluent into its sewers and sewage treatment works. As a Crown developer, discharges of sewage sludge from Water Executive sewers or sewage treatment works have not been subject to the discharge consent system laid down in the Water Act (NI) 1972; instead, the DoE(NI)'s Environment Service sets standards for discharges from the Water Executive's sewage treatment works but none have been placed on public registers. The DoE(NI)'s Environment Service has also been responsible for setting and monitoring water quality objectives; however, until 1993, this system of control operated on an informal administrative basis. The traditional system of control had many deficiencies, not least

---

[15] OJ 1992 L 337, p. 48.
[16] The law dealing with waste will form the focus of coverage in respect of pollution to land.
[17] C. 5.
[18] SI 1973 No. 70.

of which was the DoE(NI)'s dual role as 'poacher and gamekeeper' which has considerably undermined the enforcement of legislative controls operating in this context. In addition to the lack of public accountability underlying the enforcement of the legislative controls on water pollution, this system of water pollution control made almost no provision for the 'polluter pays' principle in that fees were not charged for discharge consents or for abstractions of water. Fines for water pollution offences had also become totally outdated. Provision for public consultation on the operation of the system of control was almost non-existent, and where such provision was made, the decision to consult was entirely within the discretion of the DoE(NI). Similarly, the provision of public access to information concerning the operation of legislative controls was very sparse. Although the DoE(NI) is required to maintain a register of consents issued under the 1972 Act, this does not include conditions governing discharges from DoE(NI) sewers and sewage treatment works, because, as already explained, the Water Executive is not governed by the discharge consent system laid down in the Water Act (NI) 1972. There is no provision for the maintenance of a public register of consents issued under the 1973 Order.

In stark contrast to the legislative lethargy which characterised the 1970s and 1980s, there has been a flurry of legislative activity in the context of water pollution control in Northern Ireland since the early 1990s, with the result that over the course of the past five years, the legislative landscape governing the pollution of Northern Ireland's inland, coastal and groundwaters has been considerably altered and updated. Although the impetus for such reform has come almost entirely from the obligation to implement standards adopted at European level, it is important to stress that delays in implementing EC directives concerning water pollution in Northern Ireland have been considerable, usually spanning several years, and in some cases, a decade or more. It should also be noted that even where the process of implementation has finally begun, there are many instances in which only partial implementation has been achieved. There are also a number of directives for which no implementing legislation has as yet been introduced. Thus far, there have been four principal areas of reform; namely, the introduction of new controls governing discharges of dangerous substances into coastal, inland and groundwaters, the introduction of new controls on pollution from agricultural sources, the introduction of a new system of statutory water quality control, and the introduction of more stringent controls on the treatment and ultimate disposal of urban waste water.

Control of dangerous substances

Directive 76/464/EEC[19] on pollution caused by certain dangerous substances discharged into the aquatic environment required that discharges of List I and II substances be subject to prior authorisation by September 1978, that pollution reduction programmes for List II substances would be in place by September

---

[19] OJ 1976 L 129.

1981, and that these programmes should be implemented by September 1986. Formal implementation of the requirements laid down in Directive 76/464/ EEC did not occur in Northern Ireland until the enactment of the Pollution of Waters by Dangerous Substances Regulations (NI) 1990[20] as amended by the Pollution of Waters by Dangerous Substances (Amendment) Regulations (NI) 1992.[21] The 1990 Regulations, as amended, only implement the Directive in so far as List I substances are concerned. In effect, the DoE(NI) is now obliged 'to take the appropriate steps' to eliminate pollution of inland, territorial and internal coastal waters by List I substances and in addition make it an offence to discharge such substances into such waters without the DoE(NI)'s written consent or to do so in breach of any condition attaching to the consent. The Environment Service Corporate Plan 1994–97 states that the DoE(NI) will review existing discharge consents to ensure compliance with the Directive; the review will be complete by the end of 1996. Thus far, the requirements for List II substances have not been implemented in Northern Ireland, however, the DoE(NI) proposes to adopt the Dangerous Substances to Water (List II) Directive Regulations in the near future. Although Member States were required to be in compliance with the requirements of Directive 80/68/EEC[22] on the protection of groundwater against pollution caused by dangerous substances by December 1981 and to achieve actual compliance by December 1985, formal implementation was not achieved in Northern Ireland until the enactment of Pollution of Groundwater by Dangerous Substances Regulations (NI) 1994.[23] The system of control (which governs List I and II substances) is almost identical to that outlined in relation to Directive 76/464/EEC. In essence the DoE(NI) is obliged to take the necessary steps to prohibit discharge or deposit of List I or II substances so as to allow their entry into groundwaters without DoE(NI) consent. In addition, the Department is under an obligation to take the necessary steps to prevent the introduction of List I substances to groundwater and to limit the introduction of List II substances. The Control of Asbestos in Water Regulations (NI) 1995[24] has introduced an identical system of control for the purposes of implementing Directive 87/217/EEC[25] on the prevention and reduction of environmental pollution by asbestos in so far as discharges of asbestos into water are concerned; implementation should have been completed by December 1988.

Water quality objectives

As is the case in Great Britain, EC water quality directives have completely transformed the system of control governing water quality objectives in Northern

---

[20] SR No. 38.
[21] SR No. 401.
[22] OJ 1980 L 20, p. 43.
[23] SR No. 147.
[24] SR No. 93.
[25] OJ 1987 L 85, p. 40.

Ireland from an informal system based on administrative controls to a closely regulated system of statutory control which, for the first time, makes public consultation and public access to information compulsory elements of the system of control. Member States were required to introduce formal legislation to implement Directive 75/440/EEC[26] on the quality of surface water intended for the abstraction of drinking water by June 1977 and to achieve actual compliance by June 1985. The statutory powers necessary to implement the Directive were not introduced in Northern Ireland until the adoption of the Water and Sewerage Services (Amendment) (NI) Order 1993[27] (which did not come into force until February 1994) and a further two years elapsed before the requirements of the Directive were actually implemented in Northern Ireland, but even then not completely. The Surface Waters (Classification) Regulations (NI) 1995[28] set out the classifications (DW1, DW2 and DW3) and the criteria for determining the grade of waters in waterways according to its suitability for abstraction by the DoE(NI) for supply as drinking water, however, the 1995 Regulations only give effect to the mandatory values set down in Annex II of the Directive. Water quality objectives which determine the type of treatment to which surface water should be subjected before it is put into public supply as drinking water are established under Part VI of the Water Quality Regulations (NI) 1994.[29] The provisions of Directive 79/869/EEC on sampling and analysis of surface water intended for the abstraction of drinking water should have been implemented in Northern Ireland by October 1981; thus far, no implementing legislation has been adopted for Northern Ireland.

Directive 80/778/EEC[30] on the quality of drinking water required formal implementation by July 1982 and actual compliance by July 1985. The statutory powers necessary for the implementation of the Directive were not introduced in Northern Ireland until 1993 and a further year elapsed before implementing legislation was actually enacted. The Water and Sewerage Services (Amendment) Order 1993 introduced the necessary powers in this regard and, in addition, replaced the DoE(NI)'s existing duty to provide wholesome water, which was not subject to any statutory definition, with a duty to provide wholesome water which is defined according to mandatory water quality standards set down in the Directive. The requirements of the Drinking Water Directive have been implemented for public water supplies by Part II of the Water Quality Regulations (NI) 1994[31] which defines the concept of 'wholesomeness' in respect of water which is supplied for domestic or food production purposes. Part VII of the 1994 Regulations requires the DoE(NI) to maintain detailed records of water quality for human consumption which must be available for public inspection and, in addition, to publish annual reports concerning the quality of

---

[26] OJ 1975 L 194, p. 26.
[27] SI 1993 No. 3165.
[28] SR No. 11.
[29] SR No. 221.
[30] OJ 1980 L 229, p. 11.
[31] SR No. 221.

drinking water in Northern Ireland. The requirements of the Directive have been implemented for private water supplies by the Private Water Supplies Regulations (NI) 1994.[32] The Environment Service Corporate Plan 1994–97 states that a Drinking Water Inspectorate will be established within the DoE(NI)'s Environment Service for the purposes of monitoring the Water Executive's compliance with the requirements of the Drinking Water Directive.

Directive 76/160/EEC[33] concerning bathing water required formal implementation by December 1977 and actual compliance by December 1985. The Directive was not implemented in Northern Ireland until the adoption of the Quality of Bathing Water Regulations (NI) 1993.[34] Sixteen coastal bathing waters have since been identified under the directive in Northern Ireland; 15 of these have consistently complied with mandatory requirements, but only five have consistently complied with the more stringent guide values. In effect, Northern Ireland has a 94% compliance rate as opposed to an 80% compliance rate for the United Kingdom as a whole.[35] Directive 78/659/EEC on the quality of water for freshwater fish should have been implemented in Northern Ireland by July 1980; however, as yet no implementing legislation has been introduced. In practice, the Environment Service Report 1991–93 states that 1200 km of rivers in Northern Ireland have been designated as salmonoid or cyprinid under the terms of the Directive and the most recent monitoring results available indicate that compliance with the Directive is generally good.[36] Directive 79/923/EEC concerning the quality of water for shellfish should have been implemented in Northern Ireland by November 1981 and actual compliance should have been achieved by November 1987. Once again, no formal implementing legislation has been introduced; however, in practice, the Environment Service Report 1991–93 states that a 5 km² area of Strangford Lough is designated under the Shellfish Water Directive and recent monitoring results indicate compliance with the requirements laid down in the directive.

Pollution from agricultural sources

As is the case in Great Britain, agriculture is a potent source of water pollution in Northern Ireland, however, because 80% of the land in Northern Ireland is in agricultural use, this is a particularly acute problem. Directive 86/278/EEC[37] which regulates the use of sewage sludge on agricultural land is implemented in Northern Ireland by the Sludge (Use in Agriculture) Regulations (NI) 1990,[38] while Directive 91/676/EEC[39] concerning water pollution caused by nitrates from agricultural sources, which should have been implemented by December

---

[32] SR No. 237.
[33] OJ 1976 L 31, p. 1.
[34] SR No. 205.
[35] Department of the Environment (NI), *Environment Service Corporate Strategy 1994–97*, p. 31.
[36] *Ibid.* p. 26.
[37] OJ 1986 L 181, p. 6.
[38] SR No. 245.
[39] OJ 1991 L 375, p. 1.

1993, has still not been implemented in Northern Ireland. The 1990 Regulations make it an offence to violate any of the provisions of the regulations concerning the use of sludge and septic tank sludge on agricultural land. Nitrate Directive Regulations are scheduled as forthcoming.

Urban waste water treatment

Although Member States were required to complete formal implementation of Directive 91/271/EEC[40] concerning urban waste water treatment by 30 June 1993, formal implementing legislation was not introduced in Northern Ireland until 1995 with the enactment of the Urban Waste Water Treatment Regulations (NI) 1995.[41] The 1995 Regulations require the DoE(NI) to publish a 'situation report' every two years concerning the implementation of this Directive in Northern Ireland and also to report to the Commission in this regard. The DoE(NI)'s Water Executive, which is responsible for the provision and mainten- ance of Northern Ireland's sewers and sewage treatment works, has drawn up plans designed to ensure that the requirements laid down in the Directive concerning secondary treatment of urban waste water are implemented in Northern Ireland by the deadlines set down in the directive. The DoE(NI)'s Environment Service Corporate Plan 1994–97 states that the Environment Service is currently reviewing standards for the discharge of effluent from the Water Executive's water and sewage treatment works for the purposes of ensuring implementation of the requirements laid down in Directive 91/271/ EEC. In addition, the Report states that the Environment Service has made arrangements to monitor Northern Ireland's major sewage treatment works' discharges and monitoring will be extended to all other sewage treatment works in Northern Ireland. It is important to note that not only will the Environ- ment Service expect the Water Executive to comply with the requirements laid down in the Directive by the end of 1996, the Environment Service also intends to establish a public register of these standards by the same date which repre- sents a completely new departure from the traditional position where such information was not available for public inspection.[42] Although the DoE(NI) is the body made responsible for implementing all of the requirements of the Directive and for enforcing those provision in Northern Ireland, it is doubtful whether the DoE(NI), as both a poacher and gamekeeper in this context, can be regarded as a competent body for enforcing the requirements of the Urban Waste Water Treatment Directive in Northern Ireland.

Forthcoming legislation

At the time of writing two important changes are forthcoming in the context of water pollution control in Northern Ireland, both of which have been largely

---

[40] OJ 1991 L 135, p. 40.
[41] SR No. 12.
[42] Department of the Environment (NI), *op. cit.* note 35, p. 32.

stimulated by standards adopted at EC level. In December 1993 the DoE(NI) and DANI published the *Review of the Water Act (NI) 1972: A Consultation Paper* which set out proposals designed to: (a) take account of scientific advances which have occurred since the adoption of the Water Act (NI) 1972; (b) introduce mandatory provision for public consultation in relation to applications for discharge consents to inland, coastal and groundwaters; (c) introduce a system of discharge consent fees and fees for water abstraction designed to implement the 'polluter pays' principle which will complement considerable rises in fines for water pollution offences introduced in 1993; and (d) strengthen the DoE(NI)'s powers to prevent water pollution. It is intended that the review process would culminate in the introduction of a new Order in Council in mid-1996.

In March 1996 the DoE(NI) published the draft Industrial Pollution Control (NI) Order 1996 which, when enacted, will establish a three-tier pollution control which incorporates a system of integrated pollution control for those industrial processes with the greatest capacity for generating pollution, thereby providing the legislative basis on which to implement the then proposed Directive on integrated prevention and pollution control.[43] The new control regime will require compliance in terms of the 'best available techniques not entailing excessive cost' (BATNEEC) and, in some instances, will require consideration of the 'best practicable environmental option' (BPEO).

Air pollution

EC environmental law and policy has had an important impact on Northern Ireland air pollution controls in four principal contexts, namely, the control of emissions from industrial processes, the introduction of a system of air quality standards, the control of emissions of asbestos into the air, and the control of emissions from large combustion plants.

Industrial emissions

At the time of writing (April 1996), emissions into the air from Northern Ireland's most polluting industrial processes are regulated under the system of control laid down in the Alkali &c. Works Regulation Act 1906,[44] as amended, which is based on use of the 'best practicable means'. Although Member States were required to implement the terms of Directive 84/360/EEC[45] by June 1987, the process of introducing formal implementing legislation in Northern Ireland did not commence until 1987, and is still not complete. It should be said, however, that this delay is due not only to the normal legislative delays in implementing directives in Northern Ireland, but also to the fact that the

---

[43] OJ 1996 L 275, 10.8.96.
[44] C. 14.
[45] OJ 1984 L 188, p. 20.

DoE(NI)'s proposals for implementation have been overtaken by fundamental changes in both the national and the EC's approaches to industrial air pollution control which have required the Department to revise its initial proposals for implementation.

The implementation process for Northern Ireland has spanned a number of stages to date. The first stage began in 1987 when the DoE(NI) published a consultation paper entitled *Review of Public Health and Air Pollution Controls in Northern Ireland*, which set out, amongst other things, the Department's proposals for the implementation of Directive 84/360/EEC. No formal implementing legislation was introduced as a result of this consultation process, however, by 1993, Directive 84/360/EEC was implemented in Northern Ireland in practice, but not to the exact requirements of the Directive, via the adoption of the Alkali &c. Works Order (NI) 1991[46] and the Environmental Information Regulations (NI) 1993.[47] In effect, the 1991 Order brought those plants which were not previously subject to air pollution control, but which are listed in Annex I of Directive 84/360/EEC, within the list of scheduled processes governed by the Alkali &c. Works Regulation Act 1906, as amended, while the 1993 Information Regulations made provision for public access to information concerning such processes. The second phase in the implementation of Directive 84/360/EEC in Northern Ireland began in February 1993 with the publication of a second DoE(NI) consultation paper, this time entitled *Proposals for a New System of Air Pollution Control in Northern Ireland*, which outlined the Department's proposals for a new system of air pollution control in Northern Ireland. The consultation paper proposed the introduction of a new Order in Council which would repeal the Alkali &c. Works Regulation Act 1906 in its application to Northern Ireland and replace it with a system of air pollution control which would ensure full implementation of Directive 84/360/EEC. The 1993 consultation paper proposed a two-tier system of air pollution control (APC) based on BATNEEC to be exercised by a Chief Inspector appointed by the DoE(NI) and district councils. The APC system was intended to ensure full implementation of Directive 84/360/EEC in Northern Ireland, and, while not being a formally integrated system of industrial pollution control, the DoE(NI) took the view that the existing involvement of the Department's Environment Service in the administration and enforcement of legislation governing industrial discharges to water, emissions to air, and deposits to land would effectively ensure that the holistic approach required by integrated pollution control (IPC) would be achieved. This would bring Northern Ireland industrial pollution control into line with standards applying in Great Britain under Part I of the Environmental Protection Act 1990 as amended. Since beginning its preparation on the new Order in Council, the Council of Ministers of the European Union agreed the proposed Directive on integrated prevention and pollution control (IPPC).[48] Given that

---

[46] SR No. 49.
[47] SR No. 45.
[48] *Op. cit.* note 43.

the DoE(NI)'s proposed system of APC would not provide the necessary statutory basis for the implementation of the IPPC Directive, the Department was forced to return to the proverbial 'drawing board' to extend the scope of the proposed Order in Council so as to provide for a system of IPC in Northern Ireland for those industrial processes with the greatest capacity for generating pollution. In March 1996 the DoE(NI) published the draft Industrial Pollution Control (NI) Order 1996 and a compliance cost assessment, which, when enacted, will introduce a considerably strengthened three-tier regime of industrial pollution control in Northern Ireland. The proposed system of control incorporates a system of integrated pollution control for those processes with the greatest capacity for generating pollution and requires compliance in terms of BATNEEC, and, in certain instances, consideration of the BPEO. In effect, the draft Industrial Pollution Control (NI) Order 1996 will ensure full implementation of the Air Framework Directive 84/360/EEC in Northern Ireland and will provide the legislative basis for the implementation of the Integrated Prevention and Pollution Control (IPPC) Directive.

Air quality control

All of the air quality directives were implemented in Northern Ireland between 1990 and 1996, however, once again, several years after the implementation date had expired. Directives 80/779/EEC,[49] 82/884/EEC,[50] and 85/203/EEC[51] concerning atmospheric concentrations of smoke, sulphur dioxide, lead, and nitrogen dioxide were all implemented by the Air Quality Standards Regulations (NI) 1990[52] as amended by the Air Quality Standards (Amendment) Regulations (NI) 1994[53] and the Air Quality Standards (Amendment) Regulations (NI) 1996.[54] Directive 92/72/EEC[55] concerning ground level ozone has been implemented in Northern Ireland by the Ozone Monitoring and Information Regulations 1994.[56]

Large combustion plants

The Large Combustion Plants (Control of Emissions) Regulations (NI) 1991[57] have implemented the requirements laid down by Directive 88/609/EEC[58] in so far as emissions from existing large combustion plants are concerned. Once again implementation was late (in this instance a year after the deadline for

---

[49] OJ 1980 L 229.
[50] OJ 1982 L 378, p. 15.
[51] OJ 1985 L 87.
[52] SR No. 145.
[53] SR No. 339.
[54] SR No. 23.
[55] OJ 1992 L 297, p. 1.
[56] SR No. 440.
[57] SR No. 449.
[58] OJ 1988 L 336, p. 1.

implementation had expired), and incomplete. Implementing legislation for new plants has yet to be enacted in Northern Ireland.

Emissions of asbestos into the air

Directive 87/217/EEC[59] on the prevention and reduction of environmental pollution by asbestos should have been implemented in Northern Ireland by December 1988; however, the process of implementing the requirements of this Directive in so far as emissions of asbestos to air are concerned was not completed in Northern Ireland until 1993. In effect, Directive 87/217/EEC is implemented by a combination of three sets of regulations, namely, the Control of Asbestos in the Air Regulations (NI) 1993,[60] the Alkali &c. Works Regulations Act 1906,[61] as amended, and the Control of Asbestos at Work Regulations (NI) 1988[62] as amended.

Waste

Legislation covering waste, its deposit and disposal, and the threat of soil pollution in Northern Ireland is extremely archaic. The regime which is presently in force is based on the first attempt to introduce systematic licensing controls for a waste legislative regime, the Control of Pollution Act 1974. To date the modernising impact of EC law relevant to waste has been minimal: partial or even complete non-implementation of directives having characterised the situation in the Province for many years. The provisions of the Control of Pollution Act 1974 have long since been amended and superseded (in no small part due to the requirements and influence of EC law) in England and Wales by the Environmental Protection Act 1990 and the Environment Act 1995. Northern Ireland law has however been slow to catch up with developments in the rest of the United Kingdom. Change was however set in motion, in no small part due to the recognition that the law in Northern Ireland, if hopelessly out of step with the rest of the United Kingdom, was in an even worse position in regard to EC law. A consultation exercise carried out by the DoE(NI), based on the *Review of Waste Disposal in Northern Ireland*,[63] beginning in 1993 saw the start of a concerted attempt to modernise the law.

The relevant parts of the aforementioned statutes, together with a licensing system applicable to waste carriers analogous to that introduced by the Control of Pollution (Amendment) Act 1989, are only now being implemented in Northern Ireland in the draft Waste and Contaminated Land (Northern Ireland) Order 1996, which is due to become law by the end of the year. The

---

[59] OJ 1987 L 85, p. 40.
[60] SR No. 170.
[61] C. 14.
[62] SR No. 74.
[63] Carried out by Aspinwall and Company for the DoE(NI), (DoE(NI) 1990).

draft Order, in addition to bringing the law in Northern Ireland into line with that on the mainland, will also go a considerable way towards updating the law in this sector as required by the relevant EC provisions. Some examples of the current and projected law relating to waste are outlined below.

Municipal waste

The main legislation relating to municipal waste in Northern Ireland is currently the Pollution Control and Local Government (Northern Ireland) Order 1978[64] which is similar in its approach and provisions to the Control of Pollution Act 1974. The provisions of the 1978 Order have been amplified, though not greatly enhanced, by the Waste Collection and Disposal Regulations (Northern Ireland) 1992.[65] The draft Waste and Contaminated Land (Northern Ireland) Order will entirely re-enact the licensing regime applicable to waste, introducing in Northern Ireland enhanced licensing controls, the duty of care in respect of waste, and other innovations which have formed integral parts of modern legislation in the rest of the United Kingdom.

Special waste

The controls for special waste, the Pollution Control (Special Waste) Regulations (Northern Ireland) 1981,[66] were issued under art. 17 of the 1978 Order and partially implement Directive 78/319/EEC[67] on toxic and dangerous waste. The treatment of waste oils, which form a category of special waste, was tackled by the amendment of the 1978 Order by the Waste Collection and Disposal Regulations (Northern Ireland) 1992, which partially implemented Directive 87/101/EEC[68] (which itself amended Directive 75/439/EEC)[69] on the disposal of waste oils. The requirements of both of the aforementioned Directives will be further pursued by the provisions of the draft Waste and Contaminated Land Order 1996. The DoE(NI) Environment Service is also currently considering a review of the Special Waste Regulations, although its current priority lies with updating the general regime dealing with waste.

Waste incineration

Directives 89/369/EEC[70] (on the prevention of air pollution from new municipal waste incineration plants) and 89/429/EEC[71] (on the reduction of air pollution from existing municipal waste incineration plants) are covered by the Alkali &c. Works Regulations Act 1906, as amended by the Alkali etc. Works

---

[64] SI 1978 No. 1049.
[65] SR No. 254.
[66] SR No. 252.
[67] OJ 1978 L 84, p. 43.
[68] OJ 1987 L 42, p. 43.
[69] OJ 1975 L 194, p. 23.
[70] OJ 1989 L 163, p. 32.
[71] OJ 1989 L 203, p. 50.

(Amendment) Order 1994.[72] Though these provisions allow the emission targets set by both Directives to be complied with, in practice they will be included in a more general overhaul of air pollution controls under the draft Industrial Air Pollution Control (Northern Ireland) Order 1996.[73] This change, while not affecting the substantive content of the law, will contribute to a more coordinated approach to air pollution controls. Northern Ireland legislation implementing Directive 94/67/EEC[74] on the incineration of hazardous waste will be made under regulations to be issued under the draft Order.

Transfrontier shipments of waste

The legal provisions of the Transfrontier Shipment of Waste Regulations 1994[75] provide an example of the government honouring its commitment to ensure a nationwide approach to the implementation of EC environmental law. The Regulations extend Council Regulation 259/93/EEC[76] (on the supervision and control of shipments of waste within, into and out of the European Community) and Council Directive 74/442/EEC[77] (in respect of imports and exports of waste) to the whole of the United Kingdom.

Contaminated land

The issue of contaminated land, which was the subject of an abortive legislative regime in England and Wales under the Environmental Protection Act 1990, will be tackled for the first time in Northern Ireland under the draft Waste and Contaminated Land (Northern Ireland) Order 1996. The draft Order by-passes the failed provisions and is based instead on the new controls instituted by the Environment Act 1995. In this area at least, action to ensure that Northern Ireland law is not left lagging behind that of the rest of the United Kingdom has been comparatively swift.

Conclusion

It will be apparent from the brief survey given here that environmental law in Northern Ireland is in a state of flux generally speaking, but especially in terms of discharging the government's EC law obligation to implement EC environmental directives. After two decades of neglect, it would now appear that there is cause for optimism in this context. The 1990s have been characterised by an

---

[72] SR No. 104.
[73] The Order has yet to be made.
[74] OJ 1994 L 365, p. 34.
[75] SI 1994 No. 1137.
[76] OJ 1993 L 30, p. 1.
[77] OJ 1975 L 194, p. 47.

unprecedented level of legislative activity covering all areas of environmental protection, the vast majority of which has been adopted for the purposes of implementing environmental standards adopted at European level. By the end of 1997 the legislative landscape regulating all environmental media in the Province will have been transformed almost beyond recognition into a framework of control which reflects contemporary legal and environmental values.

Part II

PRINCIPLES OF EC ENVIRONMENTAL LAW IN THE UNITED KINGDOM

Chapter 6

THE IMPACT OF SUBSIDIARITY
David Freestone and Han Somsen

Introduction

It has been said that the coming into force of the Treaty on European Union,
signed at Maastricht on 7 February 1992, ushers in a new era of EC environmental law.[1] The redrafted EC Treaty contains for the first time a basic
commitment to the promotion of 'sustainable and non-inflationary growth
respecting the environment' (Article 2). Maastricht also introduces a further
raft of changes to the way in which EC environmental law will operate, which
must be read against the background of the political commitments contained
in the EC environmental action programmes, particularly the 1993 Fifth
Environment Action Programme entitled 'Towards Sustainability'.[2] Whereas the
1987 Single European Act talked only of 'actions relating to the environment',
the Maastricht Treaty recognises the significance of Community action in this
field by calling it, for the first time, an environmental 'policy', albeit a policy
which must be firmly integrated with policies in other sectors.

However, having recognised an EC environmental policy for the first time,
the Maastricht Treaty also contains other important provisions which have led
Wilkinson to describe it as 'two steps forward, one step back'.[3] Foremost among
these is a new Article 3b of the EC Treaty that introduces the now well-known
general subsidiarity provision applicable to all areas of Community activity. The
new Article 3b provides that the Community shall take action '*only if and in so
far as* the objectives of that action cannot be *sufficiently* achieved by the Member

---

[1] For text see (1992) 31 ILM 247; (1993) 32 ILM 1693. In this article the term EC is used strictly
to denote activities conducted under what is now termed the EC (formerly EEC) Treaty. The term
European Union is an umbrella term for activities conducted under the Maastricht Treaty
including the 'two pillars' of a Common Foreign and Security Policy and Co-operation in the
Fields of Justice and Home Affairs.

[2] Fifth Environmental Action Programme (1993–99), adopted 1 February 1993, OJ C 138 17.5.93,
p. 1.

[3] Wilkinson, 'Maastricht and the Environment: the Implications for the EC's Environment Policy of
the Treaty on European Union' (1992) JEL Vol. 4, No. 2, 221.

States and can therefore by reason of scale or effects of the proposed action, be better achieved by the Community'.

The issue of subsidiarity has been the subject of a great deal of debate amongst politicians and Community officials as well as academics.[4] Despite some recent judgments where the principle of subsidiarity has been raised (mostly by the parties themselves, but also by Advocates General and—more rarely—the European Court of Justice,[5] debate about its justiciability continues.[6] Yet, irrespective of the outcome of this process, the Commission is already compelled to implement the principle. In this regard, it has expressly recognised the importance of maintaining the existing high environmental standards relating to water and air quality and has stressed the point that the application of the subsidiarity principle must not be allowed to lower those standards.[7] Indeed some have argued that the impact of subsidiarity will be to increase rather than decrease the scope of Community involvement in the sphere of the environment.[8]

This chapter looks at the way in which subsidiarity is being applied in practice and attempts a preliminary assessment of whether the results will be beneficial for the future development and effective implementation of EC environmental law. The paper first addresses the concept of subsidiarity as elaborated in the Maastricht Treaty. This is followed by an analysis of the way in which subsidiarity has been incorporated into the Commission's legislative programme; some 'subsidiarity' directives are then assessed and a few conclusions suggested.

Subsidiarity post Maastricht

It will be recalled that, prior to Maastricht, Title II of the Single European Act envisaged that environmental legislation would be based on one of two main legal grounds: Articles 130s or 100a. Article 130s, by providing specifically for the enactment of environmental legislation, freed it from the requirement that it should serve economic ends,[9] but such legislation had to be adopted by unanimous agreement of the Council of Ministers, unless (by unanimity) it

---

[4] Mackenzie Stuart, Temple-Lang, Brinkhorst, Toth, Somsen.
[5] For some recent cases see for example Case 11/95 of 10 September 1996 (not yet reported) Opinion 2/94, *Re the Accession of the Community to the European Convention* [1996] 2 CMLR 265, Case C-192/94, *El Corte Ingles SA v. Christina Blasquez Rivero* [1996] 2 CMLR 507, Case C-415/93, *Jean Luc Bosman* [1996] 1 CMLR 645, Joined Cases C-430 and 431/93, *Jeroen van Schijndel and Johannes van Veen v. Stichting Pensioenfonds voor Fysiotherapeuten* [1996] 1 CMLR 801, Case C-359/92, *Germany v. Council* [1994] ECR I-368.
[6] Toth, 'The Legal Status of the Declarations Attached to the Single European Act' (1986) 23 CML Rev 802.
[7] Commission Report, COM(93) 545, p. 17.
[8] Jan Brinkhorst, 'Subsidiarity and European Community Environmental Policy. A Panacea or a Pandora's Box?' [1993] 2 EEL Rev 8; House of Lords Select Committee on the European Communities, *Report on the Implementation and Enforcement of Environmental Legislation*, Session 1991–92, Ninth Report, HL Paper 53–1, para. 87. See also Van Kersbergen and Verbeek, 'The Politics of Subsidiarity in the European Union' (1994) 32 JCMS 215.
[9] See further Somsen, 'EC Water Directives' [1990] 1 *Water Law* 93.

chose to define those matters as ones on which decisions were to be taken by a qualified majority.[10] Action taken under Article 130s was made subject to the principle of subsidiarity,[11] namely that:

The Community shall take action relating to the environment to the extent to which the objectives . . . can be attained better at the Community level than at the level of the individual Member States.[12]

and to the general safeguard provision in Article 130t that:

The protective measures adopted in common pursuant to Article 130s shall not prevent any Member State from maintaining or introducing more stringent protective measures compatible with this Treaty.

The alternative basis for environmental legislation was provided under Article 100a, the primary source of legislation for the attainment of the single market.[13] This Article provided for action by majority vote in the Council of Ministers and, presumably in recognition of the fact that the pressures to achieve the single market might result in environmental considerations being pushed into second place, the Commission was obliged when presenting proposals for environmental action under this Article to 'take as its basis a high level of protection' (Article 100a(3)). In addition, when such action was to be taken by majority vote, Member States were specifically permitted to adopt stricter measures of domestic environmental protection.[14]

This limited impact of subsidiarity was removed by the Maastricht Treaty on

---

[10] Article 130s (second indent). For example, the Commission had for some time been proposing that the procedure for adding new substances to the annex of Directive 76/464/EEC on dangerous substances be changed (by unanimous vote) to a majority approval procedure.

[11] In fact the EC appears to have adopted such an approach in the past regarding environmental legislation: see *Progress made in connection with the environmental action programme and assessment of the work done to implement it* (Communication from Commission to Council) COM(80) 222 final, 7 May 1980.

[12] Article 130r(4).

[13] The Court, in Case C-300/89, *Commission* v. *Council*, ruled that Articles 100a and 130s were mutually exclusive and environmental legislation could not be based on both provisions simultaneously. See Somsen, 'Case C-300/89, *Commission* v. *Council (Titanium Dioxide)*' (1992) 22 CML Rev 29, 140–151.

[14] Subject, that is, to the procedure of Article 100a(4):

If, after the adoption of a harmonisation measure by the Council, acting by a qualified majority, a Member State deems it necessary to apply national provisions on grounds of major needs referred to in Article 36, or *relating to protection of the environment* . . . it shall notify the Commission of these provisions.

The Commission shall confirm the provisions involved after having verified that they are not a means of arbitrary discrimination, or disguised restriction on trade between Member States. (emphasis added)

Note also the Danish declaration attached to the Single European Act and Toth, *op. cit.* note 6.

European Union[15] which, as indicated above, contains a general subsidiarity provision applying to all areas of Community activity. The new Article 3b of the EC Treaty provides that the Community shall take action '*only if and in so far as* the objectives of that action cannot be *sufficiently* achieved by the Member States and can therefore by reason of scale or effects of the proposed action, be better achieved by the Community' and Article 3b goes on to add what effectively is a proportionality clause limiting any action by the Community after Maastricht to that which is *necessary* to achieve the Treaty's objectives (emphases added).[16]

The full implications of this shift of emphasis, which compared to the old Article 130r(4) reverses the 'burden of proof' by requiring the Community to show that Community action is both necessary and effects better achieved at Community level, is still subject to considerable debate. The few cases which so far have touched upon the principle of subsidiarity, including the most recent example relating to the Directive on working hours, as yet offer too little guidance to warrant any detailed analysis here.[17] However, the cases decided so far appear to suggest that the European Court of Justice only very marginally reviews the use of powers by the Council against Article 3b.[18] In Case C-84/94 of 12 November 1996, for example, the United Kingdom had argued that the Community legislature had neither fully considered nor adequately demonstrated whether there were transnational aspects which could not be satisfactorily regulated by national measures, whether such measures would conflict with the requirements of the EC Treaty or significantly damage the interests of Member States or, finally, whether action at Community level would provide clear benefits compared with action at national level. Thus, the United Kingdom argued, Article 118a ought to be interpreted in the light of the principle of subsidiarity and therefore could not support adoption of a directive of the nature contested in the proceedings. Responding to this argument, the Court noted:

... it should be noted that it is the responsibility of the Council, under Article 118a, to

---

[15] It is presumed that the principles enumerated in Article 130r and hence the principle of subsidiarity only apply to those measures adopted on the basis of Article 130s. There is some scope for disagreement in this respect by virtue of the principle of integration in Article 130r which stipulates that environmental goals—and arguably hence the principles listed in Article 130r—shall form a component of all other policy areas.

[16] Article 3b provides:

> The Community shall act within the limits of the powers conferred upon it by this Treaty and of the objectives assigned to it therein. In areas which do not fall within its exclusive competence, the Community shall take action, in accordance with the principle of subsidiarity, only if and in so far as the objectives of the proposed action cannot be sufficiently be achieved by the Member States and can therefore, by reason of the scale and effects of the proposed action, be better achieved by the Community.
>
> Any action by the Community shall not go beyond what is necessary to achieve the objectives of the Treaty.

[17] See Calliess, Der Schlüsselbegriff 'der ausschliessischen Zuständigkeit im Subsidiaritätsprinzip des Art. 3b II EGV', *Europäische Zeitschrift für Wirtschaftsrecht* (EuZW) Heft 20/1995 pp. 693–700.

[18] Note 5 above. Case C-84/94, *United Kingdom v. Council,* 12 November 1996 (not yet reported) at paras. 46 and 47.

adopt minimum requirements so as to contribute, through harmonization, to achieving the objective of raising the level of health and safety protection of workers which, in terms of Article 188a(1), is primarily the responsibility of the Member States. *Once the Council has found that it is necessary to improve the existing level of protection as regards the health and safety of workers and to harmonize the conditions in this area while maintaining the improvements already made, achievement of that objective necessarily presupposes Community-wide action,* which otherwise, as in this case, leaves the enactment of the detailed implementing provisions required largely to the Member States. (emphasis added)

And thus, the Court concluded in para. 55:

The argument of non-compliance with the principle of subsidiarity can be rejected at the outset. It is said that the Community legislature has not established that the aims of the directive would be better served at Community level than at national level. But that argument, as so formulated, really concerns the need for Community action, which has already been examined in para. 47 of this judgment.

The impact of subsidiarity on substantive environmental law

Although environmental legislation, particularly water and air quality legislation, has been expressly singled out for 'subsidiarisation',[19] in fact modern approaches to environmental regulation which stress holistic and eco-systems approaches are particularly susceptible to transnational management. Somsen and Sprok-kereef[20] have pointed out that some key environmental sectors such as atmospheric pollution (including emission of greenhouse gases), marine pollution and wildlife conservation can only be addressed satisfactorily at a regional or international level. Brinkhorst suggests that the principle might increase the scope for Community activity as it would lead to the birth of a new generation of environmental measures which are designed to provide encouragement rather than compulsion, such as the eco-label and eco-audit schemes.[21] The House of Lords Select Committee on the European Communities in its 1992 Report on the Implementation and Enforcement of Environmental Legislation, commenting on the poor enforcement record of EC legislation by Member States, suggested that:

Unless they [Member States] demonstrate, in accordance with the principle of subsidiarity, that they can ensure the effective implementation of Community legislation the pressure will grow for a transfer of competences to the Community itself.[22]

---

[19] See Somsen and Sprokkereef, 'Making Subsidiarity Work for the Environmental Policy of the European Community: the Role of Science' (1996) *International Journal of Biosciences and the Law* Vol. 1, No. 1 37–67.

[20] *Ibid.* 38–39.

[21] See Jan Brinkhorst, note 8 above, at 19.

[22] House of Lords Select Committee on the European Communities, *Report on the Implementation and Enforcement of Environmental Legislation*, Session 1991–92, Ninth Report, HL Paper 53–1, para. 87.

To date, despite the few judgments discussed above, the main evidence of the future impact of subsidiarity is still mainly derived from the legislative programme of the Commission and the way in which the Commission itself has signalled that it will be adapting this to subsidiarity. In this respect the Commission has drawn a distinction between new legislation and existing legislation.

With regard to new legislation, the Commission gave an undertaking to the 1992 Edinburgh European Council which was incorporated in the Inter-Institutional Agreement of 4 November 1993,[23] that the requirement that the Community demonstrate the existence of a legitimate need for each new initiative would be met by the inclusion of a written justification for Community action in all new legislative proposals; it also undertook to withdraw or revise pending proposals in the light of the same factors—some 20 proposals were subsequently reconsidered.[24]

With regard to the application of the subsidiarity principle to existing legislation, the Lisbon European Council in June 1992 asked the Commission to draw up a report on certain Community rules with a view to adapting them to the subsidiarity principle. A number of Member States, notably the French and British acting together and the German government, sent in proposals for the revision of old legislation. Among the 'families' of existing rules which were identified for revision were a number in the environment sector, regulating water and air quality. The conclusions of the Edinburgh European Council in December 1992 stated: 'On the environment, the Commission intends to simplify, consolidate and update existing texts, particularly those on air and water, to take new knowledge and technical progress into account.'[25] On water quality the Commission declared that it intends, in line with the subsidiarity principle, 'to reorient rules and regulations towards compliance with essential quality and health parameters, leaving Member States free to add secondary parameters if they see fit'.[26] Ostensibly as a result of the Franco-British submissions to the Edinburgh Council, the Commission now plans to replace much existing water legislation. The 1993 Commission Report to the Council on the Adaptation of Community Legislation to the Subsidiarity Principle sets out its legislative plan in relation to both water and air quality.

Water quality legislation

It might at this point be worth recalling an older debate of the 1970s and 1980s between the United Kingdom and the Commission over the choice between Uniform Emission Standards and Environmental Quality Objectives (EQOs). At that time, the United Kingdom argued that the setting of uniform emission standards or limit values for discharge levels of particular substances—which

---

[23] EC Bull. No. 10, 12, 129–130 (1993).
[24] Cited in *Commission Report to the European Council on the Adaptation of Community Legislation to the Subsidiarity Principle*, COM(93) 545 final, 24 November 1993, at p. 3.
[25] *Ibid.* p. 15.
[26] *Ibid.*

was the established regulatory model in continental Europe—ignored the experience of the United Kingdom in improving river quality by the establishment of more flexible EQOs which could be adjusted to the needs of various aquatic environments. The United Kingdom particularly argued that as an island state with fast flowing rivers it was the quality of the receiving waters which was crucial rather than the quality of each individual discharge. Uniform discharge levels (adopted in Brussels and applicable indiscriminately throughout Europe) overloaded some environments while not utilising the full assimilative capacity of others.[27]

In reality, neither uniform limit values nor EQOs can claim to offer ideal solutions to the problem of water pollution. The fixing of quality objectives in the majority of cases only leads to the protection of those waters which perform one of the uses for which quality directives have been adopted (and then only to the extent necessary to safeguard continued use of the waters for the relevant purposes). Even where the uses are defined in objective terms, Member States possess very considerable degrees of discretion in determining which waters are to be subject to the Community regime. The Community, meanwhile, enjoys little or no control over the selection of national waters for the purpose of the application of EC water directives other than judicial review *ex post* by the European Court of Justice which, for various reasons, is highly unsatisfactory. Where waters are significantly cleaner than required by the quality objectives, the latter may be interpreted as licences to pollute.

Furthermore, the fixing of quality objectives to protect waters from particularly toxic, bio-accumulative and persistent substances—which is at the heart of the debate between the United Kingdom and the Commission—appears to ignore the very properties of those substances. Resistance to the application of Community standards to national environments is significant and, obvious considerations like cost apart, is at least in part explained by their general aloofness, i.e. their inability to take account of local (environmental) conditions and priorities. This, combined with the discretion on the part of national authorities in implementing the directives and the difficulty faced by the Commission in supervising the implementation of quality objectives, almost necessarily leads to significant implementation deficits. Uniform limit values, on the other hand, fail to deal satisfactorily with non point and multiple sources of pollution and by definition do not take into account local environmental conditions as propagated by Article 130r(3) of the EC Treaty.

Although in the context of Directive 76/464/EEC on dangerous substances discharged into the aquatic environment the vast majority of Member States have opted to adhere to uniform limit values, as will become clear from recent proposals, environmental quality objectives appear to be celebrating the beginning of a come back. Whereas this trend undoubtedly is partly inspired by new

---

[27] On this issue see Boehmer-Christiansen, 'Uniform Emission Standards versus Environmental Quality Objectives', in Freestone and Ijlstra, *The North Sea: Perspectives on Regional Environmental Co-operation* (Graham and Trotman/Martinus Nijhoff, 1990), pp. 139–149.

insights in the sphere of environmental management, at least as important is the fundamental parallel between the technique of local standard-setting (which is what the implementation of environmental quality objectives ultimately requires) and the principle of subsidiarity.

For a combination of the reasons outlined above, it has become increasingly accepted that the Community's original policy of fixing quality objectives for waters performing certain uses in conjunction with the adoption of uniform limit values applicable to discharges of a number of agreed so-called 'black-list' substances was unsatisfactory. A more integrated, source-oriented approach was to supplement the existing regime. Important early examples are the Directives on pollution by municipal waste water and nitrates by agricultural sources[28] respectively which made a first real attempt to attack the root of the problem by seeking to change municipal waste water treatment and farming practices. Crucially, and in line with the principle of subsidiarity, Member States are to designate themselves the vulnerable zones to which these Directives apply and the less vulnerable zones where less stringent measures may be acceptable. It is not difficult to see the potential for conflict and even abuse of this approach.

Directive 96/61/EC on integrated pollution prevention and control (IPPC) is set to formalise this more integrated approach to water pollution control. Great emphasis is placed on the concept of 'Best Available Techniques' (BAT) which aims to prevent emissions to air, water and land or, where it is not practicable to do so, to minimise emission to the environment as a whole. It is expected that BAT will encourage the development and application of low emission technologies, as emission standards will be based on 'best available techniques'. The Commission started work on this Directive in 1990 and published a proposal in September 1993[29] although clear references to the need for a more integrated approach to pollution control were already contained in the Third and Fourth Environmental Action Programmes. Experience in the United Kingdom with integrated pollution control clearly influenced the Commission's thinking. The objective of the Directive is 'to provide measures and procedures to prevent, wherever practicable, or to minimise emissions from industrial installations within the Community so as to achieve a high level of protection of the environment as a whole' (Article 1). The scope of application of the Directive is determined by Annex I, which contains the sectors of industry which will be subject to the IPPC approach. Installations need a permit before they can be operated, for existing installations there exists a transitional regime. Conditions will be attached to the permits which 'normally' include limit values for the substances and preparations listed in Annex III. It becomes clear from this formulation that it is quite possible that different limit values will apply for the same substances in different Member States, a point heavily criticised by

[28] Directive 91/271/EEC concerning urban waste water treatment, OJ 1991 L 135, Directive 91/676/EEC concerning the protection of waters against pollution caused by nitrates from agricultural sources, OJ 1991 L 377.
[29] OJ 1993 C 311, p. 6, see OJ 1996 L275, 10.8.1996.

Germany.[30] These limit values, in turn, are to be based on 'Best Available Techniques', as defined in Article 2(10) of the Directive.[31] Obviously, such limit values may not lead to violation of existing EC water law. Quite strikingly, and similar to the Directives on municipal waste water and nitrate from agricultural sources, rather than traditional uniform Community standard-setting the IPPC Directive relies heavily on national authorities to perform this task, albeit in a loose Community framework.

Important insights into the nature of EC environmental law in the post subsidiarity era were also provided by the draft directive on the ecological quality of surface waters. Thus, despite the fact that it is no longer envisaged that it will become law in its present form, very similar provisions are planned to form the basis of the framework directive on water resources.[32] The directive was designed to complement the Community's water laws by controlling point sources, diffuse sources and other anthropogenic factors. The directive's aim was to maintain water quality of Community waters where it is already good and ultimately achieve good ecological water quality elsewhere.[33] Article 2(1) provided that:

water is of good ecological quality when the self purification of the water body is maintained, the diversity of the naturally occurring species is preserved and the structure and quality of the sediments are able to sustain the naturally occurring biological community of that ecosystem.[34]

The territorial scope of the draft directive is very wide. Community surface waters means all surface waters within the territory of each Member state, together with their internal waters and territorial sea as defined by international law.[35]

Somsen has pointed out that in its explanatory memorandum the Commission

---

[30] See Bongaerts, 'Integrated Pollution Prevention and Control: The Bonn Workshop' [1994] 3 EEL Rev 199–201 and Krämer, 'Integrierter und betrieblicher Umweltschutz' Dritte Osnabrucker Gesprache zum deutschen und europaischen Umweltrecht am 18/19 Mai 1995 (Koln: Carl Heymanns, 1995).

[31] Best available techniques (BAT) signifies the latest stage in the development of activities, processes and their methods of operation which indicate the practical suitability of particular techniques as the basis of emission limit values for preventing, or, where that is not practicable, minimising emissions to the environment as a whole, without predetermining any specific technology or techniques.

   Note that these 'techniques' must be 'industrially feasible, in the relevant sector, from a technical and economical point of view'. 'Available' means 'those developed on a scale which allows implementation in the relevant industrial context, under economically viable conditions, whether or not the techniques are used or produced inside the Member State in question, as long as they are reasonably accessible to the operator'. 'Best' means 'most effective in achieving a high level of protection for the environment as a whole, taking into account the potential benefits and costs which may result from action or lack of action'.

[32] COM(93) 680 final.

[33] COM(93) 680 final, p. 4.

[34] COM(93) 680 final, Article 2.1, Annex II.

[35] Subject to a *de minimis* exception for waters of insignificant size and effects, Article 10.

devotes six pages to justifying the proposal in the light of the principle of subsidiarity and only five pages to explaining its substance.[36]

Interestingly, the directive allows *Member States* to set the operational quality targets for good ecological quality as defined in Article 2 and Annex I of the directive. For this purpose they must draw up integrated programmes to meet these targets. Article 5 leaves it to Member States, by 31 December 1998, to define for all the Community surface waters located on their territory as well as for their internal waters and territorial sea the operational targets for good ecological water quality. These operational targets are fixed in accordance with Annex II, which merely lays down a 'list of representative elements'. The measures contained in the programmes will be based on the implementation of 'Best Environmental Practices' and, as far as point sources are concerned, also on 'Best Available Technology', terms which are defined in Annexes attached to the directive. Evidently, the crux of the directive is the obligation on the part of Member States to implement the measures contained in the programmes. Yet again, and in line with the spirit of subsidiarity, Article 8 leaves considerable discretion as to how this is to be achieved. Thus, Member States may ensure that the measures and practices required under the integrated programmes are legally binding on natural persons, both public and private or, alternatively, they may opt for the use of economic instruments designed to encourage natural persons and public and private undertakings to comply with the provisions of the directive.

The uniqueness of the directive resides in the fact that, unlike previous water directives, it does not impose an obligation of result in the sense that the operational targets must be achieved. The obligation, rather, is to take all the procedural steps indicated in the directive, allowing the elaboration of solutions tailored to the needs of individual waters.

The most recent thoughts on the Union's future water policy are contained in the Commission's Communication on a European Water Policy of 21 February 1996 which articulates the need for a framework directive on water resources which would make the draft directive on the ecological quality of surface waters redundant.[37] The Communication acknowledges that the hostilities between advocates of quality objectives and emission standards are far from over, admitting that the quality objectives approach may amount to a 'licence to pollute' whilst uniform limit values lack a degree of flexibility and may result in unduly stringent standards being imposed on certain environments. The proposed answer to this dilemma is the kind of zoning first introduced in the nitrate and municipal waste water Directives and further elaborated in the proposed directive on ecological quality of surface waters.

The trend towards a more integrated approach to pollution control is also embodied in the proposed framework directive in the form of integrated programmes to be drawn up by all Member States containing all those measures

---

[36] Somsen, *op. cit.* note 9, p. 174.
[37] COM(96) 59 final.

which they are required to implement as well as further development of river basin management. Integration will be further pursued between:

- water quantity and water quality issues;
- surface water management and groundwater management;
- water use and environmental protection;
- control of pollution through emission controls and through quality objectives;
- water policy and other policies.

The suggested directive will leave a number of directives unaffected such as the Bathing Water Directive, the Dangerous Substances Directive, the Drinking Water Directive, the Urban Waste Water Directive and the Nitrates Directive. This set of Directives is largely in place and already, the Commission feels, reflects subsidiarity and, arguably, a precautionary approach. The Nitrate and Municipal Waste Water Directives result directly from initiatives at the 1990 Hague International Conference on the Protection of the North Sea which explicitly endorsed the precautionary approach.[38]

On the other hand, directives to be repealed are the Surface Water Directive, the Fish Water Directives, the Groundwater Directive and the proposed ecological quality of water directive. As to the directives to be repealed, the Groundwater Directive stands out as one which needs an urgent alternative which appears to be absent from the Communication.

It appears that the 1976 Dangerous Substances Directive[39] would remain in place and to the package would be added Directive 96/61/EC on integrated pollution prevention and control (IPPC).[40]

Air quality legislation

As far as air quality legislation is concerned, current legislation is sectoral and related to source emissions (car and lorry exhausts, combustion plants etc.). The Commission's aim therefore in this area is to develop overall objectives within the context of the establishment of evaluation and monitoring procedures. The text of the first of these proposed directives, on ambient air quality, is now available.[41] This proposal and its daughter directive will replace existing air quality measures. The Commission's hope is that they will be 'much simpler than the previous legislation' despite being more rigorous.[42] It will only come

---

[38] For the text of the 1990 Hague Declaration which sets out these requirements, see Freestone and Ijlstra, *The North Sea: Basic Legal Documents on Regional Environmental Co-operation* (Graham and Trotman/Martinus Nijhoff, 1991) pp. 3–39.

[39] Council Directive 76/464/EEC on pollution caused by certain dangerous substances discharged into the aquatic environment of the Community, OJ L 129 18.5.76, p. 23.

[40] Directive 96/61/EC on Integrated Pollution Prevention and Control, OJ 1996, L 275, 10.8.1996.

[41] Proposal for a Council Directive on ambient air quality assessment and management, COM(94) 109 final. See also Mount, 'The Proposed Directive on Ambient Air Quality Assessment and Management' [1995] 4 EEL Rev 50–53.

[42] Per representative of DGXI in *Europe Environment* (1994) No. 436, 1 (quoted Mount, note 41 above, at 52).

into force when all the daughter directives are adopted. The Commission's aim for this was July 1996.[43] It has four main objectives:

1. *Establishment of ambient air quality objectives.* These objectives will be designed to limit or prevent the harmful effects of the pollutants. Limit values (Air Quality Standards—AQSs) for specified pollutants will be established which will have to be met within 10–15 years. Alert thresholds will also be established.

2. *Assessment of ambient air quality throughout the Community according to a common procedure.* Some monitoring will be mandatory. Daughter directives will establish methods for specific substances.

3. *Maintaining and improving air quality.* Air quality will be assessed as poor, improving or good. States with poor areas will be required to draw up action plans to achieve AQS within an agreed timetable.

4. *Informing the public.* If alert thresholds are reached the public must be informed. Plans to improve poor air quality must be published. The Commission will publish annual reports on poor quality areas and a triennial report on general air quality.

Conclusions

The Commission has expressly recognised the importance of maintaining the existing high standards relating to water and air and stresses the point that the application of the subsidiarity principle must not be allowed to lower those standards.[44] From this overview, the question arises whether this claim is justified in the light of the evidence to date, or whether these developments amount to the dismantling of EC environmental regulation in these sectors and its substitution with wide national discretionary powers.

It is, of course, possible that any doubts about the sincerity of Member States' belief that they are in a better position to determine which environmental standards ought to apply to which parts of their territory will prove to be entirely unjustified. Yet, it is difficult to deny the fact that the evidence to date is not encouraging in this regard.

Directive 76/464/EEC on dangerous substances released into the aquatic environment, by virtue of Article 7, required Member States to establish by 1981 the kind of plans now at the heart of the Community's latest thoughts on water and air pollution control. Yet, in its most recent report on the implementation of EC law, it reported that infringement proceedings had been commenced against all the Member States for failure to notify such programmes.[45] In the same report, it is revealed that in respect of the Urban Waste Water Directive,

---

[43] But at the time of writing the view of the European Parliament is still awaited, as well as those of Member States.
[44] Commission Report, COM(93) 545 final, p. 17.
[45] COM(95) 500 final, p. 49.

no implementing measures were communicated from Germany, Greece, Italy, Spain and the United Kingdom. In short, evidence so far appears to suggest that the subsidiarisation of environmental law may lead to an increase in instances of non-compliance.[46]

Even where Member States do adopt the programmes and standards required by the Community framework, in view of Member State discretion in respect of sampling, analysis and the continued absence of a Community Inspectorate with independent enforcement powers, Community supervision of compliance in practice of waters with these quality objectives may prove virtually impossible.

It hence appears that implementation of the principle of subsidiarity by way of the adoption of framework directives of a procedural nature which delegate the fixing of operational standards to national authorities is creating an imbalance between Member States' ever increasing responsibilities to manage and protect a common heritage, and the powers of the Community to check and if necessary enforce adherence to the minimum standards commonly agreed.

Addressing this imbalance in a way which respects the principle of subsidiarity is set to become one of the major challenges facing the European Union's environmental policy in the next millennium.

---

[46] See Macrory and Purdy, Chapter 3 above.

Chapter 7

PROPORTIONALITY AND ENVIRONMENTAL PROTECTION IN EC LAW

Owen McIntyre

Introduction

The principle of proportionality is well established as a general principle of Community law. Wyatt and Dashwood consider it an example of 'common law' principles, which 'the Court of Justice has developed . . . inspired by the national laws of the Member States, in accordance with which it interprets the explicit provisions of Community law, and evaluates the legality of acts of the institutions'.[1] Lasok describes the principle, as embodied in the German constitution, as 'an aspect of the Aristotelian distributive justice' which 'means that social burdens [imposed by law] should be distributed fairly according to the capacity of the members of the society'.[2] A much-quoted articulation of the principle as it applies in the context of EC law was provided by Advocate General Dutheillet de Lamothe,[3] who stated that 'citizens may only have imposed on them, for the purposes of the public interest, obligations which are strictly necessary for those purposes to be attained'. It is an example, according to Lasok,[4] of a well-established principle of national legal systems on which the European Court of Justice relies to secure justice for the individual. To this end, the principle ensures a proportionate relationship between means and ends in legislative measures. Interestingly, Lasok finds a comparison between proportionality and the operation of equity in English law and observes that '[T]he body of case law emerging from the process [before the ECJ] is like the ancient Equity of English law which fed on the harshness and deficiencies of the Common Law system'.[5] He further develops the analogy by noting that '[S]ince the principles applied by the Court [ECJ] in such cases are

---

[1] Wyatt and Dashwood, *The Substantive Law of the EEC* (London: Sweet and Maxwell, 1980), at p. 47.
[2] Lasok and Bridge, *Law and Institutions of the European Union*, 6th ed. (London: Butterworths, 1994), at p. 172.
[3] Case 11/70, *Internationale Handelsgesellschaft* [1970] ECR 1125, at 1146. See Lasok, *op. cit.* note 2.
[4] *Op. cit.* note 2.
[5] *Ibid.*

regarded as "superior rules of law for the protection of the individual" based on ethical precepts, it seems appropriate to describe them as "EC Equity" '.[6]

Proportionality has developed in German[7] and French[8] administrative law as a principle of sound and proper administration and its first mention in a European context was under the Coal and Steel Community Treaty.[9] Probably the earliest application of the principle by the European Court of Justice occurred in the *Fedechar* case,[10] where the Court held that, by a generally accepted rule of law, the reaction of the ECSC High Authority to an unlawful act must be proportional to the scale of the act. Stated in its broadest sense, as a 'general principle' of law, it dictates that necessary social burdens should be distributed fairly according to the capacity of members of the society to carry such burdens for the benefit of society as a whole. In those national legal systems in which the principle has developed, it has come to mean, in practice, that the individual should not have his freedom of action limited beyond the degree necessary for the public interest.[11] This construction is supported by another case concerning the ECSC High Authority[12] in which the Court stated that 'the High Authority . . . has indeed a duty to take account of the actual economic circumstances in which these arrangements have to be applied, so that the aims pursued may be attained under the most favourable conditions and with the smallest possible sacrifices by the undertakings affected'.[13] The development, by the Court, of 'unwritten' general principles, which include, *inter alia*, the principles of proportionality, legitimate expectation, and legal certainty, can be justified by reference to a variety of Treaty Articles.[14] Their incorporation into the general corpus of EC law has been described as ' . . . largely an exercise in

---

[6] *Ibid.* Other commentators perceive proportionality as being closely related to equity, see e.g. Schermers and Waelbroeck, *Judicial Protection in the European Communities*, 5th ed. (Deventer/ London: Kluwer, 1992) at p. 77.

[7] Proportionality appears to have its earliest origins in nineteenth century Prussia where the principle of *Verhaltnismassigkeit* was invoked by the Prussian Supreme Administrative Court as a check to the discretionary powers of police authorities, see Singh, *German Administrative Law: A Common Lawyer's View* (Berlin: Sringer-Verlag, 1985) at pp. 88–101.

[8] For an account of the operation and development of the proportionality principle in French administrative law, see Boyron, 'Proportionality in English Administrative Law: A Faulty Translation?' (1992) *Oxford Journal of Legal Studies* 237, at 239–249. For a general account of proportionality in German and French law, EC law, European Human Rights law and its application in English law, see Jowell and Lester, 'Proportionality: Neither Novel nor Dangerous', in Jowell and Oliver (eds), *New Directions in Judicial Review* (London: Stevens, 1988) at p. 51.

[9] See Lasok, 'Equity in the EC Legal System' (1993) *Student Law Review* 44.

[10] Case 8/55, *Fedechar* v. *High Authority* [1954–56] ECR 245.

[11] Boyron advocates the utmost caution when comparing the concept of proportionality as it exists in national legal systems or when attempting to 'transplant' the concept from one system to another as '[S]uch concepts cannot be viewed in isolation, but are integrally related to the whole theoretical framework which exists within a particular legal system', note 8 above, at 238.

[12] Case 19/61, *Mannesmann AG* v. *High Authority* [1962] ECR 357.

[13] See Harding and Sherlock, *EC Law: Text and Materials* (London: Longman, 1995), at 185.

[14] For example, Article 164, Article 173(1) and Article 215(2). See Tillotson, *European Community Law: Text, Cases and Materials*, 2nd ed. (London: Cavendish, 1996) at p. 206.

comparative law ... governed by an intent to trace elements from which Community legal principles and rules can be built up which will offer an appropriate, fair and viable solution for the questions with which the Court is confronted'.[15]

It would appear to be beyond debate that the principle of proportionality is well established in Community jurisprudence. However, it is not quite so clear how, or more precisely when, this was accepted by the European Court of Justice. In the *Handelsgesellschaft* case, the Court, recognising that the '*Verhaltnismassigkeit*' principle was a fundamental principle of German consti-tutional law, held that the system of returnable deposits, being part of Community law, could not be overridden by principles of national law, even principles of a constitutional character. However, six years later, in the *Bela-Muhle* case, the Court appears to lift the German proportionality concept (at least in so far as it applies to Article 12 of the *Grundgesetz* which safeguards the right to choose a trade, occupation or profession) directly into EC law. According to the Court, '[T]he rights guaranteed under national constitutions cannot, of course, be invoked as such before this Court because it is not for the Community Court to ensure that national law is observed. At the same time there can be no doubt that the Community legal order adopts as its own the fundamental rights which are part of the common heritage of the legal systems of the Member States. The principle that every individual has freedom to choose his trade, occupation or profession is recognised in all the Member States of the Community, although in differing terms. It must therefore follow that a similar fundamental principle of freedom exists in Community law also.'[16]

Role of proportionality in EC Law

In relation to protection of the environment, as to all Community policy objec-tives, the principle of proportionality, as it exists in EC law, fulfils two functions.

Review of Community measures

The principle of proportionality has a role in assessing the legality of Community measures. The principle provides a framework within which the European Court of Justice can determine whether EC legislation which directly imposes burdens on individuals, undertakings or economic groupings has distributed those burdens fairly. In this context, it corresponds closely to proportionality as it is found in the administrative law of several Member States. For example, the German administrative law principle of *Verhaltnismassigkeit*, which dictates that

---

[15] Kapteyn and VerLoren van Themaat, in Gormley (ed) *Introduction to the Law of the European Communities*, 2nd ed. (Deventer/London: Kluwer/Graham and Trotman, 1989), cited in Tillotson, note 14 above.

[16] Case 114/76, *Bela-Muhle Josef Bergmann KG* v. *Grows-Farm GmbH* [1977] ECR 1211, at 1234.

'State power may only encroach upon individual freedom to the extent that it is indispensable for the protection of the public interest.'[17] The *Bela-Muhle* case[18] provides an apt illustration of this application of the principle. In this case, the European Court of Justice was asked to review the legality of Commission Regulation 563/76/EEC which, with the aim of reducing stocks of skimmed-milk powder, obliged certain animal feed producers to substitute skimmed-milk powder for less expensive soya. As this measure almost trebled the price of animal feed, the Court held that it was disproportionate and, therefore, invalid. The Court stated that the measure went beyond what was necessary to reduce skimmed-milk powder stocks and that it involved a discriminatory distribution of the burden of cost between different agricultural sectors.

Regarding the validity of a Community measure, under the principle it is necessary to establish, first that the means it employs to achieve a legitimate aim correspond to that aim, secondly that they are necessary for its achievement, and, thirdly that it does not disproportionately burden any individual, sector or Member State or disproportionately affect any of the Community's general objectives. In this context it is appropriate to describe proportionality as a ground for the judicial review of EC legislation. The European Court of Justice itself has come up with various formulations of the test. One much cited, though rather vague, version describes the test as having two stages: 'In order to establish whether a provision of Community law is consonant with the principle of proportionality it is necessary to establish, in the first place, whether the means it employs to achieve the aim correspond to the importance of the aim and, in the second place, whether they are necessary for its achievement.'[19] Weatherill and Beaumont[20] opt for a slightly different European Court of Justice formulation of the test and state that it is now settled case law that in order to establish whether a provision of Community law complies with the principle ' . . . it must be ascertained whether the means which it employs are suitable for the purpose of achieving the desired objective and whether they do not go beyond what is necessary to achieve it. Futhermore . . . if a measure is patently unsuited to the objective which the competent institution seeks to pursue this may affect its legality.'[21] Much of the relevant case law stems from challenges to the validity of Community measures adopted under the Common Agricultural Policy (CAP), with proportionality providing a control on the wide discretionary powers enjoyed by the competent Community institutions under the CAP. Indeed, Lasok informs us that '[P]roportionality continues to be a favourite plea

---

[17] See Jowell and Lester, 'Proportionality: Neither Novel Nor Dangerous', in Jowell and Oliver (eds), note 8 above, pp. 52–54.
[18] Case 114/76, note 16 above.
[19] Case 66/82, *Fromoncais SA v. Fonds d'Orientation* [1983] ECR 395, at para. 8.
[20] Weatherill and Beaumont, *EC Law,* 2nd ed. (London: Penguin, 1995), p. 260.
[21] Joined Cases 279, 280, 285, and 286/84, *Rau v. Commission* [1987] ECR 1069, at 1125–1126.

in order to save the forfeiture of deposits under the Community regulations'[22] forfeiture being a common administrative penalty under CAP measures.[23]

However, the test is strict and a Community measure will not be found invalid unless it is disproportionate to a substantial degree. According to the European Court of Justice, 'the legality of a measure can be adversely affected only if the measure is manifestly unsuitable for achieving the aim pursued by the competent Community institution'.[24]

Similarly, in Case 5/73, *Balkan-Import-Export*,[25] it was held that the burdens imposed would need to be 'manifestly out of proportion to the object in view'. Generally, the Court has held that Community institutions are entitled to impose very harsh penalties for non-compliance with the requirements of Community measures. In the *Handelsgesellschaft* case[26] the Court took the view that the forfeit of deposits under Regulation 120/67/EEC was justified in that it served the purposes of the Treaty in supporting the common organisation of agricultural markets. The Court took a similarly restrictive approach when it stated that the Commission 'was not obliged to vary the severity of the measure in question according to the gravity of the failure to comply with that obligation. Such a measure cannot be regarded as out of proportion to the objective pursued'.[27] The Court, therefore, appears consistently to place great importance on ensuring compliance with Community measures. In other words, it sets a higher threshold for a finding of disproportionality where an action is brought against the Community institutions in an area of discretionary policy making. Although the Court has consistently viewed non-compliance with a licensing system established under Community legislation as grounds for the forfeiture of a deposit,[28] it has qualified this position somewhat. In the *Buitoni* case, the Court distinguished between different types of requirements and held that a failure to comply with purely bureaucratic requirements, in this case a delay in submitting a proof of import, did not justify forfeiture. The Court stated that '[T]he fixed penalty, which is applied to an infringement which is considerably less serious than that of failure of the obligation which the security itself is intended to guarantee, which is sanctioned by an essentially proportionate penalty must, therefore, be held to be excessively severe in relation to the objectives of administrative efficiency.'[29] In the *Atalanta* case the Court held that a Community provision[30] which provided that 'the security shall be wholly forfeit if the obligations imposed by the contract are not fulfilled' fell foul of the

---

[22] Note 2 above at p. 173.
[23] See, for example, Case 85/78, *Bundesanstalt für Landwirtschaftliche Marktordnung* v. *Jacob Hirsch & Sohne GmbH* [1978] ECR 2517, [1979] 2 CMLR 631; Case 122/78, *Buitoni SA* v. *Fonds d'Orientation et de Regularisation des Marches Agricoles* [1979] ECR 677, 2 CMLR 665.
[24] Case 59/83, *Biovilac NV* v. *Commission* [1984] ECR 4057, at para. 17.
[25] Case 5/73, *Balkan-Import-Export GmbH* v. *Hauptzollamt Berlin-Packhof* [1973] ECR 1091, at 1112.
[26] Note 3 above.
[27] Case 272/81, *Société Ru-Mi* v. *Forma* [1982] ECR 4167, at para. 14.
[28] For example, Case 85/78, *Jacob Hirsch & Sohne GmbH*, note 23 above.
[29] Case 122/78, *Buitoni SA*, note 23 above.
[30] Commission Regulation 1889/76/EEC, Article 5(2).

principle because it did not 'permit the penalty for which it provides to be made commensurate with the degree of failure to implement the contractual obligations or with the seriousness of the breach of those obligations'.[31] It has also held that a delay of a few hours in applying for an export licence does not justify forfeiture of the whole security.[32] In both the *Atalanta* and *Man* cases, the Court suggested that an absolute rule of total loss of security should be replaced with a discretionary rule making the level of forfeiture proportionate to the gravity of breach of contract.[33] Subsequently, the Court has distinguished between principal obligations and secondary obligations and held that only partial forfeiture of a security could be justified by non-compliance with a secondary obligation.[34]

It would appear that the principle, at least in so far as it applies to the validity of Community measures, has now, by virtue of the Treaty on European Union,[35] formally been inserted into the Treaty of Rome. Article 3b which introduces subsidiarity into the Treaty, would seem to apply the principle of proportionality expressly to Community action by stating that '[A]ny action by the Community shall not go beyond what is necessary to achieve the objectives of this Treaty'.[36]

Review of national measures

Proportionality provides a useful check to the unharmonious unilateral exercise of their competences by the Member States. In this capacity, it provides a test against which the compatibility of Member State legislation with the requirements of the Treaty can be judged. National measures often impose restrictions, justified on public policy grounds, which to some extent adversely affect EC law. In particular, such measures may restrict the 'four freedoms' guaranteed by the Treaty, i.e. free movement of goods, of persons, of services and of capital. Proportionality is used to determine whether such a restriction can be justified having regard to the legitimacy of its aims, the means employed and the extent of the restriction on Community freedoms. For example, in the *Skanavi* case,[37] the Court held that German rules which treated a person who had failed to exchange a Greek driving licence for a German licence as driving without a licence, thereby incurring harsh criminal penalties, were disproportionate. The Court was of the opinion that, in view of the importance of the right to drive a motor vehicle for the exercise of the right of freedom of movement, the German rules were disproportionate to the gravity of the infringement in

---

[31] Case 240/78, *Atalanta v. Produktschap voor Vee en Vlees* [1979] ECR 2137, at 2151.
[32] Case 181/84, *Man (Sugar) v. IBAP* [1985] ECR 2889.
[33] See Weatherill and Beaumont, note 20 above, p. 261.
[34] Case 21/85, *A Maas & Co. v. Bundesanstalt für Landwirtschaftliche Marktordnung* [1986] ECR 3537, [1987] 3 CMLR 794.
[35] Treaty on European Union (Maastricht, 17 February 1992) (1992) 31 ILM 247.
[36] Article 3b, para. 3. See further Freestone and Somsen, 'The Impact of Subsidiarity', Chapter 6 above.
[37] Case C-193/94, *Criminal Proceedings against Sofia Skanavi and Konstantin Chryssanthakopoulos* [1996] 1 and 2 *European Court Monitor* 87-89 (29 February 1996).

the light of the ensuing consequences.[38] In the *Bela-Muhle* case, though it concerned the legality of a Community measure, the European Court of Justice discussed this function of proportionality, saying that 'the Court has referred to proportionality as a criterion in a whole series of judgments relating to the freedom of movement . . . which the Treaty confers on individuals. In those cases . . . the principle of proportionality was applied as a measure of the legality of national provisions and measures restricting those rights.'[39]

The *Cassis de Dijon* case[40] clearly set out the principle's application to national measures which restrict Community freedoms. The case concerned the importation into Germany of a French liqueur which, containing only 15%–20% alcohol, infringed a German law stating that only liqueurs with a minimum alcohol content of 25% could be marketed as such. The European Court of Justice conceded that '[I]n the absence of common rules relating to the production and marketing of alcohol . . . it is for the Member States to regulate all matters relating to . . . alcoholic beverages on their own territory.' However, it immediately went on to hold that 'Obstacles to movement within the Community resulting from disparities between the national laws relating to the marketing of the products in question must be accepted *in so far as those provisions may be recognised as being necessary* in order to satisfy mandatory requirements relating in particular to the effectiveness of fiscal supervision, the protection of public health, the fairness of commercial transactions and the defence of the consumer.'[41]

This formulation of the principle has often subsequently been referred to as the 'rule of reason'.[42] In this particular case the Court found that 'the requirements relating to the minimum alcohol content of alcoholic beverages do not serve a purpose which is in the general interest and such as to take precedence over the requirements of the free movement of goods, which constitutes one of the fundamental rules of the Community.'[43] In the *Walter Rau* case,[44] which concerned a Belgian law requiring all margarine to be sold in cubic containers in order to prevent consumers confusing it with butter, the Court clearly outlined the nature of the proportionality test in this context. It stated that '[I]t is also necessary for such rules to be proportionate to the aim in view. If a Member State has a choice between various measures to attain the same objective it should choose the means which least restricts the free movement of goods'[45] and that, in this instance, the Belgian measure ' . . . considerably exceeds the

---

[38] Regarding national criminal measures impacting on the free movement of goods and persons, see Case 203/80, *Casati* [1981] ECR 2618; Case 50/76, *Amsterdam Bulb* [1977] ECR 137; Case 41/76, *Donckerwolcke* [1976] ECR 1921; Case 118/75, *Watson* [1976] ECR 1185; Case 8/77, *Sagulo* [1977] ECR 1495.

[39] Case 114/76, note 16 above.

[40] Case 120/78, *Rewe-Zentral AG* v. *Bundesmonopolverwaltung für Branntwein* [1979] ECR 649, [1979] 3 CMLR 494.

[41] *Ibid.* para. 8 (emphasis added).

[42] For example, see Steiner, *Textbook of EEC Law* (London: Blackstone Press, 1988), p. 65.

[43] Case 120/78, note 41 above, at para. 14.

[44] Case 261/81, *Walter Rau Lebensmittelwerke* v. *De Smedt PvbA* [1982] ECR 3961, [1983] 2 CMLR 496.

[45] *Ibid.* at para. 12.

requirements of the object in view. Consumers may in fact be protected just as effectively by other measures, for example rules on labelling, which hinder the free movement of goods less.'[46] The *Oosthoek* case[47] provides an example of a restrictive national measure surviving the proportionality test. The case concerned a Dutch consumer protection law which prohibited the offering of free gifts by retailers to purchasers as a sales promotion device. The Court felt that the measure did not exceed what was necessary to prevent practices which 'may mislead consumers as to the real price of certain products and distort the conditions on which genuine competition is based'.[48]

Although many of the relevant cases in this area concern national consumer protection measures,[49] the 'mandatory requirements' referred to in the *Cassis* judgment are by no means exhaustive. The Community law test of proportionality has been used to determine the validity of national measures relating to, *inter alia*, restrictions on Sunday trading,[50] the right of persons to free movement within the Community[51] and even the protection of cultural interests.[52] The *Danish Bottles* case[53] provides the first example of the principle's application in this context to a national environmental measure creating potential barriers to intra-Community trade. In this case, the Court applied the proportionality test to determine the validity of a national measure for environmental protection which effectively created a barrier to trade between Member States. It concerned a Danish national measure prohibiting the marketing of beer and soft drinks in metal cans and requiring the use of returnable containers approved by the Danish authorities. A subsequent amendment allowed the use of non-approved containers up to a limit of 3000 hectolitres per producer per year, though in such cases it was required that a special deposit-and-return system be set up. The Court found that the deposit-and-return scheme was necessary to achieve its legitimate aims and was, therefore, proportionate, but also, that the requirement to use approved containers (along with the limited possibility of using non-approved containers up to a quantitative limit and in conjunction with a special deposit-and-return scheme) was excessively restrictive and, therefore, disproportionate.

Despite its dual role, it is possible to provide a common general formulation of the principle as it functions in either capacity. It is generally accepted that to establish the proportionality of a measure three distinct tests must be applied:

[46] *Ibid.* at para. 17.
[47] Case 286/81, *Oosthoek's Uitgeversmaatschappij BV* [1982] ECR 4575, [1983] 3 CMLR 428.
[48] *Ibid.* at para. 18.
[49] See further Case 178/84, *Commission v. Germany (Re Purity Requirements for Beer)* [1987] 1 ECR 1227.
[50] Case C-145/88, *Torfaen Borough Council v. B and Q plc* [1989] ECR 3851; Case C-23/89, *Quietlynn Ltd v. Southend-on-Sea Borough Council* [1990] 3 CMLR 55, [1990] 3 All ER 207.
[51] Case C-265/88, *Criminal Proceedings against Messner* [1989] ECR 4209. See Ellis and Tridimas, *Public Law of the European Community: Text, Materials and Commentary* (London: Sweet and Maxwell, 1995), p. 552.
[52] Joined Cases 60 and 61/84, *Cinéthèque SA v. Fédération Nationale des Cinemas Français* [1985] ECR 2605, [1986] 1 CMLR 365.
[53] Case 302/86, *Commission v. Denmark (Danish Bottles)* [1988] 1 ECR 4607. See below.

1. the measure must be appropriately aimed at a legitimate objective;
2. the measure must be necessary, with no less restrictive means of achieving the objective available;
3. the measure must be proportionate or balanced, in that any injury or restriction caused should be offset by the benefits gained (by the public or community) without the measure being discriminatory.

Proportionality and Community environmental measures

Protection of the environment has long been a legitimate objective of the Community. Even before any express mandate for Community environmental action was inserted into the Treaty by the Single European Act (SEA), the European Court of Justice considered that Community measures could be validly founded on Article 100 in so far as they were aimed at the elimination of technical barriers to trade or appreciable distortions of competition.[54] Similarly, in the *ADBHU* case,[55] the Court stated that a 1975 Directive on the disposal of waste oils[56] 'must be seen in the perspective of environmental protection, which is one of the Community's essential objectives'.

Following the insertion into the Treaty of an Environment Title by the SEA, and the subsequent amendment of that Title by the Treaty on European Union (TEU), Community environmental measures may be based on Article 130s which confers an express legislative mandate on the Community to achieve the objectives set down in the Title by Article 130r. The wide legislative competence granted by this mandate is a reflection of the breadth of the objectives it may be used to pursue, which include:

— preserving, protecting and improving the quality of the environment;
— protecting human health;
— prudent and rational utilisation of natural resources;
— promoting measures at international level to deal with regional or worldwide environmental problems.

However, Community legislation relevant to the environment may also be based on a host of other Treaty provisions. For example, measures also relating to transport policy may be based on Article 84, those relating to agriculture on Article 43, those relating to fiscal measures on Article 99, those relating to commercial policy on Article 113 and, of course, those relating to the internal market on Article 100a.[57] These ancilliary powers have provided a basis for

---

[54] Case 91/79, *Commission* v. *Italy* [1980] ECR 1099.
[55] Case 240/83, *Procureur de la République* v. *Association de Défense Des Brûleurs D'huiles Usagées* [1985] ECR 531.
[56] Directive 75/439, OJ 1975 L 194, p. 23.
[57] For examples of each, see Krämer, 'Environmental Protection and Article 30 EEC Treaty' (1993) 30 CML Rev 111–143, at 112.

environmental law-making prior to the SEA and TEU amendments[58] and are likely to continue to do so as Article 130r now provides that '[E]nvironmental protection requirements must be integrated into the definition and implementation of other Community policies'.

Any Community legislative provisions on the environment adopted under these various powers may be subject to review on grounds of proportionality. Typically, this could occur indirectly by means of an Article 177 referral from a national court where an individual challenges the validity of a Community measure[59] or invokes its invalidity as a defence for non-compliance,[60] or, by means of a direct action for annulment, taken by a Member State for example, under Article 173 on grounds of 'infringement of this Treaty or of any rule of law relating to its application'. Indeed, Article 130s(5) appears to anticipate, at least with regard to the financial burdens imposed upon Member States, that some Community environmental measures may prove disproportionate in their effects. It states that:

if a measure based on the provisions of paragraph 1 involves costs deemed disproportionate for the public authorities of a Member State, the Council shall, in the act of adopting that measure, lay down appropriate provisions in the form of:
— temporary derogations and/or
— financial support from the Cohesion Fund . . .

Even though there are, as yet, no high-profile examples of a challenge to the validity of a Community environmental measure on grounds of proportionality, it is not difficult to imagine scenarios whereby individuals, economic groupings or even Member States might consider themselves excessively burdened by intrusive legislation. For example, the introduction of an energy or carbon tax[61] might, in one form or another, be argued to burden disproportionately certain economic sectors such as electricity generation, road hauliers, or airlines. Similarly, Community legislation imposing strict mandatory quality objectives for an environmental medium such as water[62] might be challenged by water companies on the ground that it goes beyond what is necessary for human and ecological safety and that it unfairly distributes the burden of achieving those objectives in the public interest.

Although it is more correctly classified as a consumer rather than an environmental issue, the current controversy concerning the Commission's ban on exports of British beef provides a useful illustration of the potential application of the proportionality principle in this context. Due to concerns over the

---

[58] For example, Directive 80/51/EEC on noise levels of certain airplanes OJ 1980 L 18, p. 26, adopted under Article 84. See Krämer, note 57 above.

[59] As occurred in *Bela-Muhle*, note 16 above.

[60] As occurred in *Internationale Handelsgesellschaft*, note 3 above and *Man (Sugar)*, note 32 above.

[61] See the Commission proposal for a directive on the introduction of an energy tax in order to limit carbon dioxide emissons, OJ 1992 C 216, p. 4.

[62] For example, Directive 76/160/EEC on bathing water, OJ 1976 L 31, p. 1 and Directive 80/778/EEC on water for human consumption, OJ 1980 L 229, p. 11.

possibility of a link between Bovine Spongiform Encephalopathy (BSE or 'Mad Cow Disease') and its human equivalent, Creutzfeldt-Jakob Disease (CJD), the Commission has acted to ban the export of British beef, veal, beef products and live cattle to other Member States and to countries outside the European Union.[63] The European Court of Justice has started preliminary hearings in relation to a challenge by the UK to the validity of the Commission's decision on several grounds, including the claim that the ban is out of proportion to the objectives of protecting human and animal health. Although at the time of writing it is possible only to speculate as to how the Court will deal with this question, it is useful to apply provisionally the principle's constituent tests to the issues involved.

First, the Court will need to consider whether the protection of human and animal health are legitimate objectives and, if so, whether the total ban constitutes an appropriate measure for achieving those objectives. In considering the legitimacy of these objectives, it is worth noting that both are expressly enumerated in Article 36 as grounds upon which prohibitions on exports may be justified. However, the maintenance of consumer confidence may also be cited as an objective which could justify more far-reaching measures.[64] Secondly, although the ban can easily be argued to be appropriate to approach the objectives, the Court will need to consider whether it is necessary. Regarding the protection of human and animal health, it could be argued that a less restrictive means of achieving these objectives is available. For example, the 1994 Commission Decision[65] which laid down rules on, *inter alia*, trimming the meat from BSE herds, removing certain tissues, labelling certain meats, and banning the export of offal, might be argued to be sufficient. However, such a measure would hardly be sufficient to achieve consumer confidence should this be accepted as a legitimate objective. Finally, the Court will have to determine whether the measure is proportionate, in other words, whether the restriction and any resulting injury is offset by the public benefits. This is patently the vaguest and most politically sensitive element of the principle's application and the one which might be expected to involve consideration of complex scientific, technical, and economic evidence. However, this element of the test may merely involve an impressionistic balancing of injury and benefits rather than a detailed

---

[63] Decision 96/239/EC, of 27 March 1996, on emergency measures to protect against BSE, OJ 1996 L 78, p. 47. The decision is based on emergency powers derived from Directives 89/662/EEC and 92/118/EEC which are concerned with animal and human health. See Elworthy, 'Crated Calves and Crazy Cows: Live Animals and the Free Movement of Goods', Chapter 18, below.

[64] The preamble to Decision 96/239/EC on emergency measures to protect against BSE, notes that 'the resulting uncertainty [on the transmissibility of BSE to humans] has created serious concern among consumers'. Other Community initiatives support recognition of 'consumer confidence' as a legitimate objective of Community consumer law-making. For example, the commentary preceding the proposed directive on the sale of consumer goods and associated guarantees refers to the maintenance of 'consumer confidence' as a necessary means of achieving the aims of consumer policy as set down in Article 129(A), see COM(95) 520 final, at 6. Similarly, at para. 4, the recitals to the proposed directive state that, by helping to create a common minimum corpus of consumer law, the directive would 'strengthen consumer confidence'.

[65] Decision 94/474/EC, of 29 July 1994 OJ L 194, p. 96. See Elworthy, Chapter 18, below.

consideration of all available evidence. In the *Second Schluter Case*[66] the Court stated that 'it does not necessarily follow that the obligation must be measured in relation to the individual situation of any one particular group of operators. Given the multiplicity and complexity of economic circumstances, such an evaluation would not only be impossible to achieve, but would also create perpetual uncertainty in the law'.[67]

Proportionality and national environmental measures

The Community's competence to legislate for the protection of the environment is by no means exclusive. Indeed, according to Krämer,[68] the principle of shared competence under the Treaty aims at optimising environmental protection. The Member States continue to enjoy environmental competence where the Community has not legislated, provided national legislation complies with the general rules of the Treaty and, in particular, with Articles 30 and 36. Also, where the Community has adopted measures, the Member States may legislate for more stringent environmental protection, where the relevant Treaty provisions so provide. Community legislation itself may expressly authorise more stringent protective measures at the national level. Therefore, the competence of Member States primarily depends on whether the Community has already legislated in the relevant area.

In the absence of Community legislation, the unilateral adoption of environmental protection measures by Member States can often constitute a restriction of free trade. Whether or not such a restriction is unwarranted must be decided in accordance with Articles 30 and 36. Article 30 prohibits quantitative restrictions on imports between Member States and, for the purposes of this Article, the European Court of Justice has widely defined such quantitative restrictions to include 'trading rules enacted by Member States which are capable of hindering, directly or indirectly, actually or potentially, intra-Community trade'.[69] Article 36 provides for exceptions to Article 30, permitting restrictions 'justified on grounds of public morality, public policy, or public security; the protection of health and life of humans, animals or plants; the protection of national treasures possessing artistic, historic or archaeological value; or the protection of industrial and commercial property' providing such restrictions do not 'constitute a means of arbitrary discrimination or a disguised restriction on trade between Member States'. However, the Court has interpreted Article 36 very restrictively, stating that the list of justifications for trade restrictions contained therein is

---

[66] Case 9/73, *Second Schluter Case* [1973] ECR 1156.
[67] *Ibid.* at para. 22. See Schermers and Waelbroek, note 6 above, at p. 78.
[68] Krämer, note 57 above, at 114–115.
[69] Case 8/74, *Procureur du Roi* v. *Dassonville* [1974] ECR 837.

exhaustive.[70] Therefore, trade restrictive national environmental measures could only be justified under Article 36 to the extent that they had as their objective the protection of health or life of humans, animals or plants. Examples include a prohibition on the marketing and use of unapproved plant-protection products[71] and measures regulating the presence of pesticides in foodstuffs[72] where neither issue was covered by provisions of Community law. However, according to Krämer, it is obvious that measures relating to environmental taxes, environmental labelling, waste prevention, environmental impact assessment, and environmental liability could not be justified on these grounds while measures to reduce discharges of pollutants to water, air or soil, to reduce the noise level of cars, or to provide for the designation of habitats would be very unlikely to qualify.[73] Any trade restrictive national environmental measures which would qualify could only be justified to the extent that they do not constitute 'a means of arbitrary discrimination or a disguised restriction on trade between Member States'.[74]

Despite having narrowly interpreted Article 36 as an exhaustive list, the Court has effectively identified further grounds on which to justify trade restrictions by referring, in the *Cassis de Dijon* case,[75] to 'mandatory requirements'. The Court stated that these mandatory requirements related '*in particular* to the effectiveness of fiscal supervision, the protection of public health, the fairness of commercial transactions and the defence of the consumer'.[76] Therefore, though environmental protection was not expressly included by the Court in this particular case, the list of mandatory requirements was clearly not meant to be exhaustive. It was only necessary that the requirements 'serve a purpose which is in the general interest and such as to take precedence over the requirements of the free movement of goods, which constitutes one of the fundamental rules of the Community'.[77] Though it was concerned with a Community measure rather than national legislation, the European Court of Justice later found that environmental protection 'is one of the Community's essential objectives' capable of justifying certain limitations of the principle of the free movement of goods.[78] Also, the view that environmental protection constituted a 'mandatory requirement' within the meaning of *Cassis de Dijon*

---

[70] Case 113/80, *Commission v. Ireland* [1981] ECR 1625, at 1638; Case 95/81, *Commission v. Italy* [1982] ECR 2187, at 2202. See Scherer, 'Regional Perspectives on Trade and the Environment: The European Union', in Lang (ed), *Sustainable Development and International Law* (London: Graham and Trotman, 1995), p. 258; Krämer, note 57, above, at 117.

[71] Case 125/88, *Nijman* [1989] ECR 3533.

[72] Case 54/85, *Mirepoix* [1986] ECR 1067.

[73] Note 57 above, at 117–118.

[74] For a detailed account of the ECJ's interpretation of the terms 'arbitrary discrimination' and 'disguised restriction', see Oliver, *Free Movement of Goods in the European Community Under Articles 30 to 36 of the Rome Treaty*, 3rd ed. (London: Sweet and Maxwell, 1996), pp. 182–185.

[75] Note 40 above.

[76] Note 40 above (emphasis added).

[77] Note 40 above, para. 14.

[78] Note 55 above.

had been expressed by the Commission as early as 1979.[79] Finally, in the *Danish Bottles* case, the European Court of Justice expressly stated, in relation to a trade restrictive national measure, that 'the protection of the environment is a mandatory requirement which may limit the application of Article 30 of the Treaty'.[80] However, any national measures taken to satisfy mandatory requirements must be proportionate. In *Cassis de Dijon*, the Court stated that '[I]n the absence of common rules ... [O]bstacles to movement within the Community resulting from disparities between the national laws ... must be accepted *in so far as those provisions may be recognised as being necessary in order to satisfy mandatory requirements* ... '.[81] This requirement was mirrored in *ADBHU* where the Court stated that trade restrictive measures prescribed by a Community directive must not 'go beyond the inevitable restrictions which are justified by the pursuit of the objective of environmental protection, which is in the general interest'.[82] In *Danish Bottles* the Court considered, in relation to the Commission's submission that the Danish rules were contrary to the principle of proportionality, that it was 'necessary to examine whether all the restrictions which the contested rules impose on the free movement of goods are *necessary to achieve the objectives pursued by those rules*'.[83] The Court considered that the deposit-and-return scheme for empty containers was 'an indispensable element' of the system intended and was, therefore, 'necessary to achieve the aims pursued by the contested rules'.[84] 'That being so', the Court found that 'the restriction which it imposes on the free movement of goods cannot be regarded as disproportionate'.[85] It is also required under the *Cassis de Dijon* formula, the so-called 'rule of reason', that, in order to remain valid, a restrictive national measure must be 'applicable to domestic and imported products without distinction'.[86] However, it should be noted that the European Court of Justice does not view this requirement as absolute but subject to limited exception or to interpretation having regard to relevant Treaty provisions. In the *Belgian Waste* case,[87] the Court did not consider a national measure which prohibited the discharge or dumping of waste[88]

---

[79] Written Question 1289/77 (OJ 1979 C 214, p. 5). See also, the Communication on '*Cassis de Dijon*', OJ 1980 C 256, p. 2. See Oliver, note 74 above, p. 243.

[80] Note 53 above, para. 9.

[81] See note 40, para. 8 (emphasis added). See the Commission Communication on '*Cassis de Dijon*', note 79 above which stated that barriers to trade resulting from differences between commercial and technical rules are only admissible if the rules are necessary, that is, 'appropriate and not excessive', in order to satisfy mandatory requirements. See Schermers and Waelbroek, note 6 above, at p. 79.

[82] Note 55 above at para. 15.

[83] Note 53 above, para. 12 (emphasis added).

[84] *Ibid.* para. 13.

[85] *Ibid.*

[86] *Ibid.* para. 6. See also, Joined Cases C-1/90 and 176/90, *Aragonesa de Publicidad Exterior SA and Publiva SAE* v. *Departamento de Salidad y Seguridad Social de la Generalitat de Cataluña* [1991] ECR 4151.

[87] Case C-2/90, *Commission* v. *Belgium* [1992] ECR 4431, [1993] 1 CMLR 365; (1992) JEL Vol. 5, No. 1, 132; Krämer, *European Environmental Law Casebook* (London: Sweet and Maxwell, 1993), p. 71.

[88] The Court considered that 'wastes, recyclable or not, must be considered as products the movement of which, in conformance with Article 30 of the Treaty, cannot in principle be prevented'. See Case C-2/90, note 87 above, para. 28.

coming from another state to be discriminatory as it was in compliance with the guiding principle of EC environmental law that 'environmental damage should as a priority be rectified at source'.[89] Therefore, proportionality, as applied under the rule of reason, requires the national measure to be non-discriminatory, as regards domestic and imported products, and necessary, that is, it must not go beyond what is required for the attainment of a legitimate objective. It would appear that the former requirement may be relaxed in relation to restrictive national environmental measures where this can be justified under the guiding principles of Article 130r(2). This might prove significant where there is scientific uncertainty as to the environmental impact of imported products, as discriminatory restrictions on such products could possibly be justified under the precautionary principle.[90]

Even where the Community has legislated in a particular sphere, Member States will often be entitled to apply national measures. The Treaty itself clearly indicates where Member States are to enjoy, at least, residual competence. Where EC secondary legislation on the environment has been introduced under Article 130s, Member States may, under Article 130t, maintain or introduce 'more stringent protective measures' provided such measures are 'compatible with the Treaty' and are 'notified to the Commission'. There is some doubt as to whether a national measure which operates in a significantly different manner to existing EC legislation would qualify as a more stringent protective measure.[91] Krämer cites the example of four Member States which have legislated to prohibit the marketing of products containing CFCs despite the fact that the relevant Community Regulation[92] only concerns itself with the production and consumption of ozone-depleting substances with the aim of eventually phasing out such substances altogether.[93] However, though these various national measures would appear to go further than and to operate differently from the regulation, none have been challenged before a national court nor objected to by the Commission.[94] Also, in relation to Article 130s harmonisation measures, Article 130r(2) states that such measures 'shall include, where appropriate, a safeguard clause allowing Member States to take provisional measures, for non-economic environmental reasons, subject to a Community inspection procedure'. This provision obliges the Community to

---

[89] Article 130r(2). See Case C-2/90, note 87 above, para. 34. See Scherer, note 70 above, p. 260; Wheeler, 'Restrictions on Waste Movements Under Community Law: *Commission* v. *Belgium*' (1993) JEL Vol. 5, No. 1, at 145; Geradin, 'The Belgian Waste Case' (1993) 18 EL Rev, at 144.

[90] See Hession and Macrory, 'Balancing Trade Freedom with the Requirements of Sustainable Development', in Emiliou and O'Keeffe, *The European Union and World Trade Law: After the GATT Uruguay Round* (Chichester: Wiley, 1996), pp. 200–202.

[91] See Scherer, note 70 above, at p. 263.

[92] Now covered by Regulation 3093/94/EC, OJ 1994 L 333, p. 1.

[93] Krämer, note 57 above, at 135–136.

[94] Krämer takes the view that, as there are no Community-wide bans of products containing CFCs, these national bans should be assessed under Article 30. He further points out that, under 'classical rules of interpretation of Article 30', such bans would inevitably be disproportionate as each, individually, would be incapable of achieving its objective, i.e. a better protection of the ozone layer, see note 57 above, at 136.

make allowance for the adoption of short-term national measures, for example, in the event of environmental emergencies or disasters.[95]

Similarly, where harmonisation measures, which have as their object the establishment and functioning of the internal market, are adopted under Article 100a, a Member State may, where it 'deems it necessary . . . apply national provisions on grounds of major needs referred to in Article 36, or relating to protection of the environment or working environment . . .'.[96] There is some uncertainty as to whether, under Article 100a(4), Member States may introduce new national measures or merely 'apply' existing measures.[97] It should be noted, however, that in *France* v. *Commission* (the *PCP* (pentachlorophenol) case),[98] Advocate General Tesauro spoke of Article 100a(4) in terms of '[T]he possibility granted to a Member State of *continuing* to apply its own rules, even though the matter had been harmonised at Community level . . .'.[99] The Member State must notify the Commission which will confirm the national provisions 'after having verified that they are not a means of arbitrary discrimination or a disguised restriction on trade between Member States'. Article 100a(4) goes on to provide that 'the Commission or any Member State may bring the matter directly before the Court of Justice if it considers that another Member State is making improper use of the powers provided for in this Article'. In the first such case,[100] France objected to a Commission decision[101] taken under Article 100a(4) which confirmed German rules prohibiting products and substances containing pentachlorophenol (PCP) which were stricter than and pre-existed Community harmonising measures. The Court annulled the contested decision on the ground that the Commission had not satisfied the obligation to state reasons as laid down in Article 190 of the Treaty and so did not need to consider the French plea that Germany had not demonstrated that the measures were proportionate, having regard to the barriers to trade which might result. However, in his Opinion, Advocate General Tesauro examined the scope of Article 100a(4) in some detail. First, with regard to the interests which a state may invoke in order to enable it to derogate from harmonisation measures, he states that 'the reasons set out in Article 100a(4) are certainly fewer in number than those considered by the Court in its decisions concerning quantitative restrictions and measures having equivalent effect, starting with the *Cassis de*

---

[95] See Scherer, note 70 above, pp. 263–264.

[96] Article 100a(4).

[97] Krämer points out that there is considerable dispute among legal authors as to whether this provision only allows the maintenance of existing provisions or whether it also allows the introduction of new provisions. He himself is of the opinion that no new national measures may be introduced under Article 100a(4), Krämer, note 57 above, at 113 and 123. Scherer, on the other hand, takes the view that, because Article 100a(4) aims at environmental protection at the highest possible level, it would allow the adoption of new national environmental regulations, Scherer, note 70 above, p. 261.

[98] Case C-41/93, *France* v. *Commission* [1994] ECR 1829.

[99] *Ibid.* at 1832 (emphasis added).

[100] Case C-41/93, note 98 above.

[101] Commission Communication 92/C334/04 of 18 June 1992, OJ 1992 C 334, p. 8.

Dijon case'.[102] Furthermore, in addition to being in pursuit of one of the objectives envisaged by Article 100a(4), national rules restricting intra-Community trade must 'satisfy the further condition of being necessary and proportionate in relation to the aim pursued' which requires that 'they must have the least possible disruptive effect on trade: the State in question must therefore demonstrate that there are no other suitable means of achieving the aim pursued in a manner less restrictive of the movement of goods'.[103] With regard to the proportionality of the German measure in this case, Advocate General Tesauro suggests that 'it would have been appropriate for the [Commission] decision to have specified to what extent the additional protection of health and the environment guaranteed by the German rules justifies the possibility of greater barriers to intra-Community trade; or, again, for it to have examined the consequences of the need to use other products instead of PCP'.[104] He further elaborates on the procedural sequence of each element of the test under Article 100a(4) by stating that '[I]t is incumbent upon the Member State to prove that those [national] provisions ... are necessary and proportionate' and that '[I]t then falls to the Commission to confirm the provisions "after having verified that they are not a means of arbitrary discrimination ... " '.[105] Therefore, Advocate General Tesauro's formulation of the test applied under Article 100a(4) corresponds closely with the principle of proportionality as applied in other contexts, in that: the measure must be aimed at a legitimate objective; it must be necessary and proportionate; and, it must not be discriminatory. A national measure which fails to satisfy this test would constitute an 'improper use of the powers provided' under the Article. Unfortunately, the Court missed the opportunity of dealing with the French submission that 'where a Member State maintains in force rules which are more restrictive than those laid down in directives adopted by the Council, this can be justified under Article 100a(4) *only by circumstances peculiar to that State*'.[106] A pronouncement on this issue might have shed considerable light on the test of 'proportionality in the strict sense'.[107] The requirement, under both Articles, to notify the Commission appears consistent with the position taken earlier by the European Court of Justice that the onus is on the Member State to justify trade restrictive measures by establishing the justification of necessity. In the *Van Bennekom* case[108] the Court stated that '[I]t is for the national authorities to demonstrate in each case that their rules are necessary to give effective protection to the interests referred to in Article 36

---

[102] Note 98 above, at 1833, para. 5.

[103] *Ibid.* at 1834, para. 6.

[104] *Ibid.* at 1839, para. 14.

[105] *Ibid.* at 1834, para. 7.

[106] *Ibid.* at 1847, para. 16 (emphasis added).

[107] Hession and Macrory perceive proportionality as encompassing at least three separate tests: effectiveness; minimum restrictiveness; and, proportionality in the strict sense. The latter 'balances not the means to the ends but two ends, where the means adopted to enforce one objective are considered against the seriousness of the infringement of an alternative objective of equal or other value'. See Hession and Macrory, note 90 above, p. 198.

[108] Case 227/82, *Van Bennekom* [1983] ECR 3883.

of the Treaty and, in particular, to show that the marketing of the product in question creates a serious risk to health.'[109]

Where the Community has legislated to provide for full harmonisation of national measures, Member States may not, according to the Court, have recourse to the exceptions provided for under Article 36 itself.[110] However, the Member State competences provided for under both Articles 100a(4) and 36 are likely to be similar as neither may be used to apply measures which constitute 'a means of arbitrary discrimination or a disguised restriction on trade between Member States'.

Krämer asserts that the European Court of Justice is of the opinion that these criteria 'are an expression of the principle of proportionality'.[111] He further argues that the words 'arbitrary discrimination' and 'disguised restrictions' on the one hand and 'proportional', as used under Article 30, are equivalent.[112] Oliver appears to concur with this view and alludes to a number of cases[113] which apply the language of proportionality to Article 36.[114] In other words, the proportionality principle applies to national measures adopted under Article 36, Article 100a(4) and under the 'rule of reason', though, fewer objectives would be considered legitimate in justifying derogations or trade restrictions under Article 100a(4) and fewer still under Article 36. If this is the case, it would appear reasonable to expect that the requirement that national measures be 'compatible' with the Treaty, contained in Article 130t, is equivalent to proportionality.

Where the Community has not legislated for full harmonisation, but rather for minimum harmonisation, in a particular area, the EC legislation itself will usually expressly provide for the introduction of more stringent national measures.[115] Examples of such legislation include measures on toxic and dangerous waste,[116] on the transport of dangerous waste,[117] on exports of dangerous waste to third countries,[118] on the notification of new chemicals,[119] and on the conservation of wild birds.[120] Article 14 of the Wild Birds Directive states that 'Member States may introduce stricter protective measures than those provided for under this Directive'. The compatibility with EC law of a Dutch measure totally pro-

---

[109] *Ibid.* at para. 40. See Krämer, note 57 above, at 126; Hession and Macrory, note 90 above, p. 200.

[110] Case C-29/87, *Dansk Denkavit* v. *Danish Ministry of Agriculture* [1988] ECR 2982. See Case C-169/89, *Gourmetterie Van den Burg* [1990] ECR 2143, at para. 8. On 'total harmonisation' of European environmental rules, see Jans, *European Environmental Law* (Deventer: Kluwer, 1995), pp. 90–98.

[111] Note 57 above, at 126.

[112] *Ibid.* at 127.

[113] Case 104/75, *De Peijper* [1976] ECR 613, [1976] 2 CMLR 271, and Case 13/78, *Eggers* v. *Freie Hansestadt Bremen* [1978] ECR 1935, [1979] 1 CMLR 562.

[114] Oliver, note 74 above, p. 185.

[115] On 'minimum harmonisation', see Jans, note 110 above, at pp. 98–103.

[116] Directive 78/319/EEC, OJ 1978 L 84 p. 43. Article 8 provides that 'Member States may at any time take more stringent measures with regard to toxic and dangerous waste than those provided for in this Directive.'

[117] Directive 84/631/EEC, OJ 1984 L 326, p. 31.

[118] Directive 86/279/EEC, OJ 1986 L 181, p. 13.

[119] Directive 79/831/EEC, OJ 1979 L 259, p. 10.

[120] Council Directive 79/409/EEC, OJ 1979 L 103, p. 79.

hibiting trade in red grouse, was examined by the European Court of Justice in the *Gourmetterie Van den Burg* case[121] and, though the Court decided the case on totally different grounds, Advocate General van Gerven argued that the question at issue was whether the stricter national measure was compatible with Article 36.[122] He was of the opinion that the Dutch measure was incompatible with Article 36 as it was disproportionate to the objective pursued since the Dutch government had a less restrictive measure available to protect red grouse.[123] Therefore, more stringent national environmental measures, even where expressly permitted under EC secondary legislation, appear subject to the principle of proportionality. Similarly, it seems reasonable to assume that the 'Community inspection procedure', alluded to in Article 130r(2), by which provisional environmental measures, adopted by Member States under safeguard clauses included in Article 130s harmonisation measures, are to be assessed, must involve a review of the proportionality of the national measures.

Scherer points out that, though one might have expected the insertion of Articles 100a(4) and 130t into the Treaty by the Single European Act to have reduced the need for such express provisions in EC secondary legislation, the insertion of the subsidiarity principle[124] may result in 'a new flexibility of EU environmental legislation, allowing Member States to establish their own environmental protection targets'.[125] He cites, as a recent example of a Community measure permitting stricter national standards, the 1994 Directive on packaging and packaging waste[126] which allows Member States under certain conditions to go beyond the targets laid down in the directive for recovery and recycling of waste.[127] Regarding the compatibility with EC law of measures unilaterally adopted by Member States, the proportionality principle would appear to define the outer limit of Member State competence. Therefore, proportionality, in this context, assists in defining the scope of the subsidiarity principle.

As a means of reviewing the validity of national environmental measures, some writers have compared the application of the proportionality principle to the 'less restrictive alternative' doctrine applied by American courts to assess the compatibility of state legislation with the United States Constitution.[128] The US court will seek to ensure that state legislators do not 'use a sledgehammer to crack a nut'. In other words, it will examine whether the state interest, however legitimate, could be achieved by a measure less damaging to free trade than

---

[121] Case C-169/89, *Gourmetterie Van den Burg* [1990] ECR 2143.

[122] [1990] ECR 2143, at 2151.

[123] *Ibid.* See Krämer, note 87 above, p. 158.

[124] Now embodied in Article 3b of the EC Treaty as inserted by the Treaty on European Union, OJ 1993 C 224, note 35 above.

[125] Note 70 above, p. 264.

[126] Directive 94/62/EEC, OJ L 305 20.12.94, p. 10.

[127] Note 70 above, pp. 264–265.

[128] See Neville Brown and Kennedy, *The Court of Justice of the European Communities*, 4th ed. (London: Sweet and Maxwell, 1994), p. 327.

the one adopted.[129] The Federal High Court of Australia has applied a similar principle in two recent cases where unilateral state action adversely affected interstate trade: *Cole* v. *Whitfield*[130] which concerned state measures for the conservation of crayfish, and *Castlemaine Tooheys Ltd.* v. *South Australia*,[131] which concerned state environmental protection legislation which imposed a mandatory deposit of five cents on non-refillable beer bottles.[132] In *Castlemaine Tooheys*, the Court found that '... neither the need to protect the environment... nor the need to conserve energy resources offers an acceptable explanation or justification for the differential treatment given to the products of the Bond [non-state] brewing companies'[133] and that the measures were not 'appropriate and adapted to the resolution of those problems' but rather were 'disproportionate to their achievement'.[134]

Conclusion

Gráinne De Búrca, in her authoritative analysis of proportionality as developed and applied by the European Court of Justice, concludes that, in either context, the test 'essentially takes the form of a structured weighing of interests' where 'the Court appears to consider the interest of the complainant which is adversely affected on the one hand, as against the interest of the Community or Member State in adopting the challenged measure, on the other'.[135] She describes the test as involving three stages: 'first, whether the measure was an appropriate and effective way of achieving its legitimate aim; secondly, whether the measure was a necessary way of achieving its aim, in that there was no less restrictive alternative; and, thirdly, whether, even if the first two stages are satisfied, the adverse effect on the interest or right affected was disproportionate or excessive when weighed against the aim of the measure', and, further, identifies the second of these stages as the most prominent in the reasoning of the Court.[136]

Most importantly, however, she identifies, from detailed analysis of the case law of the European Court of Justice in a wide variety of areas, the various factors which will lead the Court to apply the test in either a 'deferential or a rigorous manner'.[137] A 'deferential' application of the principle, that is, one which is more deferential to the acts of the relevant legislative authority, will

---

[129] See Sandalow and Stein, *Courts and Free Markets* (Oxford: Clarendon Press, 1982), Vol. 1, p. 28.
[130] (1988) 165 CLR 360.
[131] (1990) 169 CLR 436.
[132] See generally Staker, 'Free Movement of Goods in the EEC and Australia: A Comparative Study', 1990 10 YEL 209–242; Geradin and Stewardson, 'Trade and Environment: Some Lessons from *Castlemaine Tooheys* (Australia) and *Danish Bottles* (European Community)' (1995) 44 ICLQ. 41–71.
[133] Note 130 above, at 477.
[134] *Ibid.* at 473.
[135] De Búrca, 'The Principle of Proportionality and its Application in EC Law' 1993 13 YEL 105–150, at 146.
[136] *Ibid.*
[137] *Ibid.* at 147–149.

involve a looser or less strict formulation of the test. According to de Búrca, this approach is more likely to be taken where the measure challenged is one which pursues an important aim, where the subject-matter of the measure is one in which the decision-makers are given broad discretionary powers, and one for which they bear clear political responsibility, or, where the interest or right affected is something other than an important, legally recognised one of a fundamental nature, and is restricted in a manner which is not unduly severe.[138] A deferential approach is more likely to be taken with regard to a national measure which infringes a basic Community rule where it relates to: 'a nationally sensitive or ideologically contentious matter which is not of itself within the sphere of Community competence except in so far as it affects the operation of other Community rules; a complex political objective which requires specialised knowledge, experience, and appreciation of varied national requirements; an area in which there are as yet no harmonised European-wide or internationally agreed standards of protection for certain interests; or, an area in which a finding of disproportionality would impose a considerable financial burden on the State.'[139] On the other hand, the European Court of Justice is more likely to apply a rigorous or strict proportionality test, and so, to look more closely for the existence of less restrictive alternatives, where a very important right or Community interest is affected, and where the adverse or restrictive impact is considerable. Such an approach is also more likely where the aim of national legislation 'is clearly out of line with agreed international standards on a specific matter' or 'where the Court suspects that an alleged State aim is not in fact the real or primary aim of the restrictive measure, but that the real aim is one which is contrary to Community objectives'.[140]

These factors, which comprise the substantive core of the proportionality principle, will apply equally to the review of Community or national environmental measures and should be considered by decision-makers at either level when exercising legislative competence and by any party contemplating a challenge to environmental measures they consider unduly onerous or restrictive.

---

[138] *Ibid.* at 147.
[139] *Ibid.*
[140] *Ibid.* at 148.

Chapter 8

SAFE SCIENCE? THE PRECAUTIONARY PRINCIPLE IN UK ENVIRONMENTAL LAW[1]

Jane Holder

Introduction

To some the environment is a robust system capable of absorbing and assimilating considerable change before harm occurs. An alternative view is that ecological processes are delicately balanced and easily disrupted and thus any unintended changes should be avoided. The precautionary principle is an expression of the latter perspective. One understanding of the principle is that substances or activities which might be detrimental to the environment should be regulated even in the *absence* of conclusive evidence of their harmfulness; lack of full scientific evidence should not be used as a reason for postponing measures to prevent environmental degradation.[2] The conceptual premise of the principle is that the damaging effects of human activities may become irreversible before the scientific community can agree the precise nature or scope of their impact; taking precautionary action can help avoid this. The principle therefore has significance primarily for science,[3] but it also has political and legal implications.

The principle is the product of an international legal culture and fits well into the broad sweep of international declarations. It has been adopted as a guiding principle of Community environmental policy in Article 130r(2) of the EC Treaty and thereby constitutes, in some way, part of environmental law in the United Kingdom; its exact status, though, is the subject of some disagreement. For the purposes of this Chapter, its impact in UK law indicates the

---

[1] I would like to thank Justin Wray, Sue Elworthy, and Jeffrey Jowell for their comments on this chapter.

[2] A single, precise definition of the principle does not exist. For an account of the varying definitions and readings, see Freestone, 'The Precautionary Principle', in Churchill and Freestone, *International Law and Global Climate Change* (Dordrecht/London: Martinus Nijhoff/Graham and Trotman, 1991), p. 36.

[3] See Wynne, 'Uncertainty and Environmental Learning: Reconceiving Science and Policy in the Preventive Paradigm', (1992) 2 *Global Environmental Change* 111–127 and Wynne and Meyer, 'How Science Fails the Environment' (1993) New Scientist 33–35.

extent of integration of different strata of environmental law—international, Community, and national.

I address several questions concerning the impact of the principle. Does EC law impose a legal obligation on Member States to adopt precautionary measures? Is it possible to apply the principle to actions which have at their base harm to human health caused by environmental damage as opposed to damage to the environment *per se*? How does the principle interact with other Community principles such as subsidiarity? I begin by assessing the principle as an instrument of policy making in international, EC, and British environmental law. I then examine the treatment of the principle in several British cases, broadly classed as 'environmental'. Since these suggest only limited application of the principle, I consider why it has not been better accepted in this context and consider whether it might be so in the future. This is not to say that the principle of precaution is unproblematic. There is another side to the argument for precaution which is worth airing before addressing these specific issues.

Principles of precaution

Environmental problems are typified by uncertainties in scientific knowledge. These include simply lack of data: the consequences of polluting emissions are not always clearly established, and the cumulative nature of pollutants from diverse sources means that effects may be seen only after long periods of time. Of greater complexity is uncertainty arising from the variability of natural processes. Natural systems operate by processes and are subject to chaotic fluctuations which are not adequately modelled, nor even understood in traditional scientific terms.[4] The precautionary principle encourages an acceptance of these uncertainties by changing the role of scientific data: according to the principle, once environmental damage is threatened action should be taken to control or abate possible environmental interference even though there may still be scientific uncertainty as to the effects of the activities. The precautionary principle appears, if not to make sense of uncertainties in the environmental field, then at least to provide a so-called 'common sense' strategy for dealing with these. In this respect, the principle questions assumptions about rational decision-making—that experts present scientific knowledge neutrally and objectively and that policy makers make decisions on the basis of such knowledge. It acts as a practical manifestation of theoretical inquiries into the construction of scientific knowledge,[5] promoting a less quantitative and absolute model of

---

[4] Wynne, note 3 above. See also Bodansky, 'Scientific Uncertainty and the Precautionary Principle' (1991) 33 *Environment* 4–5, 43–45.

[5] See Habermas, 'The Scientization of Politics and Public Opinion', in *Toward a Rational Society* (London: Heinemann, 1971) pp. 62–80; Barker, Peters and Guy, *The Politics of Expert Advice: Using and Manipulating Scientific Knowledge* (Edinburgh: Edinburgh University Press, 1993); Schrecker, *The Political Economy of Environmental Hazards* (Ottawa: Law Reform Commission of Canada, 1984); and Scott 'Continuity and Change in British Food Law', (1990) 53 MLR 785–801.

scientific methodology than that currently accepted. The principle also appears to give credence to more subjective, intuitive perceptions of risk,[6] and might foster participation in decision-making. From this perspective, the principle is radical, amply capable of destablising what counts for the traditional structure and use of scientific knowledge.

An alternative view is that precaution upholds the status quo, and represents a deeply conservative, Luddite reaction to social advances and ecological change. The principle's usual refrain (action even in the absence of certain scientific knowledge) can be inverted (no action unless one knows for certain the consequences). Its critics argue that by institutionalising caution, the precautionary principle imposes a doctrine of limitations: 'It offers security but in exchange for lowering expectations, limiting growth and preventing experimentation and change.'[7]

The former, more favourable, view of the precautionary principle usually prevails, at least in environmental law literature. The principle has become a leitmotiv of the environmental movement, due to its origins in pollution control legislation and because it appears to offer a way out of the maze of conflicting scientific and 'expert' opinion. The application of the principle is therefore as much a political as a scientific or legal issue: it is concerned with the divisive issues of how one deals with environmental risk and how those at risk are protected. This political nature is demonstrated most clearly by the subject-matter of cases in which the principle has most recently been invoked—the legality or otherwise of measures at the EU level banning the import of British beef,[8] and, at the international level, French nuclear testing in the Mururoa and Fangatanfa Atolls in the South Pacific.[9]

The conservative, and leftist/anarchist interpretations of the principle may differ on the progressive, or otherwise, quality of the principle. But, in legal terms at least, the principle can legitimately be labelled as radical. It may yet require the rethinking of accepted rules of causation, and the standard and structure of proof. Taking the latter as an example, a strong version of the principle might reverse the normal burden of proof. Defendants may then be made responsible for deeds which others may have committed if they are not in a position to prove that their actions could *not* have caused the alleged environmental damage.[10] Such changes are legitimately regarded as dramatic since loosening causal links, for example by relaxing the rigid legal requirements of proof, is capable of transforming *individual* liability into *collective* constel-

---

[6] On 'civic science', see Schwing and Albers, *Societal Risk Assessment: How Safe Is Safe Enough?* (New York: Plenum, 1980).

[7] Füredi, 'The Dangers of Safety' (1996) *Living Marxism* 16, at 17.

[8] Commission Decision 96/239/EC, OJ L 78 28.3.96, p. 47 on emergency measures to protect against BSE. See further, Elworthy, Chapter 18, below.

[9] International Court of Justice, Communiqué No. 95/29, 22 September 1995, see particularly dissenting opinion of Judge Weeramantry.

[10] Teubner, 'The Invisible Cupola: From Causal to Collective Attribution in Ecological Liability', in Teubner, Farmer and Murphy (eds) *Environmental Law and Ecological Responsibility: The Concept and Practice of Ecological Self-Organisation* (Chichester, Wiley, 1994), p. 19–20.

lations of liability.[11] In terms of regulatory action, the principle might require that an actor prove in advance that a proposed action will *not* cause harm to the environment. This has led to conservative, or regressive, strains of thought being identified with the principle. Conversely, the principle also commits regulators to take positive, precautionary action in some circumstances. Some states already advance such a version of the principle, for example that measures should be taken 'even where there exists no causal link between the emissions and the effects',[12] or 'if there are reasons to believe that damage or negative effects could be caused even if there is inadequate or inconclusive scientific evidence to prove the existence of a causal link between emissions and effects'.[13]

The principle might therefore be capable of shifting the burden of proof of causation for litigation or environmental regulation purposes from those alleging harm from a pollutant or substance to those engaged in the polluting activity.[14] This would change the prevailing perception of many activities as being relatively harmless, to being capable of great harm to human health and the environment. Shifting the burden of proof in such a way might more generally strengthen a view of the environment as a vulnerable rather than a robust system.

German origins and international declarations

The potential significance of the precautionary principle for science and law (even beyond that concerned with environmental protection) defies its humble origins. The principle originates in the German concept of *Vorsorgeprinzip*, which is understood as the need to act against risks which are not yet proved, or even to act in the absence of risk. *Vorsorgeprinzip* was first included as part of German environmental policy in 1976:

Environmental policy is not fully accomplished by warding off imminent hazards and the elimination of damage which has occurred. Precautionary environmental policy requires furthermore that natural resources are protected and demands on them are made with care.[15]

---

[11] *Ibid.*
[12] Ministerial Declaration of the Third International Conference on the Protection of the North Sea, The Hague, March 1990.
[13] Nordic Council Conference on Marine Pollution, Final Document, Copenhagen, October 1989.
[14] One example of the reversal of the burden of proof in line with the precautionary principle is the Oslo Commission Decision 89/1 in relation to the dumping of industrial waste at sea: '... the dumping of industrial wastes in the North Sea shall cease ... except for those industrial wastes for which it can be shown ... both that there are no practical alternatives on land and that the materials cause no harm to the marine environment'. OSCOM Decision 89/1, 14 June 1989.
[15] *Umweltbericht 76—Fortschreibung des Umweltprogramms der Bundesregierung vom* 14.7.76 BT-Drs. 8/3713.

Although at first the principle appeared not to give rise to specific measures, the *Waldsterben*, the death of large areas of forest in Germany, led to it being applied to air pollution legislation as a means by which more stringent controls could be justified legally and politically.[16]

The *Vorsorgeprinzip* was introduced into international law by its inclusion by the German government into the Bremen Declaration at the First Conference on the North Sea in 1984. More than a decade later, uncertainty surrounds the exact legal status of the principle in the international field. Birnie and Boyle[17] consider that the number of interpretations of the principle, and the novel and untested effects of some of its applications, mean that it is not yet a principle of international law. That its legal status remains elusive is broadly the view also of Gundling[18] and Handl.[19] But there is an argument that the principle has fairly recently crystallised into a principle of international environmental law. Freestone[20] sees support for this in its common occurrence in legal materials concerning a range of environmental sectors such as the protection of the marine environment,[21] and global environmental problems such as the depletion of the ozone layer,[22] and climate change.[23] For Cameron, the coming of age of the precautionary principle took place at the United Nations Conference on Environment and Development (the 'Earth Summit') in Rio de Janeiro in 1992. The most significant appeal to precaution was made in Principle 15 of the Rio Declaration on Environment and Development, a short statement of principles concerning sustainability.[24] The principle was also referred to in two Treaty texts signed at Rio: the Frame-

[16] von Moltke, 'The *Vorsorgeprinzip* in West German Environmental Law', in Royal Commission on Environmental Pollution, Twelfth Report, *Best Practicable Environmental Option* (London: HMSO, 1988) Cm. 310, Appendix 3, p. 60; see also Boehmer-Christiansen, 'The Precautionary Principle in Germany-Enabling Government', in O'Riordan and Cameron, *Interpreting the Precautionary Principle* (London: Earthscan Publications/Cameron May, 1994).

[17] Birnie and Boyle, *International Law and the Environment* (Oxford: Clarendon Press, 1992), p. 98. See also, Hohmann, *Precautionary Legal Duties and Principles in Modern International Environmental Law* (Dordrecht/London: Martinus Nijhoff/Graham and Trotman, 1994); and Sands, *Principles of International Environmental Law* (Manchester: Manchester University Press, 1995).

[18] Gundling, 'The Status in International Law of the Precautionary Principle', (1990) *International Journal of Estuarine and Coastal Law* Vol.5, Nos.1–3, 23–30.

[19] Handl, 'Environmental Security and Global Change: the Challenge to International Law', in Handl (ed) (1990) 1 Yb Int'l Env L Part I, 3.

[20] Freestone, 'The Road from Rio: International Environmental Law After the Earth Summit' (1994) JEL Vol. 6, No. 2, 193–218, at 215.

[21] Ministerial Declaration of the Third International Conference on the Protection of the North Sea, The Hague, 8 March 1990; Recommendation 89/1 of the Paris Commission (PARCOM), 22 June 1989.

[22] For example, Montreal Protocol on Substances that Deplete the Ozone Layer, Montreal, 16 September 1987 (1987) 26 ILM 1541, as amended, London, 29 June 1990.

[23] Final Ministerial Declaration of the Second World Climate Conference, Geneva, 7 November 1990, para. 7.

[24] Rio Declaration on Environment and Development, Adopted by the United Nations Conference on Environment and Development (UNCED) at Rio de Janeiro, 13 June 1992, UN Doc. A/Conf. 151/26 (Vol. 1) (1992) 31 ILM 874, Principle 15: 'In order to protect the environment, the precautionary approach shall be widely applied by states according to their capabilities. Where there are threats of serious or irreversible damage, lack of scientific certainty shall not be used as a reason for postponing cost-effective measures to prevent environmental degradation'.

work Convention on Climate Change[25] and the Convention on Biological Diversity.[26]

The International Court of Justice has recently carved out a place for the precautionary principle as customary international law,[27] on ruling on New Zealand's request to the Court to examine the situation of France conducting a new series of nuclear tests in the South Pacific. Judge Weeramantry accepts the role of the principle in such cases as a means of dealing with evidential problems and, furthermore, ties its practical application to the achievement of sustainable development.[28] Although this is a *dissenting* opinion, it suggests the possibility of greater acceptance of the principle by the international community in the future:

Where a party complains to the Court of possible environmental damage of an irreversible nature which another party is committing or threatening to commit, the proof or disproof of the matter alleged may present difficulty to the claimant as the necessary information may largely be in the hands of the party causing or threatening the damage.

The law cannot function in protection of the environment unless a legal principle is evolved to meet this evidentiary difficulty, and environmental law has responded with what has come to be described as the precautionary principle—a principle which is gaining increasing support as part of the international law of the environment . . .

It is a principle of relevance to New Zealand in its application to this Court and one which inevitably calls for consideration in the context of this case.

New Zealand has placed materials before the Court to the best of its ability, but France is in possession of the actual information. The principle then springs into operation to give the Court the basic rationale for considering New Zealand's request and not postponing the application of such means as are available to the Court, to prevent on a provisional basis, the threatened environmental degradation, until such time as the full scientific evidence becomes available in refutation of the New Zealand contention.

A principle of the EC

The precautionary principle is described as guiding Community policy making in the second sentence of Article 130r(2) of the EC Treaty.[29] The precautionary principle and the other principles listed in this paragraph are

---

[25] Article 3(3) United Nations Framework Convention on Climate Change (Rio de Janeiro) UNGA, A/AC.237/18 (Part II)/Add.1.

[26] Preambular para. 9 Convention on Biological Diversity, UNEP/Bio.Div.Conf./L.2.

[27] McIntyre, 'The Precautionary Principle—A Principle of Customary International Law?', talk given at SPTL Conference, Cambridge, September 1996.

[28] *Op. cit.* note 9.

[29] Article 130r(2):'Community policy on the environment shall aim at a high level of protection taking into account the diversity of situations in the various regions of the Community. It shall be based on the precautionary principle and on the principles that preventive action should be taken, that environmental damage should as a priority be rectified at source and that the polluter should pay.'

described as contributing to the achievement of the objectives of Community environmental policy set out in Article 130r(1): preserving, protecting, and improving the quality of the environment, protecting human health, prudent and rational utilisation of natural resources, and promoting measures at international level to deal with regional or worldwide environmental problems. Crucially, this inclusion of prescriptive principles of policy making is novel;[30] no other Community policy is governed by equivalent principles of action.

Unusually, the Community did not clarify the meaning of the precautionary principle in an environmental action programme, prior to its formal inclusion in the EC Treaty by the Treaty on European Union in 1993; the first reference to the principle being made in the Fifth Environmental Action Programme.[31] However, even before the Treaty had been amended to include the principle, the Community had grounded a number of measures on it: Council Decision 88/540/EEC[32] on substances that deplete the ozone layer, legislation concerned with potential or unknown risks, for example Directive 79/831/EEC[33] on the testing of new chemicals before they are marketed, and the assessment of the effects of the release of genetically modified organisms (Directives 90/219/EEC[34] and 90/220/EEC[35]); and Directive 80/778/EEC on the quality of drinking water[36] which set the maximum admissible concentrations for pesticides in drinking water at the level of detection. A more recent appeal to the principle is found in Commission Decision 96/239/EC on emergency measures to protect against Bovine Spongiform Encephalopathy (BSE or 'Mad Cow Disease')[37] in which reference is made in the preamble to uncertainty about the transmissibility of BSE to humans and the need to take action under such circumstances.

The principle might underlie all these instruments, but it remains difficult to pinpoint its exact legal status in EC law. Pescatore's classification of the mass

---

[30] Hession and Macrory, 'Maastricht and the Environmental Policy of the Community: Legal Issues of a New Environment Policy', in O'Keeffe and Twomey (eds), *Legal Issues of the Maastricht Treaty* (London: Wiley Chancery, 1994), pp. 151–167, at p. 156.

[31] *Fifth Action Programme on the Environment: Towards Sustainability—A European Community Programme of Policy and Action in Relation to the Environment and Sustainable Development* OJ C 138, ch. 2, at p. 24: 'the guiding principles for policy decisions under this programme derive from the precautionary approach and the concept of shared responsibility, including effective implementation of the "polluter pays principle" '.

[32] Council Decision 540/88/EEC, OJ L 297, p. 8 concerning the conclusion of the Vienna Convention for the Protection of the Ozone Layer, (1987) 26 ILM 1529 and the Montreal Protocol on Substances that Deplete the Ozone Layer, (1987) 26 ILM 1541, as amended London, 29 June 1990. For further details see Jachtenfuchs, 'The EC and the Protection of the Ozone Layer', (1990) 28 JCMS 261–277.

[33] OJ L 259, p. 10.

[34] EC Directive 90/219/EEC on the confinement of genetically modified organisms, OJ L 117, p. 1.

[35] EC Directive 90/220/EEC on the voluntary release of genetically modified organisms, OJ L 117, p. 15.

[36] Directive 80/778/EEC on the quality of water for human consumption OJ L 229, p. 11.

[37] *Op. cit.* note 8.

of Community law into 'geological layers' is of assistance.[38] The most shallow layer of EC law consists of policy areas where an expression of political will exists but no binding norms have been adopted, for example resolutions. A second layer is made up of areas of law described in such detail in the Treaties themselves or in relevant secondary legislation that they are capable of being applied directly in the national context. The third, deeper layer, involves law the application of which is placed with the Community, for example in the case of certain aspects of fisheries and agriculture law.

The precautionary principle, as contained in Article 130r(2) of the EC Treaty, appears to lie between the first two of Pescatore's layers: it is described in the EC Treaty itself, albeit in a general rather than detailed manner, and, although no specific binding norms on the principle have yet been adopted, it has informed the content of a number of directives. A question arises as to whether it is possible for the principle to embed in a deeper layer of EC law, and thus be capable of being applied directly in national law.

The European Court of Justice was called upon to interpret the legal status of Article 130r of the EC Treaty (including the precautionary principle) in Case C-379/92 *Peralta*[39] in the context of a preliminary ruling in criminal proceedings. Peralta was prosecuted by Italian authorities for breaching an Italian law which prohibits hydrocarbons or other harmful listed substances from being discharged into the sea (up to the territorial line). Surprisingly, Peralta sought to rely on Article 130r on the ground that the national law had the effect of forcing him to discharge the substance into the sea beyond the territorial line which 'from every point of view' is inefficient and contrary to measures adopted by the Community and contrary to obligations in international law. When asked by the national court whether the EC's environmental principles, and particularly the principle of prevention laid down in Articles 130r *et seq*, preclude this national law, the Court of Justice held that 'Article 130r is confined to defining the *general objectives of the Community in the matter of the environment*'.[40] The Court elaborated that responsibility for deciding what action is to be taken is conferred on the Council by Article 130s of the EC Treaty and that the protective measures adopted pursuant to Article 130s are not to prevent any Member State from maintaining or introducing more stringent environmental protection measures compatible with the Treaty.[41] The Court followed Advocate General Lenz's Opinion that Article 130r fails to set

---

[38] Pescatore, 'Address on the Application of Community Law in Each of the Member States', in Judicial and Academic Conference, 27–28 September 1976, Luxembourg, quoted in Curtin and Mortelmans, 'The Application and Enforcement of Community Law by the Member States: Actors in Search of a Third Generation Script', in Curtin and Henkels (eds), *Institutional Dynamics of European Integration* (Dordrecht: Martinus Nijhoff, 1994), p. 429.

[39] [1994] ECR I-3453.

[40] *Ibid.* para. 57 (emphasis added).

[41] Compare with the Court's more liberal interpretation of the principles in Article 130r in Case C-2/90, *Commission v. Belgium (Wallonian Waste)* [1993] 1 CMLR 365 in which it was held that the transport of ordinary wastes should be kept to a minimum in accordance with principles of prevention and that pollution be rectified at its source.

out any criterion for action by the Member States to protect the environment: 'action by the Member States cannot in any event be criticized in so far as it does not affect the effectiveness of the powers conferred on the Council (including the means of action provided by the Treaty, which includes the principle of prevention)'.[42]

It would appear that although the principles (including the precautionary principle) listed in Article 130r(2) are of general application, as they form only the basis of *Community* legislative action, they are probably not justiciable nor directly applicable.[43] This argument is derived from an interpretation of Article 130r as setting out principles for 'action by the Community' and not principles for the environmental policies of the Member States, and thus that Article 130r contains no binding legal rules. One consequence of this reading is that whether and how far Member States apply the precautionary principle in their own policies cannot be determined by Article 130r(2), but is to be judged rather by other provisions of Community or national law which might be based upon the principles. It is assumed however that Community action will be taken in accordance with the precautionary principle and therefore that the principle should be relevant at least to the review of the Community's discretionary decisions.[44]

Policy and practice in the United Kingdom

In international law-making, the UK government sees itself as 'strongly committed' to the precautionary approach.[45] In the North Sea Declarations, the government interpreted the principle as meaning that it applies where there is 'reasonable evidence' to suggest a causal link between emissions and effects, even though such a link has not been proven'.[46] This interpretation has meant that in the case of certain international documents the United Kingdom has unilaterally raised the threshold before regulatory action may be taken—from 'no scientific evidence' to a 'reasonable' amount of evidence.

On the domestic front, the UK government first accepted the applicability of the precautionary principle in *policy making* in a debate in the House of Lords

---

[42] Case C-379/92, *op. cit.* note 39, para. 33.
[43] Hession and Macrory, *op. cit.* note 30, at p. 156.
[44] *Ibid.*
[45] Third International Conference on the Protection of the North Sea: UK Guidance Note on the Ministerial Declaration (London: HMSO, 1990).
[46] *Ibid.* On the adoption of a precautionary approach to the disposal of sewage sludge at sea, see Jordan and O'Riordan, 'The Precautionary Principle in United Kingdom Law and Policy', in Gray (ed), *UK Environmental Policy in the 1990s* (London: Macmillan Press, 1995) p. 72; and Brown and Jordan, 'The UK Government's Response to the UNCED' (1993) 3 *Pacific and Asian Journal of Energy* 87–99.

in 1988, prior to the EC's inclusion of the principle in Article 130r(2).[47] The principle was formally adopted in the White Paper, *This Common Inheritance* (1990):

> ... Where there are *significant risks* of damage to the environment, the government will be prepared to limit the use of potentially dangerous materials or the spread of potentially dangerous pollutants, *even where scientific knowledge is not conclusive if the balance of likely costs and benefits justifies it.*[48] (emphasis added)

This statement includes a requirement to conduct a cost benefit analysis to establish an economic justification for the precautionary principle. Cost benefit analysis, premised on an assumption that there is sufficient knowledge to measure risks and calculate the appropriate response, is here combined with the precautionary principle, a main characteristic of which is the acceptance of gaps in scientific knowledge. This might lead to the non-implementation of the precautionary principle rather than its elaboration. For example, in the context of bathing waters it is the government's view that: 'because of scarce resources, nothing more should be spent to protect human health until a figure can be scientifically confirmed'.[49] The threshold for action on the basis of the precautionary principle is therefore set at a fairly high level—where a 'significant risk' of damage arises and where the 'balance of likely costs and benefits justifies it'. Alternative readings of the principle suggest a lower threshold: that action should be taken as soon as *any possible* risk is demonstrated; or, to return to the German principle of *Vorsorgeprinzip*, even in the absence of risk. The government has recently issued a number of further statements on the principle in *Sustainable Development: The UK Strategy* (1994)[50] and *Biodiversity: The UK Action Plan* (1994).[51] These amount to a bare commitment to the principle. Both resonate with references to 'sound science' – the ideal of making decisions on the basis of certain scientific knowledge, as far from a veil of ignorance as possible. The message of these documents is that, at some point in the future, scientific evidence of sufficient authority will be forthcoming to indicate the need for a particular course of action. To summarise, in policy terms the UK government's position on the precautionary principle is one of limited acceptance by reason of its assertion of the integrity, and its reliance on, sound or 'safe' science, and the tying-in of cost benefit analysis with the principle. This approach has pro-

---

[47] The Minister of State for the Environment (the Earl of Caithness) speaking in a debate on the environment in the House of Lords, 13 January 1988 (Official Report, Col. 1311): 'Environmental policy must evolve on the basis of sound science, informed debate, foresight and a proper balance between development and conservation. We accept the precautionary principle.'

[48] HM Government, *This Common Inheritance* (London: HMSO, 1990), Cm. 1200, para. 1.15.

[49] Department of the Environment, Memorandum on Bathing Water, quoted in O'Riordan and Cameron, *op. cit.* note 16, p. 128.

[50] Department of the Environment, *Sustainable Development: The UK Strategy* (London: HMSO, 1993), Cm. 2426, para. 15: 'where there is uncertainty and potentially serious risks exist, precautionary action may be necessary', and see also para. 1.20.

[51] Department of the Environment, *Biodiversity: The UK Action Plan* (London: HMSO, 1994), Cm. 2428, para. 2.18.

duced the *non sequitur* that 'sound scientific knowledge should provide the basis for precautionary action'.[52]

In practical terms, the best example of the acceptance of the principle in UK law is Part VI of the Environmental Protection Act 1990 on the release of genetically modified organisms. This Part of the 1990 Act, enacted to comply with EC legislation,[53] places obligations on those who intend to release or market genetically modified organisms to carry out risk assessments and notify the authorities. The precautionary element arises because the entire regime was put in place in advance of any observed harm from the release of genetically modified organisms, and because the regime itself seeks to scrutinise proposals for release and to consider their possible implications on the environment. In this example, an obligation of precaution is imposed on parties other than the government and on activities which extend beyond policy making.[54]

Applying the principle in British Courts

Member State institutions are bound to act in conformity with the binding rules laid down in EC law. This obligation is derived from the wording of Article 189 of the EC Treaty: that a regulation shall be 'binding in its entirety and directly applicable in all Member States'; and a directive 'shall be binding, as to the result to be achieved, upon each Member State to which it is addressed'. In the past a number of questions have chipped away at this simple statement of obligations of Member States to implement and give effect to EC law. Does EC law give rise to rights in favour of private parties that Member State institutions (including the courts) are bound to enforce against Member States themselves and possibly against other private persons? Does EC law also impose obligations on private persons that the Member States are bound to enforce, if need be judicially? Might Member States be liable to individuals for their failure to implement Community measures? As the European Court of Justice has sought to resolve these and other questions by, *inter alia*, its development of the doctrine of direct effect and, more recently, Member State non-contractual liability, a more complex shape of Member States' obligation to comply with EC law has evolved. The application of the precautionary principle in UK environmental law represents one further line of inquiry: does the obligation to act in conformity with the rules of EC law extend to complying with *principles* of Community action contained in the Treaty? This is reviewed in the context

---

[52] Department of the Environment, Memorandum on Bathing Water, quoted in O'Riordan and Cameron, *op. cit.* note 16, p. 128.

[53] Directive 90/219/EEC on the confinement of genetically modified organisms, OJ L 117, p. 1 and Directive 90/220/EEC on the voluntary release of genetically modified organisms, OJ L 117, p. 15.

[54] For a more sceptical view on the precautionary nature of this regime, see Hill, 'The Precautionary Principle and Release of GMOs', in O'Riordan and Cameron, *op. cit.* note 16.

of cases which reveal also the differing policy content, and varying judicial treatment of the principle: *Alfred McAlpine Homes (North) Ltd.* v. *Secretary of State for the Environment and Another*[55] in which there was some acceptance and legitimation of the principle; *R* v. *Secretary of State for Trade and Industry, ex parte Duddridge and Others,*[56] which offers the most explicit examination to date of the legal issues concerning the application of the precautionary principle; and *Gateshead Metropolitan Borough Council* v. *Secretary of State for the Environment,*[57] in which the court neatly sidestepped the issue. I characterise the judicial treatment of the precautionary principle according to three streams: legitimation, examination, and evasion.

Legitimation

In *Alfred McAlpine Homes (North) Ltd.* v. *Secretary of State for the Environment and Another,*[58] heard before the Court of Appeal, the Secretary of State for the Environment approved the Cheshire Replacement Structure Plan, but modified it in a manner which severely restricted the release of green belt land for housing.[59] This modification was significant because the development plan firmly guides the local planning authority when deciding whether to grant or refuse planning permission.[60] The reason the Secretary of State gave for his modifying the development plan was that he had applied the precautionary principle so as to reduce the risk of unacceptable consequences for the environment and character of Chester. Much to the building consortium's chagrin, the Secretary of State decided that future release of green belt land should not go ahead until a more thorough examination had been carried out of the likely consequences of the loss of the land on the character of the city and the long-standing protection of green belt areas. This decision rendered Alfred McAlpine Homes Ltd. unable to build on their land. In their application for judicial review of this decision before the Queen's Bench Division, Moriarty J supported the Secretary of State's cautious and restrictive approach to the release of green belt land on the following ground:

A decision to maintain the Green Belt is capable of revocation. A decision to relax the Green Belt is irrevocable. That difference, it seems to me, is capable of justifying the Secretary of State's decision in this case.[61]

This approach was followed by the Court of Appeal, although less explicit

---

[55] [1994] NPC 138.
[56] [1995] Env LR 151, (1996) P & CR 350 (CA).
[57] [1994] Env LR 37.
[58] *Op. cit.* note 55.
[59] Town and Country Planning Act 1990, s. 35(1), as amended by the Planning and Compensation Act 1991, entitles the Secretary of State to make such modifications.
[60] Town and Country Planning Act 1990, ss. 70(2) and 54A.
[61] [1993] JPEL B99.

reference was made to the precautionary principle in that court. *Alfred McAlpine Homes* illustrates that, although the precautionary principle has not been given a statutory formulation in the same manner as other principles of environmental law such as 'best practicable environmental option',[62] it has not been wholly ignored by decision-makers. The case provides a good example of the Secretary of State for the Environment applying the precautionary principle as a statement of policy and gaining judicial support for this. As the following indicates, this approach is unusual in its legitimation of the principle.

Examination

The most detailed examination of the legal status of the precautionary principle is found in *R* v. *Secretary of State for Trade and Industry, ex parte Duddridge and Others*,[63] which concerned the risk to health from electromagnetic fields (EMFs) associated with electric cables. The action was brought by three children living in an area of North East London, where the National Grid Company was laying a new high voltage underground cable. The applicants alleged that radiation emitted from the new cables would enter their homes and schools and would be of such a level that they would or might be exposed to a risk of developing leukaemia. The applicants' solicitors wrote to the Secretary of State for Trade and Industry asking him to exercise his powers under s. 29 of the Electricity Act 1989 to make regulations to protect the public from dangers and personal injury arising from the transmission or supply of electricity. The Secretary of State replied saying that he had never regarded it as necessary or appropriate to take specific measures to limit electric and magnetic fields to protect the public from the possibility of the very small risk of cancer. The applicants submitted that the correct approach of the Secretary of State is to ask himself whether there is any evidence of a possible risk of childhood leukaemia even though the scientific evidence is presently unclear and does not prove the causal connection. They therefore sought a judicial review of the Secretary of State's decision not to take action under the 1989 Act; specifically, an order of *mandamus* compelling the Secretary of State to issue regulations or guidelines to ensure that the electric and magnetic fields associated with cables to be laid as part of the National Grid did not exceed 0.2 microteslas to the nearest point of houses adjoining the cables; or at some other level at which on current research there was no evidence to suggest any possible risk to health. The applicants argued that the Secretary of State was obliged to apply the precautionary principle as a result of an obligation of EC law—specifically Article 130r(2) of the EC Treaty.

Before the Queen's Bench Division, Smith LJ held that, as a statement of

---

[62] Environmental Protection Act 1990, s. 7(4) and (7).
[63] *Op. cit.* note 56.

principle, Article 130r of the EC Treaty did not impose an obligation on the Secretary of State to consider his duties and powers under the 1989 Act in the light of the precautionary principle (Farquharson LJ concurring). Rather, Article 130r was intended to lay down principles from which future *Community policy* on the environment was to be based.[64] The case turned on the European Court of Justice's finding in Case C-379/92, *Peralta*[65] that Article 130r is confined to defining the general objectives of the Community in the matter of the environment, and therefore that the principles outlined in that Article do not impose an obligation on Member States. Before the Court of Appeal Glidewell LJ was confident that there was no need to refer the case to the European Court of Justice, as requested by the applicants, on the ground that the European Court of Justice had itself issued a ruling on the legal effect of Article 130r.[66] The Court of Appeal rejected the applicants' argument that the European Court of Justice's ruling in *Peralta* was given in the context of criminal proceedings and was thus inapplicable as a guide to determine Member States' obligations under EC law. The outcome of *Duddridge*, that decision-makers such as the Secretary of State for Trade and Industry are not bound to apply the precautionary principle, clearly limits its legal impact. Nonetheless, the case is significant in assessing the application of the precautionary principle for a number of reasons.

Duddridge raises the question whether the precautionary principle is restricted to issues of environmental harm. This was clearly the view of Smith LJ: ' . . . the principle is primarily intended to avoid long term harm to the environment itself rather than damage to human health from transitory environmental conditions'.[67] It was held that there was no basis for the action on the ground of domestic policy since government policy on the principle was intended to protect the environment itself and was not intended to apply to damage to human health caused by environmental factors. This narrow interpretation of the principle overlooks the relationship between harm to the environment and harm to human health and narrows the legitimate scope and potential of environmental law in a manner now rejected by most other legislative and policy formulations. For example s. 2 of the Environmental Protection Act 1990 adopts a holistic perspective on the relationship between human health and the environment by defining 'pollution of the environment' as 'capable of causing harm to man or any other living organisms supported by the environment'. Such an approach is similarly taken by the European Union: Article 130r(1) of the EC Treaty states that Community policy on the environment shall contribute to protecting *human health*, this thereby constituting part of the EC's environmental policy. The United Nations Environment Programme registers also that *human suffering* is a result of irreversible damage to the

---

[64] *Ibid.* at 174.
[65] *Op. cit.* note 39.
[66] (1996) 71 P & CR 350 (CA).
[67] *Op. cit.* note 56, at 158.

environment and that this should, with environmental harm, be encompassed by the precautionary principle.[68]

Duddridge addresses also what might be the evidential threshold for applying the precautionary principle. Epidemiological studies (the study of patterns of behaviour in large numbers of cases) suggest the possibility of a link between exposure to EMFs and leukaemia and that this increases progressively with the intensity of the field.[69] It was expected that the applicants would be exposed to far greater EMFs than ordinarily expected in the domestic environment.[70] However, the expert witnesses for the applicants were unable to conclude with certainty that residential EMF exposure causes leukaemia in childhood. Of great importance is that Smith LJ was prepared to accept that, if the Secretary of State is shown to be under a legal obligation to apply the precautionary principle to legislation concerned with health and the environment, the existing state of scientific knowledge about harm caused by EMFs was such as to oblige the Secretary of State to apply the principle in considering whether to issue regulations to restrict exposure to EMFs. This suggests that epidemiological evidence of a possible association between the exposure to EMFs and the development of cancers would suffice as a threshold for the application of the precautionary principle.

Of further interest is the interplay between the principle of subsidiarity (EC Treaty, Article 3b) and the precautionary principle (EC Treaty, Article 130r(2)) in the case. Appearing as an interested party, the National Grid Company relied upon Article 3b in arguing that Article 130r(2) does not impose an obligation on Member States to legislate in accordance with the precautionary principle. This argument was accepted fully by Smith LJ,[71] leading inevitably to the conclusions that some principles of EC law are more justiciable than others, and that (in accordance with its predominant status in the EC Treaty) subsidiarity is favoured. This gives Member States considerable room for manoeuvre in their application of the precautionary and other principles. Had the precautionary principle been found to be a binding rule, and thus capable of imposing obligations on Member States, and possibly granting rights to individuals, Smith LJ's dicta would suggest that this finding be set aside on the grounds of subsidiarity.[72] Such recourse to the principle of subsidiarity in this context suggests a misreading of the principle. As stated in Article 3b of the EC Treaty, the principle of subsidiarity guides law-making in the Community; it should not be

---

[68] United Nations Environment Programme (UNEP), Decision 15/27, Governing Council.
[69] National Radiological Protection Board, *Risk of Radiation-Induced Cancer at Low Doses and Low Dose Rates for Radiation Protection Purposes*, Vol. 6, No. 1 (London: HMSO, 1995).
[70] Ordinary domestic exposure is said to be in the range of 30–150 nanoteslas (the unit of measurement of EMFs); the applicants would be exposed to fields well in excess of 300 nanoteslas. It is worth noting that the Swedish government has recently issued guidance to planning authorities advising them not to grant permission for the construction of residential properties underneath high voltage electricity cables due to attendant, but not proven, risks of cancer, *The Independent*, 14 January 1994.
[71] *Op. cit.* note 56, at 174.
[72] *Ibid.*

used as a means by which the binding nature of existing Community measures might be lessened.

Individual protection and the precautionary principle

The appeal to Article 130r(2) of the EC Treaty by the applicants in *Duddridge* raises the issue of the adequacy of protection of Community rights in national courts. The key question is whether Article 130r of the EC Treaty is justiciable— whether it can have direct effects and be capable of judicial adjudication.[73] To return to the geological layers of Community law described by Pescatore, this question may be rephrased as whether Article 130r is capable of embedding in a deeper stratum, so that the precautionary principle might be directly applicable in the national context. The applicants argued in *Duddridge* that the Secretary of State for Trade and Industry was under a duty imposed by European Community law to apply the precautionary principle contained in Article 130r and therefore consider his powers and duties under the Electricity Act 1989 in the light of the duties imposed by that Article. Smith LJ construed Article 130r as a non-binding measure: the ordinary words of Article 130r and the intention of the Article (that the policy envisaged in Article 130r shall be brought into effect by the introduction of further Community measures) both pointing in this direction.

Most persuasive in Smith LJ's view was the description of the binding force of measures in EC law contained in Article 189 of the EC Treaty. Article 189 provides for the European Parliament acting jointly with the Council and the Commission to make regulations and issue directives, take decisions, make recommendations, or deliver opinions. Of these measures, Article 189 describes only regulations and directives as measures having binding force on Member States. Treating Article 189 as an exhaustive list of binding measures, Smith LJ draws from this that 'it is plain from the recital of the varying effects of different types of measure that it is not intended that a statement of policy or, still less, a statement of the principles which underlie a policy should in itself create an obligation upon a Member State to take specific action'.[74]

This narrow reading of Article 189 of the EC Treaty overlooks that the European Court of Justice has consistently found to be binding measures and acts other than those listed in Article 189 EC[75] (although prior to *Peralta*, the Court had not specifically ruled on the binding nature of principles). Most obviously, Article 189 does not include within its scope Treaty Articles; nevertheless these are clearly capable of binding Member States. A further example is that according to Article 189 recommendations have no binding force. However,

---

[73] Pescatore, 'The Doctrine of "Direct Effect": An Infant Disease of Community Law' (1983) 8 EL Rev 155, 176–177.

[74] *Op. cit.* note 56, at 168.

[75] For example, in Case 22/70, *Commission* v. *Council* ('ERTA') [1971] ECR 263 a fourth category of legal measure, 'innominate acts', was found to be binding.

the Court of Justice has held that national courts are bound to take them into consideration in deciding disputes, in particular where the recommendations cast light on the interpretation of national measures adopted in order to implement them or where they are designed to supplement binding Community provisions.[76] Recently the European Court of Justice has held that examples of 'soft law' may also produce legal effects in the Member States, thus imposing legal obligations on those Member States.[77] The Court of Justice presumes therefore that any rule of EC law is meant to have an effect.

In *Duddridge*, the applicants also attempted to rely upon Article 5 of the EC Treaty (the 'fidelity clause') which requires Member States to 'take all appropriate measures, whether general or particular to ensure fulfilment of the obligations arising out of this Treaty'. The applicants argued that Article 5 has been relied upon in a variety of situations to enforce compliance with Community obligations.[78] However, since an obligation on the Member States to adopt specific measures cannot be *created* by Article 5 in the absence of a particular provision in the Treaty or binding acts adopted by the institutions,[79] Smith LJ considered that this proposition 'begs, but does not answer, the question as to whether Article 130r EC creates an obligation on Member States'.[80] A less restrictive view of the scope of Article 5 is held by Temple-Lang.[81] Although it is undoubtedly correct that Article 5 of the EC Treaty is not capable of *introducing* obligations and duties on Member States, Temple-Lang advances that the Article does impose a duty on Member States to implement the *objectives* of the Community when the objective and the required action are sufficiently clear. Such objectives can be legal, found in or derived from the Treaty, or even policy objectives adopted by the Community institutions.[82] Arguably, as a principal tenet of Community environmental policy, the precautionary principle contributes to the achievement of the objectives of Community environmental law. Article 130r of the EC Treaty may be deemed to be a sufficiently clear description of the objectives of Community environmental policy, particularly when considered in the light of cases in which Community

---

[76] See Case C-322/88, *Grimaldi* v. *Fonds des Maladies Professionelles* [1989] ECR 4407 at 4421, (a recommendation concerning the adoption of a European Schedule of Occupational Diseases was held to have some *effet utile*: 'it must be stressed that the measures cannot be regarded as having no legal effect').

[77] See Case C-366/88, *France* v. *Commission (Re FEOGA Inspections)* [1992] 1 CMLR 205 (instructions issued by the Commission which empowered the Commission to take samples of agricultural products produced legal effects) and Case C-303/90, *France* v. *Commission* [1991] ECR I-5315, in which the ECJ upheld the French argument that a Commission prepared Code of Conduct on reporting of fraud against the Community imposed legal obligations on Member States.

[78] As established in Case 45/76, *Comet* [1976] ECR 2043, Case C-68/88, *Commission* v. *Greece* [1989] ECR 2965 and Case C-2/90, *Commission* v. *Belgium (Wallonian Waste)* [1993] 1 CMLR 365.

[79] Case 229/86, *Brother Industries* v. *Commission* [1987] ECR 3757, at 3763.

[80] *Op. cit.* note 56, at 169.

[81] Temple-Lang, 'Community Constitutional Law: Article 5 EEC Treaty' (1990) 27 CML Rev 645.

[82] *Ibid.* at 657.

objectives in other policy areas were found to impose a legal duty on Member States in conjunction with Article 5.[83]

A finding in the alternative, that Article 130r imposed a legal duty on the Member States to adopt precautionary measures, might also have had the effect that a citizen of a Member State could invoke that Article as conferring direct rights upon which they may rely in proceedings in their national courts against the government or some other agency charged with carrying out a statutory duty. It is by this doctrine of direct effect that the precautionary principle might inform national law most clearly. Also of relevance to the legal status of Article 130r of the EC Treaty is that a finding that the Article does impose an obligation on the Secretary of State to adopt precautionary measures, coupled with the possible inadequacy of existing policy and law, may possibly have opened up the way for an action for *Francovich* damages.[84]

Evasion

The potential significance of the precautionary principle was side-stepped by the English courts in *Gateshead Metropolitan Borough Council* v. *Secretary of State for the Environment*.[85] The Secretary of State granted planning permission for a clinical waste incinerator in Gateshead. The Inspector appointed to hear the appeal recommended that permission be refused. One issue taken into account by the Inspector was the local public's fear that dioxins emitted from the site would be harmful. The Secretary of State concluded that this issue could be satisfactorily addressed as part of the Integrated Pollution Control (IPC) authorisation procedure established by Part I of the Environmental Protection Act 1990. That decision was challenged by Gateshead Metropolitan Borough Council on the ground that the planning control and IPC systems were so closely linked that it would be unreasonable to grant planning permission without knowing if emissions could be adequately controlled under the IPC authorisation process. The applicants alleged that the Secretary of State's decision that these controls are adequate to deal with the emissions and the risk to human health contravened the precautionary principle. The High Court, confirmed by the Court of Appeal, decided that although the two statutory requirements overlapped, the extent of the overlap would vary on every occasion and therefore the grant of planning permission would not inhibit Her Majesty's Inspectorate of Pollution from refusing authorisation and using powers which were adequate to deal with the concerns raised. Sullivan J held:

---

[83] For example, in Case 71/76, *Thieffry* v. *Conseil de l'Ordre des Avocats à la Cour de Paris* [1977] ECR 765 it was established that even in the absence of directives on the recognition of qualifications provided for in Article 57(1) and (2) of the EEC Treaty, Member States were considered bound by Article 5 to bring about the achievement of the Community objective of freedom of establishment. See also Case 32/79, *Commission* v. *United Kingdom* [1980] ECR 2403, at 2437–2438 and 2460–2461 in which it was considered whether a Member State had a legal duty under Article 5 to adopt measures to conserve a fish stock.

[84] See Cases C-6-9/90, *Francovich* v. *Italy* [1991] I-ECR 5357. See further Hilson, 'Community Rights in Environmental Law: Rhetoric or Reality?', Chapter 4 above.

[85] [1994] Env LR 37.

. . . just as the environmental impact of such emissions is a material planning consideration, so also is the existence of a stringent regime under the Environmental Protection Act 1990 for preventing or mitigating that impact and for rendering any emissions harmless.[86]

This reasoning makes clear that the local planning authority's misgivings about the effects of a project upon the environment may be resolved by imposing conditions on an Integrated Pollution Control authorisation. The trust shown in the operation of the IPC system by Sullivan J, and endorsed by the Court of Appeal, circumscribes the means by which planning controls might prevent pollution of the environment. The judgment recognises, but nevertheless limits, the common ground between the systems of planning and pollution control.

Government policy on the overlap of pollution controls and planning regimes is stated in the White Paper, *This Common Inheritance* (1990) that '[planning] permission should not be granted if that might expose people to danger'. In *Gateshead*, this was read alongside policy on the precautionary principle, also in the White Paper, that 'where there are significant risks of damage to the environment, the government will be prepared to take precautionary action'.[87] The judgments in the High Court and the Court of Appeal suggest that there was insufficient information before the inspector to enable him to reach a fully informed decision on the risks to health which might result from the incineration plant. Left with a perceived risk to amenity, and concerns that 'the impact on air quality was not sufficiently defined', and 'fears as to environmental pollution and in particular dioxin emissions could not be sufficiently allayed', the Inspector recommended refusing permission on the basis that granting permission was an unacceptable risk to take. Neither the High Court nor Court of Appeal explicitly considered the planning regime as an evocation of the precautionary principle. However, the refusal of planning permission by the planning inspector was clearly a precautionary measure. And the applicants, Gateshead Metropolitan Borough Council, saw the planning control powers they held as the first line of defence against environmental harm: once planning permission has been granted, they argued, 'there is in practice almost no prospect of Her Majesty's Inspectorate of Pollution using their powers to refuse to authorise the operation of the plant'.[88]

The outcome of *Gateshead* is that those opposing development at the planning stage must adduce clear and conclusive evidence of the effects on health.[89] This represents a countervailing approach to the precautionary principle. This arises because, unlike other principles of environmental law, for example that the best practicable environmental option (BPEO) be used, the precautionary principle has no statutory basis, is described only in policy documents, and might

---

[86] *Ibid.* at 44.
[87] *Op. cit.* note 48, para. 1.18.
[88] [1994] Env LR 37, at 48.
[89] Macrory, 'Appeal Court Ruling on Planning and Pollution Interface' (1994) *ENDS Report*, Vol. 233, 43.

therefore be given such weight as is thought appropriate. This is reinforced by a comment made by Glidewell LJ in the Court of Appeal that the precautionary principle is a statement of common sense, but not a statement of law.[90]

Conclusions

The United Kingdom government has adopted the precautionary principle in policy statements; although its commitment to the principle is sometimes a little baldly stated and is lessened by a continuing reliance on 'safe science'. In the courts there is some acceptance of the principle. But there is also a reluctance on the part of the judiciary to entertain a broad reading of the principle by applying it to policy making, particularly in *Duddridge* and *Gateshead*. The approach in the latter cases might be accounted for by conflicting scientific opinion about the causes of the disease of concern in *Duddridge*, and the effects of the incineration of clinical waste on air quality in *Gateshead*—ironically, exactly the scenarios in which the precautionary principle is the most appropriate.

Two lines of reasoning are drawn in these judgments. One line is based on general legal principles taken from international law, EC law, and environmental law which appeal to progressive and purposive interpretations of law and is typified by the applicants' appeal to 'common sense', 'reasonableness', and, of course, 'precaution'. A second line offers a narrow, and semantic reading of the precautionary principle which is more rigorous in its approach, less sympathetic to principles of environmental law, and fails to take sufficient account of obligations of EC law.[91] One telling example is the objection of Smith LJ in *Duddridge* to the application of the principle to cases of harm to human health from damage to the environment instead of environmental harm *per se*. In the context of these cases, the discord between the narrow and broader interpretations of the principle illustrates the current limitations of environmental law in the United Kingdom: a reliance upon objective and absolute scientific proof of harm, and failure to appreciate some significant advances in EC law.

The potentially destabilising effect of the precautionary principle is therefore lessened by an interpretation of it as no more than a general indication of what might be desirable policy. One explanation for this is that the status of the 'principle' as a legal norm is capable of being misunderstood. Whilst pronouncements of objectives and principles of law and the subsequent teleological interpretation of legislation (the Code) are key characteristics of the civil law tradition of the founding Member States of the EEC, the legislature in Britain has usually resisted the use of general and guiding principles, and the judiciary similarly show some discomfort in applying them.

A further explanation is that the duty to give reasons is gaining currency in

---

[90] [1994] Env LR 37, at 44.
[91] See Alder, 'Environmental Impact Assessment—the Inadequacies of English Law' (1993) JEL Vol. 5, No. 2, 203–220, at 220 on similar reasoning in the context of environmental assessment law.

administrative law as a principle of natural justice and good administration.[92] The courts have not attempted to define a standard or uniform threshold which the reasons must satisfy. But it might well be the case that a decision of the Court of Appeal that the Secretary of State for Trade and Industry must take action to ensure the electricity supplier reduces the voltage of electricity running through certain power lines in line with the precautionary principle might fall foul of the duty to give reasons which are precise and which explain adequately why the supplier is subject to some liability or must carry out some action. This raises the question: should the duty to give reasons be lessened for environmental cases in which there is some uncertainty as to the likely effects of a course of action (or non-action)?

A conundrum also exists that in hardening the principle into a legally binding rule in such a way as to loosen causal links, the precautionary principle must constitute a precise legal 'standard', defining a threshold to determine when action should be taken. Yet at issue is the point at which authorities are justified in acting against risks which are not yet identifiable, or even in the absence of risk (for example in maintaining an environmental resource undisturbed). Calls for the setting of a specific threshold for action may further be challenged by findings that *any* exposure to ionising radiation carries the risk of cancer.[93] This lack of certainty for the threshold for action has been taken to mean that the principle should not be viewed as a legal principle at all; it should rather be seen as a means by which different regulatory responses to achieve environmental protection may be explored.

The main explanation for the narrow interpretation of the precautionary principle in the cases reviewed, and particularly the reading of the principle in *Duddridge*, is some continuing uncertainty about the legal status of principles of EC environmental policy in the United Kingdom. This is underscored by the energetic interpretation of the principle of subsidiarity by Smith LJ in *Duddridge* as meaning that Article 130r of the EC Treaty does not impose an obligation on Member States to legislate in the light of the precautionary principle. In this context, invoking the subsidiarity principle might be seen as a strategy to avoid the specific practical duties which have followed the European Court of Justice's increasingly expansive interpretation of Article 5 of the EC Treaty.

Even whilst accepting a restrictive reading of the precautionary principle as a consequence of the text of Article 130r, and the inherent limitations of the loyalty clause in Article 5, it is interesting to consider whether the precautionary principle might still become accepted as a principle of constitutional importance[94] in order to be of greater significance to those asserting harm to health

---

[92] Woolf and Jowell, *de Smith's Judicial Review of Administrative Action* (London: Sweet and Maxwell, 1995), ch 9; JUSTICE, All Souls Committee Report, *Administrative Justice: Some Necessary Reforms* (Oxford: Clarendon Press, 1988) p. 71.

[93] *Op. cit.* note 69.

[94] A parallel European principle, is that of proportionality; on acceptance of this principle, see Jowell and Lester, 'Proportionality—Neither Novel Nor Dangerous', in Jowell and Oliver, *New Directions in Judicial Review* (London: Stevens, 1988); see also Hilf, 'The Application of Rules of National Administrative Law in the Implementation of Community Law', (1983) 3 YEL 79, at 83.

than an environmental public relations exercise. This might require legislative and judicial bodies to act with care and foresight when making decisions that may have an adverse impact on the environment. But, in hardening the principle to give rise to specific legal rights and obligations, embedding it deeper in the layers of EC law, difficulties are likely to be encountered such as setting a specific threshold for action. The future impact of the principle might therefore be judged more in terms of broadening debate about the relationship between scientific inquiry and environmental law and the effects of this on questions of causality and the structure and standard of proof.

Part III

REGULATION IN PRACTICE I: POLLUTION CONTROL

Chapter 9

TESTING THE EXTENDED GATEKEEPER: THE LAW, PRACTICE AND POLITICS OF IMPLEMENTING THE DRINKING WATER DIRECTIVE IN THE UNITED KINGDOM[1]

Ian Bache and Donald McGillivray

Introduction

This chapter considers the impact of EC legislation on the law, practice and politics of water policy implementation in the UK focusing in particular on the 1980 Drinking Water Directive,[2] a directive which has prompted government ministers and others to question publicly the merits of EC intervention.[3] In our view, implementation is a key stage of the legislative process which cannot be taken as a straightforward administrative follow-on from policy decisions but a stage which can have a significant impact on policy outcomes. Here, we focus on practical rather than formal implementation.

The importance to be attached to implementation is strengthened when applied to the emerging system of governance in the European Union. Here the European Commission, charged with the responsibility of overseeing the implementation of EC policies, is in practice highly dependent on national governments for policy implementation. The implementation stage thus pro-

---

[1] We are grateful to Stephen George, Chris Hilson, William Howarth and Bernard Ryan for useful comments. The usual disclaimers apply.

[2] Directive 80/778/EEC relating to the quality of water intended for human consumption, OJ L 229, 30.8.80, p. 11 henceforth 'the Directive' or 'the 1980 Directive'. In this chapter we focus on the impact of the Directive in England and Wales.

[3] At the Environment Council in Autumn 1993, Tim Yeo, then Environment Minister, suggested that the EC should never have legislated on drinking water and would not have done so if provisions relating to subsidiarity had then been in place; see Jewkes, 'The Principle of Subsidiarity: Its Effect on Existing and Future EC Environmental Regulation' (1994) 6 *Environmental Law and Management* 165–167, at 166.

vides Member States with a second opportunity, after agreement in the Council of Ministers, to frustrate EC policy objectives it opposes.

While national governments have been regularly described as 'gatekeepers' between the EU and their domestic systems,[4] this metaphor has traditionally been applied only to policy bargaining at EU level. Here we extend this metaphor to ask whether, and if so how and to what effect, the UK government has sought to play the gatekeeper role in relation to EC drinking water law at the implementation stage.

To guide our examination of the implementation process we refer to the 'Extended Gatekeeper' framework.[5] We argue that despite the Directive setting down seemingly firm legal limits for drinking water quality in the EC, the government has still found it possible to maintain quite tight control over the drinking water sector, not least through retaining a relatively firm hand over the enforcement of drinking water law. The Directive has moved drinking water policy away from the close confines of the professional networks of engineers that previously dominated the sector, enabling new actors to gain prominence. But central government remains the dominant actor, something the Commission's recent proposals for revision of the Directive look set to consolidate rather than erode.

The Extended Gatekeeper framework

The Extended Gatekeeper framework developed from a study of the implementation of EU structural policy.[6] It is best understood as a response to attempts at a general theory of the EU policy process based largely on EU level decisions.[7] The emphasis on EU level processes in these models and under-theorisation of implementation as an integral part of the policy process provided an incomplete picture of the influence of the actors involved. Yet to provide a general model of EU policy making which accounted for implementation would be an enormous task, requiring a detailed account of the distribution of power within each of the Member States. In recognition of this, the Extended Gatekeeper approach is concerned with examining the actions of individual governments in response to specific issues or legislative measures. While this approach reduces the possibility of generalisation from case studies, it improves precision. The relevant

---

[4] Hoffmann, 'Obstinate or Obsolete? The Fate of the Nation State and the Case of Western Europe' (1966) 95 *Daedalus* 862–915; Bulmer, 'Domestic Politics and European Community Policy-Making' (1983) 21 JCMS 349–363.

[5] As developed by Bache. See *EU Regional Policy: Has the UK Government Succeeded in Playing the Gatekeeper Role over the Domestic Impact of the European Regional Development Fund?*, PhD Thesis, University of Sheffield, 1996.

[6] *Ibid.*

[7] See Moravcsik, 'Preferences and Power in the European Community: A Liberal Intergovernmental Approach' (1993) 31 JCMS 473–524; 1993, Marks, 'Structural Policy and Multilevel Governance in the EC', in Cafruny and Rosenthal (eds), *The Maastricht Debates and Beyond*, Vol. 2 in *The State of the European Community* (Harlow: Longman, 1993), 391–410.

aspects of the Extended Gatekeeper approach for this study can be summarised as follows.

1. EU policy is made in related stages which link initial policy decision to policy outcome. While in practice it can be difficult to distinguish the point in that process where policy initiation ends and implementation begins, for analytical purposes it is helpful to make a distinction between policy making at EU level and the implementation process which is largely a domestic matter (albeit supervised by the Commission).
2. When a Member State perceives its interests to be threatened by an EU policy development it will defend those interests at *all* stages of the policy process at which the threat is identified, including implementation. This is the notion of the Extended Gatekeeper.[8]
3. EU policy making involves a process of bargaining at both the EU level and the implementation stage. To understand the bargaining process, this approach utilises the policy networks approach, the main features of which are summarised below.

The policy networks approach

A policy network is defined as 'a set of relationships between organizations which are involved in policy making and policy implementation, and which are mutually dependent on each other for the resources to achieve their goals'.[9] Rhodes sets out five types of network ranging from tightly integrated policy communities to more loosely coupled issue networks. In between, on what is seen as a continuum, are professional networks, inter-governmental networks and producer networks. At one end of the continuum, policy communities are characterised by:

Stability of relationships, continuity of a highly restrictive membership, vertical interdependence based on shared service delivery responsibilities and insulation from other networks and invariably from the general public (including Parliament). They have a high degree of vertical interdependence and limited horizontal articulation.[10]

At the other end of the continuum, issue networks are distinguished by their large number of participants and limited degree of interdependence. The structure tends to be atomistic, and stability and continuity are 'at a premium'.[11]

---

[8] The definition of a Member State's interests on a particular issue may change over time and may be influenced by a range of actors within and outside government. The Core Executive Studies approach can be applied here; see Dunleavy and Rhodes, 'Core Executive Studies in Britain' (1990) 68 *Public Administration* 3–28.

[9] Rhodes, Bache and George, 'Policy Networks and Policy Making in the European Union' in Hooghe (ed), *European Integration: Cohesion Policy and Subnational Mobilisation* (Oxford: Oxford University Press, 1996) pp. 294–319.

[10] Rhodes, *Beyond Westminster and Whitehall* (London: Unwin Hyman, 1988), p. 78.

[11] *Ibid.*

Professionalised networks are dominated by one class of participant: the profession. In short, 'professionalized networks express the interests of a particular profession and manifest a substantial degree of vertical interdependence whilst insulating themselves from other networks'.[12] The inter-governmental networks Rhodes refers to are those based on the representative organisations of local authorities, while producer networks are distinguished by the prominent role of economic interests.[13]

In the EU policy networks, national governments and other actors will mobilise their resources to secure desired policy objectives within implicit 'rules of the game'. The importance of different types of resources available to governments and other actors may fluctuate across policy sectors and over time. However, constitutional-legal, political, financial and informational resources are generally of importance.[14]

All actors possess resources, though not in equal amounts. The extent to which actors possess and mobilise resources in a given network situation explains why some actors have greater influence. This distribution of resources between networks distinguishes one from another, 'both as between policy sectors within the same political system and between political systems within the same sector'.[15] Finally, policy networks may change over time, 'especially when circumstances change in such a way that the distribution of resources is affected'.[16] It is part of the task of this research to assess whether EC drinking water law has had such an impact on domestic policy networks in the United Kingdom.

EC drinking water law

The original proposal for EC legislation to regulate standards of drinking water quality dates back to 1975. Following difficult and protracted negotiations,[17] the Directive was eventually adopted in 1980. Although the Directive was enacted as a trade harmonisation measure under Article 100 of the Treaty of Rome, it has a basis also in Article 235, promoted as an 'environmental' measure to secure improved public health and with early origins in the First Action Programme on the Environment of 1973.[18] But while the standards require sources of potable supply to be sufficiently free from contamination to allow inexpensive

---

[12] *Ibid.* at pp. 78–79.
[13] *Ibid.* at p. 80.
[14] See further *ibid.* at pp. 77–94.
[15] Bache, George and Rhodes, *op. cit.* note 9.
[16] *Ibid.*
[17] Involving 52 working group meetings. See Krämer, 'The Elaboration of EC Environmental Law', in Winter (ed), *European Environmental Law: A Comparative Perspective* (Aldershot: Dartmouth, 1996), pp. 310–311.
[18] OJ C 112 20.12.73, p. 1.

drinking water treatment,[19] it is also evident, as we discuss below, that the Directive itself has had little *direct* impact on the quality of the natural aquatic environment.[20]

The standards in the Directive are based on, but in some cases exceed, guidelines from the World Health Organisation (WHO) dating from 1970.[21] The Directive lays down 62 different standards (usually Maximum Admissible Concentrations or 'MACs') for water for human consumption or for the purposes of food production, except for natural mineral waters which are covered in other legislation.[22] Non-mandatory guide levels are also set down for 29 of the parameters,[23] while Minimum Recommended Concentrations are set for four parameters in relation to softness of water. Stricter measures may be imposed by Member States.

That the terms of the Directive exceed the then WHO guidelines can be traced to concerns surfacing at the time in relation mainly to pesticides (especially DDT) and nitrate levels. The Directive itself, though, is silent as to how individual parameters were justified.[24] As Faure remarks in relation to organochlorine pesticides:

for practical reasons the standard was set at the minimum concentration . . . that could be detected by the analytical methods available at the time . . . and there was no evidence that the proposed standard was in danger of being exceeded because for many pesticides the level of analytical detection was not sufficiently sensitive.[25]

A number of suggestions have been advanced for explaining the willingness with

---

[19] Ward, Buller and Lowe, *Implementing European Environmental Policy at the Local Level: The British Experience with Water Quality Directives Volume II: Research Report* (1995), p. 97.

[20] Directive 75/444/EEC provides for the classification of surface waters used for drinking water supply, and seeks to ensure that supplies are given sufficient treatment according to quality on abstraction (OJ L 194 25.7.75, p. 26). In England and Wales see the Surface Waters (Classification) Regulations 1989, SI 1989 No. 1148. However, this measure has had little impact on improving the quality of water in the natural environment used for potable supply.

[21] World Health Organisation, *European Standards for Drinking Water*, 2nd ed. (1970).

[22] Directive 80/777/EEC on the approximation of the laws of the Member States relating to the exploitation and marketing of natural mineral waters, OJ L 229, 15.7.80.

[23] It would seem that the UK government is not greatly interested in the guide levels, although the water suppliers are reported as seeking to stay well within the imperative levels, for example by having operating systems alert concentrations well within the MAC (see Ward *et al*, *op. cit.* note 19, p. 117). In relation to the Bathing Water Directive (76/160/EEC), the High Court recently heard from the National Rivers Authority that guideline values stated there were 'not applied by the UK Government', though ultimately the judge decided that the applicants had failed to prove that the NRA had not had regard to them (see *R. v. National Rivers Authority, ex parte Moreton* (1995) *ENDS Report*, Vol. 250, 43–44).

[24] Faure, 'The EC Directive on Drinking Water: Institutional Aspects', in Bergman and Pugh (eds), *Environmental Toxicology, Economics and Institutions* (Dordrecht: Kluwer, 1994), pp. 39–87, at p. 52.

[25] Faure, 'Protecting Drinking Water Quality Against Contamination by Pesticides: An Alternative Regulatory Framework' (1995) 4(4) RECIEL 321–326, at 322.

which the UK government embraced the Directive without internal dissent.[26] Although there were initial concerns about the proposed lead standards and anticipated problems in meeting the nitrate parameter, these did not prevent adoption of a Directive which departed radically from a domestic policy tradition of 'hostility' to statutorily prescribed standards.[27]

One suggestion points to the then widely-held view that non-compliance with agreed provisions would present few legal or political difficulties.[28] Alternatively, it has been suggested that 'the idea that British water might not be clean enough to pass tests which would also have to be met by continentals with supposedly dirtier water probably did not occur to the British Government'.[29] There may be some truth in both views. While the government saw itself as a leader rather than a laggard in the provision of clean water supply, no problems were anticipated in resisting the European Commission should EC standards not be met on time. In the context of its time, this anticipation was perfectly logical, with policy implementation—as against legislative adoption—remaining low on the Commission's agenda during the first ten years of EC environmental policy.[30] Moreover, the five-year period eventually agreed for practical implementation of the 1980 Directive allowed until July 1985 for adjustments, while further room for manoeuvre was given by the possibility of delays and derogations contained within the Directive.

Implementing the 1980 Directive: the UK experience

Formal compliance with the Directive was required by July 1982. In September 1982 the UK government informed the Commission it would implement the Directive through Department of the Environment Circular 20/82. This provided, with reference to minimum standards required under the Directive, the first quantified definition of the term 'wholesome', used to describe water of acceptable drinking quality. Previously, disputes between suppliers and local authorities over the definition of wholesome had been referred to the Secretary

---

[26] Interview with Lord Clinton Davies (1993) 4 *Water Law* 177–179, at 178. More time seems to have been spent contemplating whether water authorities would have sufficient legal powers to enter properties to carry out their monitoring obligations than on how much the Directive would cost to implement: see HC Papers 1975–76, 53–I; 8–xiii; 8–xxxix; and 1978–79, 10–x; and HL Papers 1975–76, 111. At the time, the House of Lords Select Committee on the European Communities looked into the use of Article 100 in questionable areas, for example bathing water and shellfish water quality, but did not question the Directive as being *ultra vires* the powers and objectives of the Treaty of Rome ('Approximation of Laws under Article 100 of the EEC Treaty', Session 1977–78, 22 Report, HL 131, April 1978).

[27] Richardson, Ogus and Burrows, *Policing Pollution: A Study of Regulation and Enforcement* (Oxford: Clarendon, 1982), p. 42.

[28] Richardson, 'EU Water Policy: Uncertain Agendas, Shifting Networks and Complex Coalitions' (1994) 3 *Environmental Politics* 139–167, at 143.

[29] Haigh and Lanigan, 'Impact of the European Union on UK Environmental Policy Making', in Gray (ed), *UK Environmental Policy in the 1990s* (London: Macmillan Press, 1995), pp. 18–37, at p. 22.

[30] *Ibid.* p. 19. See OJ C 127 14.5.84.

of State for judgment. Thus, for the first time, quality standards were prescribed in legally-binding terms to facilitate compliance with the Directive by the then water authorities and existing private water companies in relation to supply, and local authority in relation to monitoring.[31] The provisions of the Directive were later incorporated into the Water Supply (Water Quality) Regulations 1989, made under the Water Act 1989.[32]

No account of the impact of the Directive would be complete without discussion of practical compliance. As noted earlier, an assessment of practical compliance is essential in testing the notion of the Extended Gatekeeper in the drinking water sector. We consider the key issues in regard to actual litigation below, but before this it is necessary to consider the impact of EC water law generally on the UK government's attempt to privatise the water industry in England and Wales. The episode is instructive, serving to illustrate the crucial role of EC law and institutions in national decision-making. But at the same time it also shows the continuing importance of central government, both in negotiating the privatisation legislation with the Commission and in the residual power it has sought to maintain in domestic legal provisions.

Privatisation and the Drinking Water Directive

The requirement formally to comply with the Directive had a considerable impact on the government's plans to privatise the ten water authorities in England and Wales.[33]

In its White Paper of 1986, the government had proposed the transfer of water authorities into the private sector complete with environmental regulatory powers.[34] However, the threat of legal action before the Court of Justice under an Article 177 reference, challenging the proposed status of private water companies as 'competent authorities' for certain water directives, was an obvious threat to a successful flotation.[35] Indeed, civil servants at the Department of the Environment informally approached the then Director of the Council for the Preservation of Rural England—a prominent pressure group which had sought leading counsel's opinion in the matter[36]—to assess the likelihood of

---

[31] Under the Water Act 1973, s. 11. This development is an important part of what Macrory identifies as the new policy formalism pervading UK environmental law, 'Environmental Law: Shifting Discretions and the New Formalism', in Lomas (ed), *Frontiers of Environmental Law* (London: Chancery, 1991), pp. 8–23.

[32] SI 1989 No. 1147 (as amended in 1989 and 1991), made under the Water Act 1989, s. 52. See also the Drinking Water in Containers Regulations 1994 (SI 1994 No. 743), made under the Food Safety Act 1990. Note, however, the important difference between the legal obligation to supply 'wholesome' water, and the offence under s. 70 of the Water Industry Act 1991 of supplying water 'unfit for human consumption'. The latter is a smaller category. Unlike pollution of water in the natural environment (see the Water Resources Act 1991, s. 85(6)), there is no 'technical' offence of breaching drinking water quality limits. There is, in any event, a 'due diligence' defence in relation to drinking water which there is not with water more generally.

[33] Haigh, *Manual of Environmental Law* (London: Longman, looseleaf, updated), 4.4–6.

[34] *Privatisation of the Water Authorities in England and Wales*, Cmnd. 9734 (1986).

[35] See OJ L 129 18.5.86, p. 23.

[36] Jacobs and Shanks, *Joint Advice Re: Water Authority Privatisation* (unpublished opinion).

such an action being brought.[37] The high political salience attached to privatisation forced the government in 1987 to revise its proposals, resulting in the
eventual establishment of the National Rivers Authority (NRA), responsible
for the quality of water in the natural environment, and the Drinking Water
Inspectorate within the Department of the Environment to audit drinking water
quality.[38] In effect, the privatisation programme had been slimmed-down in
response to EC requirements, with only water supply and sewerage services
transferred to the private sector. Moreover, the episode signalled the arrival of
the Commission as a significant actor in UK water policy, a position confirmed
by the government's decision to consult with the Commission over those aspects
of its privatisation legislation relating to the enforcement of drinking water
standards, 'probably the first occasion since Britain's accession to the Community that a UK government had entered into direct negotiations with the
Commission on the proposed details of a major item of its domestic legislation'.[39]

But consultation with the Commission may have failed to produce a satisfactory outcome.[40] Discussions led directly to the more stringent measures in
relation to water company compliance now contained in ss. 18–22 of the Water
Industry Act 1991 in place of rather weaker agreements entered into either
with the Secretary of State or OFWAT, the economic regulator established at
the time of privatisation.[41] In particular, water companies would only avoid
enforcement action if they entered into legally-binding undertakings with the
Secretary of State, rather than weaker agreements which the Water Bill originally
provided for. Following this re-draft, the government announced that outstanding differences with the Commission were settled: they were not. A further
opportunity to meet the terms of the Directive in the form of a House of Lords
amendment seeking to require water companies to comply with the Directive
no later than 1 September 1993 was overturned by the government in the
Commons.[42]

In October 1989 the Commission began proceedings under Article 169 of
the EC Treaty against the government and in November 1992, the Court
of Justice upheld the Commission's complaints in Case C-337/89, *Commission* v.

---

[37] Private correspondence referred to in Maloney and Richardson, *Managing Policy Change in Britain:
The Politics of Water* (Edinburgh: Edinburgh University Press, 1995), p. 67, who also note that the
Department of the Environment did not concede their view on the 'competent authority' question
until late May 1987 (p. 68).

[38] As from 1 April 1996, the National Rivers Authority became part of the Environment Agency for
England and Wales.

[39] Haigh, *op. cit.* note 33, 4.4–6.

[40] Haigh, *op. cit.* note 33, 4.4–9, notes that 'the negotiations were thus highly unusual, involving the
Commission and a Member State in a joint endeavour to arrive at a new implementation timetable
for a Directive whose legally-binding compliance date had long since passed'. The authors use
'may' here because of the uncertainty which will only be resolved by the Court of Justice.

[41] Briefly, these impose a duty on the Secretary of State to make an enforcement order against a
company contravening its legal obligations to supply wholesome water unless he is satisfied that
the contravention is trivial, that his general environmental and other obligations preclude him
from doing so, or the company has given, and is complying with, an undertaking.

[42] Haigh, *op. cit.* note 33, 4.4–6.

United Kingdom.[43] The government was found in breach of its obligations under the Directive by failing to ensure that water used for food production purposes was covered by the 1989 implementing regulations, and by failing to comply with the MAC for nitrate in 28 supply zones in England.[44] This was the first time that the United Kingdom had been found to be in breach of an 'environmental' directive, but equally important was its finding in relation to practical compliance, an area until then 'not fully explored by the Court's jurisprudence'.[45] The Court of Justice held that practical compliance is an absolute obligation, subject only to those derogations allowed in the Directive which the government was, in any case, time-barred from relying upon.[46]

While the privatisation programme was in part responsible for the government's reluctance to implement the Directive, it was the threat posed to privatisation by the Directive that ultimately furthered UK compliance. On the one hand, the financial costs of implementation threatened successful privatisation. The soon to be privatised water authorities were already committed to a multi-billion pound investment programme. This made the spreading of capital costs over time, to bring drinking water up to EC standards, a priority wherever possible. On the other hand, the risk that legal action over non-compliance might delay and ultimately frustrate privatisation secured government acceptance of the Commission's view of sampling for MACs in the Directive, an interpretation previously seen by the Department of the Environment as scientifically indefensible.[47]

The legal impact of the Directive

The prescription of mandatory standards for drinking water in the United Kingdom has both provided information and encouraged debate on the issue. Beyond this, however, the possibility of actions in both public and private law have opened up. Concerned individuals and organisations have been able to bring actions in public law to seek compliance with standards imposed under the Directive, which the European Court of Justice in Case C-337/89, *Commission v. UK*[48] clearly found as being directly effective. *Francovich*-type actions against the UK for damages consequent to infringement of rights following improper

---

[43] [1993] *Water Law* 59, (1993) JEL Vol. 5, No. 2, 273; see also comment by Holder and Elworthy at (1994) 31 CML Rev 123–135.

[44] The omission concerning food production was rectified by the Food Safety Act 1990. The government avoided an adverse ruling in relation to lead levels at 17 supply zones in Scotland because of the lack of precision over the obligation in this respect.

[45] Somsen [1993] *Water Law* 59–62, at 62.

[46] Directive, Articles 9, 10 and 20.

[47] (1987) *ENDS Report* Vol. 154, 9–10 and (1987) *ENDS Report* Vol. 155, 19–20, cited by Maloney and Richardson, *op. cit.* note 37, p. 66.

[48] *Op. cit.* note 43.

implementation would also seem possible, though causation may be difficult to establish.[49]

However, a legal action by Friends of the Earth highlights the present state of the law in relation to public law challenges over alleged non-compliance with EC drinking water standards. Subsequent to Case C-337/89, *Commission* v. *United Kingdom*, Friends of the Earth sought judicial review of the decision of the Secretary of State to accept undertakings from the water companies concerned, rather than bring enforcement action.[50] Despite the earlier ruling of the Court of Justice on the breach by the United Kingdom of its *primary* obligations under the Directive, however, the Court of Appeal held that the *secondary* duty to comply with the judgment of the European Court of Justice was not absolute but could be qualified by practical considerations. The Court was not persuaded that the government's obligations extended further than securing the agreement of the water companies to the undertakings entered into, for example by overriding existing planning legislation. However, as Hilson points out, less drastic measures might have been contemplated, for example the designation of water protection zones under s. 93 of the Water Resources Act 1991 or other, perhaps fiscal, measures for reducing nitrate levels to prescribed maxima in supplies.[51] The Court of Appeal accepted that meeting EC requirements remained the government's policy objective and it would ultimately comply with the obligations of the Directive. Perhaps especially at first instance, there was insufficient evidence to support the argument that compliance could be achieved faster than as provided for through undertakings.[52] Although speedier implementation was essentially a matter of political will, the decision leaves the compliance timetable in the control of the Secretary of State, subject to action by the Commission under Article 171 of the EC Treaty (Maastricht amendments to which have empowered the Commission to set Member States a timetable for compliance with their legal obligations, backed by possible financial penalties). However, as Hilson notes, there are 'no signs' as yet of the Commission taking this path:

At a time when the legitimacy of the Community order has been under close scrutiny and relations between the UK and the rest of the Community delicate, it would be understandable if, whilst the Commission felt safe in securing a one-off Article 169 judgement against the UK, it was not tempted to use Article 171 to order politically controversial action to achieve full compliance with Community drinking water standards.[53]

---

[49] Elworthy and Holder, 'Blue Babies, Gastric Cancers and Green Ponds: The Law's Response to the Nitrate Problem' (1996) *Int J Biosciences L* Vol. 1, No. 1, 69–90.

[50] See text accompanying note 41.

[51] See [1996] 1 CMLR 117, and further comment by Hilson, (1995) 32 CML Rev 1461, at 1467.

[52] Hilson, *op. cit.* note 51, at 1466.

[53] *Ibid.* at 1473. Significantly, recent action by the Commission in bringing out of abeyance proceedings against the United Kingdom in relation to breaches of the pesticide parameter—a reasoned opinion was issued in July 1993—suggest that such a course of action may well now be in the contemplation of the Commission (see note 66 below) since, as Hilson notes (see note 51 above, at 1474), an Article 169 action in relation to pesticides is, following *Ex parte Friends of the Earth*, 'somewhat redundant' unless taken as a necessary preliminary to action under Article 171.

Disputes over domestic arrangements for complying with EC standards are therefore likely to remain a feature of the implementation process. This is true not only for the United Kingdom, but also in most other Member States where nitrates and pesticides are used, to varying degrees, to maximise agricultural productivity.

The possibility of actions in private law pursuant to the Directive is best illustrated in *Cambridge Water Co.* v. *Eastern Counties Leather.*[54] There, the plaintiffs were forced to relocate an abstraction point for potable supply after the coming into force of the Directive made it impossible for supplies to comply with quality standards. Although ultimately unsuccessful in nuisance, negligence and the rule in *Rylands* v. *Fletcher,* due to the absence of foreseeability of damage at the time the chemicals were spilled at the defendant's tannery, the House of Lords did establish damage on the basis of the parameters of the Directive. The ensuing litigation also contributed to significant advancements in scientific understanding of the pathways of chemicals below ground.[55] However, *Cambridge Water* also provides a good example not only of how actions can be brought in tort further to the Directive, but also the limitations both of what is essentially a product quality directive and existing private law in securing environmental improvement. Had the water company succeeded in its action, damages sufficient to pay for the costs of relocation of its borehole would have been awarded, leaving the groundwater as contaminated as it was before private legal action was begun. Also, while the principal legal obligation under the Directive is merely to supply water of an acceptable standard up to the stopcock, this may not in itself be sufficient to avoid successful claims in negligence.[56] This may be particularly important in relation to instances of exceeding the revised lead parameter where this is due to customers' lead pipes.

Private prosecutions, however, are in principle ruled out by the Water Industry Act 1991 which assigns the right to prosecute for breaches of drinking water quality to the Secretary of State or the Director of Public Prosecutions. This compares with the general right to bring a private prosecution under the Water Resources Act 1991 for pollution of water in the natural environment, and

---

[54] [1994] 1 All ER 53.

[55] *Ibid.* at 65.

[56] *Read* v. *Croydon Corporation* [1938] 4 All ER 631. It might be argued, following *Budden and Albery* v. *BP Oil* [1980] JPL 586, that an action in negligence must fail where the defendant has acted in accordance with statutory standards. There, two oil companies were sued for using lead in petrol. Regulations prescribing the lead content in petrol had validly been made by the Secretary of State in 1976. The court held that, if the companies were liable and subject to injunctions limiting the lead content in their petrol to a level below that set under the Act, then 'The courts would thus necessarily be, in effect, laying down a permissible limit which would be of universal application and inconsistent with the permissible limit prescribed by Parliament. That would result in a wholly unacceptable constitutional anomaly. The authority of Parliament must prevail.' The statutory standard therefore set the common law standard in negligence. This case may be subject to criticism because it is not apparent from the enabling legislation (Control of Pollution Act 1974, s. 75) that Parliament intended to give a statutory defence to air polluters in respect of their common law liabilities. The point seems to turn on whether the Directive applies to the quality of water at the stopcock or at the customer's tap, a matter that has yet to come before the European Court of Justice.

sheds light on the role of the Drinking Water Inspectorate. Despite the government having originally recommended that 'on balance' its functions should be
transferred to the Environment Agency, the decision eventually taken was to
leave it within the Department of the Environment. There, it remains a small
unit without any legislative identity, responsible for auditing the water companies monitoring and reporting functions, and overseeing undertakings
entered into to secure compliance. In doing so it has exceeded that which is
required under the Directive, its Annual Reports being 'invaluable resources,
not only to environmental pressure groups with an interest in water quality
issues, but also to the water industry, public policy makers and the research
community'.[57] However, the Inspectorate may only recommend enforcement
action to the Secretary of State, giving enforcement a more 'political' quality
than, for example, the prosecution by the Environment Agency of a privatised
water company for breaching water pollution provisions of the Water Resources
Act 1991. By April 1997, only six prosecutions had been brought in relation to
drinking water quality, two 'technical' offences under the 1989 Regulations and
four prosecutions under s. 70 of the Water Industry Act 1991 for supplying
water 'unfit for human consumption' (of which, three actions were successful
and one action was pending). Despite evidential problems in proving epidemiol-
ogically that the water is 'unfit for human consumption' it might be queried
whether this approach to enforcement would have been followed had responsibility been exercised by a body more detached from the Department of the
Environment. In any event, the enforcement provisions established in the Water
Act 1989 are themselves revealing of government policy in this area.

Practical implications of the Directive

The EC approach to drinking water regulation expressed through the Directive
has changed long-standing British practice. Tighter regulatory controls over
water supply companies have been required, with more stringent regulatory
powers to be sought by the Commission in forthcoming proceedings.[58] A
number of developments have raised not only the quality of drinking water but
also its political salience: the shift from negotiated definitions of water quality
to precise quantifiable definitions based on MACs; improvements in sampling
methods; publicising of water quality data; and improvement programmes for
pesticide and nitrate levels in drinking water. In relation to the last of these,
the Directive not only raised the profile of an issue which had previously been
off the political agenda,[59] but has made information available to those keen to
see the issue resolved.[60]

---

[57] Ward *et al*, *op. cit.* note 19, p. 124.
[58] See note 53 above.
[59] Hill, Aaronvitch and Baldock, 'Non-decision Making in Pollution Control in Britain: Nitrate
Pollution, the EEC Drinking Water Directive and Agriculture' (1989) 17 *Policy and Politics* 227–240.
[60] Ward *et al*, *op. cit.* note 19, p. 106.

In addition to these, there has been a substantial financial cost to implementing the Directive in the United Kingdom. Although the precise cost is unclear, one estimate placed the amount spent on improvement programmes agreed since 1989 and due to be completed by 1995 at around £2 billion.[61] While some of this spending was a result of under-investment before privatisation, EC legislation has at least influenced the nature and pace of new investment, the Directive contributing to the range of water directives which, together, have necessitated investment programmes of around £30 billion since privatisation.[62]

It would be difficult to justify such measures without environmental (including public health) benefits, and there is general acceptance that the Directive has played an important part in raising the quality of drinking water in the United Kingdom. The latest report of the Drinking Water Inspectorate, for example, notes that 99.5% of all samples taken complied with EC standards, as well as additional standards set at national level.[63] This compares favourably with results of monitoring in previous years,[64] with increases in non-compliance with certain parameters such as polyaromatic hydrocarbons accounted for by additional and more focused monitoring. Other than one-off or trivial breaches, most failures are subject to water company improvement programmes. However interest groups, notably Friends of the Earth, continue to assert that a substantial proportion of British consumers are drinking water that does not meet EC standards, highlighting those areas where individual parameters—notably nitrates and pesticides—are exceeded rather than overall compliance.[65] This has recently received support from the Commission, which has described official composite UK statistics as 'not a useful figure'.[66]

Concerns over nitrate levels have been met in part by provision for Nitrate Sensitive Areas, originally under the Water Act 1989, and a positive British response to the Nitrates Directive 1991.[67] However, the government has been criticised for implementing the Nitrates Directive only in relation to areas linked to drinking water supplies and not, as the Directive envisages, to all inland water where nitrate concentrations are likely to exceed the agreed levels. Thus, 68 Nitrate Vulnerable Zones (NVZs) have been designated to contribute to the

---

[61] Reference cited in Ward *et al*, *op. cit.* note 19, at pp. 111–114.

[62] See, for example, Haigh, *op. cit.* note 33, 4.1–5.

[63] Department of the Environment/Welsh Office, *Drinking Water 1995: A Report by the Chief Inspector, Drinking Water Inspectorate* (1996).

[64] The first report of the Drinking Water Inspectorate for 1990 found compliance to be 99%, a figure which dropped slightly in 1991 before improving steadily since then.

[65] See, for example, 'Poison on tap: The first region by region guide to your drinking water', *The Observer Magazine*, 6 August 1989. The latest report of the Drinking Water Inspectorate states that 85.4% of water supply zones complied with the total pesticides standard, with 69.4% compliance for individual pesticides; *op. cit.* note 63, p. 189.

[66] 'EU Lands Court Challenge on British', Reuters Press Release, 28 June 1996. Certain methodological and legal difficulties also exist. No allowance is made in the statistics for breaches of standards which are subject to derogations under reg. 4 of the 1989 Regulations implementing Articles 9 and 10 of the Directive (see [1993] *Water Law* 192–193).

[67] Directive 91/676/EEC on the protection of waters against nitrate pollution from agricultural sources, OJ L 375 31.12.91, p. 1. See now the Protection of Waters Against Agricultural Nitrate Pollution (England and Wales) Regulations 1996 (SI 1996 No. 888), and also SI 1996 No. 908.

lowering of nitrate levels in drinking water, in contrast to, for example, the Netherlands and Denmark where the whole country is designated as a NVZ on the grounds also of preventing environmental harm through eutrophication.[68] In effect, as Elworthy and Holder remark, the government has treated the Nitrates Directive 'solely as a drinking water directive'.[69]

It is doubtful whether the Nitrates Directive would have been agreed when it was, without the prominence of contamination of water supplies by nitrates given by the 1980 Directive. Prior to the 1980 Directive, nitrate levels in UK drinking water supplies were inadequately measured, problems were neither widely recognised nor their severity appreciated, and there was little policy response. The Directive thus defined a problem otherwise unacknowledged, leading in time to further action beyond nitrate levels in water for human supply.[70] However, as Ward *et al* note, compliance with MACs has largely been through the blending of supplies from sources of high and low levels of key parameters (especially nitrate) and the opening up of new sources of supply.[71] In their detailed field study in the area of South West Water, they noted that the Directive 'has not stimulated any major regulatory moves to improve the quality of raw water sources'.[72] It may be argued, therefore, that the Directive has had little *direct* impact on the quality of water in the natural environment. It has, however, raised the visibility of certain pollutants in the environment, contributing in no small measure to further EC legislation of a more preventive nature in relation to nitrates and pesticides.[73]

Political impact of the Directive

EC drinking water law has had a number of impacts on the policy networks through which water policy is made in the United Kingdom. In particular, EC legislation has brought new issues on to the political agenda, brought new actors into the networks, affected the distribution of resources within the networks, and increased the information available to non-governmental actors. Public awareness of drinking water quality issues in particular has increased.

Whereas 'non-decision-making' was a regular feature of the UK water policy making process before EC involvement, legislative proposals for directives now 'accelerate[s] the arrival of their subject on to the political agenda, even where the proposal is relatively invisible and so not the source of public disquiet and

---

[68] See [1996] *Water Law* 71–73, at 72.
[69] See note 49 above, at 86. This may be explicable by the relatively low incidence or severity of eutrophication in the UK compared to other Member States, but Holder and Elworthy suggest a better explanation is a compartmentalised approach to public health and environmental protection that has yet to be broken down.
[70] Hill, Aaronvitch and Baldock, *op. cit.* note 59.
[71] Ward *et al, op. cit.* note 19. The *Cambridge Water* case is a good example of this, see note 54 above.
[72] Ward *et al, op. cit.* note 19, p. 135.
[73] Further measures are proposed in relation to the marketing of biocides; see COM(96) 312 final, on which the Council reached a common position on 20 December 1996.

pressure'.[74] Moreover, in relation to network change, Rhodes had previously characterised the water sector as a professionalised network 'wherein the constraints on water engineers seem particularly weak'.[75] But increased participation has now complicated matters:

water policy is now more complex and less predictable and water policy is characterized by numerous cross-sectoral linkages. The number of policy actors who might participate in some aspect of water policy is now potentially in the hundreds rather than the tens.[76]

The task of evaluating the impact of EC legislation on drinking water policy networks in England and Wales is complicated by the impact of other processes which have overlapped, the most important of these being privatisation. However, EC legislation has been instrumental in empowering interest groups within the policy networks, an important source of network change. The incorporation into UK law of the European regulatory approach of setting standards for drinking water quality has provided all actors with new informational resources, but in particular this development 'has opened up the issue to greater scrutiny by environmental pressure groups and the adversarial style of political debate they bring'.[77] Consequently, 'the traditional British approach to environmental management, characterised by flexibility, pragmatism and closed policy communities, has been on the wane'.[78]

By monitoring the implementation of EC law, environmental interest groups have become an important force at the implementation stage of the UK water policy process. By 1990, for example, one-third of all complaints made to the Commission about breaches of environmental directives were originating from the United Kingdom.[79] Interest groups were establishing their own monitoring systems, providing the otherwise 'information-starved DGXI officials'[80] with data on breaches about which it would otherwise have remained ignorant.[81]

In addition to monitoring implementation, interest groups have a significant role in shaping the policy agenda, both at national and particularly EC level. Again, EC involvement is clearly important here with the environment being 'perhaps the classic example of an issue having higher priority in Europe than in Britain and of the EC's agenda being influenced by certain enthusiastic

---

[74] Haigh and Lanigan, *op. cit.* note 29, p. 29.
[75] Rhodes, *op. cit.* note 10, pp. 78–79.
[76] Maloney and Richardson, *op. cit.* note 37, p. 161.
[77] Ward *et al*, *op. cit.* note 19, p. 124.
[78] *Ibid.*
[79] Haigh and Lanigan, *op. cit.* note 29, at p. 26.
[80] *Ibid.* at p. 29.
[81] Friends of the Earth were instrumental in reporting breaches of the Directive to the Commission, for example in relation to the government's failure to implement the Directive in relation to private water supplies. This prompted an Article 169 letter from the Commission in June 1987, leading eventually to the Private Water Supplies Regulations 1991 (SI 1991 No. 2790). Following the decision of the Court of Justice in Case C-42/89, *Commission* v. *Belgium* [1992] 1 CMLR 22, the Regulations are no longer applied to private supplies serving only a single dwelling.

actors'.[82] In short, interest groups are now consulted more widely on legislative proposals, monitor policy implementation and respond to breaches of directives by informing the Commission and, where necessary, through legal action.

In carrying out this role, interest groups both inform and feed off public opinion on environmental matters. Here also, the Directive has been important. By prescribing explicit quantitative standards, raised in political salience by privatisation, the Directive brought under the spotlight not merely issues in relation to the benefits of cleaner water, but as importantly the costs of supplying such water and on whom such costs should fall.[83]

The Directive has therefore contributed towards shifting water policy making away from the closed confines of the professionalised network, placing it in a policy arena which is more open to scrutiny and to participation. As Maloney and Richardson put it, 'Making policy in a goldfish bowl is a more accurate analogy than the old description of water policy as the private management of public business.'[84]

Recent developments

For some, EC water policy 'has become some kind of litmus test in the debate between federalists and anti-federalists as they battle over the future of the Union'.[85] As part of the move towards revision of EC environmental directives in line with its commitment to the principle of subsidiarity,[86] the Commission hosted a conference on the 1980 Directive in September 1993 to discuss revisions in the light of improved technical knowledge and scientific understanding.[87] When published in early 1995, Commission proposals for a revised directive allayed initial fears that the Directive might be wholly 'repatriated' to Member States.[88] Under the draft directive, to be adopted under Article 130s as an environmental measure for the protection of human health, the number of mandatory parameters is to be reduced from 62 to 44, allowing Member States to set standards for additional parameters or higher standards for existing ones, subject to Commission oversight. While the existing standards for nitrates and individual pesticides would remain, the cumulative standard for all pesticides would be removed. Moreover, the proposed five-fold reduction in the permitted lead level would account for the overwhelming majority of the 70 billion ECU estimated total cost to Member States of compliance. The cost of

[82] Mazey and Richardson, 'British Pressure Groups in the European Community' (1992) 45 *Parliamentary Affairs* 92–107, at 99.
[83] See, for example, Office of Water Services, *Paying for Quality: The Political Perspective* (1993).
[84] Maloney and Richardson, *op. cit.* note 37, p. 168.
[85] Richardson, *op. cit.* note 28, at 140.
[86] Cf. Freestone and Somsen, Chapter 6 above.
[87] Richardson, *op. cit.* note 28, at 152.
[88] COM(94) 612 final, OJ 1995 C 131, p. 5. The government's pre-draft position was set out in a 'non-paper' leaked to Friends of the Earth in 1993 ((1993) *ENDS Report* No. 224, 37–38); see also [1993] *Water Law* 190–191.

compliance in the United Kingdom has been estimated at around £8 billion, spread over 15 years.[89]

The draft directive would give Member States greater scope for derogations from chemical parameters. Although derogations would still not be able to constitute a potential danger to human health, it would no longer be necessary to show, as the United Kingdom failed to do before the Court of Justice, that derogations were necessary because of 'situations arising from the nature and structure of the ground', from 'exceptional meteorological conditions' or in 'times of emergency'.[90] Instead, under Article 10 of the draft directive, the Member State at most need only specify the reason for its derogation. This proposal was welcomed by the Department of the Environment and would give central government and the water companies greater flexibility in organising programmes for water quality remediation.[91]

The Commission's proposals have been backed by the House of Lords Select Committee on the European Communities. But central government continues to object to much of the detail, questioning in particular the justification for many chemical parameters and citing support for the most recent WHO guidelines which, in many instances, are more flexible than those provided for in the Commission's proposals.[92] Even if more flexible individual parameters are not eventually adopted, it may be that the new Article 10 will provide the UK government with greater flexibility in implementing measures than it enjoyed under the original Directive. Moreover, while timetabled plans for remedial work are required, the draft directive does not stipulate maximum periods within which work must be completed, calling into question the strictness of the dates for practical compliance.

Thus, while proposed changes to the Directive would not lead to a repatriation of control over drinking water standards to Member States, there are indications of a loosening of Commission control. As the proposals have yet to be agreed in the Council of Ministers, the precise nature of the revised directive remains uncertain. In any event, the real test of its significance will only be revealed fully at the implementation stage.

Concluding discussion

A dominant feature of the implementation of the 1980 Directive in the United Kingdom has been that of the government seeking to minimise unwanted regulation while others in the policy network have sought to maximise environmental protection. The main problem for the government in seeking to play

---

[89] House of Lords Select Committee on the European Communities, *Drinking Water*, Session 1995–96, Fourth Report, HL Paper 31.
[90] Directive, Articles 9.1(a), 9.1(b), 10.1.
[91] Further Evidence from the Department of the Environment, *op. cit.* note 89, p. 17.
[92] Department of the Environment, *The Government Response to the Report of the Select Committee on the European Communities on COM(94) 612 Final*, April 1996.

this Extended Gatekeeper role was its own lack of vigilance when the Directive was originally agreed. As Maloney and Richardson put it, 'current difficulties are due to lack of foresight by Britain at the policy formulation and policy decision phases of the European policy process'.[93]

As we have seen, the government of the day did not see a threat to its ability to decide and control policy so the Gatekeeper role lay dormant until the real challenge became apparent. By this time, other actors in the network had accumulated resources which constrained the government's ability to perform this role. Of particular importance were the constitutional-legal resources the Commission was able to use to further compliance, including the resources of environmental interest groups, despite itself being severely understaffed at the time.[94] That the Directive is relatively precise in its requirements for compliance has been decisive in this. This contrasts with the study of structural policy in which the vagueness of EC regulations facilitated non-compliance.[95] But it also contrasts with many pollution control directives where provision for area designation has often been used as a 'half-way house' between emission limits and environmental quality objectives. In these instances, subject to often stringent judicial oversight,[96] central government has often been able to implement EC legislation within relatively wide parameters.

In addition to contributing to a shift in the balance of constitutional-legal resources away from central government, the Directive has also spread the balance of informational resources more evenly. The main feature of this development has been the empowerment of environmental interest groups at the expense of central government and water companies who must now operate aware that their actions can be effectively monitored.

Central government has also had to concede political resources to other actors, notably the Commission and interest groups, who are now regarded as legitimate players in the UK water policy sector and whose views must be considered. In this case, the shift in constitutional-legal and informational resources has had a direct effect on the resources of political legitimacy. Combined, the shift of resources away from central government has limited its ability to play the Extended Gatekeeper role over drinking water policy largely to that of delaying the practical implementation of measures rather than blocking them, an approach which may itself be restricted following proceedings before the European Court of Justice under Articles 169 and 171.

However, if the relatively precise requirements of the Directive were decisive in tipping the balance of resources sufficiently away from the Extended Gate-

---

[93] Maloney and Richardson, *op. cit.* note 37, p. 145.
[94] Krämer, *Focus on European Environmental Law* (London: Sweet & Maxwell, 1992), p. 219.
[95] Bache, *op. cit.* note 5.
[96] See, for example, Case C-56/90, *Commission* v. *UK* (1994) JEL Vol. 6, No. 1, 125; Case C-355/90, *Commission* v. *Spain* [1993] *Water Law* 209. At national level see *R.* v. *Secretary of State for the Environment, ex parte Kingston-upon-Hull City Council*, linked with *R.* v. *Secretary of State for the Environment, ex parte Bristol City Council and Woodspring District Council* (1996) JEL Vol. 8, No. 2, 336. See now also the decision of the European Court of Justice in Case C-44/95, *R* v. *Secretary of State for the Environment, ex parte RSPB*, [1997] 2 WLR 123.

keeper for policy implementation to be secured, recent developments indicate that national governments have learned from this experience. The subsidiarity principle has been used by Member States as an argument for repatriating some control over water policy and while the draft directive suggests this may be limited, the direction of this proposal is clearly towards greater flexibility for national governments in implementing water policy. Moreover, while it is fair to argue that the 'Europeanisation' of the UK water policy sector has had the general impact of reducing the control of central government, and has been described as the 'best example of the erosion of national autonomy',[97] this process should not be exaggerated. Even without increased flexibility in the revised directive, the Department of the Environment still plays a central role in implementing directives, the central role in the negotiation of new provisions, and retains strong control over the bringing of enforcement proceedings.

To summarise, the EC's involvement in drinking water policy has had a clear impact in legal, practical and political terms. The most prominent characteristic of this impact has been the erosion of national autonomy. However, the water sector is not insulated from other developments in the EC and in a context in which national governments are attempting to assert more control, it is possible that the near future may be characterised by a shift back towards greater national autonomy. If enacted, the revised directive may facilitate that process, although at this stage its implications are not clear.[98]

In their study of water policy in the United Kingdom, Maloney and Richardson concluded that ' "Europeanisation" is certain to continue to present a strong challenge to Britain and it seems safe to predict that a continuation of the erosion of national autonomy will continue'.[99] While we can endorse the first part of this argument, at this particular stage of uncertainty over drinking water policy specifically and the direction of EC politics more generally, we would be more cautious in predicting that erosion of national autonomy will continue to be a feature of the water sector in the immediate future.

---

[97] Maloney and Richardson, *op. cit.* note 37, p. 169.
[98] As at April 1997, little progress had been made with the draft Directive, though it had received its reading, under the cooperation procedure, in the European Parliament. The 1980 Directive is not affected by recent proposals for a Water Resources Framework: see COM(96) 59 final.
[99] *Ibid.* at p. 157.

Chapter 10

THE IMPACT OF EC ENVIRONMENTAL LAW ON LAW AND PRACTICE RELATING TO MARINE AND COASTAL WATERS

Lynda M Warren

Introduction

The seas adjacent to a coastal state comprise an important asset for that state. This is especially true for an island nation such as the United Kingdom. We use the seas for a variety of different purposes, each of which has come to be influenced to some extent by the effect of environmental laws emanating from Europe. The most obvious impact of EC law on the use of the seas around Britain is that of the Common Fisheries Policy. Although its stated objective is to preserve fish stocks by limiting catches, the Common Fisheries Policy is as much about resource allocation. Recent disputes over access to British fishing grounds by Spanish fleets[1] is indicative of the surrender of sovereignty over fisheries resources. While stock conservation certainly overlaps with environmental policy, the Common Fisheries Policy is not, at heart, an environmental law measure. It will not, therefore, be considered further in this chapter.

The conservation of biodiversity is, however, of direct relevance to this chapter. Two directives, the Birds Directive[2] and the Habitats Directive,[3] have had (and will continue to have) a marked effect on the UK approach to protected areas. Both are dealt with in detail elsewhere in this book, but are considered here in the context of marine habitats and species.

The use of the seas as a waste repository is both traditional and, probably, universal to those communities with appropriate access. What is slightly unusual about the British position on this practice is its lingering reluctance to accept that using the sea and sea bed in this way is not a valid environmental option. This is a subject area where the EC has had a profound effect on UK policy

---

[1] Case C-213/89, *R* v. *Secretary of State for Transport, ex parte Factortame* [1991] 1 All ER 70.
[2] Council Directive 79/409/EEC on the conservation of wild birds OJ 1979 L 103, p. 1.
[3] Council Directive 92/43/EEC on the conservation of natural habitats and of wild fauna and flora OJ 1992 L 206, p. 7.

and practice. Without the push from other Member States, the United Kingdom would probably still be putting complete faith in the principle of dilution as the solution to pollution. The biggest impact will come when the Urban Waste Water Treatment Directive[4] is fully implemented but the process of changing British practice dates back to the late 1970s and the Bathing Water Directive,[5] both of which are considered in detail below. Sea water quality is, of course, also heavily influenced by land-based pollution. EC legislation on water quality has clearly had an indirect impact on the level of pollution of sea water but these measures are best discussed in the context of freshwater pollution law.

The British economy is heavily dependent on the service sector. Tourism forms an important part of this sector and the recreational use of the coastal environment is crucial to the well-being of many seaside towns. Reference has already been made to the Bathing Water Directive. In the 20 years since it was adopted, the concept of categorising beaches according to their quality has broadened to encompass other characteristics such as amenity. Providing an attractive environment for the tourist is as important as providing clean water. This is largely achieved through appropriate physical planning. Planning policy and practice is an area that has always centred at the domestic, rather than the European level, before the concept of subsidiarity was even considered as a principle and EC influence on planning law has been mainly restricted to the introduction of environmental assessment procedures.[6] The Fifth Environmental Action Programme[7] makes specific reference to the management of coastal zones, however, and the issue of integrated coastal zone management, incorporating an element of physical planning, is currently being considered at EC level.

Finally, the sea provides a major trade route, especially for a maritime nation such as the United Kingdom. The importance of EC law in this aspect of marine activities is secondary to that of international law. Nevertheless, the EC has taken initiatives in matters of ship design and in identifying the needs for special measures in environmentally sensitive areas, both of which are considered below.

The Bathing Water Directive

The Bathing Water Directive was adopted in the days before the EC had given itself explicit environmental competence and was, therefore, justified as a measure on grounds of human health and distortion of trade. Its main objective was to protect the environment and public health through the reduction of pollution of bathing water and the protection of such waters from further

---

[4] Council Directive 91/271/EEC concerning urban waste water treatment OJ 1991 L 135, p. 40.
[5] Council Directive 76/160/EEC concerning the quality of bathing water OJ 1976 L 31, p. 1.
[6] Note, however, that Council Directive 85/537/EEC on the assessment of the effect of certain public and private projects (the Environmental Impact Assessment Directive) OJ 1985 L 175, p. 40 covers some maritime activities such as marine aggregate extraction.
[7] OJ 1993 C 138, p. 5, para. 5.6.

deterioration. Although not expressly a marine directive, it has had its greatest impact in this country on coastal sites. The Directive requires Member States to identify bathing waters and to test them against a list of 19 microbiological, physical and chemical parameters. A bathing water is defined, *inter alia*, as sea water in which bathing is not prohibited and is traditionally practised by a large number of bathers.[8] For most of the parameters there are quantitative values, some of which are imperative (I) and others guide (G) values. An individual bathing water passes or fails to comply—that is to meet the desired bathing water quality—if more than a specified number of samples exceed imperative or guide limits. The Directive includes some information on sampling procedures (e.g. frequency and sample depth) but does not lay down a sampling regime as such. The five microbiological parameters have attracted the greatest interest. They are designed to provide an indication of the presence of pathogens arising from sewage contamination. The most important of these parameters are total coliform and faecal coliform concentrations for which there are both I and G values. Faecal streptococci have a guide value only. Any presence of salmonella or enteroviruses constitutes a failure (I = 0) but there is not a mandatory requirement to test for these in all samples. The physicochemical parameters include colour and transparency, oxygen and nitrogen concentrations and the presence of pollutants such as pesticides and heavy metals. For most of these no I or G values are specified.

The UK government's initial response to the Directive probably did much to foster the image of this country as the dirty man of Europe.[9] Only 27 bathing waters were identified compared with about 1000 in France and in Italy. Even landlocked Luxembourg had 39.[10] Furthermore, most of the designated sites were in areas of low population such as Cornwall. None of the major holiday resorts such as Blackpool or Brighton was included. The failure to identify obvious bathing waters led to infraction proceedings before the European Court of Justice.[11] As a consequence, further sites were identified and the current list numbers over 400. The cynic could be forgiven for concluding that the original procedure to identify sites had been devised with the intention of excluding those sites that were likely to fail because of the input of raw sewage.

The government never made any secret of the fact that it considered the Directive to be flawed scientifically[12] so it is not surprising that it was not wholehearted in its support. The pathogens that cause human disease are not microbes that are easy to test for. Instead, the Directive adopts an indicative test of measuring faecal coliforms. In the government's view, however, there is no clear correlation between the concentrations of the different microbes.

---

[8] Article 1.
[9] See, for example, the comments of the House of Commons Environment Committee in its Report on the *Pollution of Beaches*, Session 1989–90, Fourth Report, 1990, Vol. 1., HC Paper 12-I, para. 19.
[10] HL Deb [564] Col. 699, *per* Lord Clinton-Davis.
[11] Case C-56/90, *Commission* v. *United Kingdom* [1994] 1 CMLR 769.
[12] See, for example, *The Government's Response to the Fourth Report from the House of Commons Select Committee on the Environment*, Cm. 1363 (London: HMSO 1990), ch. 2.

Viruses are especially problematic because they are so difficult to test for and because they behave very differently from bacteria in seawater, making any predicted correlation far less reliable.

Leaving aside concerns over the test criteria, the government had a more fundamental reservation about the Directive in that it questioned the link between sewage pollution and ill health. While it fully accepted that swimming in sewage contaminated water was repugnant aesthetically, it did not accept that it had significant adverse effects on public health.[13] It is understandable, then, that the government was unenthusiastic and sought a minimalist approach, given the enormous costs of reducing sewage pollution of seawater.

The image of a country that was trying to avoid compliance remained even after more beaches had been identified. Campaigning groups such as the Marine Conservation Society and Surfers Against Sewage were not convinced by the reports of gradually improving standards and argued that sampling regimes could distort the true picture. The government naturally denied all of this but also expressed the view that comparisons between Member States were meaningless because of the variation between sampling regimes and test techniques.

Despite these serious misgivings with the Directive, however, the government's policy has been to work towards compliance of all identified sites while at the same time pressing for changes in the legislation. The record has been impressive. From figures of 67% compliance in 1981 (one of the worst in Europe by some 20%) results have improved to 90% compliance in 1995. Further improvement is expected when the projects instigated under the Urban Waste Water Treatment Directive are up and running.

The change in official attitude must be, at least partly, due to the adverse media attention attracted by tales of dirty water and mystery illnesses. The Good Beach Guide produced by the Marine Conservation Society[14] made a full list of beaches and their quality available to the general public. Local authorities whose beaches were criticised joined the environmentalists in the push for a clean-up. The amenity award schemes such as the European Blue Flag Award[15] and the Seaside Award[16] gained government support. In the course of just ten years beach quality has been turned around from being an irrelevant nuisance to a marketable asset. At the same time, however, the government has continued to question the public health benefits of cleaning up seawater. Following several incidents in south Wales, it commissioned epidemiological research

---

[13] According to the House of Commons Environment Committee, the view dates from a Public Health Laboratory Service Study in the 1950s. *Op. cit.* note 12, para. 24.

[14] First published in 1988.

[15] This scheme, devised by the Federation of Environmental Education in Europe, is administered in the United Kingdom by the Tidy Britain Group. Flags are awarded for beaches complying with guide values for microbiological parameters. Twenty sites were granted an award in 1993 (National Rivers Authority, Fourth *Annual Report* (1994)).

[16] The Tidy Britain Group Seaside Award was introduced in 1992 to complement the European Blue Flag Award. It rewards high standards of facilities and management as well as beach cleanliness and water quality.

which concluded that there was no significant risk of serious disease arising from contact with pathogens in sewage-contaminated seawater.[17] Minor complaints, such as stomach upsets and sore throats might be caused by pollution but the evidence also suggested that seawater itself could be the causal factor.

Government policy on bathing water quality has been the subject of several Select Committee inquiries. In 1990, the House of Commons Environment Committee[18] was highly critical of government practice. An opinion more in tune with government thinking was expressed by the House of Lords Committee on the European Communities which reported on the Commission's proposals to replace the 1976 Directive with an amended version.[19] The Commission made its proposals with a view to simplifying the present test regime in the light of advances in scientific and technical knowledge. The United Kingdom was strongly in favour of reform and contributed much to this increased knowledge base.

The proposed directive[20] is justified as an environmental measure under Article 130r and is thus subject to a qualified majority procedure. The objectives remain the same but reference to the benefits to the tourism industry have been added.[21] The original 19 parameters have been replaced with 12 and the emphasis on the microbial indicators has changed. There are imperative and guide values for *Escherichia coli* and for faecal streptococci.[22] Salmonella has been dropped because its presence is not closely correlated to sewage contamination but more emphasis is given to enteroviruses and bacteriophages. A category of 'excellent quality' has been added which requires a higher proportion of samples to meet the specified values.[23] Where pollution constitutes a threat to public health, a Member State is required to close the affected bathing water. Such a threat is deemed to occur where there is a significant deviation from I values.

The House of Lords concluded that the objectives of the Commission's proposals were admirable but questioned the likely effectiveness and cost-effectiveness of the provisions proposed.[24] The general conclusion was that the imperative values in the present Directive appear to be stringent enough to protect against serious illness and there was not, in the Committee's opinion, sufficient evidence to show that either the existing or proposed values would protect against minor illnesses. There was a particular problem over the standard

---

[17] Pike, *Health Effects of Sea Bathing* (WMI 9021) Phase III. Final Report to the Department of the Environment, January 1994 (WRc plc).

[18] *Op. cit.* note 9.

[19] House of Lords Select Committee on the European Communities. *Bathing Water*, Session 1994–95, First Report, HL Paper 6-I, 1994.

[20] Commission Proposal for a Council Directive concerning the quality of bathing water COM(94) 36 final, OJ 1994 C 112, p. 3.

[21] Preamble.

[22] Article 5.

[23] Article 5(2).

[24] See the debate on Bathing Water: ECC Report, HL Deb [564] Cols. 684–708.

for faecal streptococci. The proposal is for an imperative value of 400/100 ml compared with the current guide value of 100/100 ml (there is no imperative value). Evidence before the Committee suggested that 400/100 ml was about ten times too high to have any beneficial effect on the incidence of minor gastroenteritis or respiratory infections.[25] The Committee was, therefore, concerned at the large expenditure that might be entailed in meeting standards that were arbitrary. It went further to criticise the Commission for its failure to engage the scientific community in open discussion of its proposals with the consequence that some of the details showed a disregard of current science.[26] It is worth noting that the Committee of the Regions, in its opinion on the Commission's proposal, was similarly critical.[27] Both reports were opposed to the idea of introducing an excellent category because of the likely confusion this would generate and neither showed much enthusiasm for the closure proposal.

The House of Lords conducted a further inquiry[28] into the proposals in the light of a Department of the Environment commissioned report[29] on the costs involved. This indicated that full implementation of the proposed directive in the United Kingdom would cost an extra £1.6 billion for capital expenditure over and above the £9.5 billion required to implement the existing Directive and the Urban Waste Water Treatment Directive in full. This contrasts markedly with the Commission's assertion that the proposals were cost neutral.[30] Furthermore the costs would be distributed unevenly among water companies. South West Water's area, for example, has almost one-third of identified bathing waters but less than 3% of the population.[31]

To some extent the motivation for reform of the Bathing Water Directive has lessened as the quality of bathing waters has improved. With more sites complying, there is less reason for an unenthusiastic government to question the scientific rationale. Once the improvements brought about through works undertaken to implement the Urban Waste Water Treatment Directive take effect, there is expected to be an even higher level of compliance. At this stage, the law of diminishing returns may tip the balance away from further raising of standards leaving the way clear to concentrate on better and more cost effective sampling and test regimes. The UK government, through its sponsored research in scientific and health aspects of sewage pollution, is likely to play a major part in the development of this area of EC legislation.

----

[25] *Op. cit.* note 19, paras. 19–28.
[26] *Ibid.* para. 38.
[27] OJ 1995 C 120, p. 53.
[28] House of Lords Select Committee on the European Communities, *Bathing Water Revisited*, Session 1994–95, Seventh Report, HL Paper 41 (London: HMSO, 1995).
[29] HL Deb [561] Written Answer, Cols. 70–72, *per* Viscount Ullswater.
[30] Article 130r of the EC Treaty implies that a revised directive should make no change which would either increase net public cost of compliance without a proportionate increase in public health protection or reduce that level.
[31] HL Deb [564] Col. 695, *per* Lord Dixon-Smith.

The Urban Waste Water Treatment Directive

The objective of the Directive is to protect the environment from the adverse effects of discharges of domestic and certain types of industrial sewage. Its main impact on UK law and practice has been in the regulation of coastal discharges and in the disposal of sewage sludge. The Directive is implemented by the Urban Waste Water Treatment Regulations 1994.[32]

Coastal discharges

The Directive requires Member States to introduce treatment schemes[33] to ensure that discharges comply with standards specified in the Directive. The level of treatment required varies according to the population size of the community and the nature of the receiving waters. The basic premise of the Directive is that all sewage should receive secondary treatment (i.e. removal of organic material through the use of activated sludge or biological filters) before it can be safely discharged to sea or estuary. In some cases it may be necessary to apply additional treatment because the receiving waters are particularly susceptible to pollution. 'Sensitive Areas', as these are termed,[34] are typically prone to eutrophication and so additional treatment is required to strip nutrients from discharges. At the same time it was acknowledged that the assimilative and dispersive characteristics of some receiving waters, termed 'Less Sensitive Areas' were such that secondary treatment might not be necessary to protect the environment.[35]

The size of the community, expressed in terms of population equivalents,[36] gives a measure of the quantity of sewage discharged and, hence the level of treatment required. Implementation of the requirements is to be phased in according to the magnitude of the sewage burden. The basic rule is that secondary treatment must be in place by the end of the year 2000 for populations of more than 15,000; by the end of the year 2005 for populations of more than 10,000 but less than 15,000; and by the end of the year 2005 for populations of more than 2000 but less than 10,000 where the discharge is to freshwater or an estuary.[37]

Less Sensitive Areas are to be designated following the general guidance given in Annex II. Where there is a discharge into coastal waters from populations of between 10,000 and 150,000, less stringent measures need be applied. There is a minimum requirement of at least primary treatment, however, and the

---

[32] Urban Waste Water Treatment (England and Wales) Regulations 1994 (SI 1994 No. 2841); Urban Waste Water Treatment (Scotland) Regulations 1994 (SI 1994 No. 2842) and Urban Waste Water Treatment Regulations (Northern Ireland) 1995 (SR (NI) 1995 No. 12).

[33] Article 4.

[34] Article 5 and Annex II.

[35] Article 6 and Annex II.

[36] 1 p.e. (population equivalent) means the organic biodegradable load having a five-day biochemical oxygen demand of 60g O_2 per day (Article 2(6)).

[37] Article 4(1).

decision to waive further treatment is dependent on evidence from a comprehensive study showing that there will be no adverse effect.[38] Similar provisions
apply to discharges into estuaries but here the population limits are between
2000 and 10,000.[39] In addition to these exceptions for Less Sensitive Areas,
Article 8(5) permits a further relaxation in the case of discharges into Less
Sensitive Areas in coastal waters from populations of more than 150,000. If
more advanced treatment is not beneficial on environmental grounds, it is
permissible to treat such discharges as if they came from a population of
between 10,000 and 150,000 provided that a case for derogation is accepted by
the Commission.

Sludge disposal

Article 14 of the Directive requires Member States to establish, before the end
of 1998, a scheme of authorisation for sewage sludge disposal. The criteria for
disposal are to be based on the principle that sludge should be reused wherever
possible. Disposal at sea is to be phased out before the end of 1998.

UK implementation of the Directive

Expenditure on sewage treatment works in the United Kingdom increased
dramatically in the mid-1980s after years of under-investment. The investment
programme by the water industry followed the recommendations of the Royal
Commission on Environmental Pollution (RCEP)[40] that the installation of long
outfalls was the most appropriate action to take. In making this recommendation, the RCEP had accepted that the problem of sewage in seawater was
aesthetic rather than medical.[41] Sewage would, accordingly, undergo preliminary
treatment, i.e. screening, but would otherwise be discharged without treatment.
The scientific justification for the long outfall approach was rooted in the
natural assimilative capacity of the sea. It was believed that if sewage was discharged three kilometres offshore, the dilution and the combined effect of
sunlight and seawater would break down the sewage and destroy bacteria and
viruses.[42] The House of Commons Environment Committee was sceptical
and, therefore, set up an inquiry into the pollution of beaches.[43] At about the
same time, the government announced its acceptance of the clean-up principles
in the draft directive and the long outfall policy was, effectively, abandoned.

   The main concern over the Directive is that its implementation will add
considerably to the consumer's water bill. The House of Lords Select Committee
on the European Communities considered the implications for the United

---

[38] Article 6(2).
[39] *Ibid.*
[40] Royal Commission on Environmental Pollution, *Tackling Pollution: Experience and Prospects*, Tenth
   Report, Cmnd. 9149 (London: HMSO, 1984).
[41] *Op. cit.* note 9, para. 3.
[42] HC Deb [139] Col. 1292, *per* Mr Nicholas Ridley.
[43] *Op. cit.* note 9.

Kingdom of implementing the Directive and concluded that the costs could amount to more than £2.16 billion even if all coastal waters were designated as Less Sensitive Areas.[44]

Given the increased costs associated with secondary treatment compared with primary treatment (i.e. precipitation or settlement of suspended solids) and preliminary treatment (screening for gross solids), it is clear that expenditure can be reduced if the boundary between estuaries and coastal waters is set as far inland as possible so as to maximise the potential area of Less Sensitive Areas in coastal waters. The Directive, itself, is not clear on the distinction between the two. An estuary is defined as the transitional area at the mouth of a river between freshwater and coastal waters.[45] Coastal waters are defined as the waters outside the low-water line or the outer limits of an estuary.[46] The government engaged in an extensive consultation exercise to determine criteria for the identification of Sensitive and Less Sensitive Areas and went on to publish a draft list of each.[47] It was then decided to re-examine the list of 58 'High Natural Dispersion Areas' (HNDAs, the name given to Less Sensitive Areas in the Regulations) with a view to reducing the overall cost. As a result, the boundaries of the Humber and the Severn estuaries were set further inland than originally proposed by the National Rivers Authority. This decision was challenged in judicial review in *R* v. *Secretary of State for the Environment, ex parte Kingston-upon-Hull*[48] on the grounds that the Secretary of State had failed to abide by the Directive definition of an estuary; had failed to take account of material considerations such as the salinity of the water and the topography, and/or had taken into account irrelevant factors, namely the economic consequences arising from the difference between an estuary and an area of coastal waters. The applicants claimed that an estuary was defined on objective scientific criteria such as salinity and topography and observed that the National Rivers Authority's advice, accepted in principle by the government, was that a typographical definition, based on that in the Clean Rivers (Estuarine and Tidal Waters) Act 1960, should be adopted. The respondents alleged circularity in the Directive definitions and argued that the distinction was a discretionary one. Harrison J agreed that there was an element of discretion involved but went on to hold that there must be a genuine and rational assessment having regard to all relevant circumstances. Cost of treatment dependent on a decision on the definition was not relevant: 'An area of water either is or is not an estuary regardless of what it will cost to treat waste water discharged into it.'

When the House of Lords considered the Directive, one of its main concerns was that the Directive adopted a limit value rather than a quality standard.[49]

---

[44] House of Lords Select Committee on the European Communities, *Municipal Waste Water Treatment*, Session 1990–91, Tenth Report, Vol. 1 Report, HL Paper 50-I, 1991, para. 115.

[45] Article 2(12).

[46] Article 2(13).

[47] Referred to in *R* v. *Secretary of State for the Environment ex parte Kingston-upon-Hull City Council* (1996) JEL Vol. 8, No. 2, 336, at 339.

[48] (1996) JEL Vol. 8, No. 2, 336, at 339.

[49] *Op. cit.* note 44, paras. 17–21 and 124–129.

The facts of the Humber case provide a clear illustration of the House of Lords' concerns. The National Rivers Authority acknowledged that there was no absolute need for secondary treatment of sewage discharged into the Humber and the Severn. Moving the estuary boundary was regarded as a pragmatic decision to avoid unnecessary costs to the public. If the Directive had incorporated criteria based on quality standards for the receiving waters, the problem would not have arisen.

Impact on UK practice

In 1991 24% of estuarine discharges from towns with a population of more than 2000 had no treatment; 17% had only preliminary treatment; 24% also had primary treatment and 35% had secondary treatment. Of discharges into coastal waters from towns of more than 10,000 people, 42% had no treatment; 46% had preliminary treatment; 10% also had primary treatment and just 2% had secondary treatment.[50] By this time the government had already set out its policy to treat all substantial discharges of sewage into the sea.[51] Legge[52] reports that the total cost to customers for sewerage services increased by 7% in 1993–94 in response to expenditure needed to meet the requirements of the Control of Pollution Act 1974 and the Bathing Water Directive. This work was largely completed in 1993. There were no significant cost increases in 1994–95 because the impact of this Directive is yet to be felt.

The commitment to phase out dumping of sewage sludge at sea has had a major effect on UK practice. A large proportion of the organic material in sewage effluent settles out as sludge. The problem of disposal now that the sea is no longer available as a dustbin is exacerbated by the further requirement of the Directive to introduce more secondary treatment and thus to increase the production of sludge.[53] At the time of the adoption of the Directive, about 25% of UK sludge was deposited at sea. In some regions, notably parts of Scotland, the figure rose to over 50%. The simplest alternative disposal option is to increase disposal onto agricultural land although capacity is limited. The United Kingdom already disposed of up to about 50% of its sludge in this way depending on the region. In any event, agricultural disposal is not without its own environmental problems including smell; nutrient run-off and leaching; heavy metal accumulation; and risks from pathogens.

Although the government announced plans to phase out dumping of sewage sludge at sea following the 1990 North Sea Ministerial Conference and published a programme in March 1991[54] (i.e. in advance of this Directive being adopted) it has never conceded that such measures are necessary for the protec-

---

[50] *Ibid.* at Tables 3 and 4.
[51] See *This Common Inheritance*, First Year Report, Cm. 1655, (London: HMSO, 1991), para. 9.21.
[52] Legge, '1994–95 Report on the Cost of Water Delivered and Sewage Collected' (1996) 7 Utilities L Rev 62–63.
[53] Evidence from the Department of the Environment to the House of Lords Select Committee on the European Communities gave an estimated 15% increase. *Op. cit.* note 44, para. 88.
[54] *Op. cit.* note 51, para. 9.22.

tion of the environment or even that they are environmentally sound. The evidence before the House of Lords Select Committee would seem to confirm its scepticism.[55] While some witnesses were of the opinion that any sewage sludge in the sea was unacceptable, others considered sea disposal as the best environmental option. The latter seem to have been in the majority. For example, in their final report to the Department of the Environment, WRc plc found only a minimal impact from sludge dumping at sea and the Natural Environment Research Council reported that evidence indicated that the environmental costs of this form of disposal were small in relation to other methods. On the other hand, some experts, including the Institute of Environmental Health Officers and the Royal Society for the Protection of Birds, were fully in favour of the Directive's objectives. The Committee itself expressed reservations about the scope for increasing disposal of sludge to agricultural land to any great extent.[56] Landfill was considered an unlikely option, given adverse public opinion, and the only other realistic alternative, incineration, was considered likely to be just as unpopular. It is, as yet, too soon to assess whether the objectives of the Directive have been met in a cost-effective manner but the suspicion remains that the inflexibility of the limit value approach may lead to considerable expenditure for little environmental gain.

Integrated coastal zone management

In 1992 the House of Commons Environment Committee reported in favour of a system of strategic coastal zone management founded in the principle of holistic management with integration between sectoral interests and across the land sea divide.[57] These conclusions were in general accord with the non-governmental lobby which had been campaigning for such an approach for a number of years.[58] The government was less than enthusiastic but did agree to undertake a review of relevant management plans and legislation.[59] European interest in the coastal zone arose in the context of sustainable use and a recognition of the socio-economic value of the coastal zone in the tourism industry. Coastal zone management as referred to in the Fifth Environmental Action Programme[60] sets a goal of sustainable use of the coastal zone through the development of an operational framework for integrated planning and management by the year 2000. In March 1994 the Council passed a resolution

---

[55] *Op. cit.* note 44, paras. 100–103.
[56] *Ibid.* at paras. 173–178.
[57] House of Commons Environment Committee, *Coastal Zone Protection and Planning*, Session 1991–92, Second Report, Vol. I, HC Paper 17-I, especially para. 117.
[58] See, for example, the Memorandum from Wildlife Link to the House of Commons Environment Committee, *Coastal Zone Protection and Planning*, Session 1991–92, Second Report, Vol. II, HC Paper 17-II, p. 125.
[59] The government's Response to the Second Report of the House of Commons Select Committee on the Environment, *Coastal Zone Protection and Planning* (London: HMSO, 1992).
[60] *Op. cit.* note 7.

calling upon the Commission to develop a strategy for coastal zones.[61] Progress has been slow, partly because coastal zone management is seen as akin to land use planning and, therefore, essentially an issue for Member States, and partly because the pressures on the coastal zone and, therefore, the desirability of particular legislative measures, vary considerably between Member States. In northern Member States sea level rise and coastal defence are major issues of concern. In many southern Member States the main problem is with unsympathetic development of holiday complexes for the mass tourist market. Nevertheless, the Commission has published proposals[62] for the creation of a three-year demonstration project with the ultimate aim of putting an end to the environmental deterioration of the coastline by making existing instruments more effective while, at the same time, respecting the principle of subsidiarity. Three main reasons for Community action were identified: (a) the transnational nature of many of the problems; (b) the influence of other European policies on development in the coastal zone; and (c) the need for exchange of experience and know-how. The proposal was welcomed by the Council.[63] It also received the endorsement of the Committee of the Regions[64] which, however, urged a bottom-up approach. Because the problems to be addressed are most evident at local and regional levels, it is preferable to start there. The EC contribution should be to ensure coordination of other EC controlled activities with the objectives of coastal zone management. This view is likely to be welcomed by the UK government which has expressed the opinion that any strategy arising out of the demonstration project should be broad and not over-precise in its legislative requirements.[65]

Marine conservation

UK legislation for the protection of marine habitats was long in the making and slow in implementation. Provisions for Marine Nature Reserves were made in the Wildlife and Countryside Act 1981, over 30 years after legislation for National Nature Reserves.[66] There are still only three Marine Nature Reserves[67] and the legislation has been severely criticised over the years.[68] The need to implement the Habitats Directive with respect to marine sites has led to signs of a change towards a more positive approach. The Conservation (Natural

[61] OJ 1993 C 59, p. 1. See also OJ 1994 C 135, p. 2.
[62] COM(95) 511 final.
[63] See [1996] *Water Law* 78.
[64] Opinion of the Committee of the Regions on the 'Communication from the Commission on the Integrated Management of Coastal Zones', OJ 1996 C 182, p. 12.
[65] *Op. cit.* note 63.
[66] See the National Parks and Access to the Countryside Act 1949, s. 15.
[67] Lundy; Skomer and the Marloes Peninsula; and Strangford Lough.
[68] See, for example, Warren, 'Law and Policy for Marine Protected Areas', in Rodgers (ed), *Nature Conservation and Countryside Law* (Cardiff: University of Wales Press, 1996), pp. 65–88, at p. 74.

Habitats, etc.) Regulations 1994,[69] which implement the Directive in Great Britain, provide for the identification of European Marine Sites[70] as potential Special Areas of Conservation. Responsibility for protecting the conservation interest of these sites rests with a wide range of competent bodies[71] which are required to carry out their functions so as to comply with the Directive.[72] A more limited number of relevant authorities[73] may be required to work together to produce and implement a management plan for each European Marine Site, the purpose of which is to guide their activities with respect to the site.[74] Although there are some doubts as to how these provisions will work in practice,[75] they do represent a first attempt to instigate integrated coastal zone management, albeit purely from a conservation viewpoint.

The environmental impact of shipping

It is European environmental policy with respect to pollution from shipping to follow international agreements and work for their effective implementation within the EC. The EC's involvement in this area of environmental law escalated in response to shipping accidents in the winter of 1992–93 one of which, the Braer, led to similar activity on the domestic level in the United Kingdom. In 1993, the Commission published *A Common Policy on Safe Seas*[76] and this was approved in amended form by the Council later that year.

The Report of the Donaldson Inquiry,[77] set up by the government as part of its response to the Braer incident, included details of current EC initiatives in the field of maritime safety and refers to one directive[78] and five draft directives.[79] Of these, the most important is the Port State Control Directive.[80]

The Donaldson Inquiry made a recommendation that it would be useful to identify Marine Environmental High Risk Areas (MEHRAs)[81] where there was

---

[69] SI 1994 No. 2716. See Reid, Chapter 12 below.
[70] Regulation 2.
[71] Defined in reg. 6 as including any minister, government department, public or statutory undertaker, public body of any description or person holding public office.
[72] Regulation 3(3).
[73] Listed in reg. 5 and including the nature conservation agencies, local authorities, the Environment Agency, and sea fisheries committees.
[74] Regulations 34–35.
[75] See, for example, Warren, *op. cit.* note 68, p. 86.
[76] COM(93) 66 final, OJ 1993 C 271, p. 1.
[77] *Safer Ships, Cleaner Seas*, Report of Lord Donaldson's Inquiry into the Prevention of Pollution from Merchant Shipping, Cm. 2560 (London: HMSO, 1994).
[78] Council Directive 93/75/EEC on minimum requirements for vessels bound for or leaving Community ports or carrying dangerous or polluting goods which came into force in September 1995.
[79] *Op. cit.* note 77, para. 5.70.
[80] Council Directive 95/21/EEC concerning the enforcement, in respect of shipping using Community ports or sailing in waters under the jurisdiction of the Member States, of international standards for ship safety, pollution prevention and shipboard living and working conditions (port state control) OJ L 157, p. 1.
[81] *Op. cit.* note 77, paras. 14.120–14.128.

both a navigational problem and an environmental sensitivity so that mariners could be better informed when navigating in, or near, such areas. The European Commission is clearly thinking along the same lines. In 1993 it invited Member States to identify and inform it of any Environmentally Sensitive Areas in their national territory.[82] These areas were envisaged as stretches of coastal waters where environmental characteristics were such as to merit stricter controls over shipping. The UK response was that it was difficult to provide information without knowing what sort of protection was being contemplated. In February 1996 another oil pollution incident, caused by the grounding of the Sea Empress, rekindled public interest in maritime safety. Although the majority of the Donaldson Inquiry's recommendations have been acted upon, there has been no progress on MEHRAs. It is likely that any further developments will be at the international level, under the auspices of the International Maritime Organization, rather than at European or national level.

Conclusions

The United Kingdom's approach to the protection of the coastal and marine environment has traditionally been founded on three principles—the sea's dispersive capacity; the desirability of determining regulations in accordance with environmental need—i.e. a quality standard approach rather than a limit-based, precautionary approach; and a belief in voluntary mechanisms whereby users cooperate to protect the sea. European legislation has eroded all three of these principles. The debate over the use of the sea as a waste repository was probably lost in the context of the North Sea ministerial conferences rather than the EC. Certainly, the UK's participation in the Declarations[83] arising from these conferences made it virtually impossible, politically, to hold out against subsequent proposals from Europe. The adoption of the EC's favoured mechanism of limit values rather than quality objectives is, perhaps, the least welcome aspect of European marine environmental policy from a UK viewpoint, as witnessed by the Humber estuary case. The desirability of adopting the best environmental option, taking account of both environmental and economic costs, is central to UK environmental policy. The perception that the Commission prefers a more rigid, fixed approach is the cause of much of the reluctance of the United Kingdom to endorse European environmental policy wholeheartedly.[84] As far as conservation is concerned, the United Kingdom has made a strong commitment to the conservation of biodiversity. Compliance with the Habitats Directive is part of this commitment. The fact that marine habitats are included in the Annexes therefore means that the United Kingdom

---

[82] *Op. cit.* note 76.

[83] Especially the *Ministerial Declaration of the Third International Conference on the Protection of the North Sea*, The Hague (1990).

[84] Note, in this respect, the government's response to European coastal zone management initiatives, *op. cit.* note 63.

must provide for their strict protection. If the procedures laid down in the 1994 Regulations work, this could be one of the most important influences of EC legislation on UK law and practice because it paves the way for an acceptance of wider integrated coastal zone management.

The possibility of a new framework directive on water quality is currently under consideration.[85] It is designed to produce a sustainable water policy. The objectives include maintaining a quality of water such as to sustain a good ecological state and functioning of aquatic environments. It is based on the belief that much of the quality related legislation could be put together in a single directive on water resources.

The proposals focus on freshwaters rather than marine ones and no significant changes to either the Bathing Water Directive or the Urban Waste Water Treatment Directive are expected. Assuming that the proposals proceed to the legislation stage, the most important impact for the United Kingdom is likely to be the introduction of mandatory integrated water management plans.

---

[85] Commission Communication to Council and European Parliament on European Community Water Policy COM(96) 59 final.

Chapter 11

THE IMPACT OF EC LAW ON NOISE LAW IN THE UNITED KINGDOM

Francis McManus and Tom Burns

UK noise law

Historical background

While noise has ranked as a perennial environmental problem in the United Kingdom since the industrial revolution the pollutant has attracted little legislative attention. Such an approach was no doubt based on the very nature of noise. It is invisible. It leaves no residue and therefore has no fall-out factor associated with other pollutants. Its effect upon human health is uncertain. Again, the creation of noise seems to have been tacitly accepted as the inevitable concomitant of modern life. Furthermore, until fairly recently, unlike acid rain or the state of the ozone layer, noise has traditionally not generated sustained public interest.

The nineteenth century

As far as legislative control over noise was concerned, during the ninetenth century noise control legislation took the form of local authority byelaws made either under national public health legislation such as the Public Health Acts, or local enactments. Such byelaws tended to be limited in scope and confined their attention to street noise, noise made by buskers etc. Many of the byelaws remain in existence today and complement the more sophisticated controls which will be discussed below. We may look askance at such a *laissez-faire* approach to environmental noise but there seems to have been little public support for greater parliamentary intervention in the field of noise. Local studies carried out by one of the authors in relation to Edinburgh between the years 1833–79[1] and Leith between 1833–1901, has revealed little discontent by

---

[1] See F. McManus, *Public Health Administration in Edinburgh 1833–1879*, unpublished MLitt thesis (Edinburgh: University of Edinburgh, 1984).

either the general public or public authorities who were responsible for enforcing environmental law with the state of the law relating to noise.

1960–90

It was only as late as 1960 that, after effective pressure group action, UK legislation expressly struck at the problem of environmental noise in the form of the Noise Abatement Act 1960. That statute was not particularly adventurous in that it simply allowed local authorities to treat noise amounting to a nuisance emanating from premises as a statutory nuisance. However, the 1960 Act was an important piece of legislation in that it demonstrated a commitment on the part of Parliament to dealing with the problem of environmental noise. The first attempt to adopt a holistic approach to noise control in the United Kingdom came in the form of the Control of Pollution Act 1974 (COPA). Part III of the Act placed local authorities under a duty to deal with noise nuisances emanating from premises. Special provision was made for construction site noise as well as noise from vehicles in streets. One of the most innovatory features of COPA was the introduction of the concept of noise abatement zones. Basically local authorities were given wide discretion to set up areas (which could be of any size). After such an area was set up and the noise levels emanating from the relevant premises recorded in a noise level register, it was made an offence to exceed those limits without the express permission of the local authority. Unfortunately, the power to create such areas was not embraced with tremendous enthusiasm in the United Kingdom. While there are currently about 60 noise abatement zones in England and Wales there are no such zones in Scotland. It seems that local authorities generally have been reluctant to set up noise abatement zones on the basis that the effective policing of such zones would place too great demands on the time of officials.

It must be emphasised that there is other legislation dealing with noise. Town and country planning and entertainment legislation are among the more important local authorities have at their disposal to control neighbourhood noise.

The 1990s

The early 1990s witnessed a growing awareness of the problem of environmental noise especially neighbourhood noise which was often generated by electronic equipment such as stereos, car radios, burglar alarms, etc. The Noise and Statutory Nuisance Act 1993 was an attempt to deal with this problem. The 1993 Act amended Part III of COPA (for Scotland) and Part III of the Environmental Protection Act 1990 (for England and Wales) to give additional powers to local authorities to deal with noise from such sources.

A common cause of concern has been the problem of noise at night. The Noise Act 1996 will now give local authorities power to deal with night-time noise if it exceeds a prescribed limit.

Summary of UK noise law

By way of a general overview of UK noise law one can say that it is an ugly mosaic of separate legal regimes. Arguably, the law is in a chaotic state and requires to be consolidated. It is also heavily nuisance based. Indeed, the law seems to be a victim of its historical development. Parliament has relied on the concept of nuisance as an environmental quality standard for noise in contradistinction to employing limit values. This approach contrasts sharply with the position in other jurisdictions such as Colorado, New Jersey, and Illinois where it is made an offence for noise to exceed prescribed levels.

Impact of EC noise law

The Community has never had a comprehensive noise control policy. The 1957 Treaty did not contain an explicit provision relating to the environment. When the Community later came to develop an environmental policy in the early 1970s both in response to the obvious damage that was occurring to the environment[2] and to the public demand for action, the Community had to seek 'creative' solutions to the problem of there being no constitutional basis on which to promulgate environmental laws. The early noise laws therefore had to be shaped in such a way as to be based on existing Treaty Articles such as Article 100 (trade measures); Article 84 (transport measures) or Article 235 (general powers). Thus, the Community in its early years was left with little or no choice but to focus its attention on controlling noise emissions from certain products and modes of transport, and had to justify these measures on the basis that the Community was setting standards to eliminate barriers to trade in these goods. There was also a feeling that neighbourhood noise was a local issue and therefore best dealt with by local communities.

As far as the early EC directives relating to noise were concerned they were aimed at specific mobile sources of noise namely motor vehicles, tractors (74/151/EEC as amended by 77/311/EEC) aircraft (80/51/EEC and 83/206/EEC), lawnmowers (84/538/EEC and 87/252/EEC) and construction plant (84/532/EEC). In addition the Community passed a Directive concerning the noise emitted from household appliances (86/594/EEC) and required manufacturers of such equipment to display the noise levels that their machines emit. Most of the directives are very detailed and contain not only permissible noise levels from the relevant source but also instructions on standards for the measurement of noise. Furthermore, so detailed are the provisions of the various directives that as a consequence the Member States are left with little discretion on how to achieve the relevant objectives contained in the directives. As a result many noise directives resemble regulations. Indeed, Krämer has observed that when

---

[2] The UN Conference in Stockholm on the Human Environment in 1972 led to the Heads of State in the Community issuing a Summit Communiqué which indicated that the environment would become a policy consideration for the EC (EC Comm. Sixth General Report, p. 8).

it comes to environmental directives the effect of their very detailed content has the tendency to make, ' . . . the differences between regulations and directives . . . extremely small and largely semantic'.[3] This may have ramifications as far as the enforcement of the law is concerned. In conformity with general principles which obtain in EC law this may encourage persons to challenge public authorities over any lax enforcement of EC law.[4]

Before we look at noise law in terms of specific noise sources it is important to make several general points. The early EC noise law directives were very detailed in content and therefore did not leave Member States much scope to exercise their discretion on how to achieve the various targets set by the directives. While most of the directives are of this type, the 1984 Construction Plant Directive (84/532/EEC) marked a change in policy. This was a framework directive which laid out the general principles of law applying to this range of machinery. The Directive provides for the general policy incorporated in the directive to be 'fleshed-out' by daughter directives. This approach in respect of construction plant has produced a clear and more coherent set of laws. Five detailed daughter directives covering the noise levels of compressors (84/533/EEC); power generators (84/536/EEC); powered hand-held concrete breakers and picks (84/537/EEC); hydraulic excavators (86/662/EEC) and tower cranes (84/534/EEC) have been made. This arrangement has helped to produce precise laws which can be more easily transposed into the national law and serves as a model for future legislation on any new product-based sources of noise identified by the Commission as requiring regulation. Another interesting variant to the control of noise was displayed in the 1986 Directive on noise emitted from household appliances (86/594/EEC). Here a duty was imposed on manufacturers to display the noise levels emitted from their products on the labels attached to their appliances. The Community hoped that by employing this tactic, consumers themselves, by exercising their preference for less noisy equipment would be able to pressurise manufacturers to produce less noisy washing machines or dishwashers. This serves as an interesting example of the use of an economic instrument as a means of pollution control.

Cars, buses and lorries

Among the earliest directives dealing with specific noise sources were those dealing with the noise of four-wheeled vehicles. The parent Directive 70/157/EEC was agreed before Britain joined the Community. It was closely modelled on the United Nation's Economic Commission for Europe's non-mandatory regulation 9. Motor vehicle noise was first controlled in Britain in 1970 by the Motor Vehicles (Construction and Use) Regulations 1968 made under the Road Traffic Act. On accession to the Community in 1973 Britain became subject to Directive 70/157/EEC which prescribed slightly more stringent limits for cars

---

[3] Krämer, 'Community Environmental Law—Towards a Systematic Approach' [1991] 11 YEL 151, at 158.
[4] Geddes, 'Locus Standi and EEC Environmental Measures,' (1992) JEL Vol. 4, No. 2, 29.

but less for buses and lorries. Since the Directive was 'optional' it was not necessary to tighten the British limits for cars but in order to prevent a barrier to trade, the limit for buses had to be relaxed. This was done by the Motor Vehicles (Construction and Use) Regulations 1973[5] made under the Road Traffic Act 1972. Haigh[6] points out that as far as the United Kingdom was concerned the effect of Directive 70/157/EEC was a relaxation of the noise limits for buses and lorries. Furthermore, in international terms the noise standard for vehicles was not very demanding. For example, the Californian Vehicle Code of 1971 set more stringent standards. The 1973 UK Regulations have been amended several times and the new limits are now found in reg. 55 of the Road Vehicles (Construction and Use) Regulations 1986.[7] This regulation applies to vehicles first used on or after 1 October 1983 which must comply with the limits set in Directive 77/212/EEC using either the test procedure in that Directive or the test procedure in Directive 81/334/EEC and 84/372/EEC. Vehicles first used on or after 1 April 1990 (1991 in the case of heavy lorries and some buses) are required to comply with the limits set by Directive 84/424/EEC. Directive 92/97/EEC lowers maximum permitted levels of noise levels from vehicles. These became mandatory as of 1 October 1989 in respect of vehicle certification procedures and from 1 October 1996 for the entry into service of any vehicle in the EC. It is current EC practice to revise such limits roughly every five years.

The system of national type approval for cars (which require any manufacturer before marketing a new type of vehicle to have a sample tested by the Department of Transport) was introduced by the Motor Vehicles (Type Approval) (Great Britain) Regulations 1976[8] (made under the Road Traffic Act 1972 (now the Road Traffic Act 1988)). This sets the limits of Directive 77/212/EEC for cars. The 1976 Regulations have now been replaced by the Motor Vehicles (Type Approval) (Great Britain) Regulations 1984[9] which implement the requirements of Directive 81/334/EEC.

The legal effect of EC directives relating to vehicle noise was discussed in *R v. London Borough Transport Committee, ex parte Freight Transport Association*.[10] Under Directive 70/157/EEC (the Sound Level Directive) the permissible sound levels of vehicles and exhaust systems were harmonised throughout the Community. The Directive provided that the sale, registration or use of a vehicle could not be prohibited on grounds relating to its brakes, sound level or exhaust system if the vehicle conformed to the requirements laid down by the Directive. Under s. 6 of the Road Traffic Regulation Act 1984 the traffic regulatory authority for Greater London, of which the appellant transport committee was a successor, imposed a ban on heavy goods vehicles using residential streets in Greater London at night-time without a permit. The authority imposed a condition on

---

[5] SI 1973 No. 1347.
[6] Haigh, *Manual of Environmental Policy: the EC and Britain*, (London: Longmans) 10.2–4.
[7] SI 1986 No. 1078.
[8] SI 1976 No. 937.
[9] SI 1984 No. 81.
[10] [1991] 3 All ER 915.

the grant of permits for vehicles over 16.5 tonnes requiring those vehicles which were capable of being fitted with an air brake noise suppressor to be fitted with such a suppressor. The plaintiffs, who were a national organisation representing the transport and distribution industries, sought judicial review of the air brake noise suppressor condition imposed by the authority on the grant of its permits. It was held by the House of Lords that the condition imposed by the authority requiring vehicles over 16.5 tonnes to be fitted with an air brake noise suppressor before they would be granted a permit to use residential streets in Greater London at night-time was not contrary to the Sound Level Directive since the condition was imposed for the regulation of local traffic and the protection of the environment whereas the Directive was concerned with the control of vehicles. Furthermore, the condition was consistent with the express policy of the Commission with regard to the environment and fell within the powers exercisable by the traffic regulation authorities of Member States. The condition therefore did not infringe EC law.

The setting of noise emission limit values for vehicles certainly represents the mainstay of the EC's involvement in environmental noise abatement thus far.

The Commission is currently working with a proposal on tyre noise reduction. The issue whether any new emission limit values are appropriate will also be addressed. As far as general vehicle noise is concerned the Commission is considering whether noise factors could be taken into account in relation to the existing annual vehicle tax as well as the roadworthiness test.

Civil aircraft noise

Aircraft noise poses an obvious and potentially serious environmental problem. Aircraft can give annoyance to the community either while the aircraft is in flight, or, after the aircraft has landed at the appropriate airport. The relevant statutory controls over aircraft noise can be divided roughly into those which relate to the control of noise from the flight (or navigation) of aircraft and those which specifically relate to the control of noise from aerodromes. As far as annoyance to the public by flight noise is concerned it is important that one reduces the noise which emanates from aircraft at source, that is to say, from the aircraft itself. Of prime importance in this respect is the Chicago Convention on International Civil Aviation (which deals with aviation in general), signed in 1944, to which the United Kingdom is party. Annex 16 to the Convention deals specifically with noise from aircraft. Volume 1, entitled 'Aircraft Noise' sets out criteria in relation to aircraft noise. Chapters 2 and 3 lay down standards relating to noise from subsonic jet aircraft. Chapters 5 and 6 do likewise for propeller driven aircraft. Aircraft which meet such standards are generally referred to as 'Chapter 2' and 'Chapter 3' aircraft etc. It is in relation to flight noise and noise certification that the EC has taken a progressively greater interest. A number of directives based on agreements have been made under the aegis of the International Civil Aviation Organisation. As far as the United Kingdom is concerned, the relevant provisions of the Chicago

Convention and the appropriate EC directives are implemented by noise certifi-cation orders made under s. 60(3)(r) of the Civil Aviation Act 1982. The general aim of the legislation is to phase out gradually the use of noisier aircraft.

The upshot of such a policy was that aircraft operators in the United Kingdom were first banned, in 1986, from operating non-noise certificated aircraft, that is to say aircraft which did not meet either the standards applicable for Chapters 2 or 3 in relation to subsonic aircraft, Chapter 4 for supersonic jet aircraft, or Chapters 5 and 6 in relation to propeller-driven aircraft. Such a policy was instituted by Directive 83/206/EEC which was implemented by the Air Navi-gation (Noise Certification) Order 1984[11] which came into force on 1 April 1984. The second stage was banning the addition of Chapter 2 so-called 'first generation' and therefore noisier, subsonic jet aircraft to the UK register from 1 November 1990. This was effected by the Air Navigation (Noise Certification) Order 1990.[12] The third stage consists of the phasing out of Chapter 2 aircraft from the register between 1 April 1995 to 1 April 2002. This is implemented by the Aeroplane Noise (Limitation of Operation of Aeroplanes) Regulations 1993.[13]

As far as air transport is concerned the Commission intends to develop an integrated approach to noise reduction by employing a variety of instruments. It is likely that more stringent emission limits will be imposed. Economic instru-ments will also be employed to encourage the use of aircraft which emit lower noise. Under its Transport Action Programme during the period 1997–2000 the Commission would propose a Common Framework for land use around airports.

Conclusions: The impact of EC law to date

The EC approach to the control of environmental noise has been product-related. Roughly 25 directives covering ten products have been made. The approach has been palpably piecemeal (indeed the EC's approach to noise has been scathingly referred to by Rehbinder and Stewart as, 'no more than a kind of regulatory patchwork'[14] but it has been effective nonetheless. In terms of improving the quality of the general environment the EC's influence has been most significant in relation to reducing noise from vehicles including aircraft. This is an area where the EC is continuing to devote particular attention. Further reductions of noise emissions from various sources such as cars, trucks, aircraft, cranes, mowers etc. is part of the Community's Fifth Action Programme on the Environment.[15] Indeed, the Community is contemplating more use being made of economic instruments in this particular sphere. In its Green Paper, *Towards Fair and Efficient Pricing in Transport,* the use of road noise incentive schemes based on an annual tax or road pricing is suggested as a way forward.

---

[11] SI 1984 No. 368.
[12] SI 1990 No. 1514.
[13] SI 1993 No. 1409.
[14] Rehbinder and Stewart, *Environmental Protection Policy* (Berlin: Walter de Gruyter, 1985), p. 203.
[15] OJ C 138 17.5.93, p. 56.

As far as railway noise is concerned the imposition of track charges to take account of noise is also a possibility.

Generally speaking, the existing body of EC noise law is highly detailed but narrowly focused. Critics such as Krämer[16] have observed that the standards set in the various noise directives reflect the current state of the art in manufacture and do not stretch the producers to innovate to reduce noise emissions dramatically. Furthermore, the fact that the EC has regulated for different types of products and set special standards for each has contributed to the incoherence of the law and the multiplicity of standards in the United Kingdom. There is also the concern that the EC, by pre-empting state action in setting noise limits for products, has prevented the United Kingdom from acting more swiftly and effectively in those areas.

The future direction of EC noise policy

While no doubt some benefit to the environment has accrued from the various directives on noise (indeed it is likely that the Community will continue its current approach in respect of transport and products as far as noise is concerned) one of the outstanding weaknesses of the EC approach to noise has been the lack of a coherent policy. Things may be about to change in the near future, however.

The Fifth Action Programme on the Environment[17] recognises noise as an urban problem. Importantly, it is regarded as a danger to human health not merely a nuisance. Noise is also seen as a pressing environmental problem and accorded priority. In conformity with the principle of subsidiarity, responsibility for the quality of the urban environment and for undertaking the necessary remedial measures will be a matter for the competent local authorities. Article 5(5) provides that:

Pursuant to the principle of subsidiarity, responsibility for the quality of the urban environment (including noise control) and for undertaking the necessary remedial or improvement measures will be a matter for competent authorities, primarily the local authorities ... The purpose of Community policy must therefore be to encourage local authorities to rise to the challenge and to assist them to find the best way of doing this.

The Community proposes to set targets for environmental noise whereby no person should be exposed to noise levels which endanger health and quality of life. Under Article 130s the standards that will be set will be 'minimum standards'. This does not imply, however, that such standards will be lax. By the provisions of Article 130r the Community is committed to 'aim at a high level of protection' and by Article 130t Member States are allowed to maintain or introduce even more stringent standards. The proposal is significant in that no

---

[16] Krämer, *EC Treaty and Environmental Law*, 2nd ed. (London: Sweet and Maxwell, 1995), p. 14.
[17] *Op. cit.* note 15, p. 52.

such right has thus far been recognised in any UK noise legislation. The Community recognises that night-time exposure of the population to noise levels in excess of L_{eq} dB(A) 65 should be phased out and at no point should a level of 85 dB(A) be exceeded. Again, the proportion of population at present exposed to levels between 55–65 dB(A) should not suffer any increase in these levels. Furthermore, the proportion of population at present exposed to levels less than 55 dB(A) should not suffer any increase above that level. In order to attain these objectives the Commission proposes to collect data on noise exposure levels. The centrepiece of the Community's policy is the institution of a noise abatement programme. The programme also intends to enlist the aid of the planning system in Member States and requires better zoning around airports, industrial areas, main roads and railways. Of particular interest is the recommendation that measures be adopted to 'influence behaviour' such as driving cars, flight procedures for aeroplanes, and industrial processes operating at night.

As far as noise from equipment is concerned the Commission intends to propose a framework directive to cover more than 60 types of equipment used outdoors including construction plant, garden equipment, as well as equipment used on specific vehicles. The directive would incorporate the existing directives on noise from outdoor equipment. One innovative and indeed important feature of the new directive will be a requirement for manufacturers to label all equipment which is placed on the market bearing a guaranteed noise emission level. The intended effect of this is that the consumer would tend to chose items of the same variety which emitted less noise and therefore manufacturers would be placed under economic pressure to reduce noise from equipment. Another important feature is the collection of information on the range of noise emission values of equipment on the market, their populations as well as contribution to noise exposure.

Furthermore there is a strong possibility that in the near future the Commission will adopt a more holistic approach to environmental noise. A directive will be made, first, to establish a common noise exposure index (i.e. noise standards) throughout the Community, and, secondly, that a harmonised procedure to assess or measure ambient noise exposure in the Community from specific sources such as road traffic, railways, aircraft and industrial installations[18] is employed by Member States. The directive will, we understand, place an obligation on the relevant authorities to carry out assessments of noise at first for urbanised areas with more than 500,000 inhabitants but gradually covering lesser sized urban areas, in areas along existing traffic routes or around industrial installations where night-time noise exposure exceeds or is likely to exceed certain limits (probably 65 dB(A)). This would require national authorities to compile noise maps which will be reviewed every five years. It is likely that the ambient noise exposure levels will be required to be expressed in terms of the A-weighted equivalent continuous sound pressure level L_{Aeq} in dB(A) deter-

---

[18] Volker Irmer, *Acustica* (1996) Vol. 82, Suppl. 1, p. 98.

mined during a specified period of time according to ISO 1996:1982. This will allow the Community to obtain easily comprehensible data on noise pollution in Member States and allow its dissemination.

Where the noise in a given area exceeds the limits laid down in the directive (probably 65 dB(A) or 55 dB(A) night-time noise) it would become incumbent on the responsible authority to prepare noise abatement plans which should be designed to meet target values which would be set by the Member States. The responsible authority would be obligated to meet the targets by (in order of priority):

1. reducing noisy activity;
2. employing noise reduction at source;
3. employing noise reduction on the path of transmission;
4. employing noise reduction at the reception point.

This hierarchy reflects current Community policy on pollution control. Member States will be given wide discretion as to the devices they employ to reduce noise. Among the various instruments which may be utilised to reduce noise to meet the relevant targets are:

1. the use of products and vehicles which emit low levels of noise;
2. the banning of noisy products;
3. traffic control;
4. the use of sound barriers;
5. concentrating noisy buildings in one place;
6. the use of sound insulation.

It will be observed that the methods which can be employed by the relevant authority include regulation involving criminal sanction commonly found in pollution control as well as the use of the control of development of land.

The relevant noise maps will be required to be made available to the general public. The maps would contain a description of the relevant area together with details about the main noise sources in the area as well as a description of the noise control measures the authority has adopted. The implications of this are significant in that the directive will force national and local authorities to adopt stricter standards than those which obtain at present. The other significant result would be that pressure groups would be given the opportunity to challenge public authorities who have a responsibility for noise. In recent years there has been some public disquiet about the unwillingness of local authority environmental health departments to enforce noise control legislation especially at night.

From a UK point of view the outstanding feature of the new proposals is that they eschew the concept of nuisance which is firmly ingrained in our domestic law relating to nuisance and which is not really understood by the general public. The fact that the public are uncertain that any given state of affairs constitutes a nuisance in law and therefore falls to be dealt with in terms of Part III of the Environmental Protection Act 1990 has a detrimental effect on the accountability of enforcing authorities to the electorate. On the other hand the introduction of fixed standards for various forms of noise coupled with a duty imposed on local authorities to make relevant information public would give, in theory at least, the public the opportunity to ascertain if the law was being enforced.

Another advantage of employing fixed standards to deal with the problem of noise instead of using nuisance law is that there is a difference between the law of nuisance north and south of the Border. Whereas in English law liability for nuisance is strict,[19] liability in Scots law only lies if culpa (or blame) can be proved.[20] Given that the courts accord the word 'nuisance' as used in statute its ordinary meaning at common law[21] the upshot of this is that we will have different interpretations of the word 'nuisance' in Scotland and England. Parliament never intended such a disparity! Furthermore, the Scottish courts have as yet to articulate the concept of culpa in terms of nuisance generally. The courts may find it especially difficult to do this in terms of noise nuisance.

The distinct unwillingness of local authorities to employ noise abatement zones seems to indicate that local authorities have a dislike of the use of fixed standards for noise largely on the basis that they are difficult to enforce. It would therefore be likely that the ambient levels set by the EC may be embraced with little enthusiasm by local authorities. Another disadvantage of fixed limit values is that they are inflexible and their application may result in overkill in certain areas, that is to say, that fixed ambient noise standards may not be warranted in certain localities.

Finally, if ambient noise levels are introduced into the United Kingdom, noise law, which is complicated enough at present, would become more so. For example, as far as England and Wales are concerned, we would have a situation where noise from industrial installations could be dealt with either as a statutory nuisance or in terms of the EC ambient noise exposure limits. If the factory was situated in a noise abatement zone the factory noise would come within an additional legal regime. Furthermore, night-time noise from dwellings in the same locality would come within the scope of the Noise Act 1996. In short while the proposed directive is well-intentioned, and if properly enforced, would undoubtedly redound to the benefit of the community in general it would result in the addition of more substantive law to an area of law which is over-complicated at present.

Noise in the workplace

Noise in the workplace can present a serious potential problem to employees.

---

[19] *Cambridge Water Co.* v. *Eastern Counties Leather plc* [1994] 2 WLR 53.
[20] See, e.g., *RHM Bakeries* v. *Strathclyde Regional Council* 1985 SC (HL) 17; *Kennedy* v. *Glenbelle Ltd* Inner House, 1996 SCLR 411.
[21] See e.g. *National Coal Board* v. *Thorne* [1976] 1 WLR 543.

Directive 86/188/EEC was the first directive specifically aimed at controlling noise in the workplace. The Directive applies to all workers except those in sea and air transport. The Directive requires employers to assess and, where necessary, measure noise levels to identify workers and workplaces to which the directive applies. Noise exposures are required to be reduced to the lowest levels reasonably practicable. Where noise levels are likely to exceed 90 dB(A) employers are required to give employees adequate information, and where necessary, training on, *inter alia*, potential risks to hearing, and the wearing of personal ear protectors. Ear protectors are required to be made available to employees where levels actually exceed 90 dB(A). The Directive goes on to provide that where the daily personal noise exposure exceeds 90 dB(A) the reasons for the excess level must be identified and measures taken to reduce the level as far as reasonably practicable. Personal ear protectors must also be worn. Where noise exposures exceed this level appropriate signs must be displayed and access restricted to the appropriate area. Member States are required to ensure that new plant or substantial changes to existing plants complies with the general requirement to reduce noise exposure to the lowest level reasonably practicable. Adequate information must be made available about the noise of machinery which exceeds 90 dB(A).

The original exposure limit set in the draft directive was 85 dB(A). However, this level was not acceptable to the UK Health and Safety Commission which made this clear in a consultative document published in 1981. The final Noise in the Workplace Directive indeed changed the limit to 90 dB(A) as stated above. The provisions of the Directive were implemented in the United Kingdom by the Noise at Work Regulations 1989.[22] However the implementing regulations do not fully implement the terms of the Directive relating to the provision of ear tests on the basis that such tests are available to everyone under the National Health Service. The Commission began infringement proceedings against the United Kingdom with the issue of an Article 169 letter in early 1991.[23]

Conclusions

The main thrust of EC noise law to date has been its pronounced emphasis on controlling noise from products and vehicles. While existing directives have concentrated on various noise sources which have presented environmental problems, the legislation has also been driven by the desire to permit the free movement of goods throughout the Community. However, the Fifth Action Programme on the Environment and the proposed directive on ambient noise represent a marked shift in emphasis from a product-related

---

[22] SI 1989 No. 1790.
[23] See Haigh, *op. cit.* note 6, 10.8–3.

approach to one which is patently 'people-centered' in that the proposed directive's purpose is explicitly orientated to preventing damage to human health.
Indeed this new initiative serves as a good example of the Community's
increasing interest in matters environmental as well as human health.[24]

---

[24] Since this chapter was written, the European Commission has published a Green Paper on Future
Noise Policy, COM(96) 540 final.

Part IV

REGULATION IN PRACTICE II:
NATURE CONSERVATION

Chapter 12

NATURE CONSERVATION LAW
Colin Reid

In considering the impact of the EC on nature conservation law in Great Britain[1] two items stand out for consideration, the Birds Directive of 1979[2] and the Habitats and Species Directive of 1992,[3] but there are other areas in which the EC has also made its mark. In some cases this has been by direct intervention, e.g. in relation to trade in endangered species, while in others, e.g. agricultural policy, the impact has been indirect, but nonetheless significant. Beyond the legal rules coming from the EC, a variety of plans, programmes and grant schemes also play their part in shaping what is happening in relation to nature conservation across Europe, but it is the legal measures which form the focus of this chapter.[4]

Although an incidental impact through the regulation of trade might have been conceivable, it is unlikely that the founders of the Community imagined that their creation would play any direct part in the conservation of wild species and habitats. The initial absence of any provision in the Treaty authorising legislation in this field would appear to have been a serious obstacle to any initiatives prior to the insertion of the Environment Title[5] by the Single European Act. However, as in other areas of environmental law, this did not prevent the Community from taking action, although the strict legality of the early measures may be questioned. The Birds Directive, for example, was authorised under the residual power granted by Article 235 of the Treaty on the basis that:

---

[1] As usual, the legal position in Northern Ireland is rather different and it is not discussed here (cf. Morrow and Turner, Chapter 5 above).

[2] Directive on the conservation of wild birds, Directive 79/409/EEC of 2 April 1979 (OJ 1979 L 103, p. 1).

[3] Directive on the conservation of natural habitats and of wild fauna and flora, Directive 92/43/ EEC of 21 May 1992 (OJ 1992 L 206, p. 7).

[4] Examples include the CORINE programme classifying habitats (Commission of the European Communities, *CORINE: Examples of the Use of the Results of the Programme 1985–1990* (1993)); see generally Bennett (ed), *Conserving Europe's Natural Heritage: Towards a European Ecological Network* (London: IEEP, 1994) and Davies, 'The Environment Agency' (1994) 14 YEL 313, at 317–323.

[5] Articles 130r-130s, subsequently amended by the Maastricht Agreement.

the conservation of the species of wild birds naturally occurring within the European territory of the Member States is necessary for the attainment, within the operation of the common market, of the Community's objectives regarding the improvement of living conditions, a harmonious development of economic activities throughout the Community and a continuous and balanced expansion.[6]

It is difficult to see exactly why such steps were absolutely necessary for these purposes, and if so, why the necessity was limited to the conservation of wild birds and did not extend to wild plants and other animals. Any such doubts, though, are in the past. The revised Treaty clearly makes provision for far-ranging environmental measures, and it was under the new powers that the Habitats and Species Directive was made.

The direct impact of EC law on nature conservation in Great Britain has not been as great in this field as in many other areas of environmental law. There are two main reasons for this. First, there is a long history of legal measures in this country designed to protect wildlife, particularly birds, with broad protective measures dating back to the Wild Birds Protection Act 1872.[7] Accordingly, there was already a legal framework here which could readily accommodate the EC measures, especially those dealing with species protection. The second reason is that the EC measures are based on an international treaty to which the United Kingdom is already a party in its own right. The Convention on the Conservation of European Wildlife and Natural Habitats was agreed in Bern in 1979 under the auspices of the Council of Europe.[8] Both the Birds and the Habitats and Species Directives draw heavily on the Bern Convention for their overall provisions and wording, and the main UK legislation in this field, the Wildlife and Countryside Act 1981, was introduced to give effect both to the Convention and to the Birds Directive. The presence of a modern, comprehensive piece of legislation, drafted in the light of the EC measures and the international convention which inspired them, has meant that much of the law here complies with EC law without the need for further adjustment, with most difficulties lying at the margins.

There is however a clear distinction between the provisions on species protection and those offering protection to habitat. In the latter field, the measures in the UK have been largely discretionary, with the possibility of protection being overridden by other considerations, e.g. economic development. This is not the approach which has been adopted by the EC, where, although protection is not absolute, much higher hurdles have to be surmounted before sites identified as worthy of protection can be put at risk in pursuit of other objectives. It follows that more far-reaching changes in the law and in practice have been required to give effect to the habitat provisions of the Species and Habitats Directive than have been necessary to accommodate the restrictions on killing

---

[6] Preamble to Directive 79/409/EEC OJ L 103, p. 1 (the text in the Official Journal is worded slightly differently and does not make grammatical sense).

[7] See generally Reid, *Nature Conservation Law* (Edinburgh: W. Green/Sweet and Maxwell, 1994), pp. 4–11.

[8] See Lyster, *International Wildlife Law* (Cambridge: Grotius Publications, 1985), ch. 8.

and taking individual birds and animals. Before considering these, though, it is worth examining some of the less direct ways in which EC law has had a significant effect on conservation in this country.

Agriculture

Nature conservation is about much more than the protection of a handful of sites and species designated as being of particular value. Indeed there is a danger that the greater the attention paid to such special sites and species, the less the care taken to ensure the health of the wider countryside. The single greatest factor affecting the survival of wildlife in the countryside is agricultural practice, and as agricultural policy has been a central aspect of the EC since its foundation, this is where the EC has probably had the greatest impact on conservation in this country. Until recently, policy throughout western Europe has been directed towards the maximisation of agricultural production. In Britain this led to highly specialised agricultural units which produce high yields but require large fields for intensive crop growing or industrial buildings for intensive livestock rearing, in all cases calling for substantial use of fertilisers, pesticides and herbicides. Such practices are very destructive of the 'traditional' countryside (hedgerows, ponds, varied habitats) and the flora and fauna which it supports.

Now, however, it has been realised that this policy has been too successful and the EC is faced with an overproduction of many products which cannot be sold at a worthwhile price on the open market but must still be paid for to prevent agricultural collapse leading to the depopulation of large parts of rural Europe. Moreover, the environmental harm being done by the incentives to ever-higher production has been realised. There is still a long way to go, but agricultural policies do now contain an element of environmental concern.[9]

Two examples can be given. The first is the creation of Environmentally Sensitive Areas.[10] The origin of these lies in an EC Regulation[11] seeking to improve the efficiency of agricultural structures but which also allowed Member States to introduce schemes to encourage the use of environmentally beneficial agricultural practices in areas of ecological or landscape importance. The scheme adopted here provides for the designation by the agriculture ministers, after consultation with the conservancy councils, of areas where it appears particularly desirable to conserve or enhance the natural beauty of the area, to conserve the flora, fauna, geological, or physiographical features of the area, or to protect buildings or other objects of archaeological, architectural, or historic interest, and where these aims are likely to be facilitated by the mainten-

---

[9] The Treaty requires that 'Environmental protection requirements must be integrated into the definition and implementation of other Community policies' (Article 130r(2)), but as yet environmental issues are having only a marginal effect in most areas.
[10] Agriculture Act 1986, s. 18; see Reid, *op. cit.* note 7, pp. 173–175.
[11] Regulation 797/85/EEC Article 19 (OJ 1985 L 93, p. 1).

ance or adoption of particular agricultural methods. Within these areas, agreements can be made with those having an interest in agricultural land whereby in exchange for prescribed payments that person agrees to manage the land in accordance with the agreement. These payments are designed to encourage farmers to continue with traditional less-intensive farming methods, making up for the additional income which might otherwise be gained by switching to more intensive methods of production.

The second example is the more varied set of measures deriving from the agri-environment programme. The main legislative measure, Regulation 2078/92/EEC,[12] sets out the objectives of the aid scheme as including the promotion of: the use of farming practices which reduce the polluting effect of agriculture; an environmentally favourable extensification of crop farming; ways of using agricultural land which are compatible with protection and improvement of the environment; the upkeep of abandoned farmland and woodlands where necessary for environmental reasons; and long-term set-aside of agricultural land for reasons connected with the environment.[13] The embracing of such environmental objectives within agricultural policy is to be welcomed, but remains only a minor feature in the mass of policies and support schemes which are founded solely on considerations of finance and productivity.

Within Britain the opportunity created by the agri-environment programme has been taken through the introduction of a number of grant schemes specifically designed to further conservation.[14] Thus under the Habitats (Scotland) Regulations 1994[15] farmers can receive aid if in relation to certain habitats they set aside land for 20 years in order to establish or improve the habitat, or agree for ten years to use farming practices compatible with the environment. For each habitat (waterside, upland scrub, damp lowland grassland and marsh communities, dry lowland grassland, coastal heath) there are detailed management rules which must be observed if the grant is to be paid. Similar measures have been adopted in the rest of Britain.[16] As with the Environmentally Sensitive Areas, this should provide a real incentive to manage at least part of the countryside in a way compatible with nature conservation, but there is still a long way to go before the whole Common Agricultural Policy can be seen as an ally of conservation.

A similar need exists to ensure that fisheries policy takes nature conser-

---

[12] OJ 1992 L 215, p. 85.

[13] Article 1.

[14] See generally Rodgers, 'Environmental Gain, Set-aside and the Implementation of EU Agricultural Reform in the United Kingdom' in Rodgers (ed), *Nature Conservation and Countryside Law* (Cardiff: University of Wales Press, 1996), pp.111–137.

[15] SI 1994 No. 2710 (as amended).

[16] For England, the Habitat (Water Fringe) Regulations 1994 (SI 1994 No. 1291); Habitat (Former Set-Aside Land) Regulations 1994 (SI 1994 No. 1292); Habitat (Salt Marsh) Regulations 1994 (SI 1994, No. 1293). For Wales, the Habitat (Broadleaved Woodland) (Wales) Regulations 1994 (SI 1994 No. 3099); Habitat (Water Fringe) (Wales) Regulations 1994 (SI 1994 No. 3100); Habitat (Coastal Belt) (Wales) Regulations 1994 (SI 1994 No. 3101); Habitat (Species-Rich Grassland) (Wales) Regulations 1994 (SI 1994 No. 3102). See also the Countryside Stewardship Regulations 1996 (SI 1996 No. 695). All of the measures here are subject to frequent amendment.

vation issues fully into account, but here there has been even less progress in reflecting broader conservation goals. The Common Fisheries Policy includes comments on the environment, but remains far from reflecting a deep commitment to conservation or sustainability in its broadest sense:

The objective is to control the ecological impact of fishing but not to eliminate it altogether. A balance has to be struck between economic needs and the protection of the environment.[17]

Policy continues to be driven by the structural problems of the industry and the need to conserve commercial species rather than any wider conservation goals, and little progress has been made even to tackle some of the obviously damaging effects of current policy, e.g. the dumping back into the sea of species which cannot lawfully be landed but are caught as fishermen target other species which they can legitimately sell.

Many other measures in this area also have the potential to affect nature conservation. The laws on plant and animal health, on the movement of animals and plants within and outwith the Community, on the handling and use of pesticides and herbicides are examples. The greatest impact, though, remains that of the overall thrust of agricultural and fisheries policy. Some awareness of environmental considerations and of the need to ensure sustainable policies and practices is beginning to emerge, but major changes will be required before agricultural policy can be seen as the ally and protector of the countryside, rather than a driving force behind continued destruction of biodiversity and wildlife.

Pollution

Nature conservation is also affected by the Community's general policies on pollution control. Anything which reduces harmful emissions is bound to have an impact on the general health of the countryside, and the Community's adoption of legislation on a whole host of matters, from global warming and ozone depletion to the levels of noise made by lawnmowers, helps to protect the environment. To the extent that these have forced a raising of standards in the UK, conservation here has benefited from such measures.

Water pollution is an area in which the Community's contributions can be seen to have an obvious impact here. Although most provisions have not been specifically directed at nature conservation, such measures as those seeking to prevent discharges into water of dangerous substances,[18] clearly benefit all plants and animals relying on the aquatic environment. The effect on wild flora and

---

[17] Directorate General for Fisheries, *The New Common Fisheries Policy* (Luxembourg: 1994) p. 41.
[18] Directive 76/464/EEC (OJ 1976 L 129, p. 23) as amended and supported by supplementary provisions, e.g. on mercury, Directive 82/176/EEC (OJ 1982 L 81, p. 29) and cadmium, Directive 83/513/EEC (OJ 1983 L 291, p. 1).

fauna is sometimes more directly addressed, perhaps most clearly in the measures against pollution by nitrates from agricultural sources. The pollution of drinking water by excess nitrates is clearly undesirable, but the preamble to Directive 91/676/EEC[19] makes it clear that the measure was considered necessary to protect not only 'human health' but also 'living resources and aquatic ecosystems'. In identifying the 'vulnerable zones' within which special measures are to be taken to protect waters, the criteria to be applied include 'whether freshwater lakes, other freshwater bodies, estuaries, coastal waters and marine waters are found to be eutrophic or in the near future may become eutrophic' if action is not taken.[20] Eutrophication itself is defined wholly by ecological criteria,[21] with no specific link to human health or to any proposed use of the waters, so that protective measures can be taken wholly on the basis of conserving the wild flora and fauna dependent on the existing state of the water. This Directive has been implemented in Great Britain,[22] although so far reliance has been placed on the use of agreements rather than stronger powers of coercion to achieve restrictions in the various forms of potentially damaging agricultural practices.

This is just one example of how the EC's more general environmental policy can have an impact on conservation. Much environmental policy remains driven by concern for human health, rather than deeper ecological concern, but clearly environmental improvements are likely to be of benefit to wild flora and fauna. It is now time to turn to those measures more directly addressing nature conservation issues.

Trade in endangered species

The EC has contributed to international measures to protect endangered species. The Community itself and all of the Member States are parties to CITES, the Convention on International Trade in Endangered Species.[23] This Convention establishes a series of requirements for import and export permits in order to control the trade in certain species which are endangered or may become so if their exploitation is not carefully regulated. The main EC measure, Regulation 3626/82/EEC,[24] not only meets all of the requirements of the Con-

---

[19] OJ 1991 L 375, p. 1.

[20] Directive 91/676/EEC, Annex 1.

[21] *Ibid.* Article 2(i).

[22] Control of Pollution Act 1974, ss. 31B-31D; Water Resources Act 1991, ss. 94–96; the detailed rules for England are contained in the Nitrate Sensitive Areas Regulations 1994 (SI 1994 No. 1729) as amended by the Nitrate Sensitive Areas (Amendment) Regulations 1995 (SI 1995 Nos. 1708 and 2095) and the Protection of Water Against Agricultural Nitrate Pollution (England and Wales) Regulations 1996 (SI 1996 No. 888).

[23] See generally, Favre, *International Trade in Endangered Species: A Guide to CITES* (Dordrecht, London: Nijhoff, 1989) and Lyster, *op. cit.* note 8, ch. 12.

[24] OJ 1982 L 384, p. 1; to be replaced from June 1997 by Regulation 338/97/EC (OJ 1997 L 61, p. 1). The detailed lists of species which are covered are constantly being adjusted; the most recent major reformulation being in Regulation 558/95/EEC (OJ 1995 L 57, p. 1).

vention but goes beyond them by including some additional species and by requiring both import and export permits in some cases where the Convention itself requires only an export permit for some.

For the United Kingdom, this means that there are two sets of legislation implementing CITES. The Endangered Species (Import and Export) Act 1976 preceded the measures taken at Community level and still applies to aspects of trade with those outwith the Community, whereas the EC Regulation, supported by domestic regulations creating offences and giving powers of search,[25] also takes effect. A significant element of the EC Regulation is that Member States must recognise the decisions of the relevant authorities in other Member States and that once a permit has been granted it is valid throughout the Community.[26] States are entitled to take stricter measures than those prescribed by the Community, provided that these comply with the Treaty, in particular that they do not amount to arbitrary discrimination or disguised trade restrictions, and apply equally to non-Member States.[27]

This perhaps illustrates one of the ways in which the Community does have a significant impact on nature conservation law in this country. Whatever the motive behind their adoption, measures which are adopted here but can affect other Member States are only valid if they comply with the Treaty, not only with its environmental provisions but also with those provisions seeking to guarantee free trade and free movement of goods. Measures which interfere with these goals can be justified, but must meet the test of proportionality. Thus when Germany imposed an almost total ban on the import of live crayfish in order to protect its native populations from disease, the European Court of Justice held that it had acted unlawfully as this desirable goal could have been achieved by less drastic measures, more closely targeted at the actual risks which were to be avoided.[28] Thus any UK measure to control trade in endangered species must be in compliance with the EC law not only on this specific point but in its more general application.

The EC has also adopted other measures to protect species beyond its borders. The commercial importation of whale products is banned by the requirement for a licence for any import of any meat, oil or other products derived from cetaceans, or of goods treated with such products, coupled with a provision that no such licence is to be granted for commercial purposes.[29] The commercial importation of the skins of whitecoat pups of harp seals and of the pups of hooded seals is also prohibited,[30] and the licence requirements for the importation of raw or worked ivory from the African elephant were very strict even before such trade was essentially banned under the CITES arrangements.[31]

---

[25] Control of Trade in Endangered Species (Enforcement) Regulations 1985 (SI 1985 No. 1155).
[26] Regulation 3626/82/EEC, Article 9.
[27] *Ibid.* Article 15.
[28] Case C-131/93, *Commission v. Germany* [1994] ECR I-3303.
[29] Regulation 348/81/EEC (OJ 1981 L 39, p. 1).
[30] Directive 83/129/EEC (OJ 1983 L 91, p. 30).
[31] Regulation 2496/89/EEC (OJ 1989 L 240, p. 5).

Species protection

In examining the two main EC measures directed at nature conservation, the Birds and the Habitats and Species Directives, it is convenient to look at the species protection provisions separately from those concerning the protection of habitat. The former have had much less impact on the law here as by the time that the Community was considering its first steps in this field, Britain already had the framework for granting legal protection to wild flora and fauna. Earlier measures relating to birds had led to the comprehensive Protection of Birds Act 1954, while protection had been extended to some other creatures and to some plants by the Conservation of Wild Creatures and Wild Plants Act 1975. When the law was thoroughly revised in the Wildlife and Countryside Act 1981, the changes took into account the terms of the Bern Convention on which both the Birds Directive and the more recent Habitats and Species Directive are based. It is therefore difficult to assess the extent to which the Birds Directive itself played a part in influencing the law, although clearly the fact that obligations had been converted from ones binding in international law only to ones which could be more effectively enforced in the Community legal system played a significant part in persuading the government that the time had indeed come for the law in this area to be revised.[32]

As the 1981 Act contains measures in keeping with the key provisions protecting most wild birds and allowing limited hunting of others, it is essentially only at the margins that there have been difficulties over compliance with the Birds Directive. However, since 1981 there have had to be some adjustments to the law in order to ensure that the European provisions are observed.

Both the 1981 Act and the Directive allow for the killing of pest species, but whereas the 1981 Act granted general permission for 'authorised persons'[33] to kill the species listed in Part II of Sch. 2 to the Act,[34] the Directive's terms are more limited. The derogations which it permits must specify the methods by which the killing is to take place as well as the species affected, and annual reports are required on the effect of the derogation.[35] The 1981 Act's general authorisation to kill the listed species was considered to fall foul of these requirements, particularly as it left the authorities with no effective way to control or monitor its operation, and accordingly the legal basis for dealing with pest species has been changed. No species is now listed in Part II of Sch

---

[32] It has been suggested that some of the species protection measures in the Birds Directive may have direct effect, but not the habitat protection ones as these leave some discretion to Member States; *Kincardine and Deeside District Council* v. *Forestry Commissioners* 1992 SLT 1180, at 1187.

[33] In effect the owners and occupiers of land and those authorised by them or by local authorities or other statutory bodies: Wildlife and Countryside Act 1981, s. 27(1).

[34] *Ibid.* s. 2(2).

[35] Directive 79/409/EEC, *op. cit.* note 6, Article 9.

2[36] and permission to kill these birds now comes in the form of a licence granted by the relevant minister under the terms of s. 16 of the Act, which provides for licences to be granted for a variety of specific reasons, authorising acts normally prohibited under the Act's preceding terms. This change was, however, one of legal form rather than of substance, as the initial licences granted immediately after the change granted permission to any 'authorised person' to kill or take the same species as had been listed in Part II of Sch. 2, using any method not prohibited under the 1981 Act, in effect achieving exactly the same scope of authorisation as before.

Further change has been necessary to ensure that the 1981 Act more completely matches the Directive. The Wildlife and Countryside Act 1981 (Amendment) Regulations 1995[37] make a number of further changes to ensure that the circumstances in which such licences can be given match those permitted in the Directive. The authority responsible must be satisfied that there is no other satisfactory solution before a licence is granted, it is now expressly stated in the British provisions that the methods which are authorised must be specified, and in some cases it is expressly stated that the licence must be granted on a selective basis and in relation to a small number of birds.[38] The discrepancies between the 1981 Act and the Directive are thus gradually being eliminated, and so far the United Kingdom has been able to avoid the experience of so many other Member States of being the subject of proceedings for non-compliance with the species protection terms of the Birds Directive.[39]

A different approach towards implementation has been taken with the Habitats and Species Directive. The terms of the Birds Directive were taken into account when comprehensive British legislation was being drafted, so that there is a single piece of legislation dealing with this topic, incorporating the requirements of the Directive into the broader terms of the law in this country. For the Habitats and Species Directive, there has been no attempt at incorporating and integrating the Directive's provisions into the existing legal background. Instead the United Kingdom has made the Conservation (Natural Habitats &c.) Regulations 1994[40] which give effect to the Directive by introducing measures, frequently using the same words as the Directive, which overlap with existing provisions. This almost direct transposition of the EC measures into domestic law should reduce the opportunities for discrepancies between the two, but makes life much more difficult for those who have to work with the law. Two overlapping but quite different sets of provisions have to be consulted to work out what the law is, and it may be difficult to identify where the new provisions

---

[36] Wildlife and Countryside Act 1981 (Variation of Schedules 2 and 3) Order 1992 (SI 1992 No. 3010).
[37] SI 1995 No. 2825.
[38] *Ibid.* reg. 3, adding new subsections to s. 16 of the 1981 Act.
[39] See Wils, 'The Birds Directive 15 Years Later: A Survey of the Case Law and a Comparison with the Habitats Directive' (1994) JEL Vol. 6, No. 2, 219–242, at 235–239.
[40] SI 1994 No. 2716.

actually change the legal position as opposed to restating it in different words. For example, is there a legally significant difference between the two offences of 'intentionally' killing certain protected species of animal,[41] and 'deliberately' killing them?[42] Two separate lists of protected species must be borne in mind, and the appropriate provisions applied to each. This approach may be easier and more certain for the government, saving the trouble of working out how the existing law must be amended to comply with the Directive and reducing the risk of being taken before the European Court of Justice if complete compliance is not achieved, but it causes much more work, confusion, and difficulty for the users of the law.

The measures giving effect to the species protection provisions of the Directive do alter the law here, but only for those species protected under the Directive, which are only some of those covered by the Wildlife and Countryside Act 1981. Apart from minor changes in wording, such as the use of 'deliberately' instead of 'intentionally' or 'keep' instead of 'have in one's possession', there are a number of ways in which the 1994 Regulations go beyond the law set out in the 1981 Act. For plants the important point is that the law now penalises those who 'pick, collect, cut, uproot or destroy'[43] protected plants as opposed to merely those who 'pick, uproot or destroy'[44] them, so that someone collecting ripe seed without damaging the plant itself can now be punished. For animals, one significant change is that it is now an offence to damage or destroy the breeding site or resting place of the protected species,[45] whereas under the 1981 Act such conduct is only criminal if intentionally carried out.[46] A defence exists under the 1994 Regulations for acts which are the incidental result of a lawful operation and which could not reasonably have been avoided,[47] but changes in the law may be required, as this defence is drawn wider than any equivalent exception in the Directive itself, which allows derogations only on a number of specified grounds and where there is no satisfactory alternative and no detriment to the survival of the relevant population at a satisfactory level.[48] Other differences between the 1981 Act and the measures taken to implement the directive include an extension of the prohibited means of killing or taking certain species,[49] the extension of such prohibitions to certain species of fish,[50] and express provision to grant licences for action taken in relation to conserving wild animals or plants or introducing them to certain areas.[51]

---

[41] 1981 Act, s. 9(1).
[42] 1994 Regulations, reg. 39(1).
[43] *Ibid.* reg. 43(1).
[44] 1981 Act, s. 13(1).
[45] 1994 Regulations, reg. 39(1).
[46] 1981 Act, s. 9(4).
[47] 1994 Regulations, reg. 39(3).
[48] Directive 92/43/EEC, Article 15.
[49] 1994 Regulations, reg. 41.
[50] *Ibid.* Sch. 3.
[51] *Ibid.* reg. 44 and 1981 Act, s. 16(1)(ca) and (cb), as added by the Wildlife and Countryside Act 1981 (Amendment) Regulations 1995 (SI 1995 No. 2825).

All of these changes may be significant in individual cases, but they do not fundamentally alter the nature of the law here. The two Directives have required some tightening up of the law, particularly in relation to the granting of exceptions to the protective measures, but the overall approach in the European and domestic measures has been essentially the same. In relation to habitat protection, however, a much greater difference of approach is to be seen.

Habitat protection

It is in relation to habitat protection that EC law is having its greatest impact on the law here. There have long been provisions in British law endeavouring to identify and protect habitats of value, but the British approach has been one of seeking to balance the conflicting interests in a site. Nature conservation is one of these, but is not the only one and may be overridden by other considerations. In contrast, and although they stop short of giving absolute protection to a site, the EC provisions make it clear that on the designated sites conservation is to have the highest priority and it is only in exceptional circumstances that damaging operations can be allowed to take place.

The British approach is typified by the law relating to Sites of Special Scientific Interest.[52] These sites are designated for their special value, but there is no absolute protection given to them. The protective measures amount to no more than requiring formal notification and a four-month delay before damaging operations are carried out, and it is quite permissible for the planning authority to grant planning permission for development which wholly destroys the site, provided that it can show that it has reasonably considered that other relevant considerations outweigh the conservation interest. Even if stronger measures are taken,[53] these amount to further prohibitions on damaging conduct and it is only if a management agreement is made or compulsory purchase resorted to that the future management of the site to preserve its value can be ensured.

The approach in EC law is different. The measures in the Birds Directive[54] have now been amended[55] so as to be in line with those in the Habitats and Species Directive, and both place much more importance on the conservation of the selected sites.[56] The latter Directive sets out the criteria for designating Special Areas of Conservation and requires that the necessary conservation measures be taken, including management plans, so as to meet the ecological requirements of the site. Sites are to be protected from damage or

---

[52] Wildlife and Countryside Act 1981, s. 28; see Reid, *op. cit.* note 7, pp. 155–165.
[53] E.g. making a nature conservation order under s. 29 of the 1981 Act.
[54] Directive 79/409/EEC, Article 4.
[55] Directive 92/43/EEC, Article 7.
[56] *Ibid.* Articles 3–11.

deterioration,[57] and any projects which may damage the site are to be permitted only after thorough examination and once it is shown that there is no alternative and that the project is justified by 'imperative reasons of overriding public interest', only a limited range of such reasons being acceptable for priority sites.[58] Protection is thus not limited to preventing specific damaging operations on the site and is not discretionary. Effective measures must be taken to ensure the conservation of the site from all threats and only in truly exceptional circumstances can harmful development be permitted.

The priority given to effective protection over any competing interests in the site is clearly demonstrated by the two leading cases on the Birds Directive, Case C-57/89, *Commission* v. *Germany*[59] and Case C-355/90, *Commission* v. *Spain*[60] in both of which it was made clear that the Member State must ensure that valuable sites are effectively protected. The application of this approach in the British context has been confirmed by the European Court of Justice in the Lappel Bank Litigation.[61] Again it is made clear that conservation must be given a high priority. Although Member States have discretion in determining which areas are to be designated as Special Protection Areas under the Birds Directive, this discretion is to be exercised on biological criteria alone, disregarding economic considerations, and any action to damage or reduce the site must be justified in accordance with the strict tests laid out in the legislation and be accompanied by the requisite compensatory measures.[62] The British government's argument that the conservation issues can be balanced with economic considerations at all stages of the designation and protection process is thus firmly rejected.

The need to ensure the more effective protection required by the EC measures is now reflected in the 1994 Regulations implementing the Habitats and Species Directive, but only in an indirect way. The existing law did have the capacity to enable strong protective measures to be taken if the Secretaries of State and conservancy councils were prepared to act, ultimately authorising the compulsory purchase of a site, and the starting point of the implementing Regulations is an obligation on these ministers and bodies to 'exercise their functions . . . so as to secure compliance with the requirements of the Habitats Directive'.[63] This obligation should ensure that there is now greater readiness actually to exercise the stronger powers which are available in relation to conservation. More detailed provisions are made to ensure compliance. There

---

[57] The reference to 'deterioration' is significant as this can clearly be the result of natural or diffuse processes, not the specific 'potentially damaging operations' which are at the core of the prohibitions in relation to SSSIs.

[58] Directive 92/43/EEC, Article 6.

[59] [1991] ECR I-883 (*Leybucht Dykes*).

[60] [1993] ECR I-4221 (*Santona Marshes*).

[61] Case C-44/95, *R* v. *Secretary of State for the Environment, ex parte Royal Society for the Protection of Birds*; [1997] 2 WLR 123; the prior British proceedings are reported at (1995) 7 Admin LR 434.

[62] See Directive 92/43/EEC, Article 6.

[63] Conservation (Natural Habitats &c.) Regulations 1994 (SI 1994 No. 2716), reg. 3(2). See further Ball, Chapter 13, and Purdue, Chapter 14, pp. 248–252.

is provision for the control of potentially damaging operations on European Sites,[64] parallel to the measures for SSSIs[65] but with the power to amend the list of such operations after the original notification[66] and to make byelaws.[67] Special nature conservation orders can prohibit activities unless the consent of the relevant conservancy council has been obtained,[68] in contrast to the effect of nature conservation orders under the existing law, which can serve only to delay operations.[69]

Existing law is further altered by the measures to give effect to the strict tests which must be met before activities which may damage a European site can be permitted.[70] In keeping with the terms of the Directive, any project which may have a significant effect on a European site (including activities not on the site itself) must be assessed and can be given official permission only if it will not adversely affect the integrity of the site. If an adverse effect is likely, then approval can be given only if there is no alternative and the project is required by imperative reasons of overriding public interest; in relation to priority habitats only a limited range of such reasons are acceptable. Likewise, existing permissions must be reviewed according to the same criteria and where necessary modified or revoked. Specific measures incorporate these tests into a range of specific regimes for authorising development (town and country planning, roads, discharge consents etc.), but these tests and restrictions are of general application.

The effect of this is that although the control of harmful activities still makes use of regulatory frameworks which are essentially discretionary, the discretion of the relevant authorities is now greatly restricted. For European sites, nature conservation does not count as simply one factor to be balanced with any competing interests, but is given clear priority which can only be overcome in exceptional circumstances. As a matter of law, not just ministerial guidance etc., it is no longer permissible to allow economic considerations to justify harm to a protected site. Moreover, the justification for any departure from this level of protection is subject to examination by the European Commission[71] and Court of Justice.[72] This amounts to a major shift in law and policy, although, as the government's approach in the Lappel Bank case demonstrates, may take some time to be embraced fully by all of the relevant authorities.

---

[64] These are Special Protection Areas for birds and Special Areas of Conservation designated under the Birds and Habitats and Species Directives, and sites undergoing the process of designation; 1994 Regulations, reg. 10.

[65] *Ibid.* regs. 18–20.

[66] *Ibid.* reg. 18(2).

[67] *Ibid.* regs. 28–31.

[68] *Ibid.* regs. 22–27.

[69] Wildlife and Countryside Act 1981, s. 29; see Reid, *op.cit.* note 7, pp. 165–170.

[70] Part IV of the 1994 Regulations.

[71] E.g. Commission Opinion 96/15/EEC (OJ 1996 L 6, p. 14) on whether the proposal for a new road across a priority habitat in Germany does meet the test of 'imperative reasons of overriding public interest' in terms of the Habitats and Species Directive.

[72] E.g. Case C-57/89, note 59 above.

The legislation is thus in place to give effect to most of the Habitats and Species Directive, although some clear problem areas remain, e.g. it is widely accepted that the measures introduced on marine conservation fall well short of the Directive's requirements. As with the species protection measures, one can expect that in the years to come there will be a gradual adjustment of the law here to ensure that the gaps and inconsistencies are resolved. The bigger question, though, is whether the legal framework will in fact be used to achieve the level of conservation which the Directive demands. Will planning authorities give nature conservation the weight which is required, not just for European sites but for the wider countryside?[73] Will the government's proposals for Special Areas of Conservation fully meet the requirements of the Directive, especially for rivers and marine areas? Will the legal steps which are available in fact be taken in order to prevent the deterioration of sites? In short will it be accepted that nature conservation has to be given virtually absolute priority, forcing all other considerations to be set aside, whatever the financial cost?

A further issue deserves brief mention here. There is concern, already justified by some indications from the conservancy councils,[74] that all that is being done to place emphasis on the European sites, may end up weakening the protection for other designated sites in this country. The concentration of resources and effort on identifying and protecting European sites and their higher legal status may tend to diminish the attention and standing of those SSSIs and other conservation sites which are not given this added designation. There is a danger that in view of their lower status and weaker protection such sites will be seen as expendable, so that the gain of stronger protection for certain sites will be won only at the expense of lesser protection for others.

Conclusion

European Community law has affected nature conservation in Great Britain in several ways. There have been major indirect effects. Agricultural measures have significantly affected the countryside and only recently and to a limited degree have they given any regard to conservation issues. Environmental policy in general has assisted the health of the environment, requiring action in areas where the British government was slow to respond. Now significant measures directly addressing conservation issues are shaping the law here, adding a new dimension to the legal arguments and requiring several sets of legislation to be consulted before the legal position is clear. Giving effect to these measures has not required a fundamental recasting of the legal mechanisms, but rather a change in practice. To meet the EC requirements there must be a shift in attitude from a discretionary basis, with conservation doing battle with com-

---

[73] See Directive 92/43/EEC, Article 10 and 1994 Regulations, regs. 3(4) and 37.
[74] See, for example, the priorities set by Scottish Natural Heritage in their published *Plans and Progress 1995–96*.

peting interests on more or less level terms, to a situation where conservation must clearly be given greater priority. In relation to species protection, the effect has been limited, e.g. requiring the tightening of the terms of exceptions to the law, but there has had to be a much larger shift in approach in relation to habitat protection. The legal framework itself has not fundamentally changed, but the balance of priorities within it has. It remains to be seen how thoroughly this new balance will be reflected in practice.

Chapter 13

HAS THE UK GOVERNMENT IMPLEMENTED THE HABITATS DIRECTIVE PROPERLY?

Simon Ball

In the law of nature conservation, European and international obligations have been extremely important in the development of the law.[1] The latest major European contribution comes through Directive 92/43/EEC on the conservation of natural habitats and of wild fauna and flora (the Habitats Directive),[2] which lays down some very specific requirements concerning the protection of designated sites. The central feature of the Directive is the creation of a coherent ecological network of special areas of conservation (SACs), which will make up a system of 'European sites' known as Natura 2000. The special protection areas (SPAs) classified under the Wild Birds Directive[3] will be incorporated into this network and these European sites are to be given very strong protection indeed. The Habitats Directive also includes some more general duties, such as that relating to the management of certain important landscape features,[4] and some obligations in relation to species,[5] but this chapter will concentrate on the central Natura 2000 obligations.

At one stage the British government envisaged that the Habitats Directive could be implemented without new legislation. It initially suggested that the town planning system and the existing law relating to the protection of sites of special scientific interest (SSSIs) would be sufficient to ensure implementation. However, that view was modified in the light of the decisions of the European Court of Justice in the cases *Commission* v. *Spain*[6] and *Commission* v. *Germany*.[7] Accordingly, the Conservation (Natural Habitats, Etc.) Regulations 1994[8] were made to implement the Directive's requirements. The Regulations create a new

---

[1] See Reid, Chapter 12 above.
[2] OJ 1992 L 206, p. 7.
[3] Directive 79/409/EEC (0J 1979 L 103, p. 1).
[4] Article 10.
[5] Articles 12–16.
[6] Case C-355/90 [1993] ECR I-4221, the *Santoña Marshes* case; see comment at [1993] *Water Law* 209.
[7] Case C-57/89 [1991] ECR I-883, the *Leybucht Dykes* case.
[8] SI 1994 No. 2716.

category of protection, the special nature conservation order, under which it is possible for a form of permanent protection to be provided.[9]

These Regulations adopt what could be termed a minimalist approach. They engraft on to the existing SSSI, nature conservation order and town planning mechanisms the additional protections required for 'European sites' by the directive. In other words, although there are some additional controls and restrictions, there is a continuing reliance on the twin systems of SSSI protection and planning control. It will be argued that the Directive, interpreted in the light of the two European Court of Justice cases noted above (which concerned similar protective provisions in the Wild Birds Directive) effectively requires a form of absolute protection for some European sites and a very strong presumption against damage for others. The British town planning system and the SSSI system do not envisage absolute protection, the former because it is a system based on compromise and the latter because of the voluntary philosophy that underpins it. By basing the implementation of the Directive on these systems the Regulations are arguably flawed in concept.

When it comes to the protection of marine SACs and SPAs the position is even clearer. The Regulations do address the issue of marine sites,[10] but do not provide an adequate framework for protection.[11] However, this aspect of the subject is not dealt with in detail in this chapter.

It will also be argued that, whatever the position with regard to formal compliance (in respect of which it is relevant that the Regulations frequently use the exact, often rather opaque, wording of the Directive), the Regulations have a number of specific defects in them. These defects mean that the Directive is unlikely to be implemented properly in practice.[12] For example, the success of the Regulations depends on the willingness of the government at three stages:

1. the initial identification of SPAs and candidate SACs (a sense of reluctance can be discerned in the events leading to the *Lappel Bank* case[13] and in the saga of what is reputed to be the largest European colony of great crested newts in southern Peterborough);
2. the making of special nature conservation orders under the Regulations (it is clear from the whole scheme of protection that the government envisages special nature conservation orders as instruments of last resort to be used only when absolutely necessary); and
3. the decision whether to refuse consent for activities where appropriate.

In addition, the 1994 Regulations do not grapple fully with the question of

---

[9] See generally Reid, Chapter 12 above, 'Habitat Protection' and Purdue, Chapter 14 below, 'The Birds and Habitats Directives'.
[10] See regs. 3(3) and 33–36.
[11] Warren, 'Law and Policy for Marine Protected Areas' in Rodgers (ed), *Nature Conservation and Countryside Law* (Cardiff: University of Wales Press, 1996), especially pp. 79–82.
[12] The importance of implementation in practice is clearly seen in Case C-337/89, *Commission v. UK* [1992] ECR I-6103 (the *UK Drinking Water* case); see [1993] *Water Law* 59.
[13] Case C-44/95, *R v. Secretary of State for the Environment, ex parte RSPB* [1997] 2 WLR 123.

deterioration of sites through such things as pollution (as to which see Article 6(2) of Directive 92/43/EEC and the *Santoña Marshes* case) and rely in an unrealistic fashion on the ability of various public regulatory bodies (including the nature conservation bodies) to anticipate problems before they happen.

The Birds Directive

The Birds Directive includes two separate obligations relating to habitat. Article 3 imposes a general obligation on Member States to act so as to preserve, maintain or re-establish a sufficient area of habitat for all the species of wild birds listed in Annex I[14] and to strive to avoid pollution or deterioration of these habitats. Article 4 requires further conservation measures for Annex I birds, in particular the classification (i.e. designation) of suitable sites as *special protection areas* (SPAs) for the conservation of these species. In recognition of the importance of Western Europe for migratory species, this duty also applies to key breeding, moulting, wintering and migration sites for *all* regularly occurring migratory species. In *Commission* v. *Spain*,[15] the European Court of Justice decided that the Spanish government was in breach of the Directive by failing to designate an important wetland area, the Santoña Marshes. In essence, this case establishes that there is a duty to designate an area as a SPA where it fulfils the objective ornithological criteria laid down in the directive. This conclusion was re-emphasised by the European Court of Justice in *R* v. *Secretary of State for the Environment, ex parte RSPB*,[16] in which it was held that economic considerations can play no part in the designation of a SPA or the determination of its boundaries; the only criteria which can be used to determine whether a designation should be made are the ecological ones in Article 4(1) and (2) of the Directive.

In relation to SPAs, Member States are required to take, under Article 4(4), 'appropriate steps to avoid pollution or deterioration of habitats or any disturbances affecting the birds, in so far as these would be significant having regard to the objectives of this Article'. In *Commission* v. *Germany*[17] in an important judgment concerning an area known as Leybucht Dykes, the European Court of Justice decided that the only exceptions to Article 4(4) were where the works were necessary for reasons of public health or public safety (which was actually the situation in the case itself), and that works could not be permitted for economic or recreational reasons. The immediate effect of this decision was reversed by Article 7 of the Habitats Directive, which brought the Birds Directive into line with the less restrictive exceptions laid down in Article 6 of that directive (see below), but it illustrates the tendency of the European Court of

---

[14] Annex I includes 175 species or sub-species and is by no means limited to the rarest birds.
[15] Case C-355/90 [1993] ECR I-4221.
[16] Case C-44/95 [1997] 2 WLR 123 (the *Lappel Bank* case).
[17] Case C-57/89 [1991] ECR I-883, (1992) 4 JEL Vol. 4, 139.

Justice to adopt a fairly robust interpretation of environmental directives. The point is reinforced by the *Santoña Marshes* case, which suggested that Article 4(4) is sufficiently clear to be directly effective in relation to the duty to avoid pollution or deterioration of SPAs, although it appears that the duty to classify in Article 4(1) is not directly effective.[18]

Notwithstanding the partial reversal referred to above, the implication is clear—SPAs (whether actually classified or merely fulfilling the criteria) are to be given very strong protection, although it does fall short of absolute protection.

The Habitats Directive

The main focus of the Habitats Directive is on the creation of a 'coherent European ecological network of special areas of conservation'[19] to be called Natura 2000. In other words, although there are some significant provisions on the protection of species, the emphasis is on the protection of designated sites. Natura 2000 is to be made up of three types of site:

1. those hosting the natural habitat types listed in Annex I to the Directive;
2. those comprising the habitats of the (rare) species listed in Annex II; and
3. the SPAs designated under the Birds Directive.

The general idea is to maintain (or where appropriate restore) these habitat types and species' habitats to a position where for the foreseeable future they are stable or increasing.[20]

Leaving aside the SPAs (which are discussed above), the procedures for producing the list of Natura 2000 sites are complex.

(1) By 5 June 1995, Member States were required by Article 4(1) to send the Commission a list of proposed sites, identifying whether they are in category 1. or 2. above. This list is to be drawn up by reference to the criteria laid down in Annex III (Stage 1): in relation to Annex I sites this covers such things as the representativeness, area, degree of conservation and global importance of the site for the habitat type concerned, whilst in relation to Annex II sites it covers the size in national terms, degree of isolation, degree of conservation and global importance of the site for the species concerned. In *Biodiversity: The UK Action Plan*,[21] it is estimated that of the species and habitats listed in the Directive some 75 habitat types and 40 taxa of animals and plants occur within the United Kingdom.

(2)   The Commission is then under a duty to draw up, by 5 June 1998, a draft

---

[18] See Somsen, 'Member States' Obligations under Directive 79/409' [1993] *Water Law* 209.
[19] Article 3(1).
[20] *Ibid.*
[21] Cm. 2428, (London: HMSO, 1994.)

list of 'sites of Community importance' (Article 4(2)). This selection process will take account of the criteria set out in Annex III (Stage 2): these include such things as the relative national importance of the proposed site, its geographical location, its area, and the global ecological value of the site in respect of the biogeographical region it is in.[22] In other words, not all the sites proposed by a Member State will be listed by the Commission.

In addition, the Commission will produce a separate list of those sites which host one or more of the *priority* habitat types or species which are identified in Annexes I and II (these sites can be termed 'priority sites'). According to Annex III (Stage 2) such sites *must* be considered as sites of Community importance, with the proviso that, under Article 4(2), a Member State which has more than 5% of its territory covered by priority sites may request the Commission to apply the criteria more flexibly.

(3)   Under Article 21 the draft list is to be considered by a committee of representative experts appointed by the Member States before adoption by the Commission—the EC Council will arbitrate over any disagreements between the Commission and the committee.

(4)   Article 5 provides for a bilateral consultation process between the Commission and a Member State where the Commission considers a priority site has been left off a Member State's list. In the event of a dispute over a site remaining unresolved, the EC Council will decide the matter. However, since this decision can only be taken unanimously, the usefulness of this procedure must be questioned, as the Member State concerned will presumably veto the selection of the site.

(5)   Once the Commission has adopted the list of sites of Community importance, under Article 4(4) Member States are under a duty to designate any site on the list as a *special area of conservation* (SAC) as soon as possible and no later than six years from the adoption of the list. The full list of SACs will therefore be in existence by 5 June 2004 at the latest.

(6)   There are some continuing procedural duties under the Directive. Under Article 9 the Commission is under a duty to review the Natura 2000 list in the light of the Directive's objectives (this could include de-classifying a site), whilst under Article 17 detailed implementation reports are required from the Member States and the Commission. Finally, the Annexes can be altered by a qualified majority vote in the EC Council (Article 19).

Protection provided by the Habitats Directive

Article 6 contains the central protections laid down by the Directive. The two

---

[22] Article 1(c)(iii) lists five biogeographical regions: Alpine, Atlantic, Continental, Macaronesian and Mediterranean.

following duties apply to sites *adopted* by the Commission as sites of Community importance and to SPAs designated under the Birds Directive:

1. under Article 6(2), Member States are required to take appropriate steps to avoid the deterioration of the sites and 'significant' disturbance of the species for which the areas have been designated (this duty also applies on an interim basis to sites subject to the Article 5 consultation procedure); and

2. under Article 6(3), 'any plan or project not directly connected with or necessary to the management of the site but likely to have a significant effect thereon . . . shall be subject to appropriate assessment of its implications for the site . . . [T]he competent national authorities shall agree to the plan or project only after having ascertained that it will not adversely affect the integrity of the site concerned . . .'.

However, Article 6(4) provides for an exception. If (and only if) there is no alternative solution, a 'plan or project' affecting a site may be carried out for 'imperative reasons of overriding public interest, including those of a social or economic nature'. For priority sites the exception is more limited—only three types of exception can be relied upon:

1. considerations relating to human health or public safety;
2. considerations relating to 'beneficial consequences of primary importance for the environment', which is not defined; and
3. other reasons of overriding public interest only if they are accepted by the Commission.

This appears to retain the position set out in the *Leybucht Dykes* case for priority sites, whilst watering down the protection for other sites.[23]

In any situation where the exception in Article 6(4) is relied on, the Member State has to take any compensatory measures necessary to ensure the protection of the overall coherence of Natura 2000 and must inform the Commission of those measures.

In addition, a wider obligation to adopt necessary conservation measures (which may include a management plan for the site) arises once a site is formally designated by the Member State as a SAC.[24] Rather oddly, this obligation does not apply to SPAs designated under the Birds Directive.[25]

Finally, two other articles of the Directive require a mention. Article 10 requires Member States to 'endeavour, where they consider it necessary', to encourage the management of certain important features, such as linear fea-

---

[23] One anomaly which is of importance for the United Kingdom is that there are no priority bird species, thus reducing the possibility of birds benefitting from the stronger controls applicable to priority sites.

[24] Article 6(1).

[25] This is perhaps as well, since the 1994 Regulations do not include a reference to management plans for terrestrial sites, although in *Biodiversity: The UK Action Plan op. cit* note 21, ch. 4.64, it is stated to be government policy that a summary management plan be produced for each biological SSSI by 2004.

tures (i.e. rivers, hedges, field boundaries, etc.) or areas functioning as stepping stones (e.g. ponds, small woods or areas of fragmented heath).[26] Article 11 places Member States under a general duty to monitor the conservation status of *all* habitats and species.

The Conservation (Natural Habitats, Etc.) Regulations 1994

The Conservation (Natural Habitats, Etc.) Regulations 1994[27] seek to implement the provisions of the Habitats Directive in British law. In general terms, the government has sought to 'continue to work as far as possible under the voluntary principle, seeking the involvement and active co-operation of those involved who live and work in rural areas and at sea'.[28] Its approach has been a minimalist one in which it has tried to engraft on to existing mechanisms the additional protections that are required by the Directive. In essence, this means that, although there are *some* additional controls and restrictions, there is a continuing reliance on the twin systems of SSSI protection and planning control. As pointed out above, these are both systems with an in-built tendency towards compromise. It also means that the existing defects in these systems identified earlier may doom such an approach to failure from the start, irrespective of any extra measures that may be added.

The Regulations were made under the European Communities Act 1972, s. 2(2). As such they can do no more than simply implement the Habitats Directive. It also means that they must be interpreted in the light of the Directive.[29] In recent years it has become government practice to avoid the difficulties involved in correct transposition of directives into domestic law and the resultant threat of infringement proceedings for non-compliance by simply repeating the words of the directive. One result is that implementing regulations such as these tend to include phrases of unparalleled opaqueness and unintelligibility.[30] Another is that it puts the onus of ascertaining whether implementation has been adequate on to those who wish to challenge the government's (or any other public body's) interpretation, in effect requiring them to bring appropriate judicial review actions. A third result is that responsibility for interpreting the directive shifts from the government (through the transposition process) to the courts. In the first instance this means the UK courts, though obviously the intention is that the domestic courts will take the

---

[26] This obligation is implemented by reg. 37 of the 1994 Regulations.

[27] SI 1994 No. 2716; the Regulations apply to Great Britain, but similar implementing measures have been adopted for Northern Ireland in the Conservation (Natural Habitats, Etc.) Regulations (NI) 1995 (SR No. 380).

[28] Draft Conservation (Natural Habitats, Etc.) Regulations 1994 compliance cost assessment, para. 38.

[29] Regulation 2(2); see also the *von Colson* [1986] 2 CMLR 430 and *Marleasing* [1992] 1 CMLR 305 cases.

[30] See also Reid, Chapter 12 above, at note 42.

opportunity to refer suitable matters to the European Court of Justice under Article 177 of the EC Treaty.[31]

The Regulations stick to the procedures and timetable set out in the Directive fairly closely. For example, reg. 7 requires the Secretary of State to propose a list of sites on or before 5 June 1995, whilst reg. 8 requires the Secretary of State to designate sites adopted by the Commission as SACs 'as soon as possible and within six years at most'. Regulation 10 establishes the concept of a 'European site' and, in accordance with the Directive, defines it to mean:

1. a SAC;
2. a site adopted by the Commission as a site of Community importance;
3. a SPA designated under the Birds Directive; and
4. a site subject to consultation under Article 5 of the Directive (although in this last case the protection is limited in the same way as under the Directive).

The Secretary of State will draw up a public register of European sites (Article 11) and notify them to the nature conservation bodies (Article 12),[32] which will then notify local planning authorities, owners and occupiers and anyone else the Secretary of State may direct (Article 13).

Amendments to nature conservation law

The 1994 Regulations then proceed to lay down the protective measures that apply to European sites. Essentially, these mirror existing nature conservation controls, repeating their structure and only adding extra controls where necessary. Thus, regs. 16 and 17 provide for management agreements over European sites and adjacent land; under reg. 28 byelaws may be made for terrestrial European sites as if they were nature reserves (in fact there is a slight extension to the law here, as the byelaws may also cover surrounding or adjoining sites); and reg. 32 provides compulsory purchase powers.

Regulations 18–21 mirror the SSSI system. In keeping with the voluntary principle, no absolute restrictions are imposed, but to fit in with the Directive there are three significant departures from the provisions which apply generally to SSSIs under s. 28 of the Wildlife and Countryside Act 1981:

1. the nature conservation body may amend the original list of potentially damaging operations (thus extending the protection afforded to the site);
2. the process through which the nature conservation body grants consent for potentially damaging operations is structured; and

---

[31] This is exactly what has happened in the case of the RSPB's challenge to the non-designation of Lappel Bank as a SPA (see *The Guardian*, 10 February 1995). However, the general impression in environmental cases has been that the lower courts are very reluctant to make references under Article 177—see, for example, *R v. Poole DC, ex parte Beebee* (1991) JEL Vol. 3, 293, *R v. Swale BC, ex parte RSPB* (1991) JEL Vol. 3, 135 and *Twyford Parish Council v. Secretary of State for Transport* (1992) JEL Vol. 4, 273. In each of these cases it is strongly arguable that the judge was incorrect in his interpretation of EC law, yet did not make a reference.

[32] English Nature, Scottish Natural Heritage and the Countryside Council for Wales.

3.   existing consents must be reviewed and may be withdrawn or modified.

In relation to an application for consent to carry out a potentially damaging operation, if it appears to the nature conservation body that a *plan or project* is likely to have a significant effect on the site, it must carry out an appropriate assessment and may only give consent if the plan or project will not affect the integrity of the site. If it considers there is a risk that the operation will be carried out anyway (i.e. without consent), it must notify the Secretary of State, who may choose to make a special nature conservation order (see below). In accordance with Article 6(3) of the Directive, these duties do not apply where the operation is directly connected with or necessary to the management of the site, which will exclude a large number of potentially damaging operations.

It is important to recognise what has *not* changed. Even for European sites there is only a four-month temporary ban on potentially damaging operations; only owners and occupiers are restricted in their activities; the maximum fine for breach of the law remains £2,500; and a planning permission still outranks the nature conservation status of the site. Compared to the existing law on SSSIs, the changes are pretty minor. Accordingly, it must be asked why these minor changes could not have been made for all SSSIs.[33]

Special nature conservation orders

Regulations 22–27 of the 1994 Regulations mirror the law on nature conservation orders (s. 29 of the Wildlife and Countryside Act 1981) by creating 'special nature conservation orders'. In this case there is a major change, which is that the ban on potentially damaging operations is permanent. Under the 1981 Act the ban lasts only for three months, or 12 months if negotiations are taking place for a management agreement or the purchase of the site by the nature conservation body. This feature of the special nature conservation order is arguably the central feature of the whole Regulations, since it means that for the first time there is such a thing as a designation that may stop a damaging activity completely.

However, it is not quite as simple as that. At the outset, the Secretary of State has a discretion whether or not to make a special nature conservation order, although this discretion is not unfettered because reg. 3(2) requires all nature conservation functions to be exercised so as to secure compliance with the Habitats Directive.

Once a special nature conservation order has been made, regs. 22–27 lay down the following, somewhat tortuous, procedures:

1.   If it appears to the nature conservation body that a *plan or project* is likely to have a significant effect on the site, it must carry out an appropriate assessment and *must refuse* consent if the plan or project will affect the integrity of the site. Reasons must be given for a refusal.

---

[33] In this context, it is important to understand that all European sites will already be SSSIs.

2. The owner or occupier may then refer the matter to the Secretary of State, who may direct the conservation body to grant consent, but only if (a) there are no alternative solutions and (b) the plan or project must be carried out 'for imperative reasons of overriding public interest' (these are defined as in the Directive and include the more restrictive test for priority sites). If consent is granted, appropriate compensatory measures are required. The all-important corollary is that consent must be refused if either (a) or (b) is not satisfied.

The effect is that there is now a mechanism through which absolute protection can be ensured, but there are some tricky hurdles to negotiate and its operation is seen very much as a last resort.

Amendments to planning and other controls

The 1994 Regulations also make some important amendments to planning and other regulatory controls in relation to European sites. The following requirements apply in similar fashion to such things as planning permissions, discharge consents, pollution authorisations,[34] waste management licences, and authorisations under the procedures relating to the construction of highways or roads and consents for pipelines and electricity works.[35]

1. Under reg. 48, where a plan or project is likely to have a significant effect on a European site, before giving permission the relevant regulatory agency is required to consult with English Nature or its equivalent and to carry out an appropriate assessment of the implications of the plan or project for the site.[36]

2. The agency must agree to the plan or project only if it will not adversely affect the integrity of the site, unless the provisions of reg. 49 are satisfied. These repeat the exceptions laid down in Article 6(4) of the Habitats Directive. If the agency proposes to rely on reg. 49 it must inform the Secretary of State, who may prohibit the plan or project, either temporarily or permanently. Under reg. 53, if approval is given on the basis of an overriding public interest, compensatory measures must also be taken to ensure that the overall coherence of Natura 2000 is protected.

3. Existing consents, permissions etc. must be reviewed as soon as reasonably practicable. This review should look at the position as if the application had just been made. If the integrity of the site is adversely affected, the agency should use its normal powers of revocation or modification, paying compensation if that would be the usual position. There is a special set of regulations to similar effect where planning permission would otherwise be

---

[34] For example, under the Environmental Protection Act 1990, Part I.
[35] For example, under the Pipe-lines Act 1962, the Transport and Works Act 1992 and the Electricity Act 1989.
[36] This does not require a formal environmental assessment.

granted by a development order, or in an enterprise zone or simplified planning zone.[37]

Three practical criticisms may be made of these very wide powers. First, the process of reviewing existing consents will be very time-consuming for the regulatory agencies concerned. Secondly, the liability for compensation where existing rights are revoked may prove very significant.[38] Thirdly, many of the powers rely on the agencies anticipating a likely effect, which may prove beyond them, particularly in relation to developments some distance away from the protected site.

In relation to applications for planning permission, the 1994 Regulations are supplemented by Planning Policy Guidance Note 9 (PPG9).[39] This creates some additional protections as a matter of policy, for example in paras. 13 and 38, which state respectively:

For the purpose of considering development proposals affecting them, potential SPAs and candidate SACs included in the list sent to the EC Commission should be treated in the same way as classified SPAs and designated sites.

Environmental assessment will normally be required where a Ramsar site or a potential or classified SPA, or a candidate, agreed or designated SAC could be affected.

But, more importantly, the 1994 Regulations and PPG9 create what is in practice a presumption against development on a European site. Such a presumption has been seen by some commentators as 'semi-confiscatorial',[40] because it effectively prevents an owner realising the development value of land. This raises an important issue concerning the relationship between the protection of nature conservation sites and private interests, since it is arguable that if owners' rights are to be abrogated in this way, they should have formal rights to object to a designation and rights to compensation. Interestingly, whilst there are no such rights in relation to SSSIs and European sites, they do exist where a s. 29 nature conservation order or a special nature conservation order is made.[41]

Has the Habitats Directive been implemented fully?

It is very difficult to give a definite answer to this question.[42] The 1994 Regu-

---

[37] See regs. 60–67.
[38] The high cost of compensation is exactly why no action was taken for many years over the damage to Thorne Moors (incidentally, at one time a candidate SPA).
[39] PPG9: *Nature Conservation*, October 1994.
[40] Hockin, Ounsted Turner and Lund, 'Conservation of Migratory Birds and Protection of Their Habitat' [1992] LMELR 178.
[41] Wildlife and Countryside Act 1981, Sch. 11 and s. 30; 1994 Regulations, Sch. 1 and reg. 25.
[42] Except in relation to marine sites, where the essentially administrative (as opposed to legislative) and voluntary mechanisms for ensuring implementation appear to fall a long way short of adequate implementation.

lations appear formally to satisfy the requirements for the designation of SACs and to ensure that the important protections in Article 6(3) and (4) of the Directive are transposed into domestic law. However, it remains unclear whether some of the wider obligations in the Directive are covered properly. Article 6(3) and (4) (and the 1994 Regulations that implement them) only apply to *plans and projects*, when much that is damaging to sites occurs in a more unplanned manner. Article 6(2), which deals more generally with deterioration of habitats, is not dealt with specifically. Instead, it is implemented through the general obligations imposed on regulatory agencies (namely reg. 3(4), which simply requires all agencies to 'have regard to' the requirements of the Directive, and regs. 48–53 discussed above). As noted above, there are some practical difficulties concerning these Regulations, which call into question whether full protection will happen in practice.

There is another angle to the question. Reasoning from the *Santoña Marshes* case,[43] it is probable that the procedure whereby the Commission draws up the final list of sites of Community importance will deprive the requirement to designate sites of direct effect. However, as the requirement under Article 6(2) to avoid deterioration of habitats is effectively the same as in Article 4(4) of the Birds Directive, so it is likely to be of direct effect. The potential implications of this point for a situation where a European site actually suffers damage are immense.

This question of practical implementation also raises some other issues. For example, the success of the one mechanism for absolute protection, the special nature conservation order, depends on the willingness of the Secretary of State to make such orders, whilst the success of the whole system depends on the initial identification of SPAs and candidate SACs. Critics could be forgiven for thinking that, given the minimalist legal approach to implementation adopted by the government in the Regulations, there will also be a minimalist policy approach when there are specific threats to sites. In this context it is relevant to note that the whole structure of the 1994 Regulations ensures that the appropriate mechanism for challenge to any decision is judicial review, which is prohibitively expensive for many potential objectors and fraught with evidential difficulties.

Have the Directive and the Regulations improved the legal protection of habitat? Notwithstanding the above qualifications, there is little doubt that the law is stronger than it was before the Regulations were made, at least as far as very important sites are concerned. However, by creating special protections for European sites, resources (both financial and human) will arguably be channelled into the protection of those sites at the expense of 'ordinary' SSSIs. The creation of a category of sites with a higher protection also has the effect of downgrading other sites in the minds of decision-makers, which would be a retrograde step.

---

[43] See note 6 above.

Conclusion

The following conclusions can be suggested:

(1)   The voluntary principle embodied in the Wildlife and Countryside Act 1981 does not recognise sufficiently the ecological interest implicit in nature conservation legislation.

(2)   Even in its own terms the 1981 Act does not work properly, as the loopholes, gaps and figures on loss and damage illustrate.

(3)   The government has chosen to improve the protection for European sites without plugging these gaps and loopholes. It does not seem sensible to engraft a new regime on to one that does not work. It would have been better to draft wholly new legislation in which all sites were protected to a higher standard. As it is, the legislative protection is improved for the most important sites only: it is arguably downgraded in practice for some of the others.

(4)   The Habitats Directive and the 1994 Regulations give a greater recognition to the ecological interest than before, in particular by providing a form of absolute protection for certain key sites. It appears that, in formal legal terms, the main obligations in the Directive relating to terrestrial sites have been implemented.

(5)   However, it is clear that in practice the government will adopt the least onerous solution which is consistent with compliance with the Directive— absolute protection will only be afforded where it is absolutely necessary.

(6)   Given the above attitude, the history of the failure of the 1981 Act and the fact that many of the powers in the regulations rely heavily on an unrealistic level of ability to anticipate problems before they happen,[44] it is unlikely that the Directive will be fully implemented in practice. This could give rise to challenges based on both UK and EC law.

At the time of his death Simon Ball was working on preparing this chapter on the basis of the paper given at the conference at University College London in November 1995. This version was prepared by Professor Colin Reid of Dundee University, using the available drafts. Rather than developing points in a way which he might not have wholly supported, the approach taken has been to use Simon's words as far as possible, even where this leaves arguments briefly stated or expressed in a way similar to some of his other works, most notably his chapter 'Reforming the Law of Habitat Protection', in Rodgers (ed), *Nature Conservation and Countryside Law* (University of Wales Press, 1996). The only significant addition has been to add a comment on the *Lappel Bank* decision.

---

[44] For example, reg. 20(4), which envisages the nature conservation body anticipating a risk that a damaging operation will be carried out without consent.

Part V

REGULATION IN PRACTICE III: LAND USE

Chapter 14

THE IMPACT OF EC ENVIRONMENTAL LAW ON PLANNING LAW IN THE UNITED KINGDOM

Michael Purdue

Introduction

The first statute to have the term 'town planning' in its title dates back to 1909[1] and the Town and Country Planning Act 1947 provided England and Wales with an extremely radical, flexible, and comprehensive system of anticipatory control.[2] The scheme has been continually amended by successive Planning Acts but the overall framework has remained the same. The striking characteristic is the amount of discretion it gives to the regulating authorities. This is because both the definition of *what* needs permission and *why* permission can be granted or refused is extremely open-ended. The control goes well beyond the built environment, and by including any 'material change of use'[3] potentially encompasses most human activities. The local planning authorities are authorised to determine applications on the basis of 'any material considerations' as well as the policies in the development plans.[4] The courts have given a very wide meaning to 'material considerations' and it undoubtedly includes the effect, adverse or otherwise, which the development will have on the environment.[5]

The United Kingdom can therefore claim to have adopted the preventive

---

[1] Housing, Town Planning, &c. Act 1909.
[2] The Town and Country Planning Scotland Act 1948 extended an essentially similar scheme to Scotland.
[3] See Town and Country Planning Act 1990, s. 55.
[4] Though the status of the development plan policies have been recently upgraded by the insertion of s. 54A into the Town and Country Planning Act 1990.
[5] In a seminal paper given to the Oxford Joint Planning Law Conference in September 1991, Stephen Tromans pointed out that there is in fact very little direct authority on the materiality of pollution; see 'Town and Country Planning and Environmental Protection: The Planning Balance in the 1990s' [1991] JPEL 6. This is probably because it has always been thought as self-evident and because the earliest cases always talked in terms of the damage to amenities rather than pollution.

principle long before such alliterative principles became fashionable and before
Article 130r required European Community (EC) policies on the environment
to be based on 'the principles that preventive action should be taken'. It is not
therefore surprising that for some time it seemed that planning law and practice
was one of the high points in the United Kingdom which were not going to be
affected by the rising tide of EC law.

Yet, even without an explicit treaty basis, a large amount of EC legislation
had been issued concerning the environment. The directives which have had
the most direct impact on UK land use planning have been enacted either
under Articles 100 or 235 or a combination of these two Articles. Since then
the Single European Act has given the EC an express role in protecting the
environment and the Treaty on European Union further consolidated and
refined the remit of the Institutions on environmental matters. In this regard
it is significant that the amendments made by the Treaty on European Union
referred for the first time to town and country planning and land use. However
Article 130s does this for the purpose of distinguishing between the legislative
process for measures concerning town and country planning and land use
where the unanimity rule applies and the European Parliament only has a right
to be consulted, and the process for other environmental measures where
decisions are to be taken by qualified majority voting and the Parliament is
more positively involved through the cooperation procedure. The need for
unanimity means that it is less likely that Article 130s will be used to enact
measures specifically concerning town and country planning especially since
the principle of subsidiarity has been elevated by the Treaty on European Union
to an overarching limitation on the powers of the Community.[6] However as Redman[7]
has pointed out, Article 100a (where qualified majority voting applies) could
still be used to harmonise town and country planning matters so far as this was
thought necessary for the establishment and functioning of the internal market.

Nevertheless there are still only a small number of EC laws which directly
affect the way the planning powers are operated. The most important directives
are the Environmental Assessment Directive (85/337/EEC), the Birds Directive
(79/409/EEC), the Habitats Directive (92/43/EEC), and the Waste Framework
Directive (75/442/EEC) as amended in 1992. The Directive on freedom of
access to information (90/313/EEC) has also imposed obligations to make
available environmental information to the public: these obligations directly
affect the information made available on planning matters. There is, however,
also the indirect impact that EC environmental law can have on planning
practice by directly changing the law on specialist forms of pollution control.

---

[6] The power to enact environmental measures, provided by the Treaty of the Single European Act,
was always conditional to the objectives set out in Article 130r being more attainable at Community
level than at the level of the individual states but the new wording is much more restricting as
well as being a general principle covering all powers and objectives of the Community; see Article
3b. For an assessment of the changes introduced, see Wilkinson, 'Maastricht and the Environment'
(1992) JEL Vol. 4, No. 2, 221.
[7] See Redman 'European Community Planning Law' [1993] JPEL 999, at 1000.

The nature of this indirect impact turns on the difficult relationship between planning law and such specialist regimes and it is this indirect impact which will be addressed first.

The indirect impact of EC environmental law on planning law

The Planning Policy Guidance Note 23 (PPG23) 'Planning and Pollution Control' attempts to sum up the relationship between the planning system and other pollution control systems by stating that they are separate but complementary; see para. 1.2. They are separate in that the planning authority is given the responsibility of determining whether the site is suitable for the proposed process, while the other regulatory regimes are concerned with controlling particular aspects of how that process is operated. Yet in determining whether the proposed development is an acceptable use of the land, the planning authority must make some assessment either of the proposed development's potential for pollution or the level of pollution from existing neighbouring developments. The difficulty is in determining the extent to which the planning authority must rely on the specialist pollution regimes in making that assessment. PPG23 argues that:

The planning system should not be operated so as to duplicate controls which are the statutory responsibility of other bodies. (para. 1.3)

and later states that:

Planning authorities will need to consult pollution control authorities in order that they can take into account the scope and requirements of the relevant pollution controls. Planning authorities should work on the assumption that the pollution control regimes will be properly applied and enforced. They should not seek to substitute their own judgment on pollution control issues for that of the bodies with the relevant expertise and the statutory responsibility for that control. (para. 1.34)

The consequence must be that the more strenuous and detailed the pollution control regime, the less scope for the planning authority to make autonomous judgments on the pollution aspects. It is not that pollution ceases to be relevant to planning decisions but that the planning authority may rely not only on the advice of other regulators but also assume that pollution will be kept to an acceptable level. In this way, the existence and the stringency of pollution controls can be used as an argument for leaving outstanding issues concerning environmental pollution to the specialist pollution regime. The importance of EC law is that it will often be the driving force behind the setting up of more strict pollution controls.

The litigation in *Gateshead Metropolitan District Council* v. *Secretary of State for the Environment*[8] is both an endorsement of such an approach and a good illustration

[8] (1994) JEL Vol. 6, No. 1, 93 and [1995] JPEL 432 (CA).

of the importance of EC law. In this case the Secretary of State for the Environment granted planning permission on the grounds that unresolved questions concerning the level and impact of emissions from a proposed incinerator could be resolved satisfactorily by the need to obtain a further consent under Part I of the Environmental Protection Act 1990. A challenge to the legality of this decision was rejected both in the High Court and in the Court of Appeal.

The Deputy Judge Jeremy Sullivan QC in the High Court stated that:

> It is clear beyond doubt that the environmental impact of emissions to the atmosphere is a material consideration at the planning stage. In support of that proposition one need look no further than the Town and Country Planning (Assessment of Environmental Effects) Regulations 1988. It follows, in my judgment that the Secretary of State could not lawfully adopt a policy of hiving off all consideration of such environmental effects in their entirety to the EPA regime. But just as the environmental impact of such emissions is a material planning consideration, so is the existence of a stringent regime under the EPA for preventing or mitigating that impact and for rendering any emissions harmless. It is too simplistic to say 'the Secretary of State cannot leave the question of pollution to the EPA'. (at page 99)

In the Court of Appeal, Glidewell LJ (with whose judgment Hoffman and Hobhouse LJJ agreed) expressly approved the Deputy Judge's views as to the significance of the existence of another stringent regime.[9]

Several of the features of the new system of integrated pollution control, relied upon by the Secretary of State in the *Gateshead* case, can be traced to EC law. Thus the concept of ensuring that preventive action is based on the Best Available Technology Not Entailing Excessive Cost (BATNEEC)[10] is connected to the requirement in the Directive on atmospheric emissions from industrial plants (84/360/EEC) which required that 'all appropriate preventive measures against air pollution be taken, including the application of best technology provided that the application of such measures does not entail excessive cost'.[11] Then the inclusion of *cadmium*[12] as a prescribed substance, where there is a specific duty to employ BATNEEC to ensure that such a substance is not released or at least rendered harmless,[13] is a direct result of this substance appearing on the Red List set out in Directive 76/464/EEC on dangerous substances in water. Finally, although not strictly relevant in the *Gateshead* case, conditions should be imposed on any authorisation to ensure compliance with 'any directions by

---

[9] (1996) 71 P & CR 350 (CA). While Glidewell LJ came to the same conclusions as the Deputy Judge, he did so for different reasons as the appeal was argued on a different basis from the arguments put to the Deputy Judge. He nevertheless described the judgment of Jeremy Sullivan as 'careful and admirable'.

[10] See s. 7(1)(a), (2)(a) and (4)(a) of the Environmental Protection Act 1990.

[11] Of course it can be argued that the old standard of BPM was as strict but the government seems to have accepted that BATNEEC was a tougher standard; see Purdue, 'Integrated Pollution Control in the Environmental Protection Act 1990: A Coming of Age of Environmental law?' (1991) 54 MLR 534, at 544.

[12] One of the Inspector's reasons for recommending refusal was that the discharge of cadmium was unacceptable onto rural/agricultural areas.

[13] See Environmental Protection Act 1990, s. 7(2)(1)(a).

the Secretary of State given for the implementation of any obligations of the United Kingdom under the Communities treaties . . .'.[14]

A possible drawback of shifting the responsibility for preventing pollution to the specialist pollution controls systems is that it could undermine the effectiveness of the planning system in *preventing* development which could cause pollution. In *Gateshead* it was argued that the granting of permission would mean that authorisation under the Environmental Protection Act 1990 would have to be granted even if the application of BATNEEC would still result in harm being caused to the environment. Glidewell LJ in the Court of Appeal, having stated that what increases in pollution were acceptable and how far they could be kept to acceptable levels by BATNEEC were issues clearly within the competence of Her Majesty's Pollution Inspectorate, said:

If in the end the Inspectorate concluded that the best techniques etc would not achieve the results required by section 7(2) and 7(4) it might well be the proper course would be for them to refuse an authorization. (at page 440)

This view is supported by s. 6(3) of the 1990 Act which gives the regulator an express power to refuse permission.

On the other hand the judgments in *Gateshead* equally indicate that subject to challenges on grounds of rationality or unreasonableness, the local planning authority could rely on its own judgment and refuse permission on the grounds that the level of pollution would be unacceptable. Similarly although the Department of the Environment as a matter of policy may deplore the use of planning conditions which duplicate pollution controls,[15] the case law suggests that such planning conditions would not be invalid on this ground alone.[16]

Of course the need to refuse planning permission to protect the environment may be urged by other public bodies with responsibilities for the environment. In particular under art. 10 of the Town and Country Planning (General Development Procedure) Order 1995, the Environment Agency has the right to be consulted on applications for certain categories of development. The content of the representations will often be influenced or determined by EC standards. Thus Directive 80/68/EEC on groundwater requires certain substances to be prevented from entering groundwaters and the former National Rivers Authority made clear that it would object to any development proposals which have the potential to pollute groundwater.[17] An obvious example is an application for the winning or working of minerals which could result in the pollution of groundwater. Wastes from mines or quarries are still not directly

---

[14] See *ibid.* s. 7(2)(b).
[15] See Circular 11/95 on 'The Use of Planning Conditions in Planning Permissions', at para. 77.
[16] See *Ladbroke (Rentals) Ltd* v. *Secretary of State for the Environment* [1981] JPEL 427, *Newham London Borough* v. *Secretary of State for the Environment* [1986] JPEL 607, and *Unicorn Inns* v. *Secretary of State for the Environment* [1993] JPEL 932.
[17] See National Rivers Authority, *Policy and Practice for the Protection of Groundwater* (Bristol: NRA, 1992).

subject to licensing control by the Environment Agency[18] and so the Agency will still have to rely on planning authorities to ensure that the appropriate conditions are attached to the planning permission to prevent the introduction into groundwater of the substances listed in the Directive.[19] Any objections based on EC law would undoubtedly be material considerations of great weight and indeed could be taken to require the planning authority to ensure that there was compliance with the Directive.

Just as complementary regulatory regimes driven by EC laws can indirectly affect the way the planning system is operated, so positive requirements of EC law can drive planning policies. The Circular 17/91 on the 'Water Industry Investment: Planning Considerations' points out that the need to implement the Bathing Water Directive (91/271/EEC) and the Drinking Water Directive (80/778/EEC) requires planning permission being granted for the development of new sewerage treatment works and water treatment works. The Circular urges local planning authorities to identify in their development plans suitable sites and to facilitate planning applications. Actions by the European Commission under Article 169 have resulted in the United Kingdom being held by the European Court of Justice to be in breach of both Directives.[20] Further in *R v. Secretary of State for the Environment, ex parte Friends of the Earth Ltd.*[21] the English courts held that the breach of the primary obligation meant that the United Kingdom was under a secondary duty to ensure compliance *as soon as possible*. The courts however equally held that there was no evidence that the Secretary of State was not doing all that was possible even though it was accepted that he was only seeking to secure a result as *soon as practicable*.[22]

The interesting question is the extent to which the need for compliance with Community obligations requires a Member State to ensure that planning permission is granted as soon as possible. Friends of the Earth argued in the Court of Appeal that the government could have speeded things up in respect of the development of new treatment works by introducing legislation dispensing or abridging the need for normal land acquisition and planning procedures. This argument was unanimously rejected by all three of their lordships who considered that such action would conflict with both the rights of third parties (*per* Balcombe LJ) and with environmental, conservation and recreational interests (*per* Roch LJ) and with the need to protect public safety (*per* Pill LJ). These views must be correct in that the duty to do all that is

---

[18] This is because waste from any mine or quarry is excluded from the definition of controlled waste by virtue of s. 75(7) of the Environmental Protection Act 1990. This part of the definition of controlled waste has not been changed by either the Waste Management Licensing Regulations 1994 or the Environment Act 1995.

[19] See in this regard Minerals Planning Guidance, Note 2, at para. 101.

[20] See Case 337/89, *Commission v. United Kingdom* (1993) JEL Vol. 5, No. 2, 273 and Case C-56/90, *Commission v. United Kingdom* (1994) JEL Vol. 6, No. 1, 125.

[21] (1995) JEL Vol. 7. No. 1, 80, and for the Court of Appeal *The Times*, 8 June 1995.

[22] See my analysis of the case 'The Possible Will Take a Long While—Enforcing Compliance of the Drinking Water Directive' (1995) JEL Vol. 7, No. 1, 92. Also see case analysis by Hilson (1995) 32 CML Rev 1461.

possible to comply with the Directive must mean all that is possible without violating other rights and legal duties. The European Court of Justice has itself held that the powers of the Community institutions are qualified by the need to respect what are termed 'general principles of law' which include funda-mental human rights and other principles of administrative legality. Further in a series of decisions the Court has held that in implementing EC law, Member States must respect human rights.[23]

While the need to obtain planning permission as soon as possible should not be taken to authorise the overriding of existing laws and legal safeguards, such a need is undoubtedly a material consideration in determining a planning application. Also it is worth noting that governments have in the past pushed through the authorisation of projects where they considered this to be in the national interest. For example the power to grant permission by special development orders[24] has been used to grant permission for exploratory drilling by NIREX by the Town and Country Planning (NIREX) Special Development Order 1986. So, the problem will be to strike the right balance between the need to push through the programme of works expeditiously without jeopard-ising other interests which may be of equal or more importance than the need to provide drinking water of the required standard. The Department of the Environment is well aware of this dilemma as the Circular 17/91 'Water industry Investments: Planning Considerations' advises that environmental assessments may be appropriate[25] and that:

It is important that, in considering development proposals expeditiously, local planning authorities should nevertheless assess and weigh thoroughly all material considerations and any conflicting demands.

Finally it is worth noting that at a much more general level EC Regulations on the depletion of the ozone layer, Regulation 594/91/EEC and 3093/94/EC can be seen to have influenced the development of the principle of sustainable development in planning policies.

The Waste Framework Directive

Implementation of this Directive has resulted in several significant amendments to the Town and Country Planning legislation.

The Directive objectives

Articles 3 to 5 impose certain duties on the Member States. These duties are

---

[23] See Case 249/86, *Commission* v. *Germany* [1989] ECR 1263, Case 63/83, *R* v. *Kent Kirk* [1984] ECR 2689 and Case C-5/88, *Wachauf* v. *Germany* [1989] ECR 2609.
[24] See s. 59 of the Town and Country Planning Act 1990.
[25] Waste water treatment plants have since been added to Sch. 2 to the Town and Country Planning (Assessment of Environmental Effects) Regulations 1988.

referred in Article 7 as 'objectives' and they have been reproduced in the Waste Management Licensing Regulations 1994 as the 'Relevant Objectives'.[26] These objectives are summarised in PPG23:

The objectives in article 3 of the Directive deal with the need to minimise waste so far as possible, and to encourage materials recycling and energy recovery. This is in line with the Government's Sustainable Development Strategy (Cm 2426) that policies should encourage methods of waste management that have the least overall environmental impact taking into account the potential for energy or material recovery. The objectives in Article 4 deal with the need to protect the environment and should be considered in the context of the impact of potentially polluting developments on land use and the amenity of the area. Finally the objectives in article 5 are concerned with establishing an integrated network of disposal installations which will enable self-sufficiency at both the national level and EC level, and disposal in accordance with the proximity principle. (See paragraph 2.9.)

Article 7 requires waste management plans to be drawn up in order to attain the three objectives and Articles 9 and 10 state that a system of permits for the disposal and recovery of waste must be set up for the purposes of implementing the objectives in Articles 4 and 5 and the policies in the plans drawn up under Article 7.

The Waste Management Licensing Regulations 1994 implement the Directive by dividing up the responsibilities for drawing up both the waste plans and for issuing the permits between the local planning authorities and the other pollution control authorities (mainly the waste regulatory authorities in England and Wales). So the Directive objectives bite directly on local planning authorities both with respect to their plan-making functions and on their development control functions. This is effected by imposing on planning authorities as 'competent authorities' the duty to discharge 'their specified functions, in so far as they relate to the recovery or disposal of waste with the relevant objectives'.[27] The 'specified functions' cover actions which can result in planning permission being granted and the preparation and approval of development plans.[28] The Regulations try to avoid duplication by providing that this duty does not 'require a planning authority to deal with any matter which the relevant pollution control authority has power to deal with'. Circular 11/94 and PPG23 then give guidance as to what aspects of the relevant objectives should be covered by the planning authorities and which by the pollution authorities.

Guidance on the status of these objectives has been provided by the European Court of Justice in *Comitato Di Coordinamento Per la Difesa Della Cava* v. *Regione Lombardia*.[29] This decision concerned the old wording of the 1975 Directive and the main issue was whether Article 4 could be enforced directly by individuals against the state. The plaintiffs were arguing that the Italian regulations, by

---

[26] See para. 4 of Sch. 4 to the 1994 Regulations.
[27] See Sch. 4, paras. 2(1) and 3.
[28] See para. 3 which defines 'specified functions' as 'The taking of any specified action'. Paragraph 1 in turn defines what is meant by 'specified action'.
[29] [1994] ECR I-483.

providing only for the disposal of waste by tipping, were inimical to the Directive, which requires measures to be adopted to encourage recycling. The Court did not go into this argument but held that:

... the provision at issue [Article 4] must be regarded as defining the framework for the action to be taken by the Member States regarding the treatment of waste and not as requiring, in itself, the adoption of specific measures or a particular method of waste disposal. It is therefore neither unconditional nor sufficiently precise and thus not capable of conferring rights on which individuals may rely as against the state. (at para. 14)

The wording of the present Article 4 is essentially the same except that it now extends to the recovery of waste. So the Department of the Environment is probably correct in arguing that the judgment applies equally well to Article 4 of the amended Directive and presumably to the other objectives.[30] The approach taken by the Court has been criticised for being too rigid and for not taking into account the special nature of environmental directives.[31] However, in the case of the Directive itself, this absence of direct effect is in itself of no practical importance as the duties have been transposed almost verbatim into UK law. What is important is the interpretation that the courts will give to the legal effect of the objectives; remembering that as the source of the UK regulations are EC law, our courts would be bound to follow any interpretation given by the European Court of Justice.[32] Circular 11/94 argues that the objectives are not absolute requirements. This raises the very difficult question of the extent that a Member State can fall short of achieving the objectives. Advocate General Darmon's Opinion in the *Lombardia* case gives some help on this point. He appears to accept that there is an inherent conflict between the duty to draw up plans for 'suitable disposal sites' (previously set out in Article 6 but now to be found in the duty to 'establish an integrated and adequate network of disposal installations' in Article 5) and the duties under Article 4 to ensure that waste is disposed of without endangering human health and without harming the environment. Thus he states:

Those are the limits to which the freedom of action of those authorities is subject, although any measure for the disposal of waste is *inherently liable to produce pollution*, whatever the method adopted. (para. 37, my emphasis)

On the other hand it is clear that the Directive objectives do impose limits on the discretion of the competent authorities and in the case of Article 4, those limits are imposed in absolute terms. It therefore seems reasonable to interpret

---

[30] See para. 1.28 of Annex 1 to Circular 11/94.
[31] See Holder, 'A Dead End for Direct Effect?: Prospects for Enforcement of European Community Environmental Law by Individuals' (1996) JEL Vol. 8, No. 2, 322–335.
[32] In Case C-106/89, *Marleasing SA* v. *La Comercial International de Alimentación SA* [1990] I-ECR 4135 the European Court of Justice held that the national court was under a duty to interpret national legislation as far as possible to conform with the requirements of EC law. Where there is conflict between the wording of the national law and the directive, it would seem to follow that the national court will have to accept the interpretation given by the European Court of Justice.

the Directive as requiring the authorities to do all that is practical[33] to achieve
the objectives.

The development plans

As well as imposing all the relevant objectives on planning authorities when
they are carrying out their functions regarding development plans, the Waste
Management Licensing Regulations 1994 specifically modify Part II of the Town
and Country Planning Act 1990 so that unitary plans, structure, and local plans
must include policies in respect of suitable waste disposal sites or installations.[34]
In the case of county councils in England there is already a duty to prepare
'waste local plans' which should contain detailed policies regarding the deposit
of refuse or waste.[35] Again the Waste Management Licensing Regulations 1994
require such waste policies to include *detailed* policies in respect of suitable
disposal sites or installations.

In formulating its waste policies in any local plan or in Part II of a unitary
plan, the local planning authority is required to have regard to any waste
disposal plan for its area drawn up under s. 50 of the Environmental Protection
Act 1990.[36] Otherwise there is no explicit guidance in the Town and Country
Planning Act 1990 as to what the detailed policies in the waste local plan should
cover. Regulation 2(2) of the 1994 Regulations however makes clear that the
fact that an aspect of the relevant duties is covered in the waste disposal plan,
excludes any *duty* on the local planning authority to cover that aspect in the
development plan policies. On the other hand the need to have regard to
the policies in the waste disposal plan indirectly has the effect of bringing
into the waste local plan aspects of those relevant duties primarily the responsibility of the pollution control authorities.

So, while PPG23 emphasises that the waste disposal plans are primarily about
management aspects of treating and disposing of controlled wastes and the
development plans are primarily about land use issues, there is considerable
overlap between the two set of policies.[37]

Article 7 of the Directive imposes a requirement to draw up waste management plans to attain all the objectives set out in Articles 3 to 5. However it is
clear that it is the Article 5 objectives which are most relevant to development
plans. This is because Article 5 requires the establishment of 'an integrated and
adequate network of waste disposal installations' and as PPG23 points out

---

[33] The fact that the duties are imposed as objectives would suggest that it is the lesser duty of doing
all that is practical rather than the higher duty of all that is possible; see on this *R v. Secretary of
State for the Environment, ex parte Friends of the Earth* [1995] Env LR 11.
[34] See Sch. 4, para. 7(1).
[35] See s. 38 of the Town and Country Planning Act 1990 but note that such wastes policies can be
contained in the minerals local plan.
[36] See the Town and Country Planning (Development Plan) Regulations 1991, reg. 9. Section 50
was repealed by the Environment Act 1995 but waste disposal plans which have already been
determined remain in force until replaced by the national waste strategy drawn up by the Secretary
of State under section 44A of the 1990 Act.
[37] For example see para. 2.23 of PPG23 which lists the contents of waste local plans.

'(T)hese objectives are clearly concerned with the need for waste disposal facilities and their location.' The first stages must therefore involve the adoption of location policies in the development plans and the determination of planning applications to develop waste disposal facilities. The main constraints on the content of the policies in the development plans imposed by Article 5 are the need to ensure self-sufficiency in waste disposal both for the EC as a whole and for individual Member States and the need for waste to be disposed of in one of the nearest appropriate installations. In this respect PPG23 must be right in concluding that these Article 5 objectives are not absolutes[38] as these objectives are qualified by the need to take into account geographical circumstances and the need for specialised installations for certain types of waste. Nevertheless Article 5 does have the effect of imposing on local planning authorities a legal obligation to meet the demands for waste disposal generated in its own area.

Article 3 is concerned with the objectives of minimising the amount of waste (and particularly harmful waste) and to ensure its recovery by recycling and energy recovery. It however, gives the competent authorities a large measure of discretion as to how they go about achieving the objectives as it only requires the member state to 'take appropriate measures to encourage' those objectives. Of all the three sets of objectives, Article 3 only applies to the plan-making stage but Circular 11/94 states that:

It will normally be for WRAs [now the Environmental Agency] to implement these provisions through their waste management plans under section 50 of the Act (though planning authorities should ensure that their development plans are at least not inconsistent with these objectives). (para. 1.34 of Annex 1)

PPG23 however advises planning authorities that in drawing up their waste local plans they should take account of any relevant polices for waste minimisation and the opportunities for energy recovery.[39] PPG23 is also proactive in that it is stated that planning polices should encourage methods of waste management that have the least overall environmental effect taking into account the potential for energy or material recovery. This leads controversially to a policy of encouraging incineration with energy recovery as having an important contribution to beneficial re-use of waste.[40]

As we will see Article 4 is mainly concerned with actual implementation of policies but clearly the policies in the plans in allocating sites should reflect the duty imposed by Article 4 to prevent pollution. This is reflected in PPG23 which advises that the planning policies should encourage methods of waste management that have the least overall environmental impact.[41] This statement, of course begs the question as to the extent that Article 4 allows *any adverse*

---

[38] See para. 7 of Annex 6.
[39] See para. 2.23.
[40] See para. 2.24.
[41] See para. 2.24.

environmental impact. This question is fundamental to the way development control powers are exercised and that issue is discussed below.

Development control

Article 4 of Directive 75/442 on waste is described by PPG23 as the key objective which underlies the whole Directive[42] and it imposes clear constraints on the development control powers of planning authorities. The objective is:

... to ensure that waste is recovered or disposed of without endangering human health and without using processes or methods which could harm the environment, and in particular:

— without risk to water, air, soil, and plants and animals,
— without causing a nuisance through noise or odours,
— without adversely affecting the countryside or places of interest.

Interpreted literally it would mean that in determining a planning application to develop a landfill site the local planning authority should not only try to minimise pollution but should ensure that *no* pollution will result. PPG23 would seem to accept such a meaning when it states:

This effectively means that planning decisions taken on or after 1 May 1994[43] must implement the objective in article 4 of ensuring that waste is recovered or disposed of without harming the environment, and in particular without endangering human health or causing a nuisance through noise or adversely affecting the countryside or places of special interest. (para. 5.5)

Later in PPG23, however, it is stated that '(I)t is difficult to implement this objective literally since authorities cannot be absolutely sure that the processes or methods used could not in any circumstances harm the environment' and reliance is then placed on the fact that in the *Lombardia* case the European Court of Justice ruled that Article 4 indicated a programme to be followed in the performance by Member States of more specific obligations. Circular 11/ 94 similarly states that:

WRAs and other authorities responsible for controlling the disposal and recovery of waste would have difficulty in permitting any operations if they had to be sure that there would be *no* risk to air, soil, or animals. (para. 1.26 of Annex 1)

This is obviously true but nevertheless the objective is drafted in absolute terms. So while a public body cannot be absolutely sure of achieving such an objective, this does not alter the absoluteness of the objective itself. For example the Article 4 objective can be compared with s. 4(2) of the Environmental Protection

---

[42] See para. 3 to Annex 6.
[43] This is the date that Sch. 4, Part I, para. 2 of the Waste Management Regulations 1994 takes effect.

Act 1990 which imposes on the regulatory authorities the duty to use their functions 'to prevent or *minimise* pollution of the environment' (my emphasis). A more important qualification, as indicated above, is the extent to which the other Directive functions are only capable of being achieved by defaulting to some extent on Article 5. So in a case where there is a clear risk that the method of disposal or recovery will cause some damage to the environment in the terms of Article 4, it is suggested that EC law imposes a duty on the decision-maker to justify this risk on the grounds that there is no other practical way that the other directive objectives can be achieved.

In the United Kingdom the position is complicated by the split in jurisdiction between the planning authorities and the Environment Agency. In the case of waste management licences under Part II of the Environmental Protection Act 1990, it is a precondition of the granting of a licence that either a grant of planning permission is in force or that there is either an established use certificate or lawful development certificate in force.[44] Further, while a waste management licence can be refused on the grounds of pollution of the environment or harm to human health, where a grant of permission is in force, a licence cannot be refused on the grounds of serious detriment to the amenities of the locality. The rationale for this is clearly that matters of amenity will have already been considered at the planning stage. So it must follow that the elements of the Article 4 objectives which concern local amenity are exclusively a matter for the planning authority. The obvious difficulty is that it is extremely difficult to separate out in Article 4 what are matters of local amenity and what are matters of human health and pollution. While adverse affects to the countryside or places of special interest would seem to be primarily for the planning authority, the adverse impact of the development on the environment and nuisances through noise or odours equally affect local amenities. Circular 11/94 takes the view that it is for the planning authorities to determine to what extent they are required to discharge their functions with the relevant objectives but does advise that planning authorities should:

ensure that waste is recovered or disposed of without using processes or methods which could harm the environment and in particular without causing nuisance through noise or adversely affecting the countryside or places of special interest.

It was noted earlier how, in the case of the relationship between development control and Integrated Pollution Control, the *Gateshead* decision had established that the planning authority could leave it to the other regulatory body to ensure that the level of damage to the environment was acceptable. In the case of waste disposal and recovery, the position is very different in that the planning authority must be satisfied that the alternative body will ensure not an acceptable

---

[44] See s. 36(2) of the Environmental Protection Act 1990. Established use certificates were replaced by lawful development certificates by the Planning and Compensation Act 1991 but any established use certificates continue to have legal effects; see Planning and Compensation Act 1991 (Commencement No. 11 and Transitional Provisions) Order 1992.

level of pollution but that as far as practical there is *no* pollution. Also because of the wording of the Environmental Protection Act 1990 there is no clear demarcation as to which aspects can be left to the other body and which are exclusively matters for the planning authority. The Waste Management Licensing Regulations 1994 attempt to solve the problem of permissions and licences granted before 1 May 1994, by giving the licensing authority new powers to review licences to ensure that they do not cause 'serious detriment to the amenities of the locality'.[45] Whether this is sufficient to comply with Article 4 is doubtful since a waste disposal or recovery operation could 'adversely affect the countryside' without causing serious detriment to amenities.

Apart from the problems arising from past consents, in future local planning authorities will have to be very careful how they go about determining planning applications for waste disposal and recovery proposals. The difficulty of balancing the need to provide facilities with the need to protect local amenities has always existed but at least in legal terms the authority had flexibility as to how it came to what it considered to be the correct balance. The Directive objectives may in the words of the European Court only provide a framework but it is a framework which imposes important constraints on their discretion.

Environmental assessment

The present Directive

In the course of a reply to a question in the House of Lords as to when the government proposed to implement the EC Directive on Environmental Assessment (85/337/EEC), the Earl of Caithness commented that:

The planning systems in Great Britain already ensure that the environmental implications of new development are considered before permission is granted. (House of Lords *Hansard*, Vol. 492, No. 1380, 27 January 1988)

In fact until the implementation of the Directive there existed no legal guarantee that environmental implications would be considered; at least at any depth or in a systematic way. It is true that the environmental implications were 'material considerations' which, if apparent, had to be regarded and local planning authorities have for some time had a power to direct the applicant to supply further information about the proposed development.[46] There was however no obligation on either the developer or the local planning authority to research or analyse the environmental implications of a particular development. So it is clear that the Directive forced an important change in both the law and practice of land use planning.

---

[45] See the 1994 Regulations, Sch. 4, para. 9(7) which amends s. 36(3).

[46] This power is now found in reg. 4 of the Town and Country Planning (Applications) Regulations 1988, though it is not clear whether an application is valid if the applicant fails to provide the additional information as directed.

The government also hoped that the new obligations could be slotted pain-lessly into the existing development control system and that the number of applications which would require environmental assessment would be small. The first hope was largely fulfilled except that it was not recognised that the existing system of development control allows many projects, which could have a significant impact on the environment, to go ahead without express permission and that grants of permission can result in other ways than by an express planning application. The government has therefore frequently had to produce amending delegated legislation to block off loopholes in the planning system.

The Town and Country Planning (Environmental Assessment and Unauthor-ised Development) Regulations 1995 are a good example of the plugging of such a loophole. An appeal against the issue of an enforcement notice is also a deemed application for a grant of permission for the alleged breach of planning control and the outcome of an appeal is often a grant of permission. Thus in *Cheshire County Council* v. *Secretary of State for the Environment*[47] land had been used for the tipping of waste materials without either a grant of planning permission or a waste disposal licence. On appeal it was accepted that there were strong planning objections to the tip because of its effects on an environmentally sensitive area and its impact on local amenities. Yet planning permission was granted on the grounds that this would lead to a disposal licence and conditions could then be imposed which would help limit the existing risk of serious pollution. Whatever the merits of this decision, the development of an instal-lation for the disposal of controlled waste in an area of Special Country Value for Landscape would appear to warrant an environmental statement as being likely to have a significant impact on the environment. Under the new Regu-lations the local planning authority, when issuing the enforcement notice, would have also been required to give notice that the 1995 Environmental Assessment Regulations applied and any appeal would have to be accompanied by an environmental statement unless the Secretary of State makes a direction that he considers that one is not required.[48] The Secretary of State also has powers to require an environmental statement on an appeal if he considers that such a statement is required.[49] As with ordinary applications for planning permission, the ultimate consequence is that the Secretary of State is prohibited from granting permission on appeal unless he has first taken into account the state-ment and any representations in connection with that statement and states this in his decision.[50]

In the case of unauthorised development the fact that the development has already taken place may make it easier to evaluate the environmental impact but as *Cheshire* shows this may lead to priority being given to counteracting the effects of the project rather than its prevention, when prevention is the basic

---

[47] [1996] JPEL 410.
[48] See regs. 4 and 5 of the Town and Country Planning (Environmental Assessment and Unauthor-ised Development) Regulations 1995 (SI 1995 No. 2258).
[49] See reg. 7.
[50] See reg. 3.

rationale of environmental assessment.[51] This is perhaps inevitable but it emphasises the need for local planning authorities to exercise their powers to stop
unauthorised development which is a threat to the environment.[52] It also draws
attention to the gap in the present procedures as there is no requirement that,
once consent for a project has been granted, there will be monitoring of its
impact on the environment and measures taken to mitigate any unforeseen
impacts. This could be only be done under present planning law by granting a
limited period permission.

The numbers of projects that require environmental assessment have
exceeded the government's original expectations; though as John Zetter points
out in Chapter 15 below, the numbers are still very small compared to the
annual number of planning applications. Also it may be that a considerable
number of projects, which should be subject to environmental assessment,
escape because local planning authorities fail to apply the regulations properly.
Thus Wood and Jones in research commissioned by the Department of the
Environment concluded that:

It is apparent . . . that, nationally, a potentially large number of projects falling within
the indicative criteria and thresholds has not been formally subjected to EA.[53]

This is in some ways inevitable because the Directive gives no direct guidance
as to what is a *significant* adverse impact. For example, as Mertz has pointed
out, the development of an out-of-town superstore might have little direct
environmental impact but the indirect effects could be very large.[54] The judicial
decisions of the courts of the United Kingdom on the Directive indicate that
third parties would have little success in using judicial review to force a more
strict reading of the need for assessment. The jurisprudence of the courts has
already been subject to considerable criticism and it is not proposed to go over
that ground again here.[55] It is worth however emphasising that it has been
held that:

. . . the decision whether any particular development is or is not within the schedule
descriptions is exclusively for the planning authority in question subject only to *Wednes-*

---

[51] See preamble to the Directive.
[52] See para. 19 of Circular 13/95, 'Town and Country Planning (Environmental Assessment and
Unauthorised Development) Regulations 1995'.
[53] Wood and Jones, 'The Impact of Environmental Assessment on Local Planning Authorities'
[1992] JEPM Vol. 35, No. 2, 115, at 119. Also see Wood and Jones, *Monitoring Environmental
Assessment and Planning* (London: HMSO, 1991).
[54] See Mertz, 'The European Economic Community Directive on Environmental Assessments: How
Will It Affect United Kingdom Developers?' [1989] JPEL 483, at 491.
[55] See Alder, 'Environmental Impact Assessment—The Inadequacies of English Law' (1993) JEL
Vol. 5, No. 2, 203, and Ward, 'The Right to an Effective Remedy in European Community Law
and Environmental Protection: A Case Study of United Kingdom Judicial Decisions Concerning
the Environmental Assessment Directive' (1993) JEL Vol. 5, No. 2, 221.

bury challenge. Questions of classification are essentially questions of fact and degree not law.[56]

Moreover the English courts have taken the line that breaches of the procedures will not automatically invalidate the eventual decision if no prejudice is caused.[57]

The actual impact of the Directive on decision-making in development control is inevitably very hard to evaluate. Most commentators would however accept Zetter's view that it has helped to increase the degree to which environmental considerations are taken into account. Wood and Jones found that in two-thirds of their case studies the proposal was modified as a result of suggestion made during the environmental assessment process and that of the 20 applications where a planning decision was made two-fifths were refused.[58] Of course as they accept it is possible that such modifications and refusals might have taken place without formal environmental assessment, but the studies strongly suggest that the process itself makes a significant positive impact on the environment!

Future reforms

As John Zetter explains the Council of Ministers have now adopted Directive 97/11/EC which amends the current Directive. These amendments by increasing the number of Annex I projects (where environmental assessment is mandatory) should increase the number of developments subject to assessment. The amendments should also help to ensure that the granting of planning permission is properly justified. First, developers will be required to provide a description of the main alternatives to the project and an indication of the main reason for the developer's choice, taking into account the environmental effects.[59] At present the developer only has to provide an outline of alternatives *where appropriate*. Where an environmental assessment is needed the existence of alternative sites would certainly be a material consideration[60] but there is no obligation on either the developer or the local planning authority to provide information on alternative sites. The new provision will put the onus on the developer to provide that information but the local planning authority will also have to ensure that the developer complies. Secondly, local planning authorities will have to give reasons for granting development consent where consultation with the environmental agencies (such as English Nature) or even the general public has resulted in an 'unfavourable opinion'. This in substance will require reasons to be given for a grant of planning permission when at present there is no statutory requirement to give reasons. Thirdly, the decision should provide

---

[56] Per Simon Brown J in *R* v. *Swale BC, ex parte RSPB* (1991) JEL Vol. 3, No. 1, 135, at 142, but see criticisms made of this approach by Grant (1991) JEL Vol. 3, No. 1, 150, at 151.

[57] See on this *R* v. *Poole DC, ex parte Beebee* (1991) JEL Vol. 3, No. 2, 293 and *Twyford Parish Council* v. *Secretary of State for the Environment* (1992) JEL Vol. 4, No. 2, 273.

[58] *Op. cit.* note 53, 124–125.

[59] See the new point 2 in Annex III to the Directive.

[60] See *Greater London Council* v. *Secretary of State for the Environment and London Docklands Development Corpn* (1985) 52 *P & CR* 158.

a description where necessary of the measures to avoid, reduce, and if possible offset the major adverse effects. Together these provisions should help to raise the standard of decision-making connected to environmental assessment.

A more far-reaching reform is the proposal by the Commission for Strategic Environmental Assessment (SEA) which would require environmental assessment of any policies, plans or programmes, which were likely to affect the form or location of development. Several commentators have argued that it is a weakness of the present system that the impact of a project is only considered when it is about to be implemented.[61] Planning Policy Guidance Note 12 already recommends that proposed development plan policies should be subject to such appraisal[62] and it seems that already 110 environmental appraisals of development plans have been completed.[63] In this regard it is important to note that the government has now committed itself to the principle of 'sustainable development' and this principle is now a common feature of the government's planning polices.[64] Once a policy is contained in an adopted development plan, it will be given the extra legal status conferred by s. 54A of the Town and Country Planning Act 1990.[65] This is in contrast with the status of an environmental statement which at present only has to be considered by the local planning authority, though as already noted the amendments made to the 1985 Directive require reasons to be given for its decision.

The Birds and Habitats Directives

A process by which areas of land can be designated for their special properties or characteristics is a common feature of planning law. Such a designation does not normally prevent planning authorities from granting permission for development within such areas. Thus in the case of Sites of Special Scientific Interest (SSSIs) the need to protect the site is in law just one material consideration which may be outweighed by other material considerations such as economic need. At most the statute may, as in the case of listed buildings or conservation areas, require *special regard* or *special attention* to be given to the desirability of preserving the building or preserving or enhancing the character or appearance of the conservation area.[66] The significance of the Birds and Habitats Directives (79/409/EEC and 92/43/EEC) is that the designation of

---

[61] For example see Sheate, *Making An Impact: A Guide to EIA Law and Policy* (London: Cameron May, 1994). See further Sheate, Chapter 16.

[62] See para. 5.52 and paras. 6.1–6.25.

[63] See Earthy and Dodd, 'First Step on the Road to Environmental Appraisal', in *Planning*, 15 March 1996, p. 20.

[64] See PPG1 General Policy and Principles, para. 1; PPG2 Green Belts, para. 2.10; PPG6 Town Centre and Retail Developments, paras. 1 and 2; PPG13 Transport, para. 1.11; PPG20 Coastal Planning, para. 1.1 and 1.2; and PPG23 Planning and Pollution, para. 1.10.

[65] See Purdue, 'The Impact of Section 54A' [1994] JPEL 399, which explains the new provision.

[66] See respectively ss. 66 and 72 of the Planning (Listed Buildings and Conservation Areas) Act 1990.

land as a Special Protection Area (SPA) under Article 4 of the Birds Directive
or as a Special Area of Conservation (SAC) under Article 3 of the Habitats
Directive substantially limits the powers of planning authorities to grant permission for developments which have been assessed as adversely affecting the
integrity of the site[67] concerned.[68] The protection also extends to sites which
although not designated yet as SPAs or SACs have been agreed as sites of
Community importance and have been adopted by the Commission or have
been put on a list by the Commission as being sites hosting priority natural
habitat type or priority species.[69]

The Directives allow for permission to be granted in such a case only where:

the plan or project must nevertheless be carried out for *imperative reasons of overriding*
public interest, including those of a social or economic nature. (my emphasis)

Moreover there must be an absence of *alternative solutions* and the Member
State must take all compensatory measures necessary to ensure that the overall
coherence of Natura 2000[70] is protected. Where the site hosts a priority natural
habitat type or a priority species, an even greater justification is required if
permission is to be granted. In such circumstances the overriding public interest
can only relate to:

human health or public safety, to beneficial consequences of primary importance for
the environment or further to an opinion from the commission to other imperative
reasons of overriding public interest.[71]

Of course there can and will be disagreements over whether a particular development will adversely affect the integrity of a site and it is essentially for the
competent national authority, i.e. the local planning authorities in most cases,
to make this judgment. However the British regulations ensure that, where an
application is likely to have a significant effect, there is a process of assessment
similar to environmental assessment and that the appropriate nature conservation body is consulted. Also PPG9 on Nature Conservation makes clear that
the government will supervise closely how the local planning authorities carry
out their development control functions with regard to SPAs and SACs. It is
there stated that:

The Secretary of State will normally call in for his own decision planning applications

---

[67] This term is not defined but PPG9 on Nature Conservation defines it as 'the coherence of its
ecological structure and function across its whole area that enables it to sustain the habitat,
complex of habitats and/or the levels of populations of species for which it was classified'; see
para. C10 of Annex C.
[68] See Articles 6 and 7 of the Habitats Directive and reg. 48 of the Conservation (Natural Habitats
etc.) Regulations 1994 (SI 1994 No. 2716). See further, Ball, Chapter 13.
[69] See Articles 4(5) and 5(4) respectively of the Habitats Directive.
[70] Natura 2000 is the European Network of Special Areas of Conservation and Special Protection
Areas provided for by Article 3(1) of the Habitats Directive.
[71] See Article 6(4) of the Habitats Directive.

which are likely significantly to affect sites of international importance; he will have regard to the advice of English Nature on which applications are likely to have such effects. Where a planning application likely to affect is not called in, the government expects the papers inviting local authority members to take a particular decision to indicate clearly that the relevant factors have been fully addressed, whether or not the authority is minded to allow the development. Planning authorities should be prepared to explain their reasons, particularly if they do not decide the case in accordance with the recommendations of English Nature. Regulation 49 requires an authority proposing to allow development which would adversely affect an SPA or SAC to notify the Secretary of State in advance. (para. C9 of Annex C)

So to adopt the terminology of Davis,[72] while the local planning authorities retain an amount of discretion, it is *confined* by EC rules so that the decision-maker is forced to proceed through a series of algorithms.[73] The administrative procedures adopted by the Department of the Environment should also ensure that the discretion is also *structured* and *checked* through the need for openness as to why the permission is being allowed and the readiness of the Secretary of State to call-in the application.

The extent of the restriction on the power to grant permission can be illustrated by the example of the *Lappel Bank* decision. The European Court of Justice has taken the same view as the Advocates General's Opinion in Case C-44/95, *R v. Secretary of State for the Environment, ex parte Royal Society for the Protection of Birds*:[74] economic considerations play no part whatsoever in the deciding whether to classify land as a SPA. Article 6(4) however now expressly provides that social or economic interests can amount to 'imperative reasons of overriding public interest' which can be a justification for allowing development which it is accepted will adversely affect the integrity of the site. This means that once a site has been designated as a SPA, permission can be granted for development on economic grounds which will undermine the whole purpose of designation. This led the United Kingdom to argue in the *Lappel Bank* case that this would give rise to unnecessary administrative action if a site were to be first classified and then subject to an immediate derogation procedure. Advocate General Fennelly answered this argument by pointing out that:

The difference between on the one hand deciding not to classify a site as a SPA and, on the other, classifying the site and subjecting it, even immediately to a derogation procedure, is not one of the comparative administrative burden. If a site which qualifies for classification as a SPA under Article 4(1) or (2) is not classified, then the site will not benefit from the protective restrictions laid down by Article 6(3) and (4) of the Habitats directive and in particular the requirements of Article 6(4) that an ecologically destructive project may only be carried out 'in the absence of alternative solutions' and that 'the Member State ... take all compensatory measures necessary to ensure that the overall coherence of Natura 2000 is protected'.[75]

---

[72] See Davis, *Discretionary Justice: A Preliminary Inquiry* (Baton Rouge: Louisiana State University Press, 1969).

[73] See the flow chart set out in PPG9 at para. C10.

[74] [1997] 2 WLR 123, (1997) JEL Vol. 9, No. 1, 157.

[75] See para. 97 of his Opinion.

It may well be that on the facts of *Lappel Bank* these protective restrictions would have been met since the United Kingdom argued that there was no other way that the viability of the port could be secured and the amount of land taken was very small. The importance is that the decision-maker has to show that these safeguards have been satisfied. In the case of a SAC which hosts priority natural habitat or a priority species, it is clear that social or economic considerations *cannot* normally be used as a justification.[76]

As with the Environmental Assessment Directive, the government has also had to amend the categories of permitted development to ensure that they cannot be used to carry out development which would be likely significantly to affect SPAs and SACs.[77] Existing express planning consents present more of a problem, as their revocation could give rise to a substantial liability to pay compensation. Although this is not expressly required by the Directives, the 1994 Regulations require that, where, by the date a site becomes protected, planning permissions have already been granted, local planning authorities must review such planning permissions if the development would be likely to have a significant effect on a site either individually or in combination with other development. The consequence is that the same procedures and tests have to be applied as if it were a new development proposal. If the integrity of the site would be adversely affected and the development authorised does not fulfil the conditions under which a new development proposal could be allowed under reg. 49, the permission will have to be revoked or modified.[78]

Legislative action was needed to ensure that enforcement against unauthorised development could not result in the granting of planning permission for development which would damage sites protected by the Directives. This is covered by reg. 54 which applies the need to consider the effect on European sites in considering whether to grant permission on appeal against an enforcement notice. The Department has also urged local planning authorities to use their wide powers to take pre-emptive action against unauthorised development.[79]

The Directives do not directly prevent development plans being drawn up which envisage development which could adversely affect the integrity of SPAs and SACs. This issue arose in the decision of *Retail Developments* v. *Purbeck District Council*[80] where it was alleged that the local planning authority in adopting a local plan had failed to take into account the impact of the EC Directives. The facts were complicated because the applicants (who were rival developers) were objecting to a proposal for a supermarket which was dependent on a by-pass being built. This by-pass would affect a cluster of SSSIs. In particular the Deputy Judge, Malcolm Spence, held that the SSSIs for Sandford Heath and Holten

---

[76] It could be that social or economic reasons could amount to 'other imperative reasons of overriding interest' which can be used as a justification if this is the view of the European Commission; this however seems doubtful.

[77] This is done by regs. 60–63 of the 1994 Regulations.

[78] See regs. 50–53.

[79] See para. C17 of Annex 3 to PPG9.

[80] Decided on 14 October 1994 but as yet only summarised in [1995] JPEL B37.

Heath were proposed SPAs which hosted priority habitats and once designated as SPAs would gain the highest protection under Article 6(4)(a) of the Habitats Directive as it applies to the Birds Directive. This raises the interesting issue as to whether a SPA can host a priority habitat or a priority species since no birds are listed in Annex II to the Habitats Directive. The problem arises because of the way Article 7 applies the obligations in Article 6(2), (3), and (4) to the Birds Directive. This is a point which one day may have to be referred to the European Court of Justice but it would seem to follow that where a SPA includes priority habitats or priority species the higher protection will apply. On the other hand the Deputy Judge simply said that the higher protection would apply to the SSSIs because they were 'Temperate Heath and Scrub' when Annex I makes clear that only certain of those habitats are priority habitats.

Despite holding that the SSSIs would be subject to the higher protection of the Habitats Directive, the Deputy Judge went on to hold that this did not mean that the local planning authority had erred in law in adopting the local plan. He basically held that the authority had been aware of the legal effect of the EC Directives and that, even when the SPAs were finally designated, there would still be a chance of satisfying Article 6(4) and of getting permission for the road. He concluded that:

It appears to me that the District Council are fully entitled to pursue the course they are pursuing, albeit fraught with some risk. Any other course would be more unsatisfactory, they are entitled to think.

The court was obviously reluctant to interfere, especially at the behest of a rival developer, but the case does illustrate the need to carry out environmental assessments at the plan-making stage.

The Environmental Information Directive

The system of town and country planning in the United Kingdom is already reasonably transparent and open. The policies, whether in the development plans, planning policy guidance notes or supplementary guidance notes are generally made available to the public. In the case of development control there is a system of planning registers under which both the applications and the grants of planning permission are available for inspection at the offices of the local planning authorities. Perhaps more importantly all applications now have to be given publicity of some sort and the public normally have a right to be present at council, planning committee, and sub-committee meetings where applications are being determined and to have sight of the agenda, connected reports, and background papers.[81] In the case of the latter there are the standard

---

[81] See ss. 100A-K of the Local Government Act 1972 as amended by the Local Government (Access to Information) Act 1985. In this regard note the recent decision of R v. *Rochdale MBC* [1997] JPEL 337.

powers to exclude the public whenever it is likely that confidential information would be disclosed in breach of an obligation of confidence and the public may be excluded if it is likely that 'exempt information' such as information about employees or commercial contracts will be disclosed. Equally at the appeal stage the Planning Inquiries (Attendance of Public) Act 1982 requires that at any planning inquiry oral evidence shall be heard in public and documentary evidence shall be open to inspection except where the Secretary of State is satisfied that public disclosure would be contrary to the public interest. On the other hand a report by the Council for the Protection of Rural England concludes that 'inflated photocopying charges, limited opening hours, restrictive procedures, and expensive publications are deterring the public from exercising their rights to comment on development proposals and local authority development plans'.[82] So the actual practice may fall short of both the law and the spirit of the law.

The main importance of Directive 90/313/EEC on freedom of access to environmental information to planning practice is that it fills in whatever gaps there exist in the public's existing right to know. In this respect Article 3(7) is very important as it makes clear that where rights to environmental information already exist in the Member States but these fall short of what is required by the Directive, the greater rights set out in the Directive prevail. The most obvious gap is environmental information which local planning authorities receive as a result of consultation or in some other way. It could clearly be an advantage for environmental pressure groups to be able to get access to environmental information to fight planning applications and appeals. Thus, when at last there is a public inquiry into whether planning permission should be granted for a deep repository for radioactive waste at Sellafield, objectors may try to use the Directive to get access to information as to how NIREX went about deciding what were the best sites for such a development. The main problem in this regard is that local planning authorities may not disclose information supplied by a person who is not under a duty to disclose and who has not consented to disclosure.[83] So the scope of the rights will basically turn on the what is environmental information, the kind of public bodies who are required to make it available, and how wide is the exception made for information relating to matters which are *sub-judice* or under inquiry.

'Information relating to the Environment' is defined by Article 2(a) as:

... any information in written, visual, aural or data-base form on the state of water, air, soil, fauna, land, and natural sites, and on activities (including those which give rise to nuisance such as noise) or measures adversely affecting or likely so to affect these, and on activities or measures designed to protect these including administrative measures and environmental management programmes.

---

[82] See *Public Access to Planning Documents* (London: CPRE, 1994).
[83] See Article 3(2) of the Directive and reg. 4(3)(c) of the Environmental Information Regulations 1992 (SI 1992 No. 3240).

This definition is then reflected in the Environmental Information Regulations 1992 which purport to implement the Directive.[84] In *R* v. *British Coal Corporation, ex parte Ibstock Building Products Ltd.*[85] Harrison J rejected the argument that the 1992 Regulations only applied to information which in itself relates to the environment and not to matters which may lead to such information. He therefore held it included information which was necessary to evaluate the quality of other information on the environment; in that case the name of the informant that munitions had been deposited in an old mine. It could therefore be similarly argued that information as to what alternative sites have been investigated is within the scope of the Directive and the Regulations, as such information is needed to evaluate other environmental information about the site which is the subject of a development proposal.

While all planning authorities are clearly subject to the Directive, the blurring of the line between the state and private individuals caused by privatisation has left it uncertain whether bodies such as British Gas plc or NIREX are included. Article 6 of the Directive makes clear that the definition of public authorities extends to 'bodies with responsibilities for the environment and under the control of public authorities'. The issue is similar to the question as to which bodies are subject to vertical direct effect of directives as being emanations of the state. In this regard in *Griffin* v. *South West Water Services Ltd.*[86] the water company was held by the English High Court to be a body against which directives were directly enforceable on the grounds that it was a body:

which has been made responsible pursuant to a measure adopted by the state for providing a public service under the control of the state and has for that purpose special powers beyond those which result from the normal rules applicable to individuals.

The test under Directive 90/313/EEC itself is different in that it must only be shown that the body has public responsibilities for the environment and is under the control of a public body with such responsibilities. The obvious difficulties will be deciding what amounts to a public responsibility and control by public bodies. In the case of the newly privatised utilities such as the water companies, it is certainly arguable that they are subject to the Directive. Section 3 of the Water Industry Act 1991 imposes general environmental duties on the water companies and as the *Griffin* case made clear they are subject to important control powers exercisable by the government. The position of bodies such as NIREX and British Nuclear Fuels is more problematic as while they are controllable by central government through the shares held in such companies, they do not have any statutory responsibilities for the environment.[87] In the *British Coal Corporation* case while British Coal denied that the Regulations applied to

---

[84] See SI 1992 No. 3240, reg. 2(2).
[85] (1995) JEL Vol. 7, No. 2, 297.
[86] [1995] IRLR 15.
[87] These bodies are not set out in the list of the bodies which the government considers are subject to the directive; see Department of the Environment Consultative Paper.

them, they did not pursue the point in order to keep down the length of the hearing. So Harrison J did not go into the issue.[88]

Article 3(2) provides that information may be refused where it affects:

matters which are or have been, sub judice, or under inquiry (including disciplinary enquiries), which are the subject of preliminary investigation proceedings.

Regulation 4(2)(b) transposes this into UK law as:

information relating to, or anything which is or has been the subject of any legal or other proceedings (whether actual or prospective).

Regulation 4(5) then defines 'legal proceedings' as including proceedings at any local or public inquiry. This wording, if taken literally, would enable information to be withheld whenever the information related to a planning application as this could be the subject of an appeal. As Harrison J commented in the *British Coal Corporation* case this would seem to negate the purpose of the Directive as one would think it was intended to bite on a planning inquiry where one of the plain purposes is to determine the effect of a development on the environment. So it is submitted that the Regulations do not properly implement the Directive and it is intended only to apply to judicial and quasi-judicial proceedings where the interests of individuals may be prejudiced by the disclosure of information.

In this regard Richard Burnett-Hall has argued that:

Inspectors holding public enquiries [sic] are frequently not lawyers, nor need they be, their role is either to assemble facts on which a recommendation to the Secretary of State is made or they have delegated to them the power to make a policy decision on his behalf—clearly a matter of public administration. Since derogations from the broad provisions of EC legislation are to be construed restrictively, it is strongly arguable that this limitation has not been satisfactorily transposed from the directive into United Kingdom legislation.[89]

Harrison J left the question open as to whether regulation 4(2)(b) applied where there was a public inquiry into a planning appeal. He did however hold that it did not apply to the particular circumstances as the information only related to a planning application and it was not sufficient that there might be an appeal if permission was refused. So at least there should be no blanket restrictions on the disclosure of environmental information at the application stage of a development project.

---

[88] The British Coal Corporation is included in the government's list of bodies to which the Directive applies; see Department of the Environment Consultative Paper.

[89] See Burnett-Hall, *Environmental Law* (London: Sweet and Maxwell, 1995) at 20-022. Also see Birtles, 'A Right to Know: The Environmental Information Regulations 1992' [1993] JPEL 615, and Charlesworth, 'Examining the Applicability of the Environmental Information Regulations 1992: A Strange Case' (1995) JEL Vol. 7, No. 2, 301.

Conclusions

Evaluation of the impact of EC environmental law on UK planning law is made difficult by the large size and complexity of the subjects which are being examined. It is however hoped that this chapter has shown that the impact is of increasing importance. The nature of that impact is varied. It is undoubtedly helping to increase the importance of environmental considerations in the operation of the planning system. At the same time it has had the effect of diminishing the traditional discretion of the planning authorities in making decisions by restricting the power of the authorities to grant permission which is clearly detrimental to the environment. Yet EC law can also indirectly limit the role of planning authorities in passing judgment on specialised pollution questions and can even impose pressures to grant permission for development which damages the environment because of other environmental priorities.

Finally one obvious way in which UK planning law has been affected by EC law, albeit not environmental law, is the need to adopt the metric equivalents of imperial measures. In *R* v. *Secretary of State for the Environment, ex parte Kirkstall Valley Campaign Ltd.*[90] it was pointed out that permission was granted in terms of square feet rather than square metres. Sedley J responded by declaring that:

... in paragraph 25 of the grant the figures expressed in square feet are to be regarded as having been multiplied by 0.0929 and expressed in square metres. Admittedly a factor of 0.0929 is an ellipsis of the full formula contained in the Annex to the 1979 Directive, which requires the application of a factor of $0.0929 \times 10{-}1$, but for those educated this side of the channel I trust that it represents a sufficient compliance with the obligations created by the European Communities Act 1972.

Such is the reach of EC law!

---

[90] [1996] 3 All ER 304.

Chapter 15

ENVIRONMENTAL IMPACT ASSESSMENT: HAS IT HAD AN IMPACT?

John Zetter

Introduction

This chapter, after introducing the Council Directive on the assessment of the effects of certain public and private projects on the environment (85/337/EEC),[1] reviews its impact under five headings. These cover the number of regulations; the number of environmental assessments undertaken; the number of directions by the Secretary of State; the number of infraction proceedings; and the costs involved and an assessment of the effect on the timescale of the development process. Before the conclusion and a postscript on recent amendments to the Directive come some reflections on the European legislative process arising from the negotiations on those amendments.

The Directive

Council Directive 85/337/EEC (hereafter referred to as the Directive) was notified to Member States of the then EEC on 3 July 1985, to come into effect three years from that date. It had a long pedigree, being mentioned in each of the first three quinquennial EC Environment Programmes in 1973, 1977 and 1983.

The Directive is a comparatively short piece of law consisting of 14 Articles and three Annexes, made under both Articles 100 and 235 of the Treaty establishing the European Economic Community (known colloquially as the Treaty of Rome). This reflects the dual aim of the Directive in harmonising laws to achieve a more level playing field in competition terms (Article 100), as well as the 'catch all' provision (Article 235) in the absence of a specific reference to the environment in the Treaty.

The Directive is concerned only with development projects and is procedural in its focus. This was confirmed by Advocate General Elmer in 1995 when he

---

[1] OJ 1985 L 175, p. 40.

emphasised 'that the provisions of the Directive are essentially of a procedural nature'.[2] A wide discretion is left to Member States on its precise implementation, for example, on whether to integrate the requirements into existing legislation; the power to exempt specific projects (in exceptional cases); and the choice of public consultation procedures.

The main Articles are concerned with the provision of information and public consultation. Article 3 lists the 'factors' on which the environmental impacts of projects have to be assessed:

1. human beings, flora, and fauna;
2. soil, water, air, climate, and the landscape;
3. the interaction between these factors; and
4. material assets and the natural heritage.

Article 5, linked to Annex III, lists the information the developer has to provide. As a minimum this must include:

1. a description of the project comprising information on the site, design, and size of the project;
2. a description of the measures envisaged in order to avoid, reduce, and, if possible, remedy significant adverse effects;
3. the data required to identify and assess the main effects which the project is likely to have on the environment; and
4. a non-technical summary of the above.

The nub of the Directive is in Annexes I and II, linked to Article 4. Annex I lists nine types of projects where environmental impact assessment is compulsory. Annex II lists 13 categories of development, including modifications to Annex I projects, which need environmental impact assessment where, in line with Article 4, 'they are likely to have a significant effect on the environment'. In these cases there are two qualifying judgments which have to be made, on both the likelihood and degree of significance.

Article 6 deals with consultation procedures with environmental agencies and the general public. Member States are given the duty to:

1. determine the public concerned;
2. specify the places where the environmental information can be consulted;
3. specify the way in which the public may be informed;
4. determine the manner in which the public is to be consulted; and
5. fix appropriate time limits for the various stages of the environmental impact assessment procedure.

Following on from this Article 9 also allows Member States to decide on the detailed arrangements for informing the public about the decision taken. The

---

[2] Opinion of Advocate General Elmer, Case C-431/92, *Commission* v. *Federal Republic of Germany* [1995] ECR I-2189, at 2208, para. 35(3).

information made available must include the content of and any conditions attached to the decision.

In terms of wider consultation, Article 7 deals with the procedures for projects which are likely to have significant effects on the environment in another Member State. The environmental information gathered under Article 5 has to be made available to the other Member State and serves as a basis for consultation between the two states concerned.

Initial UK attitude

A comprehensive town and country planning system has been in effect in the United Kingdom since 1948. To quote a document contemporary to the Environmental Impact Assessment Directive coming into force, the purposes of the planning system were to meet 'the needs of development and the interests of conservation'.[3] This was emphasised in the circular which accompanied the UK regulations implementing the Directive—'in the UK there is already a highly developed body of planning and pollution control legislation which is designed to ensure that the environment and other consequences of individual proposals are fully considered before permission is given'.[4]

On this basis the initial attitude of the British government was that the Directive constituted an unnecessary set of additional regulations which would not make a useful contribution to improving environmental quality in the United Kingdom. As Article 100 of the Treaty of Rome, under which the regulations were considered, requires unanimity this attitude was maintained for some time. However, in the end the UK government voted to accept the regulations not wishing to block what the other countries wished to agree to and also seeing advantages in the improvement it might lead to in environmental conditions elsewhere in Europe.

The long held view that the Directive did not add much to procedures in some countries was generally confirmed by Advocate General Elmer's recent opinion that procedures in place could involve 'extensive examination of the project and the objections put forward against it'[5] equivalent to those required by the Directive.

Implementation

In the United Kingdom the Directive was implemented under the European Communities Act 1972. This provides for including the United Kingdom in the European Community and, therefore, no new primary legislation was required. The provisions of the Directive were therefore incorporated in secondary legis-

---

[3] Department of the Environment, *The Future of Development Plans* (London: HMSO, 1989).
[4] Department of the Environment, Circular 15/88, 'Environmental Assessment' (London: HMSO, 1988).
[5] Case C-431/92, *Commission* v. *Germany*, cited at note 2 above, at 2209, para. 35(4).

lation, the Town and Country Planning (Assessment of Environmental Effects) Regulations 1988[6] and related instruments.

However, when the opportunity was taken to extend Schedule I to the 1988 Regulations to include a new type of project and Schedule II to the 1988 Regulations to include three new types not covered by the Directive, this had to be done under powers in the Planning and Compensation Act 1991 (15). The European Communities Act 1972 only allows for the exact translation of European law into British law.

Major impacts

Number of regulations

To date it has taken 40 regulations to implement the Directive in the United Kingdom (see Appendix 4, of this book, below). This apparent complexity stems from a number of causes. First, the government decided to link implementation of the Directive to existing regulations, rather than introduce a new consent procedure. This eased the introduction of the new provisions as users of the systems were already familiar with the procedures. The main existing legislation used was the Town and Country Planning Acts for which consent for most of the projects covered by the Directive is required. Secondly, because the Planning Acts are different in each country, separate regulations are needed in England and Wales, Scotland, and Northern Ireland.

However, certain categories of development, most notably large power stations and long distance oil and gas pipelines are not covered by the planning system. So there is a need for separate regulations linked to other consent regimes. Beyond that certain types of development covered by the Directive are not subject to any consent regimes and there was a need to fill the gaps. This has most notably been done for permitted development under the general development order.[7]

The process of amending UK legislation to accord with the Directive continues. This was done most recently for enforcement appeals.[8] Other points still to be tackled include intensive agriculture in semi-natural areas, afforestation (other than projects receiving grant aid for which regulations already exist) and Crown immunity. Because planning (or other) permission is not required in these cases the trigger, where necessary, for an environmental statement does not exist.

---

[6] Town and Country Planning (Assessment of Environmental Effects) Regulations 1988 (SI 1988 No. 1199) (the '1988 Environmental Assessment Regulations').

[7] Town and Country Planning (General Permitted Development) Order 1995 (SI 1995 No. 418).

[8] Town and Country Planning (Environmental Assessment and Unauthorised Development) Regulations 1995 (SI 1995 No. 2258).

Number of environmental impact assessments

In the first report on the implementation of the Directive in the United Kingdom[9] it was recorded that there were more cases than anticipated. In the first 18 months there were 153 assessments, over 80% covering Sch. II projects.

Since that time the number of cases has increased significantly and is now estimated to be 2300, seven years after the Directive came into force.[10] Of these approximately 75% arose under planning legislation, with the next highest category being 10% under highways legislation. Waste disposal cases accounted for nearly 25%, with the next largest categories being roads and industrial and urban projects (approximately 20% each) and mineral extraction (14%). Approximately 80% of the cases were in England. To put the figures in perspective the average is approximately 250 cases a year under the Planning Acts compared to a total annual number of planning applications in the period concerned (in England) of approximately 500,000.

Linked to the number of cases of planning proposals requiring environmental impact assessment are the number of determinations on whether such an assessment is needed. The total number of cases since the Directive came into effect in the United Kingdom seven years ago is approximately 165. The average of just over 20 cases per year compares to an average annual number of planning appeals (in England) in the period of approximately 900.

Infractions

Article 169 of the EC Treaty requires that 'If the Commission considers that a Member State has failed to fulfil an obligation under the Treaty, it shall deliver a reasoned opinion on the matter after giving the State concerned the opportunity to submit its observations'. If the Member State does not comply with the reasoned opinion within the period laid down by the Commission the latter may bring the matter before the European Court of Justice.

The Commission receives a large number of complaints alleging breach of environmental directives. They are obliged to investigate these. The Environmental Impact Assessment Directive has given rise to the largest number of such complaints Community wide. Of those concerning the United Kingdom, a significant number have concerned the so-called 'transitional' cases. These have been of two types. The first category of cases are those where the applications for consent had been made before 3 July 1988 but the decision not issued until after that date. The second concern applications for consent made between 3 July 1988 when the Directive came into force and 15 July 1988 when the 1988 Environmental Assessment Regulations came into force.

The first type of case has been the subject of two Opinions by Advocates General which concur that Member States are not bound to make the projects

---

[9] Wood and Jones, *Monitoring Environmental Assessment and Planning* (London: HMSO, 1991).
[10] Glasson *et al*, *Changes in the Quality of Environmental Assessment Statements for Planning Projects* (London: HMSO, 1996).

covered by the Directive which were not approved by 3 July 1988 subject to an environmental impact assessment, but could restrict the obligation to projects for which the consent procedure had not yet been initiated.[11] The Elmer Opinion cited at note 2 above suggests that, so long as the consideration of environmental effects was consistent with the Directive and there was sufficient opportunity for public involvement, the second category is also not seriously at issue.

Despite the large number of Commission inquiries relating to British cases, the UK government has received only one reasoned opinion. No British environmental impact assessment (EIA) cases have been submitted to the European Court of Justice.

Costs and timescale

Returning to the point that British planning procedures already were considered to be as rigorous as the Directive, it is difficult to calculate whether any serious additional costs are involved. The most common figure quoted is £35,000.[12] Where figures were available, the cost of preparing the majority of Environmental Statements was in the range £10,000 to £50,000. Other unpublished research, while reinforcing the difficulties of disentangling such costs suggests that they range from 0.1% to 0.5% of total development costs. The Commission have estimated that EIA procedures add less than 1% to the costs of development. The report to the EU on the implementation of the Directive expressed the opinion that the costs of carrying out an assessment for an environmental (impact) statement were typically a small fraction of 1% of the project costs, exceptionally rising above 1%. Also there was very little overall effect on the timescale.[13]

In the United Kingdom the planning regulations were amended to extend the eight-week period for the consideration of planning applications to 16 weeks in the case of those applications accompanied by an environmental impact assessment. However, these cases are usually of a complex nature and might well have exceeded the eight-week period whether or not the 1988 Environmental Assessment Regulations had been in force. There is also a three-week period which the local authority is given to judge whether an assessment is required in connection with the planning application.

European legislation

To enact primary legislation in the United Kingdom, a Bill is first introduced

---

[11] Case C-396/92, *Bund Naturshcutz in Bayern eV, Richard Stahnsdorf and Others* v. *Freistaat Bayern* [1994] ECR I-3717, Opinion of Advocate General Gulmann, 3 May 1994.
[12] Wood and Jones, *op. cit.* note 9.
[13] *Report from the Commission of the Implementations of Directive 85/337/EC on the Assessment of the Effects of Certain Public and Private Projects on the Environment*, COM (93)28 final.

into the House of Commons or the House of Lords. It has a formal First Reading, there is then a general debate on the principle of the legislation at Second Reading followed by detailed scrutiny, line by line in Committee, report, and finally a Third Reading. Then the same process is gone through in the other House. Most of the bills are initiated by the government, but private members can and do introduce Bills, particularly in the Lords. If a private member comes near the top of the ballot and the legislation is not too controversial it can sometimes be piloted into law.

European legislation is made differently. The key features in the process need to be highlighted as they are very little known. This is surprising as EC law takes precedence over national law and Member States are required to implement European directives and regulations. As far as the Department of the Environment is concerned the vast majority of environmental legislation now comes from the European Union.

So how does European legislation arise? The first and most important point is that only the Commission has the right of initiative. Member States and the European Parliament do not. This has been the case ever since the Community was founded. One can argue about whether or not this should be changed. Generally the United Kingdom has taken the view that it should not, partly because of administrative simplicity. We do not want to clutter up the legislative process with proposals from a wide range of sources.

This does not mean that Member States have no say in what comes forward. The Community works by cooperation. If there is a perceived need for legislation, though it may take a little time, something will be done. The drive to push through the single market was very much a key objective of British policy. We have been and are working closely with other countries on subsidiarity, ensuring that only those things that need to be done at Community level are done at that level.

Also, there are plenty of opportunities to influence the content of legislation. That is why the process of consultation is so important, and why the increased use by the Commission of Green Papers is welcomed. The development of informal consultative groups with Member States and with industry, non governmental organisation (NGOs), and others where appropriate is also welcome. Commissioners too are sensitive to what goes on in their home countries. They are committed to serving only the EU. One of the ways they do so is by reflecting differing national concerns and undercurrents back to their colleagues in the College of Commissioners. Looking for a common way forward that respects differing national practices and traditions requires contributions from a wide range of sources.

Once a draft directive has been prepared and agreed by the College it is not immediately taken up by the Council of Ministers. It needs first of all to find favour with a Presidency. Some directives, that amending the existing Environmental Impact Assessment Directive for example, linger for well over a year. Presidencies cannot of course simply ignore what the Commission has put forward: that would not be *communautaire*. Arrangements for coordination between Presidencies, because each Presidency lasts for only six months, are not always what they might be. But it is true to say that the process has an inbuilt momentum towards legislation. Presidencies want to be able to point to their successes.

So the draft directive is remitted to officials to discuss in a Working Group. The lead here is taken by the National Representatives in Brussels, who are professional negotiators. Their job is to make sure that they have and understand a brief from their capitals. The United Kingdom has a well-established tradition of overnight briefing which is the envy of many others. Officials need to know therefore what the key national policy issues are and what is negotiable. This latter point is the big difference from British legislation. Here there is an open debate about the merits or otherwise of the individual clauses. In the case of European legislation it is explicitly a negotiation between Member States and with the Commission.

When the experts have ironed out the main difficulties and come up with a draft that looks an acceptable compromise it goes to COREPER, which is the high level Committee of Permanent Representatives from each Member State, and then to the Council of Ministers. They cannot of course deal with the details: there is not time. They can only concentrate on three or four big issues on each dossier, so the detail needs to have been settled beforehand.

Decisions in Council on environmental legislation are usually taken on the basis of qualified majority voting. That is to say each country has a particular number of votes broadly reflecting the size of its population, and there is a threshold that has to be exceeded for legislation to be passed. So if a Member State does not like a proposal it will spend a lot of time ensuring sufficient support from other countries to create a blocking minority. This was originally two large and a small Member State—there are obviously other combinations— but since enlargement it now requires two large and two small states. There is that murky area of the Ioannina Agreement where if the minority is not quite that, then it is possible for Member States to ask for a pause for reflection. That has not been tested yet.

Land use planning matters require unanimity. In practice this has never been tested in the courts. The majority view is that environment impact assessment is not a planning matter but an environmental one and therefore agreement to directives, etc., only requires a qualified majority. However, the British government considers that there are strong arguments for the contrary view.

But it is important not to convey the wrong impression. A Member State has to be able to carry the day on the balance of the arguments. Generally if there is a point which is clearly of importance to an individual Member State, and which does not involve an issue of principle for other Member States, then the Council will try to be accommodating.

And if one finds European legislation difficult or ambiguous, then think on this. The text could have been settled in French on the basis of a German draft as a result of a discussion at 3 am in a third language between the British and Spanish representatives. This is how things happen in the real world. The resulting ambiguity or lack of clarity is then carefully translated by the *juristes-linguistes* into every one of the Community languages, with each Member State watching like a hawk to make sure that the others do not steal an advantage in the translation. With carefully crafted compromises they cannot be remitted to officials to straighten out the drafting.

Now that the Maastricht Treaty has come into force there is an entirely different set of arrangements with the European Parliament, with the co-decision procedure for single market legislation, as well as the cooperation procedure for specifically environmental legislation. Co-decision and cooperation both represent an increase in the European Parliament's influence. But there is a wider debate at the Inter-Governmental Conference about how matters should be handled with the future of the Community's institutions under examination.

Conclusions

The real test of the Environmental Impact Assessment Directive, in its own terms, would be whether the standard of environmental decision-making on major projects is now more similar across the EC and whether, as a result, the quality of the environment has improved. In the United Kingdom and elsewhere there has certainly been an increase in the degree to which environmental considerations are taken into account in reaching planning decisions. Whether this would have happened anyway, given the increased environmental awareness of the European public, is difficult to judge. The most that can be confirmed is that because of the Directive environmental information is now presented and the public consulted in a more systematic way.

Certainly there has been a vast increase in the number of regulations. However, the total number of environmental assessment cases and appeals to the Secretary of State on whether environmental assessment is required are small, as are the number of infraction cases. Generally increased costs and longer timescales are unlikely to be significant.

Postscript

Since the Conference at which this chapter was first presented as a paper, Directive 97/11/EC[14] has been adopted which amends Directive 85/337/EEC. The major changes are as follows.

1. The preamble will clarify that Annex II projects (those not subject to mandatory assessment) require assessment where they are likely to have

---

[14] Council Directive 97/11/EC amending Directive 85/337/EEC on the assessment of the effects of certain public and private projects on the environment, OJ 1996, L 73, p. 5.

significant effects on the environment. Member States have three options for determining whether these projects require assessment. They may set criteria and thresholds, they may subject projects to a case by case consideration of the need for environmental impact assessment (EIA), or they may have a mixture of those two approaches. In setting criteria/thresholds or in subjecting projects to case by case consideration, Member States must take into account relevant criteria from a new Annex III and make public the results. The preamble will now make it clear that, where Member States opt for thresholds/criteria rather than a case by case approach, they will not be obliged to examine (or 'screen') projects falling below the thresholds or outside the criteria for the need for EIA.

2. Annex I, which lists projects for which EIA is mandatory, has been extended to cover 20 categories of development. Most of the additional categories are transferred from Annex II.

3. Authorities are required to give the main reasons for their decision and the main mitigation measures required.

4. The minimum information to be provided by the developer must include an outline of the main alternatives the developer has studied.

5. The Directive's requirements for consultation in the cases of proposals that are likely to affect other Member States mirror the key provisions of the Espoo Convention.[15]

---

[15] Convention on Environmental Impact Assessment in a Transboundary Context, United Nations, 1991.

Chapter 16

FROM ENVIRONMENTAL IMPACT ASSESSMENT TO STRATEGIC ENVIRONMENTAL ASSESSMENT: SUSTAINABILITY AND DECISION-MAKING

William Sheate

Introduction

Environmental impact assessment (EIA) has moved on from its earliest days. It is no longer just about reconciling the environment with economic growth (achieving a balance). The context for decision-making is now that of sustainable development which places the environment centre stage. While EIA continues to present information to decision-makers, those same decision-makers can no longer simply ignore that information. Contrary to popular re-definition by governments, sustainable development implies that if economic development would unduly compromise the environment, the environment should win through (Sheate, 1994: for details, see the references section at the end of this chapter).

Debates over environmental, social and economic sustainability do not mean that one necessarily has to be compromised over the others. EIA provides a mechanism for identifying ways forward which maximise sustainability for all three factors, allowing decision-makers to choose the options that are most sustainable in the widest sense. There is, however, an environmental and social imperative behind the concept of sustainable development. It is this, then, that now provides a new opportunity for EIA to make a real impact on decision-making. EIA in turn offers probably the best mechanism for incorporating sustainability into the decision-making process.

The historical development of EIA is instructive and provides important reminders of its original purpose. The environmentalism of the 1960s and 1970s was nothing new; it had been around since the mid-nineteenth century in the guise of 'transcendentalists' such as Walt Whitman and Ralph Waldo Emerson in the United States and the 'anarchists' in Europe such as William Morris. The re-birth of environmentalism in the 1960s also took place among different factions, namely technocentrics and ecocentrics. The technocentric approach represented a belief in the ability of people to make the world a better place. The ecocentric drew on the ideologies of the previous century, essentially bioethics (the intrinsic value of nature) and self-reliance (the importance of community identity and participation in community affairs). Ecology began to take the political centre-stage in the late-1960s, no longer being seen as the preserve of the academic. A key group of ecological planners were espousing an essentially technocentrist environmental management approach, people such as McHarg:

Man is that uniquely conscious creature who can perceive and express. He must become the steward of the biosphere. To do this he must design with nature. (McHarg, 1969)

Other writers were addressing the rising concern with resource depletion and environmental pollution, writers such as Rachel Carson in *Silent Spring* (1968), Paul Ehrlich (1972) and Garrett Hardin's controversial essay, 'The Tragedy of the Commons' (1968). The Club of Rome's report 'The Limits to Growth' (Meadows *et al*, 1972) also set the environmental cat among the economic pigeons. The UN Conference on the Human Environment, held in Stockholm in June 1972 provided a focus for many of these environmental concerns and led to the subsequent setting up of the UN Environment Programme (UNEP) to monitor environmental changes in the global commons.

It was within this context that environmental impact assessment (EIA) was born. It was seen as a mechanism for reconciling economic growth with concern for the environment, and for making that concern more explicit in decision-making. Ecology and the environmental sciences were at last coming together with land-use planning to 'design with nature'. Ecologists had begun to produce some alarming statistics, for instance on species extinction, showing what was being done to the natural heritage. Links with economics were also being made, showing that poor environmental management could be costly in economic terms too, e.g. through soil erosion, chemical pesticides. EIA was a natural consequence of the politicisation of the environment.

And so NEPA was born. In 1969 in the United States the National Environmental Policy Act was passed, an Act that was to set the EIA scene worldwide for the next two decades. For the first time, it introduced in legislation a requirement that an impact statement be made of the likely significant effects on the environment of major, federal actions. Australia introduced EIA in 1974 in its Environment Protection (Impact of Proposals) Act. In Europe, although a number of EC Member States had introduced their own EIA system during the late 1970s (West Germany, 1975; France, 1976), a formalised EC-wide system was not introduced until 1985.

EIA in Europe

The development of EIA legislation in the European Community and the United Kingdom has a long and often tortuous history, one which is being revisited in the current debates about strategic environmental assessment (SEA). The idea of SEA is nothing new in the EC; the same debates were being had in the 1970s and now, 20 years on, are still being tossed into the arena. A detailed analysis of the history and development of the EIA Directive can be found elsewhere (Sheate, 1984), but some key events and issues in the past are worth examining since they shed considerable light on activities today and where EIA is going.

It is instructive to look, briefly, at why the EC ever got involved in environmental policy in the first place; the original Treaty of Rome was anything but an explicitly environmental treaty and in the 1970s, of course, reference was still to the European Economic Community (EEC).

The objectives of the original Treaty of Rome are set out in Article 2:

The Community shall have as its task, by establishing a common market and progressively approximating the economic policies of Member States, to promote throughout the Community a harmonious development of economic activities, a continuous and balanced expansion, an increase in stability, an accelerated raising of the standard of living and closer relations between the States belonging to it.

Part of the preamble to the Treaty of Rome also states:

Affirming as the essential objectives of their efforts the constant improvement of the living and working conditions of their peoples.

In theory, since there is no mention of the environment explicitly in the Treaty of Rome, environmental protection could only be implemented for the purposes of achieving the objectives of the Treaty, i.e. through the approximation of economic policies and the proper functioning of the common market. A suitably dynamic and, at times controversial (von Moltke, 1977) interpretation of the Treaty and its preamble enabled the Community to agree its First Programme of Action on the Environment in 1973 (OJ, 1973). In this, the provisions of the Treaty were qualified in the form of:

. . . in accordance with Article 2 of the Treaty . . . which cannot now be imagined in the absence of an effective campaign to combat pollution and nuisances or of an improvement in the quality of life and the protection of the environment.

and

Whereas improvement in the quality of life and the protection of the natural environment are among the fundamental tasks of the Community; whereas it is therefore necessary to implement a Community environment policy.

The First Action Programme was adopted by the Council of Ministers on 22 November 1973 in response to a call from the Heads of State and Government in 1972 to take action concerning the environment and that 'economic expansion is not an end in itself'. (CEC, 1972). At that meeting the Council accepted that:

effects on the environment should be taken into account at the earliest possible stage in all technical planning and decision-making processes

and

that more account is taken of environmental aspects in town planning and land-use.

Over subsequent Action Programmes the emphasis on prevention rather than cure grew, and it was in that context that EIA came to be seen as central to the Community's environmental policy. Although many other aspects of the Community's environmental policy could be regarded as forms of fire-fighting (e.g. the setting of pollution emission limits which had to be met within a certain timescale) EIA was to be the cornerstone of a more preventive approach by the EC; after all, not only does it make good environmental sense, there are also good economic grounds for such an approach.

Early work on an EIA initiative in Europe began in 1975 with the Commission stating that an EIA procedure should be drawn up and adopted under the Second Action Programme (OJ, 1977). Coincidentally, a seminar was also organised at about the same time by the European Environmental Bureau and the European Council for Environmental Law (CEDE) in Louvain, Belgium to discuss ways of implementing environmental impact statements in Europe (Mitchell, 1975). The European Commission commissioned a number of reports on EIA, in particular from Manchester University (Lee and Wood, 1976, 1977, 1979) and later from the Batelle Institute (Batelle, 1978) on which a proposal for a directive was eventually based.

Drafting of the Directive began internally in the Commission during 1977 and 1978, along with discussions in two meetings of a Group of Experts (Lee and Wood, 1984). In November 1979 the Commission organised a symposium on EIA methods, the conclusions of which were to be used in drafting the proposed Directive. It was not until 1980, and after 20 internal drafts, that the proposal for the Directive was officially published (OJ, 1980).

The proposal for the Directive was intended to establish procedures for requiring EIA of certain public and private projects. This position had not been arrived at without considerable controversy, not least over whether project-level assessment was really the best place to start on an EIA initiative, or whether plans and programmes would not have been a more effective and appropriate level for Community-wide action.

The European Commission was at pains to secure a firm legal foothold for the EIA Directive since it was seen as the cornerstone of the Third Action

Programme, and because it was intent on avoiding the weight of litigation experienced in the United States. It was felt that development at the project level had a more direct impact in terms of distortion of competition than did plans and programmes and was therefore more readily justified under the Treaty of Rome (Stuffman, 1979). That assertion is in itself a moot point. When the draft Directive was first published in the Official Journal (OJ, 1980) the Commission appears to have been confident enough in the harmonisation basis for the Directive to have been able to dispense with Article 235 of the Treaty as a justification (which allows action to be taken where the Treaty has not made express provision) and depend solely on Article 100 (approximation of laws). However, when the Directive was finally agreed in 1985 Article 235 had reappeared in a supporting (or perhaps 'belt and braces') role.

There were, of course, other reasons why plans and programmes were not included. At the time there was little methodological expertise in assessing plans and programmes (though that was also to some extent true of projects) and the procedures for formulating plans and programmes were seen as being too disparate between Member States. However, this should not have been a real obstruction to progress. 'The methodological objection to beginning with plan and programme assessment cannot be taken seriously . . .' (Wandesforde-Smith, 1978). Indeed, it was the development of the project EIA Directive which provided the impetus in many Member States and elsewhere to develop methodologies and practice for project EIA. Nor, in the early 1990s, did the lack of methodological expertise prevent the UK government from requiring local authorities to assess the environmental implications of their development plans. It was left to the local authorities to work out how to meet the requirement.

The final agreement of the project Directive in 1985 had been no easy matter, the United Kingdom and Denmark in particular having held out for some years with objections in principle or to parts of the Directive. The United Kingdom had continuously vetoed agreement until November 1983, by which time it had negotiated sufficient amendments to make it acceptable (or believed it had) and was under considerable pressure from other Member States and the House of Lords (who had produced a favourable and influential report on the proposed directive) (UK House of Lords, 1981). The Danish eventually resolved their problems over the potential conflict with national Parliamentary decision-making over development projects.

The difficulties and controversies described above are just a taste of the many years of dispute over the draft directive. Much debate centred around the detailed drafting of the text, especially the different nuances that could be read into different translations, but also the compatibility of terminology and detail between Member States; whether annex lists were appropriate; and the contents of the annex lists: which projects should be subject to mandatory assessment (Annex I) and which should be subject to assessment when likely to have significant environmental effects (Annex II). Agricultural projects were just one category which see-sawed between the annexes from one draft to another (Sheate and Macrory, 1989).

From the beginning, there was a general desire on behalf of the European Commission and Member States to avoid what was seen as the excessive litigation in the United States which had resulted from the EIA system established under the National Environmental Policy Act 1969 (NEPA). It was felt that the US focus on the scope and content of the environmental impact statement (EIS), and its prominence in the EIA process, was the cause of this litigation and therefore the Directive was drafted without explicit reference to a specific document, but instead refers simply to the provision of information which is to be taken into account in the decision-making process. Developers and Member States were keen to prevent the establishment of further sources of delay in obtaining project consent. In fact, it is quite probable that an EIA Directive would never have been agreed had this approach not been taken.

However, the European approach appears to have reflected some misunderstanding of the US system of enforcing EIA legislation and the important procedural role of the EIS. Litigation has proved to be a crucial means of enforcing EIA requirements in the United States and perhaps EC Member States should reflect on the fact that, more than 25 years later, they have yet to establish an equally effective means of enforcement.

Directive 85/337/EEC on the assessment of the effects of certain public and private projects on the environment was agreed and notified to Member States in July 1985 and formal compliance was due on 3 July 1988. Although legally confined to EC Member States a number of other European countries have chosen to establish similar procedures or are considering doing so. The Directive is a procedural one, which seeks to ensure that before a decision is made about whether consent should be given to go ahead with a development a minimum level of information about the likely significant effects on the environment has been provided to the 'competent authority' (for example, a local authority or government minister) making the decision. It does not in itself require a Member State to refuse to give consent for a project even if it is likely to be highly damaging to the environment. In principle, the Directive applies equally across all policy sectors by providing a framework within which Member States must act.

Projects likely to have significant effects on the environment by virtue *inter alia* of their nature, size or location must be made subject to an assessment of their effects before consent is given. There are two lists of projects: Annex I projects require EIA in all cases and include major chemical works, power stations, motorways etc.; Annex II projects must be subject to assessment where Member States consider their characteristics so require. Annex II covers the majority of development projects subject to various criteria and thresholds according to the individual Member State. This leads to considerable variation throughout the EC in the extent to which the Directive is implemented and its effectiveness in requiring EIA for any project likely to have significant effects on the environment—the ultimate test. Inevitably, these discrepancies in implementation occur both within sectors and among sectors across the Community. The direct and indirect effects of the proposed project on the following four factors must be identified, described and assessed, where appropriate:

- human beings, fauna and flora;
- soil, water, air, climate and the landscape;
- the interaction between the first two groups;
- material assets and the cultural heritage.

Information supplied by the developer and gathered as a result of consultations must be taken into account in the decision-making process. Although the Directive studiously avoids reference to a formal impact statement, such a document is mentioned in the implementing legislation of many Member States. The developer must supply a minimum level of information and may supply additional information where appropriate. The minimum information is:

1. a description of the project with information on site, design and size;
2. the data required to identify and assess the main effects which the project is likely to have on the environment;
3. a description of the measures envisaged to avoid, reduce and possibly remedy significant adverse effects;
4. a non-technical summary of the above information.

Annex III provides further guidance on information to be supplied, including where appropriate an outline of the main alternatives studied and the reasons for the developer's choice. The description of effects should consider direct effects and any 'indirect, secondary, cumulative, short, medium and long term, permanent and temporary, positive and negative effects of the project'.

The public must be consulted before the project is initiated (Article 6(2)), though not necessarily earlier, i.e. before consent is given. However, there is some confusion here since Article 8 requires information gathered pursuant to Articles 5, 6 and 7 to be taken into consideration in the development consent procedure. That would imply that the public must be consulted before *consent* is given, not just before the project is *initiated*, and indeed this has now been clarified in the agreed amendments to the Directive. Any request for development consent and the information supplied by the developer must also be made public. There are also arrangements for consulting other Member States where a project is likely to have transboundary impacts. The decision and reasons must also be made public.

The Directive requires the European Commission to publish a report on the application and effectiveness of the Directive after five years from notification. This five-year review report was due in July 1990, but was only published in April 1993 (Commission of the European Communities, 1993). The Commission is required to send the report to the European Parliament and the Council. The publication was delayed well beyond its intended date of 3 July 1990, partly through delays in implementation, but also as a result of delays within the Commission and the need to gather Member States' comments on the draft report.

The review produced a useful snapshot of implementation throughout the

Community as of 1991. The lengthy delays in publishing the final report, however, made the detail somewhat less useful than might otherwise have been the case had it been published on time. The report identified where a number of improvements should be made. It concluded that the EIA process is, in many cases, not starting early enough, i.e. too often it is bolted on to the planning and design process rather than being integral from the beginning, and that there is often inadequate quality control of the environmental statement and the EIA process as a whole. Adequate mitigation measures are frequently missing from the planning and design of projects. Consultation in some cases and in some Member States is weak, and the availability of environmental statements is sometimes poor. The review also concluded that the contribution of the EIA process to decision-making and the role of monitoring project implementation are not as clear or as effective as they could be. This last point is particularly disturbing, since EIA is essentially about improving the quality of decision-making by making it more informed.

Many of the individual Member State annexes include recommendations for improving implementation in the Member State, some of which may be achieved through amending the Directive itself. One of the recommendations identified in the UK annex was that consideration should be given to the establishment of an independent statutory body to set and maintain standards relating to the EIA process. No action has yet taken place on this issue, nor does it seem likely. The review report formed the basis for the Commission to bring forward proposals for amending the Directive. These amendments have been in the pipeline for some considerable time, and were finally approved on 3 March 1997 (97/11/EC, OJ L 73, 14.3.97), the Council of Ministers previously having reached a common position on them in December 1995. The amendments include:

- screening criteria to provide consistency in determining which Annex II projects should be subject to EIA;
- scoping: early proposals for a formal scoping stage have been abandoned, scoping to take place now only if a developer asks a local authority for it;
- alternatives: to be strengthened by taking the reference out of Annex III and putting it into the main text;
- changes to the Annex lists, including significant additions to Annex I.

The most obvious omission from the amendment Directive is any reference to strategic environmental assessment, even though the limitations of project EIA are widely recognised. The amendment Directive (97/11/EC) is due to come into force in Member States by 14 March 1999.

Defining project

Defining the parameters of a development project inevitably results in difficulties in deciding what constitutes a project as opposed to a programme or plan.

A project may comprise a number of smaller sub-projects and a programme may comprise a series of projects. A plan may identify future projects or programmes or it may be a 'masterplan' covering a number of projects which are to be built or developed simultaneously or separately over a period of time. The fact that it is difficult to define precisely where the boundaries between these definitions should lie is itself an illustration of the value of a tiered approach to EIA which ensures that impacts on the environment are assessed at all the appropriate opportunities and at the degree of detail appropriate to the level of decision-making.

Until recently, EIA has been applied largely to project level decision-making, i.e. decisions about whether to go ahead with individual discrete development projects. In most cases it is not too difficult to recognise an individual project proposal, e.g. a factory, an oil terminal, an airport runway, a reservoir proposal, a housing development. However, there are cases where a development proposal comprises several discrete sub-projects (Sheate, 1995a, b; 1996). In the absence of any level of strategic environmental assessment (SEA) it is appropriate and arguably legitimate to say that the overall proposal is a 'project' made up of associated, ancillary or subsidiary projects. Where a tiered system of SEA is established, however, this semantic distinction is rendered unnecessary since such a proposal would be caught at the programme level. This problem of definition is particularly acute when it comes to linear developments such as road building, especially when related schemes come forward over a long period of time. Road building in the United Kingdom, and other EU Member States, illustrates the limitations of the EIA Directive (85/337/EEC) applying so far only to projects.

Unfortunately, there is little UK case law on the interpretation of the requirement under Directive 85/337/EEC regarding the definition of project and even less on the issue of alternatives. Most case law on EIA has been concerned with whether an assessment was required.

The first is the earliest EIA case of *R* v. *Swale Borough Council and the Medway Ports Authority, ex parte the Royal Society for the Protection of Birds*[1] in which the RSPB challenged the granting of planning permission by Swale Borough Council to the Medway Ports Authority for land reclamation of mudflats important for wintering birds (Lappel Bank), which was part of a larger scheme involving the construction of a storage area for cargo and a marina, on the grounds that it was a breach of both the EIA Directive and the Birds Directive (79/409/EEC).

The construction of a storage area for cargo and a marina might be considered to fall within Annex I (trading ports) or Annex II (harbours etc. not in Annex I). Simon Brown J held that the question must be answered strictly in relation to the development applied for, not any development contemplated beyond that.

However, he also held that the further question arising in respect of a 'Schedule 2 development' (Sch. 2 to the Town and Country Planning

---

[1] (1991) JEL Vol. 3, No. 1, 135.

(Assessment of Environmental Effects) Regulations 1988[2] which corresponds to Annex I of Directive 85/337/EEC), whether it 'would be likely to have significant effects on the environment by virtue of factors such as its nature, size or location' should be answered rather differently. He went on to say:

The proposal should not then be considered in isolation if in reality it is properly to be regarded as an integral part of an inevitably more substantial development. This approach appears to me appropriate on the language of the regulations, the existence of the smaller development of itself promoting the larger development and thereby likely to carry in its wake the environmental effects of the latter. In common sense, moreover, developers could otherwise defeat the object of the regulations by piecemeal development proposals.

The judge held that the question of whether an EIA is required or whether a project falls within Sch. 1 or 2 to the 1988 Environmental Assessment Regulations was exclusively for the planning authority to decide subject only to traditional *Wednesbury* challenge (unreasonableness).

Although the *Marleasing* decision (Case C-109/89, *Marleasing* v. *La Comercial Internacional de Alimentacion*[3]) had not yet been decided by the European Court of Justice regarding the doctrine of sympathetic interpretation (the duty to interpret national law in conformity with Community law), the principle that national legislation which is intended to implement Community measures must be interpreted in conformity with the parent Community legislation had been established in Case C-14/83, *Von Colson and Kamman* v. *Land Nordrhein-Westfalen*.[4] This principle had also been accepted and applied in the English courts on a number of occasions prior to the domestic EIA cases (Ward, 1993). The judgment in the *RSPB* case above therefore would appear to contradict key principles of EC law, i.e. it is not just for the planning authority to decide, it depends on whether the proposed project is likely to have significant effects. Arguably this also illustrates the lack of familiarity at the time of the English courts with European environmental legislation.

One of the most recent EIA cases to come before the courts is *R* v. *Secretary of State for Transport, ex parte Surrey County Council*[5] in relation to proposals by the Department of Transport to widen and add three-lane link roads alongside the M25 motorway in Surrey which would result in a highway of 14 lanes in total. Surrey County Council applied to the High Court to seek permission to bring the decision of the Secretary of State to propose the roads before judicial review on the grounds that under the EIA Directive the proposed 'improvements' to the M25 between junctions 10 and 21 should be treated as one project, not as several separate schemes as intended by the Department of Transport. Their application for judicial review was refused on the grounds that the application was premature, since there was as yet no environmental state-

---

[2] SI 1988 No. 1199 ('the 1988 Environmental Assessment Regulations').
[3] [1990] ECR I-4135.
[4] [1984] ECR 1891.
[5] (1993) not yet reported.

ment. However, MacPhearson J accepted the council's argument, adding that he would expect the environmental statement when published to take into account all the Department's plans for the M25. Should the Department fail to incorporate such plans into the assessment MacPhearson J stated that Surrey County Council would then be in a position to reapply to the court. In his decision the judge said that a new motorway over green fields could not be split up into individual schemes for the purposes of EIA, whereas an improvement of an existing motorway could be so split up. Surrey County Council have argued that it is stretching the imagination to call the proposals for the M25 simply an improvement.

This issue of definition of 'project' is a long-standing problem and has only recently come before the European Court of Justice. In Case C-431/92, *Commission v. Germany (Grosskrotzenburg)*[6] the dispute was over whether the project in question was an Annex I project in its own right (and therefore required mandatory EIA) or a modification to a project and therefore an Annex II project which may be subject to EIA. Germany argued that the construction of a new block at the power station did not constitute a project under Article 4 (1) of the Directive, but was a modification of a project under para. 12 of Annex II, which according to Article 4 (2) may, rather than must, be made subject to EIA. The Court held that, by virtue of para. 2 of Annex I, projects for thermal power stations with a heat output of 300 MW or more must undergo a systematic assessment. For the purposes of this provision, such projects must be assessed irrespective of whether they are separate constructions, are added to a pre-existing construction, or even have close functional links with a pre-existing construction. Since the project in question was a power station of 500 MW, the Court found that it was a project within the meaning of Article 4 (1) and Annex I of the Directive.

However, on the more significant issue of sub-division of projects into smaller sub-projects for EIA purposes—typical of many road proposals—the Court of Justice in Case C-392/92, *Bund Naturshutz and Others v. Bavarian Higher Regional Court*[7] avoided the question, although Advocate General Gulmann in his Opinion did not:[8]

... *the purpose of the directive should not be lost by the projects which should be subject to an environmental impact assessment being given a form which renders an environmental impact assessment meaningless. The Member States must ensure that the obligation to carry out an environmental impact assessment is not circumvented by a definition that is over-strict or otherwise inappropriate, in the light of the purpose of the directive, of the projects in respect of which application must be made.*

The important question is . . . whether, in connection with the environmental impact assessment of the specific project, there is an obligation to take account of the fact that the project forms part of a larger project, which is to be carried out subsequently, and in the affirmative, the extent to which account is to be taken of that fact.

---

[6] [1995] ECR I-2189.
[7] [1994] ECR I-3717.
[8] *Ibid.* paras. 70–72.

The subject-matter and content of the environmental impact assessment must be established in the light of the purpose of the directive, which is, at the earliest possible stage in all the technical planning and decision-making processes, to obtain an overview of the effects of the projects on the environment and to have projects designed in such a way that they have the least possible effect on the environment. *That purpose entails that as far as practically possible account should also be taken in the environmental impact assessment of any current plans to extend the specific project in hand.*

For instance, the environmental impact assessment of a project concerning the construction of the first part of a power station should, accordingly, involve the plans to extend the station's capacity fourfold, when the question of whether the power station's site is appropriate is being assessed.

Similarly, when sections of a planned road link are being constructed, account must be taken, in connection with the environmental impact assessment of the specific projects of the significance of those sections in the linear route to be taken by the rest of the planned link road (emphasis added).

The issue also arose, though was rightly rejected, in the UK courts in *R* v. *Secretary of State for the Environment et al, ex parte Greenpeace and Lancashire County Council*[9] (Yongo, 1994). The applicants for judicial review argued (perhaps rather tortuously) that the proposed thermal reprocessing plant (THORP) at Sellafield, Cumbria was actually two projects: one being the construction, and the other being the bringing into operation of the processes within THORP thereby causing emissions. The Court held that THORP was only one project, not two, and (relying on the Twyford Down case) since its commencement had begun long before the Directive came into force, that the Directive did not apply to projects in the pipeline.

The issue of project definition is critical. Unless it is resolved, road and other infrastructure EIAs in the United Kingdom and across the EU will continue to fail to address some of the potentially most significant impacts flowing from such developments. The EIA Directive will have singularly failed in its prime objective: that all direct and indirect effects of a project will have been assessed prior to consent being given.

Although the EIA Directive has undergone review, the European Commission chose not to propose any clarification to the definition of 'project', e.g. that a project means the overall project including associated or related developments, not simply the smallest component into which the project can be broken down. It should be remembered that the whole *raison d'être* behind the Directive is that:

... effects on the environment [should be taken] into account at the earliest possible stage in all the technical planning and decision-making processes ... (preamble to Directive 85/337/EEC).

This admirable sentiment cannot be achieved if EIA is applied only at the *latest* stage, i.e. individual schemes of a larger road project or upgrading of an entire route (Sheate, 1995a).

---

[9] (1994) JEL Vol. 6, No. 2, 312.

SEA Directive

There would be considerable logic in incorporating project EIA and strategic environmental assessment (SEA) into the same body of legislation rather than having a separate SEA Directive (Sheate, 1994). Indeed, in no other jurisdiction where EIA and SEA exist together (except, recently, Canada) do they do so in separate legislation. In fact, it is not too difficult in drafting terms to link EIA and SEA by amending the present EIA Directive (CPRE, 1992, Sheate, 1994). However, politically, this would be too great a leap and the Commission has been at pains to keep the draft SEA directive completely separate from amendments to the project EIA Directive. Unfortunately, the risk of inconsistency between the project EIA Directive and an SEA directive is compounded by this separatist approach. The draft SEA directive has also had a tortuous history, early drafts were under discussion within the Commission in 1990 and 1991 only to be abandoned at the Edinburgh Summit at the end of 1992 due to a UK veto. The Commission resurrected the idea a couple of years later and consulted publicly on a draft in the summer of 1995, though by that time any reference to policies had been removed, with the proposed directive applying only to plans and programmes. This was redrafted yet again in early 1996 and the Commission secured internal agreement on the new version late in 1996 (CEC, 1996). Politically, however, the prospects in the Council of Ministers, are probably far from good, even though a number of Member States are already introducing their own forms of SEA on plans and programmes. The UK government has made it clear it does not want to see formal EC legislation in this area, although it is happy to encourage voluntary 'appraisal', as it has done for development plans.

The SEA Directive is one tine of a two-pronged approach by the Commission to SEA. Reflecting the importance of integration of policies in the Fifth Environmental Action Programme, the other tine is the gradual integration of SEA requirements into other policy areas, e.g. Structural Funds (the amended Regulations in 1993 requiring a limited form of SEA), and the Trans-European Network (TEN) where the Commission is still procrastinating over how to carry out an SEA. Nevertheless, it is probably this integrating approach which holds out the best prospects for getting SEA to happen in practice, especially given the uncertainties surrounding any formal EC framework legislation on SEA.

Trans-European Network

The Trans-European Networks for Transport (TEN)—covering road, rail, air and water—are an essential part of the European Union's Common Transport Policy. In April 1994, following pressure from non-governmental organisations (NGOs) and Member States, the Commission, in a proposal for a European Parliament and Council Decision on the development of the TEN, recognised the need for a strategic environmental assessment (SEA) to ensure the European

Union was meeting its own obligations under the Maastricht Treaty (CEC, 1994). The TEN has as its main objective, to 'Ensure the sustainable and safe mobility of persons and goods within the area without internal frontiers under the best possible social conditions while contributing to the attainment of the Community's environmental objectives.'

The TEN is fundamentally linked to the completion of the single market and includes plans for some ECU 1000–1500 billion-worth of infrastructure building between 1990 and 2010. New roads alone would add a further 15,000 km of road surface across Europe. While the decision to carry out an SEA on the TEN was welcome, the objectives with which the European Commission began to explore the SEA were essentially flawed since the decision to establish the TEN had already been made.

The first concern, then, was that the SEA, if and when it happens, will occur too late in the decision-making process, after the decision to establish the TEN has been taken, instead of the SEA influencing the decision over whether the TEN should be established in the first place. Environmental safeguards have therefore failed to keep pace with the single market. The objective for the SEA suggested by the European Commission 'to provide a forecast on the overall environmental impact of the TEN when fully completed' clearly assumed the TEN would be completed or established as planned. The second objective, 'to provide a basis and criteria for the revision of the TEN with a view to their environmental improvements' indicates that the SEA is being seen primarily as a means of identifying mitigation measures to what was a fundamentally economic decision to establish the TEN, rather than as a way of avoiding environmental impact in the first place. This runs counter to the principle of SEA which, by applying EIA principles at the earliest stages, enables real, sustainable choices to be made between alternative options and so avoid impacts, not merely mitigate them. This approach is, therefore, inconsistent with the principles of sustainable development, and indeed with the EU's own Fifth Environmental Action Programme.

A SEA should be set within the overall context of sustainable development and should, therefore, consider issues such as need (as opposed to demand) and environmental capacity. The development of the TEN should not breach environmental capacity constraints (e.g. wildlife and landscape sensitive areas), should help in reducing atmospheric emissions (and meeting EU targets), and should reduce the need to travel rather than stimulate additional journeys or unsustainable freight movements (Böge, 1995). It is important that SEA is carried out for all the TEN networks (road-TERN, rail, air and water) together in order to maximise the sustainability of the final total TEN. For most criteria, e.g. atmospheric emissions or energy consumption, the rail network is likely to be more sustainable than air or road and may, for certain journeys, provide direct competition. The overall TEN should seek to shift transport from less sustainable modes such as road and air to more sustainable modes such as rail and water. This is not possible if each TEN is assessed in isolation.

Traffic forecasts are notoriously unreliable and any SEA which operates under the principles of sustainable development should recognise both environmental capacity constraints and the importance of demand management. The advantage of an SEA is that it should provide the opportunity to look at real alternatives, including managing demand rather than simply mitigating impacts caused by attempting to meet forecast demand (Sheate, 1992). However, it will also be necessary to consider parallel policies as counter or mitigation measures alongside alternatives so that the best mix of options can be identified, e.g. the use of the pricing mechanism, such as a carbon tax, traffic management and calming policies etc., to counter induced traffic through e.g. TERN designation and road improvements.

While it may be difficult—though not impossible—to elicit effective public participation at the EU level, it is quite practical and essential to do so at Member State level. It is, after all, the Member States that identify the routes in the first place. Any SEA, if it is to be credible, must make adequate provision for public and NGO participation, first at the EU level in the scoping of the SEA and then in the identification and assessment stages at Member State level, not just when the SEA has been completed.

The Commission (DGVII, Transport) is still struggling with working out how to go about the SEA. A Hearing of Experts was held in Brussels in June 1994 which, perhaps not surprisingly, failed to establish a practical methodology for carrying out the SEA. One reason, arguably, was that the Commission's objectives were somewhat different to those of many others, for instance over whether the SEA should cover operation of the network, not just the infrastructure impacts (a feeling shared by many experts at the meeting though not the Commission). There was concern, too, as to how the findings of the SEA would actually influence the nature and extent of the TEN. The Commission's prevailing view that much of the network is already in place, fails to recognise the so far unassessed impact of designating even existing routes as part of a strategic network, e.g. on traffic flows and type of traffic, let alone upgrading them.

Following continuing disagreement between the Council of Ministers and the European Parliament a compromise Decision was finally reached on 17 June 1996 enabling the European Commission to release an additional ECU 250 million earmarked for priority projects in 1996 (Transport Europe, 1996). The compromise Decision now includes a specific environmental article (Article 7a) which emphasises the need to meet the requirements of Directive 85/337/EEC in respect of projects, and instructs the Commission to 'develop potential methods of analysis for strategically evaluating the environmental impact of the whole network' and to develop methods for corridor analysis. Many members of the European Parliament, however, remained unhappy about the weakness of the environmental protection provisions in the Decision (European Parliament, 1996).

Conclusions

So what are the prospects for EIA and SEA? EIA is now fully established as an integral part of development project planning and decision-making. Increasingly, it is being seen as the most appropriate vehicle for improving public involvement, even if on a voluntary basis, in land-use planning. Some commentators (e.g. Mayda, 1996) have argued that EIA/SEA are no longer appropriate terminologies in the context of sustainable development and that what is needed is integrated or sustainability assessment which brings together economic, environmental and social forms of assessment. There is a danger here, however, that the original objectives of EIA—of making the environment more explicit in decision-making—is lost, masked by the inevitably more dominant considerations of economic appraisal and social factors. Sustainable development actually now provides an environmental and social imperative; the integration of these aspects is already widespread, exemplified by the increasing use of participatory techniques and consideration of community impacts within EIA/ SEA. We should be careful of being sucked into an overly integrated approach (attractive though it may be) which loses the distinct environmental perspective which EIA provides and in which the environment is not truly integral (cf. the New Zealand Resource Management Act, for example), or is unaccompanied by substantial changes in the way in which policy is formulated (i.e. a more objectives-led approach). Otherwise, we revert to 'business as usual' as many governments now interpret sustainable development to mean. If there was real prospect of a change from economics-led policy formulation to sustainable objectives-led formulation there might be a stronger case for fully integrating all approaches (which was the intention in the New Zealand context). Since that seems highly unlikely in most cases, it is essential that the environment continues to be given specific, public recognition within existing or modified decision-making processes. EIA/SEA still provides the best mechanism for doing that.

As experience of EIA has grown most local authorities, consultants, NGOs and other commentators have recognised the limitations of project EIA and the need for SEA. The consequence of this has been that SEA is being developed because it has to be and in response to greater public expectations. While some Member States may be reluctant to see EC legislation in this area, in practice SEA is likely to happen with or without it (though probably quicker with). In the United Kingdom, environmental appraisal of development plans is a form of SEA by any other name and now widely practised by local authorities. The Department of the Environment is also looking at extending it to Regional Planning Guidance (RPG) which would begin to create a tiered system of EIA/SEA. The SEA pigeons will really have come home to roost when its principles are applied to the real problem areas, such as transport—internationally, nationally, regionally and locally. We still have some way to go.

References

Batelle Institute (1978), *Rapport Final de L'Etude Selection des Projects Destines à Etre Soumis à une Evaluation d'Impact Sur L'Environnement*, CEC, ENV/513/78, French translation, Brussels, July 1978.

Böge, S (1995), 'The Well-travelled Yogurt Pot: Lessons for New Freight Transport Policies and Regional Production', *World Transport Policy and Practice*, Vol. 1, No. 1, 7–11.

Carson, RL (1968), *Silent Spring* (Boston: Houghton Mifflin).

Commission of the European Communities (CEC) (1972), 'Declaration Finale' of the Heads of State of Government, EC Bull., October 1972, No. 10, point 8.

Commission of the European Communities (1993), *Report from the Commission of the Implementation of Directive 85/337/EEC*, COM(93) 28 final, Vol. 12, Brussels, 2 April 1993.

Commission of the European Communities (1994), *Proposal for a European Parliament and Council Decision on Community Guidelines for the Development of the Trans-European Transport Network*, COM(94) 106 final, 7 April 1994.

Commission of the European Communities (1996), *Proposal for a Council Directive on the assessment of the effects of certain plans and programmes on the environment*, COM (96) 511 final, 4 December 1996.

Council for the Protection of Rural England (CPRE), (1992) *'Mock' EC Directive on Environmental Assessment: Proposals for Amending EC Directive 85/337/EEC.*

Ehrlich, PR and Ehrlich AH (1972), *Population, Resources, Environment: Issues in Human Ecology* (San Francisco: Freeman and Co.).

European Parliament (1996), 'Trans-European Networks', *Session News: The Week*, 15–19 July, 14–16.

Hardin, G (1968), 'The Tragedy of the Commons', 162 *Science*, 1243–1248.

Lee, N and Wood, C (1976), 'The Introduction of Environmental Impact Statements in the European Communities', CEC, ENV/197/76, May 1976.

Lee, N and Wood, C (1977), 'Methods of Environmental Impact Assessment for Major Projects and Physical Plans', CEC, ENV/36/78, December 1977.

Lee, N and Wood, C (1977), 'Environmental Impact Assessment of Physical Plans in the European Communities', CEC, ENV/37/78, December 1977.

Lee, N and Wood, C (1979), 'Environmental Impact Assessment and the Preparation of Economic Plans and Programmes in the European Communities', CEC, ENV/740/79, November 1979

Lee, N and Wood, C (1984), 'Environmental Impact Assessment Procedures Within the European Community', in Roberts, R and Roberts, T (eds), *Planning and Ecology* (London: Chapman and Hall).

Mayda, J (1996), 'Reforming Impact Assessment: Issues, Premises, and Elements', *Impact Assessment*, Vol. 14, No. 1, 87–96.

McHarg, I (1969), *Design With Nature* (New York: Natural History Press).

Meadows, DH, Meadows, DL, Randers, J, and Behrens, WW, (1972), *The Limits to Growth, A Report for the Club of Rome's Project on the Predicament of Mankind* (London: Earth Island Ltd.).

Mitchell, B (1975), 'The Environmental Impact Statement: Report of a Seminar held in Louvain', Belgium, 12 December 1975, EEB/ECEL.

von Moltke, K (1977), 'The Legal Basis for Environmental Policy', 3 *Environmental Policy and Law* 136–140.

Official Journal of the European Communities (1973), First Programme of Action on the Environment, OJ C 112 20.12.73, Vol. 16.

Official Journal of the European Communities (1977), Second Action Programme, OJ C 139 17.5.77, p. 1.

Official Journal of the European Communities (1980), Proposal for a Council Directive Concerning the Assessment of the Environmental Effects of Certain Public and Private Projects, OJ C 169 9.7.1980, COM(80) 313 final).

Official Journal of the European Communities (1985), Council Directive on the Assessment of the Effects of Certain Public and Private Projects on the Environment, OJ L 175 5.7.85.

Official Journal of the European Communities (1997), Council Directive 97/11/EC of 3 March 1997 amending Directive 85/337/EEC on the assessment of the effects of certain public and private projects on the environment, OJ L 73, 14.3.1997.

Sheate, WR (1984), *The EEC Draft Directive on the Environmental Assessment of Projects: Its History, Development and Implications*, Unpublished MSc thesis, University of London, Imperial College.

Sheate, WR (1992), 'Strategic Environmental Assessment in the Transport Sector', *Project Appraisal*, Vol. 7, No. 3, 170–174.

Sheate, WR (1994), *Making an Impact: A Guide to EIA Law and Policy*, 2nd edition (London: Cameron May).

Sheate, WR (1995a), 'Amending the EC Directive 85/337/EEC on Environmental Impact Assessment', *European Environmental Law Review*, Vol. 4, No. 3, 77–82.

Sheate, WR (1995b), 'Electricity Generation and Transmission: A Case Study of Problematic EIA Implementation in the UK', *Environmental Policy and Practice*, Vol. 5, No. 1, 17–25.

Sheate, WR (1996), 'The Search for a UK Nuclear Waste Disposal Facility: A Case Study of Disputed "Project" Definition under the EC Directive 85/337/EEC on EIA', *Environmental Policy and Practice*, Vol. 6, No. 2, 75–86.

Sheate, WR and Macrory, RB (1989), 'Agriculture and the EC Environmental Assessment Directive: Lessons for Community Policy-Making', 28 *Journal of Common Market Studies* 68–81.

Stuffman, C (1979), Minutes of evidence taken before the European Communities Committee (UK House of Lords, Sub-Committee G, Environment), 23 January 1979, evidence heard in private.

Transport Europe (1996), Trans-European Networks: Inter-institutional Compromise on Policy Guidelines, Supplement to *Transport Europe*, June 1996.

UK Department of the Environment (1991), *Policy Appraisal and the Environment: A Guide for Government Departments* (London: HMSO).

UK Department of the Environment (1993), *Environmental Appraisal of Development Plans: A Good Practice Guide* (London: HMSO).

UK House of Lords (1981), Select Committee on the European Communities (Sub-Committee G, Environment), *Environmental Assessment of Projects*, Session 1980–81, Eleventh Report, with minutes of evidence, 3 February (London: HMSO).

Wandesforde-Smith, G (1978), 'Environmental Impact Assessment in the European Community', Pre-print to publication (in 1979) in *Zeitschrift für Umweltpolitik.*

Ward, A (1993), 'The Right to an Effective Remedy in European Community Law and Environmental Protection: A Case Study of United Kingdom Judicial Decisions Concerning the Environmental Assessment Directive', *Journal of Environmental Law*, Vol. 5, No. 2, 221–244.

Yongo, T (1994), 'A Note on the THORP Case', *Environmental Judicial Review Bulletin*, Vol. 1, No. 1, 8–10.

Part VI

POLICY CONFLICTS

Chapter 17

FREE MOVEMENT OF GOODS AND THE ENVIRONMENT

Laurence Gormley

Introduction

The potential for conflict between the principle of the free movement of goods and the very legitimate interests of environmental protection has long been recognised in EC law. As will be apparent from what follows, however, the approach to reconciling these competing interests has not always been characterised by intellectual coherence, legal certainty or even elegance.

Environmental protection in relation to the free movement of goods was not recognised in the original EEC Treaty but is a creature of judicial creation as one of the headings of the rule of reason applied in the application of Articles 30 and 34 of the EC Treaty which respectively prohibit quantitative restrictions and measures having equivalent effect on imports and exports. Although the European Court of Justice has always rightly insisted that Article 36 of the EC Treaty must be strictly interpreted and is limited to the grounds specified therein, it has developed the rule of reason as an equitable recognition that legitimate measures justified on grounds of *inter alia* environmental protection may be acceptable in EC law, despite the fact that they are capable of restricting trade between Member States, in the absence of EC legislation guaranteeing the interest concerned. Thus the rule of reason is a temporary acceptance—pending Community action—of national measures. It is clear that such measures *do* constitute barriers to trade which in principle infringe Article 30 of the EC Treaty. Unlike the Court's recent about-turn in its reasoning relating to the non-discriminatory local regulation of socio-economic life which now appears to be taken outside the ambit of Article 30,[1] the rule of reason operates very

---

[1] See Cases C-267 and 268/91, *Keck and Mithouard* [1993] ECR I-6097, see, *inter alia*, Chalmers (1994) 19 EL Rev 385; Gormley (1994) 5 *European Business Law Review* 163 and (1996) 19 Fordham Int'l LJ 866; Joliet (1995) Columb. JEL 436; Mattera (1994) RMUE 117; Ross, in Caiger and Floudas (eds) *1996 Onwards: Lowering the Barriers Further* (Chichester: 1996), 45; Roth (1994) *Europarecht* 50; Steindorff (1994) *Zeitschrift für das gesamte Handelsrecht* 149; Tesauro (1995) 15 YEL 1; Van Gerven (1996) 2 Columb. JEL 217; VerLoren van Themaat (1996) *Sociaal-economische Wetgeving* 398, and Weatherill (1996) 33 CML Rev 885.

much as an evaluation of the legitimacy of trade-restricting measures. A key point in relation to the rule of reason has always been that it only applies to non-discriminatory measures and that the Court will look behind the face of the measures to their effects: apparent non-discrimination cannot serve as a cloak for disguised or indirect discrimination,[2] although, as will be explained below, it seems that the Court finds that in the case of environmental protection discrimination will not be fatal to a rule of reason justification. Discrimination itself is of course a sufficient although not a necessary criterion for an infringement of Article 30.

Initially the Court's recognition of environmental protection was only implicit. Thus, in Cases 3, 4 and 6/76, *Kramer et al.*[3] the Court accepted that although certain measures taken with a view to conserving the resources of the sea could restrict production in the short term, they were necessary in order to ensure an optimum yield from fishing in the long term.[4] Environmental protection was then speedily recognised by the Commission as falling within the ambit of the rule of reason.[5] This view entirely accords with the concepts of the rule of reason being a recognition of the need to accept—albeit on a provisional basis pending guarantees at the Community level—that measures taken in certain general interests may deserve precedence over the requirements of the free movement of goods.

Local grab measures: restrictions on exports

Taking developments effectively chronologically, it is appropriate to turn first to deal with local grab measures affecting exports. These cases are of wider importance because the Court had refused to accept Advocate General Capotorti's invitation in earlier cases to apply the case law on Article 30—the basic principle in *Dassonville*[6]—to measures applicable irrespective of the destination of the product in interpreting Article 34 of the EC Treaty. Thus for such measures to infringe Article 34 it has to be shown that they have as their specific object or effect the restriction of exports and thereby the establishment of a difference in treatment between the domestic trade of a Member State and its export trade in such a way as to provide a particular advantage for national production or for the domestic market of the Member State in question at the

---

[2] Case 207/83, *Commission* v. *United Kingdom* [1985] ECR 1201, at 1212.
[3] [1976] ECR 1279.
[4] [1976] ECR 1279, at 1313.
[5] In its Communication on the consequences of the *Cassis de Dijon* judgment (OJ 1980 C 256, p.2) and in its answer to Written Question 1285/77 (OJ 1979 C 214, p. 5) on the prohibition of non-re-usable bottles. On this problem in the United States, see Stein and Sandalow in Sandalow and Stein, *Courts and Free Markets* (Oxford: 1982) Vol. I, pp. 27–28 and the judgment of the US Supreme Court in *Minnesota* v. *Clover Leaf Creamery Co. et al.* 449 US 456 (1981).
[6] Case 8/74, *Procureur du Roi* v. *Dassonville et al.* [1974] ECR 837, at 852.

expense of the production or of the trade of other Member States.[7] The application of this criterion is well demonstrated in the waste oils judgments.

In the first waste oils judgment, Case 172/82, *Syndicat National des Fabricants
Raffineurs d'Huile de Graissage et al* v. *GIE 'Inter-Huiles' et al*[8] the Court considered
Article 34 in parallel with Directive 75/439/EEC[9] on the disposal of waste oils.
The French rules[10] for the recovery of waste oils provided that collectors had
to deliver waste oils to approved undertakings for disposal and that the latter
had to treat the waste oils in their own facilities on pain of having their approval
withdrawn. This impliedly prohibited the export of waste oils—including export
to other Member States—and, accordingly, there was no provision for undertakings authorised in other Member States to be able to carry out the disposal.
Although the Court agreed that Article 5 of the Directive did allow Member
States to grant an exclusive right to an undertaking to collect or dispose of
waste oils within a particular zone, it noted that the preamble to the Directive
made clear its intention to create 'an efficient and coherent system of treatment
for waste oils which will neither create barriers to intra-Community trade nor
affect competition'. Accordingly, the power to grant an exclusive right within a
zone did not automatically authorise the governments of the Member States to
establish barriers to exports. Moreover, in any event, such a partitioning of
the markets was neither contemplated in the Directive nor compatible with the
objectives set out therein.[11] This conclusion was reinforced by the citation of
the discrimination criterion. It seemed that the special advantage accruing
to the domestic market was that the undertakings authorised by the French
government were able to acquire waste oil for disposal at a low, regulated price,
an advantage available because of the implied prohibition of sales to foreign
undertakings. The judgment was clearly based on the provisions and aims of the
directive, and the mention of the discrimination criterion was purely ancillary.[12]
Although in this case an advantage could clearly be shown for the domestic
market, it was not strictly necessary for the Court to have referred to the
discrimination criterion. It could have left matters with the conclusion that

---

[7] Case 15/79, *PB Groenveld BV* v. *Produktschap voor Vee en Vlees* [1979] ECR 3409, at 3419; Case 155/
80, *Oebel* [1981] ECR 1993, at 2009 (Advocate General Capotorti's approach can be seen at [1979]
ECR 3409, at 3419 and [1981] ECR 1993, at 2016).

[8] [1983] ECR 555.

[9] OJ 1975 L 194, p. 23.

[10] Contained in Decree 79–81 (JORF 1979, p. 2900) and implementing orders (JORF 1979, pp. 2901
and 2903).

[11] [1983] ECR 555 at 565–566. In the same sense, see the Opinion of Advocate General Rozès
[1983] ECR 555, at 579. As she put it, 'nothing in the rules established by the Directive justifies
sacrificing the principle of free circulation in favour of the protection of the environment or the
conservation of energy. All those objectives must be attained concurrently.'

[12] Evans erroneously claims that no reference was made to the discrimination criterion: (1983) 32
ICLQ 577, at 587. The Court also noted that even if the approval granted to an undertaking had
to be seen as a grant of an exclusive right within the meaning of Article 90(1) of the Treaty, that
would not permit the Member States to escape from the obligation to comply with other provisions
of EC law. This is particularly clear, of course, from the provisions of Article 90(1) itself: 'Member
States shall neither enact nor maintain in force any measure contrary to the rules contained in
this Treaty . . .'

the French rules operated in such a way as to amount to a total prohibition of exports. An attempt was made to justify the French rules on the ground of environmental protection, the need for which had been noted in the pre-amble to the Directive, but this was decisively rejected by the Court on the ground of proportionality. The need to ensure the protection of the environment could be just as adequately met through sale to an authorised undertaking in another Member State as it could through sale to an authorised undertaking at home.

In a judgment on very similar facts in Case 295/82, *GIE 'Rhône Alpes Huiles' et al* v. *Syndicat National des Fabricants Raffineurs d'Huile de Graissage et al*,[13] the Court made it plain that it was not merely approved collectors of waste oils who were entitled to deliver to approved undertakings for disposal, holders of waste oils were also entitled to make such deliveries. These two waste oils cases are very clear examples of what may be called 'local-grab' measures which are perhaps the clearest type of measures which can fall within the discrimination criterion in Article 34.

The final challenge to the waste oils regime in France came in Case 240/83 *Procureur de la République* v. *Association de Défense des Brûleurs d'Huiles Usagées (ADBHU)*[14] in which the Court considered first the validity of Directive 75/439/EEC itself. The Court observed first that the principle of freedom of trade was not to be viewed in absolute terms but was subject to certain limits justified by the objectives of general interest pursued by the Community provided that the rights in question were not substantively impaired. It concluded that there was no reason to conclude that the Directive had exceeded those limits. Viewing the Directive in the perspective of environmental protection, which—even before the Single European Act—the Court considered to be one of the Community's essential objectives, it was evident, particularly from the third and seventh recitals in its preamble, that any legislation dealing with the disposal of waste oils had to be designed to protect the environment from the harmful effects caused by the discharge, deposit or treatment of such products. More-over, from the provisions of the Directive as a whole it was clear that care had been taken to ensure that the principles of proportionality and non-discrimination would be observed if certain restrictions proved necessary. In particular, Article 5 of the Directive permitted the creation of a system of zoning 'where the aims defined in Articles 2, 3 and 4 cannot otherwise be achieved'.

In the second place, as far as the free movement of goods is concerned, the Court stressed that the Directive had to be construed in the light of the seventh recital in its preamble, which stated that the treatment of waste oils must not create barriers to intra-Community trade. As has already been observed, in the first waste oils judgment the Court had ruled, dealing with the same zoning scheme, that an exclusive right to treat waste oils did not automatically authorise the governments of the Member States to establish barriers to exports. Indeed,

---

[13] [1984] ECR 575.
[14] [1985] ECR 531.

such a partitioning of the markets was not provided for in the Directive and would be contrary to its objectives. Accordingly, the measures prescribed by the Directive did not create barriers to intra-Community trade, and that in so far as those measures, in particular the requirement that permits must be obtained in advance, had a restrictive effect on the freedom of trade and of competition, they nevertheless were not permitted to be either discriminatory or to go beyond the inevitable restrictions which were justified by the pursuit of the objective of environmental protection, which is in the general interest. That being so, Articles 5 and 6 of the Directive were not incompatible with the fundamental principles of EC law.

The remaining relevant point for present purposes in this judgment is whether the Directive 75/439/EEC, in implementation of which the French legislation was adopted, justified the prohibition of the burning of waste oils. The intervening governments argued that the uncontrolled burning of waste oils would contribute significantly to air pollution and, consequently, that a prohibition of oil-burning in any plant which does not incorporate adequate safeguards was in conformity with the objectives of the Directive. Furthermore, the disposal of waste oil by burning, carried out by persons authorised for that purpose, had to be the subject of rules and inspections. Given that the main aim of the Directive was the disposal of waste oil in a manner which was safe for the environment, Article 2 made it incumbent upon the Member States to pursue that aim. Article 3 provided that Member States had to take the necessary measures 'to ensure that, as far as possible, the disposal of waste oils was carried out by recycling (regeneration and/or combustion other than for destruction)' and Article 4 required Member States to prohibit any deposit, discharge or processing of waste oils in such a way as to cause harmful effects on water, soil or air.

In order to ensure compliance with those measures, Article 6 provided that any undertaking which disposed of waste oils had to obtain a permit granted by the competent national authority, if necessary after an inspection of the installations, with a view to imposing the conditions required by the state of technical development. In addition to that prior inspection, subsequent checks were provided for by Articles 11 and 12, by virtue of which undertakings were required on the one hand to provide information concerning the disposal or deposit of waste oils or residues thereof, and, on the other, to be inspected periodically, particularly as regards their compliance with the conditions of their permits. Accordingly, the Directive required Member States to prohibit any form of waste-oil disposal which has harmful effects on the environment; to that end the Directive compelled Member States to set up an effective system of prior approval and subsequent inspections. The inevitable conclusion was, therefore, that the prohibition of the burning of waste oils in conditions other than those permitted under legislation such as the French legislation was not inconsistent with Directive 75/439/EEC.

Outside the strict field of environmental protection, but relevant for it, is

Case 169/89, *Gourmetterie Van den Burg BV*[15] in which the Court examined whether the prohibition by virtue of Article 7 of the Vogelwet [Law on Birds] on the importation and keeping of red grouse, lawfully shot and killed in the United Kingdom was justified on the ground of the protection of health and life of animals. The exception referred to in Article 6(2) of Directive 79/409/ EEC on the conservation of wild birds applied to red grouse, which were referred to in Annex III/1 to the Directive. The purpose of the prohibition laid down in Article 7 of the Vogelwet was the preservation of wild birds and in particular the protection of all species of birds occurring in the wild state in Europe, subject to certain exceptions which did not, however, include red grouse.

While this judgment in fact concerns Article 36 of the EC Treaty rather than environmental protection as such, the result is clearly capable of application to the rule of reason justifications as well. The Court noted that it was not disputed that the Vogelwet constituted a prohibition on imports and that the red grouse was a species which did not occur within the Netherlands. As far as Article 36 was concerned, the Court noted its consistent rulings[16] that a directive providing for full harmonisation of national legislation deprives a Member State of recourse to that article. Examination of Directive 79/409/EEC showed that, although red grouse could, in accordance with Article 6(2) and (3) of the Directive, be hunted within the Member State in which it occurs, Article 14 authorised the Member States to introduce stricter protective measures than those provided for under the Directive. The Directive had therefore regulated exhaustively the Member States' powers with regard to the conservation of wild birds. The Court then turned to define the scope of the powers conferred on the Member States by Article 14, having regard to the principal criteria on which the Community legislature had relied.

First of all, Directive 79/409/EEC granted special protection to migratory species which constituted, according to the third recital in its preamble, a common heritage of the Community. Secondly, in the case of the most endangered birds, the Directive provided that the species listed in Annex I had to be the subject of special conservation measures in order to ensure their survival and reproduction. It followed from those general objectives laid down by Directive 79/409/EEC that the Member States were authorised, pursuant to Article 14, to introduce stricter measures to ensure that those species are protected even more effectively. With regard to the other bird species covered by Directive 79/409/EEC, the Member States were required to bring into force the laws, regulations and administrative provisions necessary to comply with the Directive, but were not authorised to adopt stricter protective measures than those provided for under the Directive, except as regards species occurring within their territory.

Next, the Court noted that the red grouse was neither a migratory species

---

[15] [1990] ECR I-2143.
[16] E.g. Case 29/87, *Dansk Denkavit ApS* v *Danish Ministry of Agriculture* [1988] ECR 2965.

nor a seriously endangered species set out in Annex I to the directive. Moreover, Regulation 3626/82/EEC on the implementation in the Community of the Convention on international trade in endangered species of wild fauna and flora[17] did not refer to the red grouse as an endangered animal within the meaning of that Convention. Accordingly, the Court concluded that Article 36, read in conjunction with Directive 79/409/EEC, had to be interpreted as meaning that a prohibition on importation and marketing could not be justified in respect of a species of bird which did not occur in the territory of the legislating Member State but was found in another Member State where it could lawfully be hunted under the terms of the Directive and under the legislation of that other state, and which was neither migratory nor endangered within the meaning of the Directive. The Court thus set its face against exportation of national views about what should be protected, at least in circumstances in which Community legislation exhaustively regulated the field: the possibility of stricter national measures provided for by the Community legislation was confined to species occurring on a Member State's own territory.

Local grab measures outside the sphere of Community legislation

All the judgments discussed above deal with environmental protection in relation to Community legislation; they do not deal with national environmental legislation in fields not covered by Community action. In such circumstances it has traditionally been difficult to see how there is a place for the rule of reason—even environmental protection—in view of on the one hand the equal applicability requirement if it is to be relied upon, and on the other hand the maintenance of a discriminatory effects criterion in relation to Article 34. It may be, though, that this objection must now be set aside. The key problem, as far as exports is concerned, is how far may a Member State seek to protect environmental interests properly those of other Member States. Can you export your standard of environmental protection? Can you insist that even goods destined for export conform to national requirements or are treated in a way prescribed by national law? The answer to these questions can be gleaned from two major judgments which in fact formally relate to health protection and road safety.

In Case 118/86 *Openbaar Ministerie* v. *Nertsvoederfabriek Nederland BV*[18] the Court, dealing, as regards intra-Community trade solely with Articles 34 and 36 of the EC Treaty (as the only relevant provisions of Community legislation simply duplicated those Articles) held that it was not incompatible with Council Regulation 827/68/EEC on the common organisation of the market in certain products listed in Annex II to the Treaty, and Council Regulation 2777/75/EEC on the common organisation of the market in poultry meat, for national

---

[17] OJ 1982 L 384, p. 1.
[18] [1987] ECR 3883, [1989] 2 CMLR 436.

rules laid down in the interests of the protection of the health and life of humans and animals to provide that only holders of a licence to operate a rendering plant issued by the administrative authorities could collect and process all waste products of animal origin and that producers of poultry offal must dispose of it, as a waste product of animal origin, only to authorised licence-holders. However, in so far as they affect intra-Community trade, the Court found that such rules would be compatible with Articles 30, 34 and 36 of the EC Treaty only in so far as they did not place in the way of imports from and exports to other Member States barriers other than those justified under Article 36 of the EC Treaty by a concern to secure compliance, in the national territory, with health provisions governing the collection and transportation of products regarded as harmful to health.

In Case C-55/93, *Van Schaik*[19] the Court dealt with a challenge to the impossibility for foreign garages to be authorised as testing entities to conduct the Dutch Ministry of Transport Roadworthiness test. A charge was made for the periodic test, unless it was carried out at the same time as repair or maintenance operations. This case was principally dealt with in relation to services, the argument being that car owners could not take advantage of lower prices charged by foreign garages. The Court noted that the grant by the Dutch authorities of recognition to garages established in other Member States involved the extension outside national territory of rights and powers pertaining to the exercise of state authority and, thus, was not covered by Article 59 of the EC Treaty.

The Dutch Supreme Court also raised the question whether the loss of custom by the foreign garages in the field of maintenance services on account of the fact that they could not issue Dutch test certificates in the course of maintenance work on Dutch-registered vehicles meant that the Dutch regulations were incompatible with Article 62 of the EC Treaty. The Court recognised that the regulations could lead owners of Dutch-registered cars to dispense with the services of foreign garages—even if their charges were in certain respects lower—and thus forgo the opportunity of purchasing abroad any spare parts which might be required, as it was less practical and less expensive to have repairs and maintenance undertaken at a garage which, when repairing or servicing the vehicle could also carry out the periodic test free of charge. However, the Court found that the regulations could be justified by the requirements of road safety, which constituted overriding reasons relating to the public interest capable of justifying barriers to the freedom to provide services. The requirement that vehicles undergo a periodic test served the interests of road safety. The effectiveness of those tests was assured, in particular, by various requirements relating to the solvency and professional competence of the authorised garages, and by supervision of the tests carried out, which could only be

---

[19] [1994] ECR I-4837. Although this principally deals with services, the principle is still illustrative for the purposes of this discussion. See also Case 50/85, *Schloh* v. *Auto Contrôle Technique Sprl* [1986] ECR 1855.

undertaken on Dutch territory and by the Dutch authorities. The Court noted that this national-based approach was also that of Directive 77/143/EEC on roadworthiness tests for vehicles and their trailers. Whilst, as a result of the incomplete harmonisation in the field, mutual recognition of test certificates issued by other Member States in respect of vehicles registered in those States was assured, there was no obligation on one Member State—in view of the large number of verification processes and procedures—to recognise in respect of cars registered in its territory test certificates issued in other Member States. Even though, at the relevant time, the Directive applied only to certain categories of vehicles, it expressly permitted Member States to extend the requirement of a periodic roadworthiness test to other vehicles and the Dutch authorities had exercised that right. Accordingly, Articles 59 and 62 of the EC Treaty posed no obstacle.

It would seem, then, that provided that a measure is necessary and justified (thus also proportionate) on grounds known to EC law, a Member State is entitled, in the absence of Community legislation occupying the field, or, if authorised under such legislation, to protect the interests of the Member State of destination and thus is entitled to insist that products be treated in accordance with its national requirements. Such a conclusion also flows—again in so far as Community legislation has not occupied the field—from the old judgment in Case 46/76, *Bauhuis*.[20] In view of the *Wallonian Waste* judgment,[21] it seems highly likely that the same conclusion must apply in relation to environmental protection as in relation to Article 36, even though, save in that judgment, the approach to the rule of reason has been even stricter than the strict approach the Court takes in relation to Article 36.

Preventing access to local markets: restrictions on imports

The obvious starting point in relation to restrictions on imports is Case 302/87, *Commission* v. *Denmark*[22] on the Danish measures requiring the use of re-usable containers for beer and soft drinks and permitting only a limited use of non-approved non-metal containers provided that a deposit and return system was established. The Court's judgment concentrated on the question whether the measures could be justified on the ground of environmental protection. Everything turned on proportionality. The Court thus examined first whether the rules were necessary for the purpose of environmental protection. The system of deposit and return was felt to be an indispensable element of a system designed to ensure the re-use of containers; accordingly its necessity was not in doubt and nor were the restrictions it imposed on the free movement of goods.

---

[20] [1977] ECR 5. See Gormley, *op. cit.* note 1, 178–179.
[21] Case 2/90, *Commission* v. *Belgium* [1992] ECR I-4431, [1993] 1 CMLR 365. This judgment is discussed below.
[22] [1988] ECR 4607.

The Court then turned to the requirement to use only approved containers. Practical reasons of handling and storage space, said the Danish government, justified the need for restriction to approved containers. Nevertheless, the Court noted that the Danish government could refuse authorisation even if an importer were prepared to ensure the re-use of returned containers. In such circumstances foreign producers seeking to market their drinks in Denmark would have to manufacture or purchase containers of a type already approved; this would lead to substantial additional costs and make importation extremely difficult. The Danish government, to get round this problem, had changed its rules to allow a producer to market up to 3000 hectolitres of beer and soft drinks in non-approved containers, as long as a deposit-and-return system was established. While the general system had a high success rate, as any approved container could be returned to any retailer of beverages, non-approved containers had to be returned to the retailer who sold the beverage concerned. Thus a comprehensive system could not be established for non-approved containers. However, given that a system of returning non-approved containers was capable of protecting the environment and, as far as imports were concerned, affected only limited quantities of Danish consumption (owing to the restrictive effect on imports of the requirement that the containers be returnable) the Court concluded that a restriction on the quantity of products which could be marketed was disproportionate to the objective pursued. The result was, therefore, that the broad system was upheld in the interests of environmental protection and the quantitative restriction on imports of non-approved containers for which a deposit-and-return system was set up had to be abolished. It appears that any attempt to prevent the importation of non-approved containers would be deemed excessive if the importer were to make appropriate deposit-and-return arrangements.

The initial reactions in certain circles in Brussels to this judgment were warnings of doom and gloom and market fragmentation through national environmental measures; others were pleased that the Court had upheld the essentials of the Danish system. Others complained that the handling by the Commission of the whole proceedings was an object lesson in the consequences of having too many cooks. The decision to fight on bottles but not on cans seems an illogical compromise and it may well be that the Commission could have got more out of the Danish government by settling before going to court. In any event, this case is another one of the very rare instances in which the Court has found, on the facts, that the national rules were—largely— justified on the grounds made out. If the judgment sent one signal, it was a plea for the Community institutions to get their act together on environmental protection measures. That was perhaps also the signal from what is now the leading, if virtually untenable, judgment in the *Wallonian Waste* case.

Snatching defeat from the jaws of victory

In Case C-2/90, *Commission* v. *Belgium*[23] the Court's reasoning is reminiscent of a horse that collapses a furlong from home, having succesfully negotiated all but the final fence, only to reveal, as it jettisons its rider, while attempting the final hurdle, that it has neither backbone nor legs to carry it towards the winning post. The only explanation for the collapse of the horse in this instance is that it has been intellectually nobbled: coherent reasoning has been sacrificed on the altar of political sensitivity. The Court was faced with a measure of the Wallonia regional council which prohibited the storage, deposit or discharge within the region of waste originating outside it, whether elsewhere in Belgium or abroad.

In relation to hazardous waste covered by Directive 84/361/EEC[24] the Court found that the complete system established at Community level did not permit Member States to prohibit totally the movement of such waste; accordingly the total prohibition of importation of hazardous waste into Wallonia was incompatible with EC law.

The Court then considered the effects of the Wallonian measure on movements of waste not covered by the Directive. It expressly accepted that waste—even non-recyclable and non-reusable—constituted goods within the meaning of Article 30.[25] Turning to the question of justification in the interest of environmental protection, the Court noted the special nature of waste as a product and the danger to health and the environment which its accumulation constituted. In principle, therefore, the interest of environmental protection was well founded. There remained the hurdle of the fact that the measure discriminated against waste from other Member States which was no more harmful than waste from Wallonia. In seeking in vain to overcome this hurdle, the Court tried to have it both ways: on the one hand reaffirming that the rule of reason was available only to equally applicable measures; yet on the other hand looking at the specific nature of waste in order to determine whether the measure was discriminatory. Thus it noted that Article 130r(2) of the EEC Treaty established, with regard to Community action relating to the environment, the principle that environmental damage should as a priority be rectified at source. This led the Court to be pleased to conclude that it was up to each region, commune or other local authority to take measures necessary to ensure the reception, treatment and disposal of its own waste. Accordingly, such waste had to be

---

[23] [1992] ECR I-4431. This discussion of this judgment is based on part of the author's inaugural lecture in Groningen on 15 June 1993.

[24] OJ 1984 L 326, p. 31, as amended by Directive 86/279/EEC (OJ 1986 L 181, p. 13) and adapted to technical progress by Directive 87/112 (OJ 1987 L 48, p. 31).

[25] See Case 72/83, *Campus Oil Ltd.* v. *Minister for Industry and Energy* [1984] ECR 2727, at 2747 and *City of Philadelphia* v. *New Jersey* 437 US 617, 98 SCt 2531. This was accepted even though the waste matter had no inherent value and was not considered by the Court to be an object of commerce. The free movement of goods principle in EC law is not restricted to goods which are or are capable of being articles of commerce, see Case C-215/87, *Schumacher* v. *Hauptzollamt Frankfurt-am-Main-Ost* [1989] ECR 617 at 638–639.

disposed of as close as possible to the place of production so that its transport was reduced to the minimum necessary.[26] From these factors the Court found that, in view of the differences between waste produced in one place and that produced in another and in view of its connection with the place where it was produced, the measure was non-discriminatory in nature and thus the rule of reason justification stood. The priority given to environmental interests over the free movement of goods is evident but it is only by irrelevant reasoning that the Court was able to claim that the measures were non-discriminatory and thus apply the rule of reason justification. The Court's purported reasons go to the necessity for the measures, not to the question of their discriminatory effect. The result was that imports of hazardous waste into Wallonia could not be entirely prohibited because of Directive 84/631/EEC but imports of non-hazardous waste[27] could be. The absurdity of such a situation is evident.

It might be argued that the result of this judgment and of that in the *Danish Bottles* judgment (see note 22 above) is that the understandable attention given to environmental concerns makes manifest the need for Community level action to prevent market fragmentation, but even the new Community action is extremely weak as far as shipments of waste within Member States is concerned.[28] Another disturbing feature of this judgment is the view that differences in the nature of waste and in the place of production of the waste made the measure non-discriminatory. This is particularly peculiar in view of the starting point of the reasoning, namely that all types of waste were 'goods' and as such in principle benefited from the right to free movement. The intellectual contortions to uphold the Wallonian measure defy belief. To say that a measure which is blatantly discriminatory is not discriminatory because of the interest advanced to justify or because of the nature of the product represents a complete failure to cope with and apply principles of EC law in circumstances in which the political fall-out is perceived as being too strong. Comparision with the judgment in Case C-21/88, *Du Pont de Nemours Italiana SpA* v. *Unitá Sanitaria Locale No. 2 di Carrara*[29]—a case on all fours with the *Wallonian Waste* judgment, involving an obligation to source a certain percentage of supplies from companies established in the Mezzogiorno, disadvantaging foreign companies but also Italian companies established outside that region—demonstrates how untenable the contention that the measure was non-discriminatory really is.

It is difficult to resist the conclusion that coherence in the case law on Article 30 has been scarcely helped by the *Wallonian Waste* judgment. This judgment reflects the current reticence by the Court to adopt a coherent policy approach to Article 30. In *Keck and Mithouard*[30] the result is correct but based on absent

---

[26] The Court also noted that this was consistent with the principles of self-sufficiency and proximity laid down in the Basle Convention of 22 March 1989 (well after the contested Wallonian measures were enacted) to which the Community was a signatory. But the Convention was not yet in force at the date of the judgment.

[27] I.e. waste not covered by Directive 84/631/EEC.

[28] See Regulation 259/93/EEC (OJ 1993 L 30, p. 1), Article 13.

[29] [1990] ECR I-889, [1991] 3 CMLR 25.

[30] See note 1 above.

legal reasoning; in the *Wallonian Waste* judgment the result is politically correct and legal reasoning is simply stood on its head. In any event, these judgments scarcely enhance the Court's authority or reinforce the impression that it carries out its obligation to ensure that the *law* is observed.

Community measures to prevent proliferation of barriers to trade

Other chapters in this book address the Community's legislative activities in the environmental field, but there is a more general measure the impact of which should not be overlooked, namely Directive 83/189/EEC.[31] This Directive establishes a procedure for the provision of information in the field of technical standards and regulations. Perhaps the most high profile instance, as far as the United Kingdom is concerned, of the Commission submitting observations, which a Member State took into account, is the measures adopted in the United Kingdom relating to furniture safety requirements in response to people dying as a result of fumes from furniture fillings given off during fires.[32] The observations do not, of course, bind the Member State concerned, but failure to take them into account may lead to infringement proceedings being commenced under Article 169 of the EC Treaty for breach of Article 30 or 34.

Article 9 of Directive 83/189/EEC, however, means that the Commission or another Member State can react rather more strongly and more quickly if necessary, to require postponement of the introduction of the draft measure, which may well result in the Commission announcing its intention to propose that the Community itself act in the field concerned. A highly politically charged example of this was the saga relating to furs from animals commonly caught in leg-hold traps. The background to this was the draft regulation notified by the United Kingdom. This met much resistance, particularly from the Canadians, and was subsequently withdrawn by the UK government (in fact because of perceived trade interests relating to a possible submarine contract, which, in the event, never materialised). But that did not stop the Commission making its own proposal for Community action.[33]

Finally, it might be noted that in the environmental field, as in other areas, the Commission has been willing to use the possibility of issuing mandates to the European standards institutions CEN and CENELEC to draw up a European standard; examples include the mandate in the field of environmental manage-

---

[31] OJ 1983 L 109, p. 8 (most recently substantively amended by Directive 94/10/EEC (OJ 1994 L 100, p. 30) and the Act of Accession 1994.

[32] SI 1988 No. 1324 (amended by SI 1989 No. 2358 and SI 1993 No. 207).

[33] Which became Regulation 3254/91/EEC (OJ 1991 L 308, p. 1, as amended by Regulation 1771/94/EEC, OJ 1994 L 184, p. 3, and implemented by Regulation 35/97/EEC, OJ 1997 L 8, p. 2). See further the proposal for a Council decision on an International Agreement between the Community, Canada and Russia on humane trapping standards, COM (97) 17 final. For an example of action by the Commission in the context of infringement of the requirements of Directive 83/189/EEC, see Case 317/92, *Commission v. Germany* [1994] ECR I-2039.

ment systems, and a planning mandate on packaging and packaging waste, both of which were issued in 1994.[34]

Conclusion

The very real concern that the free movement of goods should not weaken the legitimate interest of environmental protection runs through the case law of the Court as a central aspect, yet the Court has been certainly less than clear in its approach which is on occasions characterised by a lack of logic and coherent reasoning, save where the application of Community legislation itself is concerned. Given that the clear message is that Community action must sort out the mess—like the Gods in the final scene of Brecht's *Good Person of Szechwan* the Court departs on a pink cloud, leaving everyone to sort out the problems—the plea in relation to the environment is that the need for Community action is paramount.[35] The results can clearly be better achieved at Community than at local level—certainly if the environment is to be protected within the single market rather than within an artificially fragmented market.

---

[34] The latest report on the operation of Directive 83/189/EEC is that for the period 1992–94, COM(96) 286 final.

[35] In relation to the problems in the development and enforcement of Community environmental policy, see Williams (1994) 14 YEL 351. See further, Cross (1995) 15 YEL 79 on subsidiarity and the environment, and Okowa (1995) 15 YEL 169 on the Community and international environmental agreements.

Chapter 18

CRATED CALVES AND CRAZY COWS: LIVE ANIMALS AND FREE MOVEMENT OF GOODS

Sue Elworthy

Introduction

The export of cattle and beef from the United Kingdom to other Member States of the EU has, over the last two years, opened up debate about the impact of EC law in the United Kingdom more than any other issue since Britain joined the EEC in 1972. The subject is not however generally perceived as being one covered by *environmental* law. This in itself is interesting since the relationship between humans and other animals is a central issue in environmental ethics but environmental lawyers have so far been content to allow the boundaries of their discipline to be drawn around pollution, planning and nature conservation. Animals only come within this narrow definition if they are wild. I would like to try to extend the frontiers of environmental law to encompass animal husbandry. There are two reasons for this: first, we are unlikely to take proper responsibility for the well-being of wild species so long as we treat our domestic farm animals purely instrumentally; and second, the ways in which we keep our farm animals have direct and important effects on the undoubtedly *environmental* media of soil and water as well as on wild fauna and flora.

The two *causes célèbres* around which the impact of EC law in the United Kingdom has been discussed have been the export of live calves and the BSE infected beef crisis. I will discuss the live calf export trade first and then the BSE crisis to try to unravel the different strands in the legal tangle that first led to riots in England and has now complicated the relationship between Britain and the rest of the EU. I suggest that both intensive rearing of calves and the BSE epidemic are symptoms of an agricultural policy that fails to take proper account of the welfare of animals or of consumers. Despite recent attempts to integrate environmental concerns into agricultural policy[1] the health of the wider environment is still at risk from intensive farming, and the BSE crisis may have further adverse environmental consequences.

---

[1] Council Regulation 2078/92/EEC, OJ L 215 30.7.92, p. 86.

I carried out research for this paper on South Uist in the Outer Hebrides; one of the most remote regions of Europe. During this time I helped crofters prepare their stock for the autumn sale and travelled with a stock lorry to Inverness. This social research was part of a larger project intended to enable me to assess attempts to use law to integrate environmental concerns into the Common Agricultural Policy of the EU.[2] I draw on this experience where appropriate.

Exporting live calves

Veal is not much eaten in Britain but is a favourite meat in many EU Member States where consumers are prepared to pay a premium price for white meat from young calves and for quality veal from free range calves who have just left their mothers. British farmers responded to these market demands and by 1994 had developed a significant export trade in live calves.

Veal has a very short shelf life so continental butchers buy it 'on the hoof' enabling them to 'bank' the calves for slaughter close to the consumers. In the EU there are two distinct 'banking' systems; in northern countries where very young calves are reared in crates and in southern countries where the demand is for calves which had been kept outside with their mothers but are subsequently crated until slaughter. Before the Commission's ban on cattle exports from Britain, very young calves were exported for crate rearing, and stock exporters from north west Scotland, in particular, had successfully marketed their older calves in southern Europe and had achieved a reputation for first class veal.

Under Title I, Article 9 of the EC Treaty, one of the fundamental freedoms of the Community is the free movement of goods. This raises the question, asked by many in Britain concerned with animal rights, as to whether a calf can rightly be called a 'good'. Both UK and EC law are quite clear on this point. UK law essentially follows Roman law where a distinction is made between wild animals (animals *ferae naturae*) and domestic ones (animals *domitae naturae*). Domestic animals are treated in the same way as any other moveable property, being fully owned throughout their lives.[3] In EC law, Title II, Article 38 of the EC Treaty states that the common market shall extend to agriculture and trade in agricultural products. 'Agricultural products' means the products of the soil, of stock farming and of fisheries and products of first stage processing directly related to these products.

Only an extreme animal liberationist would suggest that cattle should not be kept on farms at all, so the animal welfare issues are the conditions in which they are kept whilst on the farm and how they are transported, either from farm to farm or to slaughter.

---

[2] Elworthy 'Legal Obstacles to Integrating Environmental Concerns in the Common Agricultural Policy' in Van Dael (ed) *Recente Ontwikkelingen in Het Europees Milieurecht* (Antwerp: Kluwer Rechtwetschappen, 1997).

[3] See Reid, *Nature Conservation Law* (Edinburgh: W. Green/Sweet and Maxwell, 1994), p. 12.

Rearing calves in veal crates

All the Member States ratified the European Convention on the protection of animals kept for farming purposes, and the Community approved the Convention in 1978.[4] Nearly ten years later, in 1987, the European Parliament called on the Commission to make proposals for minimum standards for the intensive rearing of veal calves.[5] At last the Council adopted Directive 91/629/EEC laying down minimum standards for the protection of calves.[6] The standards are, indeed, minimal.

UK law governing animal husbandry developed quite independently from EC law and, so far as calf rearing is concerned, in several important respects is more demanding, entailing higher economic costs to the producer. It follows that if the calves are reared in the United Kingdom there is a competitive disadvantage compared with calves reared in other Member States where only the minimal standards of the Directive apply. Consequently, an export trade developed, transporting small calves from England to be reared in other Member States. Even though the minimal standards for calf husbandry in the United Kingdom are higher than in other Member States, and so more expensive, any intensive calf rearing cannot be good husbandry since it entails imposing a very restrictive regime on the calves. Any discussion of the lives of all domesticated animals must treat 'normal' as problematic since domestication entails such massive interventions by humans into the animals' lives and, with selective breeding, into their evolution.[7] There is a distinction to be drawn between the 'normal', or usual, way of life for a calf where crate rearing has become the established and accepted method and a meaning of 'normal' which attempts to constitute a standard. For farm animals a good system of husbandry will be one which allows the animals a life as close to normal conditions as possible, 'normal' in this case meaning one that allows patterns of behaviour approximating those which animals would have if they were wild. For a calf this means that it is free to run with its dam until weaned. I compare the EC standards with the British ones but my intention is to draw attention to how low the UK standards are, particularly since British agricultural ministers have been known to imply that the standards in the United Kingdom are exemplary.

Rearing can be sub-divided into feeding and watering; housing, including lighting; and frequency of inspection. Directive 91/629/EEC laying down minimal standards for the protection of calves covers all these. Article 4 requires Member States to ensure that the conditions for rearing calves comply with the general provisions laid down in the Annex. Articles 11-14 deal with feeding and watering. All calves must be fed at least once a day and when they are over two weeks old they must have access to water or other liquids. Article 11 stipulates

---

[4] Decision 78/923/EEC, OJ L 323 17.11.78, p. 12.
[5] Resolution of 20.2.1987, OJ C 76, 23.3.87, p. 185.
[6] Directive 91/629/EEC, OJ L 340 11.12.91, p. 28.
[7] See, for example, Paterson and Palmer (eds), *The Status of Animals* (Wallingford: CAB International, 1989).

that in order to ensure a positive state of health and well-being as well as a healthy growth rate, the calves' food must include sufficient iron and a minimum of dried feed containing digestible fibre. Crucially, this last important component in the diet of calves does not apply to the production of veal calves for white meat. Article 3 deals with housing and requires Member States to ensure that from January 1994, for a transitional period of four years, new purpose-built buildings or newly converted buildings should have adequate floor space for calves housed in groups to lie down and turn around. For calves housed in individual boxes or by tethering in stalls, the walls of the boxes or stalls must be perforated but the space requirements are only 'no less than 90 cm plus or minus 10% [width], or 0.80 times the height at the withers'.[8] Housing systems built before 1 January 1994 which do not meet these requirements must be phased out by the end of 2003. Those built during the transitional period have until the end of 2007 before they must meet the requirements of the Directive. Even these minimal conditions do not apply to holdings with fewer than six calves. Lighting is covered by Article 5 of the Annex which stipulates that calves must not be kept permanently in darkness but the intensity of artificial lighting is not specified. There must be lighting available which is strong enough to allow the calves to be inspected. Inspection is required at least once a day. Article 11 of the Directive allows Member States to have stricter requirements within their territories and Article 6 requires the Commission to submit a report and proposals based on the report, drawn up on the basis of an opinion from the Scientific Veterinary Committee, on the intensive farming systems which comply with the requirements of the well-being of calves, as well as the socio-economic implications of different systems.

The British law for the welfare of livestock comes under the Agriculture (Miscellaneous Provisions) Act 1968. Section 1(1) of the 1968 Act makes it an offence for anyone in control of livestock on agricultural land to cause or knowingly permit unnecessary pain or unnecessary distress to the stock. Section 3(1) gives the ministers powers to consult with appropriate people and then to prepare and revise codes of recommendations for the welfare of livestock. Section 3(4) allows failure to observe a provision of such a code to be relied on by the prosecution in proceedings against someone under s. 1.

Donald Broom's pioneering work on animal welfare[9] appears to have been acted upon in the 1991 revision of the 1983 version of the Code for Cattle.[10] Broom's definition of animal welfare is the state of an individual animal with regard to its attempts to cope with its environment.[11] Coping mechanisms include the brain/adrenal system which helps provide more energy, the endor-

---

[8] Article 3(1) second indent.
[9] See, for example, Broom 'Indicators of Poor Welfare', (1986) 142 *British Veterinary Journal*, 524–526; Broom, 'The Scientific Assessment of Animal Welfare, (1988) 20 *Applied Animal Behaviour Science* 5–19; Broom and Fraser, *Farm Animal Behaviour and Welfare* (London: Baillière, Tindall, 1989); Broom, 'Ethical Dilemmas in Animal Usage', in Paterson and Palmer (eds), *op. cit.* note 7.
[10] MAFF, *Code for Cattle*, (London: MAFF, DAFS, WOAD, MAFF Pubs, 1991).
[11] Broom (1986) *op. cit.* note 9.

phin/enkephalin system which enables the animal to cope with unpleasant situations by self-narcosis, and behavioural responses. If an individual animal copes easily, there is no welfare problem. If it develops methods for coping but has difficulty in doing so, then its welfare is poor and if it cannot cope its control systems are overtaxed and it is stressed.[12] Under Broom's definition of animal welfare, apparently docile animals may be coping by self-narcosis so are still suffering poor welfare. This state can be established by blood tests but from a stockman's point of view, inspecting calves on a daily basis, a knowledge of normal behaviour is needed for assessment. This shows the importance of the distinction between the meanings of normal as the usual and as a standard because a stockman only familiar with crated calves could mistake their apparent docility as normal. Crated veal calves, however, are Broom's paradigm example of poor welfare, for example 'contrast, for instance, veal calves in crates, and those in the fields or in groups in straw-yards, and ask what life is like for them as individuals'.[13]

The preface to the Code for Cattle draws on Broom's list of minimal needs for animal welfare. These include comfort and shelter, readily accessible fresh water and a diet to maintain the animals in full health and vigour, freedom of movement, the company of other animals particularly of like kind and the opportunity to exercise most normal patterns of behaviour, light during the hours of daylight and avoidance of unnecessary mutilation. The preface to the Code for Cattle says that 'cattle husbandry systems in current use do not equally meet the physiological and behavioural needs of the animals' but the Code is an attempt to identify areas where, unless precautions are taken, the animals' welfare could be at risk. Paragraph 42 says that all calves should have liquid food daily during the first four weeks of life and until they are eating adequate quantities of solid food and 'for normal development, unweaned calves should have access to palatable unmilled roughage and fresh clean water'. Paragraph 43 is concerned with an adequate intake of iron. If calves are individually penned they should be allowed to see other calves[14] and all cattle should at all times have enough room to groom themselves, to lie down and rise and freely stretch their legs 'thus the width of the pen for a singly-penned animal should not be less than the height of the animal at the withers'.[15] The Code requires the level of lighting during daylight hours to be bright enough for all housed cattle to be seen clearly[16] and says all housed calves should be closely inspected frequently, at least twice daily.[17]

Calves for southern Europe

In southern Europe a niche market exists for very high quality veal from older

---

[12] Broom, in Paterson and Palmer (eds), *op. cit.* notes 7 and 9, p. 82.
[13] *Ibid.* p. 86.
[14] Paragraph 15.
[15] Paragraph 35.
[16] Paragraph 30.
[17] Paragraph 49.

calves which have lived outside with their mothers. This market is partially satisfied by locally reared calves but some travel long journeys to reach it. Before the Commission's ban on exports of cattle from Britain, probably the longest journey was from the southern isles of the Outer Hebrides, the Uists and Barra, which had built up a reputation for quality meat. The calves from these islands are reared by crofters in conditions that, from an animal welfare perspective, are near ideal but the journey to slaughter was a long one. After the sale on South Uist, the calves were loaded onto lorries, driven to North Uist, ferried to the Island of Skye and then driven to Inverness. In Inverness they would be reloaded and driven to the ports of southern England for shipping across the Channel and on to the south of France, Spain, Italy and Greece. Every effort was made to complete this journey as quickly as possible to minimise the stress to the calves: a good stockman knows that the less stress a beast suffers before death the better will be the quality of the meat, so animal welfare and market forces coincide on this point. Even so, the long journey was inevitably extremely stressful.

Rules of law

In November 1994 stock exporters flew trial flights of aircraft carrying live calves from Coventry airport to the continent. An animal rights group, Compassion in World Farming, persuaded Coventry City Council to intervene to suspend the use of Coventry airport for this purpose. The stock exporters sought judicial review of this decision and obtained an interlocutory injunction restraining the council from suspending the carriage of veal calves by air from the airport. After an aircraft chartered by a stock exporting company to transport calves to Belgium crashed on coming in to land at Coventry airport in December 1994, the people of Coventry became alerted to the extent of the live calf export trade and mounted a series of demonstrations, attempting to prevent lorries loaded with calves from reaching the airport. The Assistant Chief Constable of Warwickshire had written to the airport manager expressing his concern that, should the flights resume, it would be impossible for the police to prevent people trespassing on the airport and so compromising the ground and air safety of the airport. The City Council met and decided to apply for the injunction to be lifted, and, subject to the application being successful, per- mission to use the airport for exporting veal calves be refused. The application to lift the injunction was refused and the demonstrations continued. The tragic death of Jill Phipps, a demonstrator who was accidentally run over by a lorry, brought matters to a head. Her funeral in Coventry cathedral was attended by thousands and followed over the following weeks by marches of mourners. The exporters agreed to suspend flights but applied for judicial review of the Coun- cil's decision to refuse permission to use the airport for this trade. *R v. Coventry City Council, ex parte Phoenix Aviation and Others and other applications*[18] was heard

---

[18] [1995] 3 All ER 37.

in April 1995. The council's decision to refuse the use of the airport to calf exporters was held to be unlawful on two grounds: first, that public authorities administering ports had no discretion to distinguish between lawful trades and, second, that the rule of law did not allow public authorities to respond to unlawful disruption and threats by surrendering to the protestors' demands.

As well as the protests in Coventry, the shipping of live calves and sheep from sea ports in England became a cause around which a wide spectrum of people mobilised. There were demonstrations in many ports with people trying to prevent lorries carrying stock from reaching ferries. The judicial review hearing of Coventry City Council's decision also dealt with Dover Harbour Board's decision to refuse use of the port to hauliers exporting stock for slaughter, claiming insufficient capacity, and Plymouth City Council's request to Associated British Ports, who run Millbay Docks at Plymouth, to withdraw port facilities from livestock hauliers because of the strain on police resources.

On reflection, perhaps the most interesting facet of the animal rights protests was the fierce battle over the ideological legal high ground that took place on the ground during the demonstrations in the ports. The EC fundamental freedom, the free movement of goods, was repeatedly used by the stock exporters as legitimation as opposed to the protestors' claim for the right to demonstrate. The battles in the ferry ports would not have been so fierce if the 'goods' being moved had not been live animals. Sadly, it was a clash of two perspectives on animal welfare. On the one side were the protestors trying to save the calves a long journey to slaughter and, on the other side, the lorry drivers, all stockmen, were trying to get the journey over as quickly as possible to minimise distress to the calves. From an animal welfare perspective, the free movement of goods is a fundamental barrier to reducing cruelty to animals. On a more mundane legal plane, Article 7 of Directive 91/628/EEC on the protection of animals during transport stipulates that no consignment of animals shall be detained during transport unless it is strictly necessary for the welfare of the animals.

In *R* v. *Coventry City Council*, Simon Brown LJ decided the cases on national law but, because there had been extensive argument on issues raised under EC law and because the applicants in the Coventry and Dover cases were intending to pursue claims for damages, he clarified the issues with the proviso that, given the difficulty of the questions, had the challenges turned on EC law it would have been appropriate to refer them to the Court of Justice. Article 34(1) of the EC Treaty prohibits quantitative restriction on exports, and all measures having equivalent effects. Article 36 provides a defence to this for prohibitions or restrictions on imports, exports or goods in transit justified on grounds of public morality, public health or public security; or the protection of health and life of animals. Interestingly, no animal welfare defence was argued under Article 36, so Simon Brown LJ expressed no view as to whether it could have succeeded.

The stock exporters having won the battle in the courts, the demonstrators shifted their attention to lobbying the institutions of the EU to improve the minimal standards for calf rearing so that the export of beasts to Member States with standards lower than Britain's would stop. They appeared not to appreciate that there are two distinct markets in the EU, one for white, crate raised veal and one for free range veal. Both raise serious animal welfare issues but these are more likely to be resolved if the two are not conflated. The intensive veal system raises issues about feeding, housing and lighting during rearing as well as welfare during transport but the free range veal system principally raises issues about transport and the 'banking' of live calves before they are slaughtered. The welfare problems of the free range calves could be improved if they were slaughtered close to where they are raised.

MEP Christine Oddy submitted a written question to the Council of Ministers in May 1995[19] to which the Council replied that the Commission was bringing forward the timetable for submission of the report and proposals required under Article 6 of Directive 91/629/EEC on minimal standards for the protection of calves.[20] The Commission has now issued a proposal to amend the Directive. The proposal is that from January 1998, in all newly built or rebuilt calf houses no calf over the age of eight weeks may be confined in an individual pen unless a vet has certified that it must be isolated, the width of a pen must be at least equal to the height of the calf with the length 10% longer than the calf. These space requirements will also apply for calves kept in groups. The Commission is expected to produce further proposals to cover the diets of calves.[21]

The transport of live animals in the United Kingdom is regulated by the Welfare of Animals during Transport Order 1994[22] which came into force in January 1995. This order implements Council Directive 91/628/EEC on the protection of animals during transport[23] and in many parts transposes the Directive word for word. According to the Scots hauliers with whom I discussed the order, the Directive might have been drafted adequately for pigs travelling overland, but the consequences of the implementing order for calves from the Outer Hebrides served to increase their distress dramatically.[24] Article 5 says that animals must be fed and watered before a journey and at specific intervals thereafter. The maximum interval between feeds for 'bovine' animals is 15 hours. If a ferry cannot sail because the sea is too rough, once the 15 hours have elapsed the calves must be unloaded, watered and fed on hay. The practical results of this Article, framed to improve animal welfare during transport, paradoxically can cause much distress to calves which have been raised humanely. In the Outer Hebrides the cattle are kept unconfined on common grazing lands, free to wander at will. In November 1995, when I observed a load of calves on the first stage of the export journey to southern Europe, the

---

[19] Written Question E-1288/95 (96/C 9/05), OJ C 9 15.1.96, p. 3.
[20] Answer 5 December 1995.
[21] European Information Service Issue 169, May 1996, p. 10
[22] SI 1994 No. 3249 (Animals, Animal Health).
[23] OJ L 340 11.12.91, p. 17.
[24] I travelled with a stock lorry from South Uist to Inverness during November 1995, observing the calves and discussing their welfare with the lorry drivers.

sea of the Little Minch was too rough for the planned ferry crossing. The cows who had been separated from their calves the day before were searching for them so when the calves were unloaded off the stock lorries, to comply with the feeding and watering regulations, cows rushed against the fence bellowing, in itself enough to upset the calves considerably. Furthermore, the stockmen are convinced that calves travel more comfortably over rough seas on empty stomachs: full of hay and water, they are prone to seasickness. A feasibility study to upgrade the local slaughter house to EC standards had been carried out but it had shown that upgrading would be uneconomic. This disappointed the islanders on two counts. First, the crofters only raise a few calves to whom they become closely attached and so would like to save them this gruelling last journey, particularly the first sea crossing. Second, crofting is part-time farming so the jobs in the slaughter house would have been most welcome. However the market niche they are filling is for freshly killed veal. In the preamble of the Directive this problem is referred to: 'whereas for reasons of animal welfare the transport over long distances of animals, including animals for slaughter, should be reduced as far as possible' but there is no limit to the overall length of a journey. The free movement of goods precludes such a limit.

Crazy cows

The European Court of Justice has started preliminary hearings on the legality of the Commission's ban on the export of British beef, veal, beef products and live cattle to other Member States and to countries outside the EU. The 'beef crisis' has soured Britain's relations with the Commission and other Member States so the Court of Justice will be reaching its decision against a complex political background. The legal issues are whether the Commission has the power to ban the exports to the rest of the EU, whether it has the additional power to ban them to the rest of the world, and whether the bans are pro-portional to the objectives of protecting human and animal health. The issue of proportionality is the one of most interest to environmental lawyers since it concerns appropriate action in the face of scientific uncertainty: the dilemma of the precautionary principle.

This crisis has been caused by the fear of a possible link between BSE and its human equivalent Creutzfeldt-Jakob Disease (CJD). The two diseases, BSE and CJD, are at the boundaries of scientific knowledge. BSE is thought to be trans-mitted by an infectious protein called a prion and the behaviour of prions is at the cutting edge of molecular biological research, but the suggestion is that the infectious prion made the jump from sheep with scrapie to cattle.[25] The scientific issue at the root of the crisis is whether BSE has made the jump to humans in the form of a new variant of CJD. Here the evidence has to be epidemiological, a branch of statistics that can tell us of likelihood rather than proof. By 1995,

---

[25] 'Twists and Turns on the Trail of a Killer', *The Guardian*, 21 March 1996, p. 6.

epidemiological work undertaken in Cambridge by Sheila Gore, reported in the *British Medical Journal* demonstrated an increase in the number of cases among farmers and teenagers: increases which suggested very strongly that the cases could not have happened by chance.[26]

The BSE epidemic was probably caused by feeding cattle with concentrated feed which contained sheep brains infected with scrapie, and then subsequently by incorporating the rendered remains of these cattle in the next generation of processed concentrated feed.[27] This raises the question of why cattle were being fed on animal remains? Cattle have four stomachs, the first of which breaks down cellulose. In the 1970s, scientists suggested that if this first stomach could be by-passed and protein introduced into the second stomach, milk production could be maximised. In the 1980s the price of soya and fishmeal rose sharply, so sheep remains were substituted.[28] For commercial reasons, the rendering process was also changed. Both the duration and the temperature of processing were reduced and an organic solvent extraction step was eliminated.[29]

Ironically, the BSE epidemic in Britain was declining by March 1996. Only a quarter of the number of suspected cases a week was being reported compared with the peak of the epidemic in 1993. Then Parliament was told that the Spongiform Encephalopathy Advisory Committee (SEAC), set up to advise the UK government, had concluded that a new form of CJD might have been caused by the patients eating BSE infected beef, perhaps between 1985 and 1989.

The Commission's decision to ban cattle, beef and beef products from Britain, Decision 96/239/EC of 27 March 1996 on emergency measures to protect against BSE,[30] is based on emergency powers derived from a line of directives concerned with human and animal health. Council Directive 89/662/EEC,[31] concerning veterinary and zootechnical checks applicable in intra-Community trade in certain live animals and produce with a view to the completion of the internal market, laid down the procedure for health checks. This Directive was amended by Directive 92/118/EEC[32] laying down animal health and public health requirements governing trade in and imports into the Community of products, etc. This is a framework directive with extensive annexes giving detailed rules for treatment, storage and documentation of animal agricultural products. Article 10(4) of this Directive reads:

The decisions provided for in paragraphs 2 and 3 must be taken on the basis of evaluation and, if appropriate, the opinion of the Scientific and Veterinary Committee, of the real risk of the spread of serious transmissible diseases or of diseases transmissible to man

---

[26] *Ibid.* quoting Dr. Dealler of Burnley General Hospital.
[27] Questions and Answers, *op. cit.* note 19, p. 33.
[28] Tim Radford, 'Sifting Facts and Theory at Boundary of Knowledge', *The Guardian*, 22 March 1996, p. 7.
[29] Questions and Answers, *op cit.* note 19, p. 33.
[30] OJ L 78 27.3.96, p. 47.
[31] OJ L 224 18.8.90, p. 29.
[32] OJ L 62 15.3.93, p. 49.

which could result from movement of the product, not only for the species from which the product originates but also for other species which could carry the disease or become a focus of disease or a risk to public health.

Article 9 specifies that the requirements applicable to imports of products covered by the Directive from third countries must offer at least the same guarantees as those specified in the Directive. Risk assessment is not just a technocratic exercise, nor one in which necessarily a scientific consensus is arrived at: it is also a political exercise in which the Scientific and Veterinary Committee arrives at a decision on the 'real risk' requirement of Article 10(4) by a qualified majority vote.

The Commission had adopted a series of decisions between the start of the BSE epidemic in Britain in 1989 and July 1995 with measures to protect animal and public health. The Commission Decision of July 1994[33] laid down rules about trimming the meat from animals from BSE herds to remove tissues that might have the offending protein, labelling bone-in meat, banning the export of offals, and specifying that ruminant protein destined for use in pig and poultry rations is not included in ruminant rations. This last requirement was to cover the possibility that cattle feed was still being contaminated from residues left in feed mills from producing feed intended for pigs and chickens.[34]

The preamble to Commission Decision 96/239/EC[35] on emergency measures to protect against BSE, sets out the political tensions against which the Commission adopted the Decision:

Whereas as a result of the publication of this information [on the new form of CJD and the conclusions of SERC] and the announced measures in the United Kingdom, other Member States have decided to ban the entry into their territory of live bovine animals and beef and veal from the United Kingdom;

Whereas on 22 March 1996, the Scientific and Veterinary Committee has been consulted; Whereas, under current circumstances, a definitive stance on the transmissibility of

BSE to humans is not possible; whereas a risk of transmission cannot be excluded; whereas the resulting uncertainty has created serious concern among consumers; whereas, under the circumstances and as an emergency measure, the transport of all bovine animals and all beef and veal or derived products from the United Kingdom to the other Member States should be temporarily banned; whereas the same prohibitions should also apply to exports to non-Member countries so as to prevent deflections of trade;

The Commission had to take measures because many countries outside the EU had also banned British beef so the whole European beef industry was at risk as well as Britain's. The bans by other individual Member States were, on the face of it, illegal because of the fundamental freedom of the free movement of

---

[33] OJ L 194 29.7.94, p. 96.
[34] Decision 94/474/EC, OJ L 194 29.7.94, p. 96.
[35] OJ L 78 28.3.96, p. 47.

goods. Paradoxically, given its use as an engine of devolution, the principle of subsidiarity under Article 3b of the Treaty on European Union can be read as obliging the Commission to take action in circumstances such as the beef crisis:

In the areas which do not fall within its exclusive competence, the Community shall take action only if, and in so far as, the objective of the proposed action cannot be sufficiently achieved by the Member States and can therefore by reason of the scale or effects of the proposed action be better achieved by the Community.

The issue of proportionality is more problematic. Proportionality is not a legal doctrine of the EC, nor to be found in either the EC or EU Treaties: it is however a fundamental principle of Community law that some writers claim ranks higher than even primary Community law.[36] Proportionality involves a three-part test: the measure proposed must be sufficient to achieve its objective; it must be the least restrictive measure necessary; and the benefit must be proportional to the restriction. If the protection of public health is viewed in isolation, the ban might be disproportional since it has not yet been established that the likelihood of contracting CJD from BSE infected beef is high. But in the circumstances of worldwide consumer panic about the safety of British beef, and illegal bans by other Member States, it can certainly be argued that the measure was 'necessary'. The reasoning of the European Court of Justice when it decides the UK challenge to the Commission on the issue of proportionality will be of great interest to environmental lawyers because the issue revolves around what is an appropriate response for precaution in the face of scientific uncertainty. Perhaps the Court will suggest ways in which this can be structured so that debate may be more open and rational.

Conclusion

The trade in live calves and the BSE crisis are linked; both are the result of an intensive agricultural system that treats animals as units of production rather than as fellow creatures, worthy of good animal husbandry concerned with their welfare. Both the calf exports and the British beef crisis arise out of an approach to farm animals that has been shaped by an agricultural policy that has, in turn, been unduly influenced for half a century by the agricultural inputs industry.[37] The causes of the veal trade and the BSE crisis do not lie only in Britain because the whole structure of EC agricultural policy has encouraged the developments that took place. The Common Agricultural Policy of the EEC was a response to post-war food shortages and was designed to encourage the development of the large, intensive farms that, by the early 1970s, had already become the norm in

---

[36] Bengoetxea, *The Legal Reasoning of the European Court of Justice: Towards a European Jurisprudence* (Oxford: Clarendon Press, 1993), p. 77.
[37] See Elworthy, *Farming for Drinking Water* (Aldershot: Avebury, 1994), pp. 110–112.

Britain. Then the CAP, with its system of guaranteed payments for agricultural produce, was superimposed on an already 'efficient' agri-industry in Britain, encouraging 'super production' by any means possible. Crated calves and crazed, because now cannibal, cows are the result[38] as well as deteriorating ground water quality and soils now dependent on chemical inputs for fertility.

The beef ban may have serious and long-term adverse effects on the environment in many parts of Britain if farmers change from keeping beef cattle to keeping sheep. If cattle are kept under an extensive grazing system, they make a valuable contribution to the ecology in circumstances where sheep, particularly in upland areas, are destructive. This is because cattle are catholic grazers where sheep are selective. Cattle will keep invasive plants like brackens and reed mats in check by tugging and pulling at plants and their weight, combined with their sharp hooves, breaks up the soil, aerating it and allowing their semi-liquid dung to be reabsorbed quickly.[39] If, as seems very likely where this is possible, farmers change from keeping beef cattle to intensive arable farming the consequences for the wider environment will be even more severe.[40]

---

[38] See Elworthy, *op. cit* note 37, for discussion of advertising in the farming press, including the 'high performance cow'.

[39] Lister-Kaye, 'Ill Fares the Land: A Sustainable Land Ethic for the Sporting Estates of the Highlands and Islands of Scotland' Occasional Paper No. 3 (Battleby: Scottish Natural Heritage, 1994), p. 12.

[40] Anecdotal evidence that in the last month farmers from beef producing areas are asking advisory soil science department for analysis of their soils, pers. comm.

Chapter 19

FROM RIO TO INVERNESS: ENVIRONMENT AND DEVELOPMENT IN THE HIGHLANDS AND ISLANDS 'OBJECTIVE 1' ENTERPRISE AREA

Joanne Scott

In 1993 the Highlands and Islands Enterprise area was accorded 'Objective 1' status—a privilege reserved for the Community's 'lagging' or 'backwards' regions, to assist them in their endeavours to 'catch up' with their more money rich neighbours.[1] Rarely has the old adage 'sticks and stone' been more apt. The Community goose, insensitive in its turn of phrase, nonetheless promised to lay a golden egg to the value of 311 million ECU. Some years later controversy over the proposed construction of a funicular railway on Cairn Gorm has focused attention upon an issue which has long since plagued Community structural funding, viz. the environmental sustainability of the 'development' which it promotes, and the ability of the left hand (DGXI, Environment) to see what the right hand (DGXVI, Regional Development) is doing.[2]

It is with this interface between environment and development that this chapter is concerned, focusing upon the implementation of Community structural funding in the Highlands and Islands for the programming period

---

[1] Annex I, Council Regulation 2081/93/EEC, OJ 1993 L 193, p. 5. There are five governing regulations in the area of Community structural funding: Council Regulation 2052/88/EEC, OJ 1988 L 185, p. 9 (the Framework Regulation); Council Regulation 4253/88/EEC, OJ 1988 L 374, p. 1 (the coordination regulation); Council Regulation 4254/88/EEC, OJ 1988 L 374, p. 15 (ERDF); Council Regulation 4255/88/EEC, OJ 1988 L 374, p. 21 (ESF) and Council Regulation 4256/88/EEC, OJ 1988 L 374, p. 25 (guidance section of EAGGF). These were substantially amended in 1993 by Council Regulations 2081–2085/93/EEC, OJ 1993 L 193, p. 5. Article 1 of the 'framework' regulation governing the structural funds provides that the structural funds shall contribute to six objectives, including (objective 1) 'promoting the development and structural adjustment of . . . regions whose development is lagging behind'.

[2] See editorial in *The Times*, 27 May 1996, and letters of 1 and 12 June 1996.

1994–99. It will examine the mechanics of 'environmental compatibility',[3] particularly as regards project selection, and consider the role of the European Courts in policing this interface.

Implementing the Single Programming Document for the Highlands and Islands: an environmental perspective

The Regulations governing the European Regional Development Fund require that actions under Objective 1 must be in accordance with the principles of sustainable development as well as being in agreement with environmental laws.

On 29 July 1993, the Commission adopted, by way of decision,[4] a Single Programming Document (SPD) for Community structural assistance in the Highlands and Islands Enterprise Area.[5] This sets out the strategic objectives to be pursued, the priorities and measures by which these are to be achieved, as well as detailed rules on the implementation of the SPD. The environment is accorded a high profile therein.

Included in the four strategic objectives laid down is the goal of preserving existing environmental quality and ensuring environmental sensitivity of future economic development.[6] To this end 5% of total Community funding is to accrue to the third of six priorities;[7] namely the preservation and enhancement of the environment.[8] In addition the indicative financial allocation included in the SPD provides that around 1.6% of funding will accrue to the development of tourism enterprises and initiatives related to heritage, culture and environment (under priority 2) and around 6.4% to the provision of adequate sewerage, and supplies of, and more efficient use of, water and energy (priority 6).

While one might quibble with attempts to quantify the benefits associated

---

[3] Article 7(1) of the framework regulation governing the structural funds (note 1 above) provides that 'measures financed by the structural funds or receiving assistance from the EIB or another existing financial instrument shall be in conformity with the provisions of the Treaties, with instruments adopted pursuant thereto and with Community policies, including those concerning ... environmental protection'.

[4] 94/638/EC, OJ 1994 L 250, p. 56.

[5] European Commission, *Highlands and Islands Single Programming Document, 1994–1999* (Office for the Official Publications of the European Community, Luxembourg, 1995).

[6] *Interim Guidance on Environmental Issues: Highlands & Islands, Objective 1* (Highlands & Islands Partnership Programme, Inverness, undated). Though this document notes that '[g]uidance is currently being prepared which will explain the Programme's environmental objectives in more detail and provide general advice on how projects can be designed to take environmental issues into consideration'; such guidelines have not yet been issued.

[7] These include Business Development—23.5% (priority 1), Tourism, Heritage and Culture—8% (priority 2), Primary Sectors—22.5% (priority 4), Community Development—15% (priority 5) and Communications/Services Networks—26% (not of course to be confused with infrastructure!) (priority 6).

[8] The four 'measures' which underpin this priority are (a) enhancement and protection of the environment and management schemes; (b) pollution control, waste disposal and the development of recycling systems; (c) development of environmental research and audits for the region and; (d) the development of environmental knowledge and skills training.

with environmental improvement (priority 3 will aim to deliver: 40 innovative demonstration projects, 150,000 ha of land and water subject to environmental protection/enhancement, a 10% increase in the number of people employed in the environmental sector, a doubling of the number of people trained in the environmental sector, and 18 access points to integrated environmental databases)[9] and the privileging of quantity over quality which this may appear to imply, it would, nonetheless, be obdurate to belittle the significance—practical and conceptual—of such initiatives.[10] The scale of such activities—relative at least to experience in many other Objective 1 regions during the first programming period (1989–93)—is testament, albeit only in part, to the vigilance of the Court of Auditors[11] and the tenacity of WWF (Europe) in the conduct of its 'European campaign against the structural funds'.[12] It is, however, not with an analysis of expenditure earmarked for environmental goods that this chapter is specifically concerned. It is concerned rather to examine, first, the procedures elaborated by the SPD, and elucidated subsequently by the authorities involved in its implementation, for the selection of projects to receive funding under each of the six programme priorities.

Applications for project funding should be submitted using a standard form provided by the Scottish Office. In completing the form applicants should include a summary of the proposed project's environmental implications and how these will be mitigated or enhanced, demonstrate how the proposed project fits with the environmental objectives of the SPD, and how it meets the environmental selection criteria for the relevant priority and measure. Section 22 of the form currently employed is specifically concerned with an assessment of 'environmental impacts'. In completing this section applicants are required: (a) to describe how the proposed project complies with all relevant (national and EC) environmental law,[13] any positive impacts it may produce on the environment and to explain how these are to be monitored in terms of an environmental audit; (b) to describe the results of any environmental impact study or to explain why one has not been undertaken; and (c) to detail any adverse effects the proposed project may have on the environment and of measures taken to minimise these effects. In addition it is made clear that projects will not receive approval until all relevant planning procedures have been completed, a point to which I will return.

Project applications will be considered, in the first instance, by the Manage-

---

[9] See note 5 above, at p. 64.
[10] Interviews with officials associated with the implementation of the SPD in the Highlands and Islands and with representatives of 'partner' organisations do suggest that there may be an 'underspend' problem in respect of priority 3. It is, however, too early in the programming period to comment authoritatively on this.
[11] See, for example, its Special Report No. 3/92 on the environment at pp. 7–8, OJ 1992 C 245, p. 1.
[12] In which more than 70 NGOs participated.
[13] It is interesting to note that, in the explanatory notes accompanying the form, the Community's Fifth Environmental Action Programme OJ C 138, 17.5.1993 is listed as one of the 'key directives and legislation appropriate' to the completion of this section.

ment Executive of the Highlands and Islands Partnership Programme.[14] This body will conduct an assessment of technical eligibility and prioritise applications against core criteria. In assessing technical eligibility the executive is required to determine whether the application complies with 'all relevant EC directives and UK policy'. While not wishing to appear pedantic it is relevant to observe the disjuncture between the guidance notes accompanying the application form and the technical eligibility criteria. Whereas the former refers to the Fifth Action Programme and hence encompasses EC policy as well as law, the latter is confined to appraising compatibility with EC environmental law and *national* policy, including policy in the area of environmental protection. It would, however, perhaps, be excessively fastidious to dwell on the use of the term 'directives'. That the application form refers to both EC and national 'directives' leads one to assume that this concept is being employed in a non-technical sense, to refer to the entire body of applicable environmental law, whatever its legal form (hence including the Treaty, regulations and judgments of the European Court of Justice). This observation does, however, exemplify the absence of specialist legal knowledge (above all in the field of EC law) within the programme executive. Indeed at present this small body does not include an environmental specialist, although there have been calls for the secondment of an environmental expert to the executive 'at certain times of the year (ie during the main appraisal periods)'.[15]

The urgency of strengthening the composition of the programme executive in terms of its capacity to promote 'environmental compatibility', as defined under EC law,[16] is further underlined by a realisation that the executive is also responsible for the prioritisation of bids against core criteria (in so doing it should take into account the views of informal area-based partnership groups, the establishment of which is encouraged by the implementing authority). This essentially involves the 'scoring' of project applications according to a number of predetermined criteria. A maximum of 40 (out of 225) points may be awarded in view of the 'degree of environmental sustainability' of the project. Project applications will be placed into one of the following four categories:

1. There is direct evidence that the project is environmentally sustainable and will result in a net improvement in environmental quality (40 points).
2. There is evidence that the project is environmentally sustainable and will result in no net change in environmental quality (30 points).
3. There is evidence that any negative environmental impacts will be minimised and carefully managed, and the long-term benefits of the project

---

[14] This is responsible to the SPD monitoring committee through the establishment of a Joint Management Board.
[15] See Report H&I/SPD/95/038, 'Highlands & Islands Objective 1 Programme: Summary of Recommendations from Review of Implementation Arrangements', at p. 5.
[16] See note 3 above.

and the lack of less environmentally damaging alternatives have been demonstrated (10 points).

4. There is evidence of adverse environmental impact which is required to be controlled by environmental planning and management systems (0 points).

On the basis of this 'scoring' exercise project applications will be classified, in terms of priority, as either 'high', 'medium' or 'low'. It is, needless to say, striking that evidence of adverse environmental impact results in a score of zero (as opposed to, for example, up to minus 40) being awarded.

Those projects which are deemed to be technically eligible, sufficiently prepared, and properly justified are circulated by the programme executive to one of three advisory groups and to the implementing authority (Scottish Office Development Department—SODD!). The role of the advisory groups (chaired by the Scottish Office) is to seek to:

[A]ssess the suitability and priority of all project applications, consulting any other Group where appropriate, using the agreed selection criteria and scoring systems on their first submission and make a recommendation on whether or not the request for funding should be supported.[17]

Although the functions of the three thematic advisory groups[18] are many and varied, they do not enjoy formal decision-making authority. Essentially their role is to score projects on a scale of 1 (poorest fit) to 6 (best fit) employing a range of 'key factor' criteria which have been devised in respect of each measure falling under one of the six programme priorities. It is fair to say that with the exception of the measures concerned specifically and explicitly with environmental quality (identified above), the 'key criteria' are remarkably silent on the issue of environmental quality. In a sense it is frustrating to observe that while these three groups encompass considerable expertise in the environmental sphere (including representatives from, for example, Scottish Natural Heritage, Scottish Wildlife Link and the Royal Society for the Protection of Birds, and enjoying a capacity to invite applicants to attend meetings and to discuss project applications) they, unlike the programme executive, perform a rather mechanical function which leaves all too little room for environmental appraisal. It is nonetheless important to note that the comments and recommendations of the advisory groups are forwarded to the Programme monitoring committee, alongside the 'scores' awarded in view of the 'key factor' criteria.[19] In addition,

---

[17] Report from SODD for the Objective 1 SPD monitoring committee of 22 May 1996, 'Review of Implementation Arrangements: Terms of Reference and Rules of Procedure', at p. 2.

[18] Advisory Group A considers applications under priority 6, Group B applications in respect of priorities 1, 2 and 4, and Group C applications relating to priorities 3 and 4. For a list of priorities, see note 7 above.

[19] Nonetheless my impression is that recommendations are premised closely upon the scores achieved by project applicants in the 'prioritisation against core criteria' exercise conducted by the programme executive and the results of the 'key factor' exercise conducted by the advisory groups themselves.

the advisory groups should, wherever possible, issue recommendations and conclusions by consensus. In the absence of such consensus the monitoring committee is to be advised of the majority and minority 'views' of this participating in the advisory groups.[20]

The monitoring committee, in practice, enjoys authority to determine the fate of applications for funding. It should do so, wherever possible, by consensus, taking into account not only the views of the programme executive and the advisory groups but also of the local area based partnership groups. Following the recent review of SPD implementation arrangements the monitoring committee is comprised as follows:

- Commission (as appropriate)
- Scottish Office and other government departments (as appropriate)
- Local authorities (seven representatives)
- Highlands & Islands Enterprise Network (five representatives from HIE and the Local Enterprise Companies)
- Scottish Natural Heritage (one representative)
- Scottish Tourist Board (one representative)
- Voluntary sector (two representatives from Scottish Council for Voluntary Organisations)
- Commercial sector (one representative from Highlands & Islands Airports)
- Further Education sector (one representative—Principal of Thurso College)

In addition it is possible that an additional member, a representative of the newly formed[21] Scottish Environmental Protection Agency (SEPA) will be included in the near future.

The monitoring committee is charged, *inter alia*, with ensuring compliance with regulatory provisions, including those relating to the eligibility of measures and projects,[22] and compliance with other Community policies.

Scottish Natural Heritage (SNH) is the only environmental body currently represented on the committee, though with the agreement of the Convener (SODD) the committee may call upon the advice of non-members and may also invite non-members to attend Committee meetings. Though the voluntary sector is represented through the participation of delegates from the Scottish Council for Voluntary Organisations, environmental non-governmental organisations active in the region do not enjoy direct representation. SNH is a statutory body,[23] which inherited the functions of the Nature Conservancy Council for Scotland and the Countryside Commission for Scotland. Its members are appointed by the Secretary of State for Scotland, on terms determined by him.[24]

---

[20] See note 17 above.
[21] Established on 1 April 1996 pursuant to the Environment Act 1995.
[22] It was observed earlier that an assessment of technical eligibility includes an appraisal of compliance with 'EC Directives and UK Policy'.
[23] Natural Heritage (Scotland) Act 1991.
[24] See the Constitution annexed to the Natural Heritage (Scotland) Act 1991.

The Chairman and Deputy Chairman of SNH are appointed by the Secretary of State who is also responsible, on such terms and conditions determined by him (with Treasury approval), for the appointment of its first Chief Officer. Subsequent appointment to the role of Chief Officer is made by the members of the body, with the approval of the Secretary of State. The Secretary of State for Scotland enjoys broad discretion to remove a member who is unfit or unable to discharge his or her functions or otherwise 'unsuitable' to continue as a member. SNH is obliged to prepare annual reports and accounts which are presented to the Secretary of State for Scotland. The accounts are forwarded by him to the Comptroller and Auditor General and subsequently, together with a report thereon, laid before both Houses of Parliament. The Secretary of State for Scotland enjoys power to give directions to these bodies of a general or specific nature as regards the exercise of their functions and it shall be the duty of the body in question to give effect to such directions and, in respect of certain specified matters, the approval of the Secretary of State must be sought. Their grants fall for the determination of the Secretary of State, subject to Treasury approval and the Secretary of State may attach conditions thereto. In so far as they are accountable they are accountable to the institutions of central government. The public does not enjoy, in relation to SNH, a right to inspect a register of members' interests, to attend board or committee meetings, to inspect minutes of meetings, nor to see policy papers or documents for meetings.[25]

SNH's aims are, broadly (a) to secure the conservation and enhancement of, and (b) to foster understanding, and facilitate the enjoyment of, the natural heritage of Scotland.[26]

SNH is thus charged with responsibility both for conservation and for recreation and amenity, a combination which offers the opportunity for an integrated approach to be taken on many countryside and environmental issues ... [but which] may lead to internal conflicts in areas where recreational pressure is damaging fragile environments.[27]

In addition SNH is to have regard not only to issues of sustainability but also to a number of other considerations; for example, the needs of agriculture, fisheries and forestry, and the need for social and economic development, the interests of owners and occupiers of land, and of local communities. While not intending, even for a moment, to cast aspersions on the integrity of individual SNH representatives on the monitoring committee, it would nonetheless be

---

[25] Weir and Hall, *Democratic Audit: Ego-Trip—Extra-Governmental Organisations and their Accountability* (London: Charter 88 Trust, 1994).
[26] Natural Heritage (Scotland) Act 1991, s. 1(1).
[27] Reid, *Nature Conservation Law* (Edinburgh: W. Green/Sweet and Maxwell, 1994), at p. 56.

naive to overlook the intensity of this body's structural links with central government and the degree of its (not least financial) dependence upon it.[28]

The monitoring committee is, wherever possible, to reach decisions by consensus. However, the Commission's internal guidance on the role of desk-officers[29] (of which there is only one with responsibility for the Highlands and Islands) provides that on 'issues concerning the eligibility and conformity of operations with the Regulations governing Community structural policies . . . and in areas where stated Community policies could be affected the Commission has a non-negotiable right of veto'.[30] To this extent it is salient to note that while a representative of DGXVI (regional development) has regularly attended the Highlands and Islands SPD monitoring committee meetings, no representative from DGXI has, as yet, done so. This fact serves to reinforce relatively well-known arguments pertaining to the limited capacity of the Commission to perform a function of environmental 'watch-dog', particularly as regards 'implementation in practice' as opposed to 'black-letter implementation'.[31]

Though the guidance notes accompanying the ERDF application form state that '[b]efore an Application Form is submitted the proposal should have been approved fully by all other relevant decision-making bodies', in practice the monitoring committee has been prepared to grant conditional approval subject to the fulfilment of planning requirements. It appears that the monitoring committee is reluctant to become directly embroiled in controversial environmental disputes, preferring to view their resolution as the responsibility of statutory planning authorities. Of the three project applications currently under review with acknowledged environmental sensitivity (the Cairn Gorm funicular, a land reclamation project in respect of mudflats on the Moray Firth, and a mobile telecommunications project involving the construction of a large number of signal receivers), the monitoring committee seems to be happy to defer to national/local development planning procedures (unless of course the Commission decides to intervene to veto any such applications which until now it has refrained from doing so). Such deference is not problem free.

---

[28] In fact SNH does appear in general to have played a robust role in relation to nature conservation and has been criticised more than once for prioritising this aspect of its work over its concern with recreation and amenity. Nonetheless its recent 'volte-face' in relation to the Cairn Gorm funicular (in contrast, for example, to the RSPB (Scotland), WWF (Scotland), and the National Trust for Scotland), might be construed as exemplifying the difficulties it faces in view of the 'mixed' nature of the aims it pursues. Equally, however, its decision to condone 'with reluctance' the proposed funicular may be viewed as a rational response to the terms of the management agreement currently being drawn up between the Highland Region and the chair-lift company (see note 42 below).

[29] 'Guide à l'usage des rapporteurs', document interne, DGXVI discussed in McAleavey, *Policy Implementation as Incomplete Contracting: the European Regional Development Fund* (PhD thesis, Florence: European University Institute, 1995) at 285–286.

[30] McAleavey, *op. cit.* note 29, at 286.

[31] See in general, Macrory, 'The Enforcement of Community Environmental Law: Some Critical Issues' (1992) 29 CML Rev 347 and Chapter 3 above, and in relation to structural funding, Scott, *Development Dilemmas in the European Community* (Buckingham and Philadelphia: Open University Press, 1995), ch. 4, and Krämer, *Focus on European Environmental Law* (London: Sweet and Maxwell, 1992).

While this is hardly the place to explore the complexities and merits of Scots planning law two observations serve to exemplify the shortcomings associated with excessive deference to the planning system. The first relates simply to the scope of the concept of 'development' in respect of which planning permission is required. Development is defined as 'the carrying out of building, engineering, mining or other operations in, on, over or under the land or the making of any material change in the use of any buildings or other land'.[32] Certain activities are declared not to involve development and hence as not subject to planning permission. These include (most crucially) the 'use of land for the purposes of agriculture or forestry (including afforestation) and the use for any of those purposes of any building occupied together with the land so used'.[33] Moreover, in certain circumstances planning permission is deemed to have been granted and hence no application need be submitted.[34] This is particularly salient in so far as it extends to development in Enterprise Zones[35] and Simplified Planning Zones.[36] As such the planning system may be seen as less than comprehensive, not least in substantive areas of crucial importance to Community structural funding.[37]

The second point relates to the broad discretion enjoyed by planning authorities in respect of applications for planning permission. In certain situations this discretion may be such as to enable planning permission to be granted for an operation which is incompatible with the requirements of EC law. This can be illustrated with reference to the Wild Birds Directive.[38] The Special Protection Areas to be designated under this measure have been implemented through recourse to existing national designations including Sites of Special Scientific Interest. In such areas planning permission may be granted for damaging operations where (having had regard to the interests of conservation) there are economic or recreational requirements which outweigh nature conservation considerations, or where the development will not threaten the survival or reproduction of the birds in the area.[39] Yet the European Court of Justice has held that Member States may not reduce the size (or, by implication, diminish the quality) of Special Protection Areas other than on exceptional grounds corresponding to a general interest which is superior to the interest represented by the ecological objective underlying the objective. Neither economic nor

---

[32] Town and Country Planning (Scotland) Act 1972, s. 19(1).

[33] *Ibid.* s. 19(2)(e).

[34] The main source of deemed planning permission is the Permitted Development Order—Town and Country Planning (General Permitted Development) (Scotland) Order 1992 (SI 1992 No. 223) (as amended).

[35] Local Government Planning and Land Act 1980, s. 179 and Sch. 32 (as amended).

[36] Town and Country Planning (Scotland) Act 1972, ss. 21A–21E and Sch. 6A (as amended); Town and Country (Simplified Planning Zone) (Scotland) Regulations 1987 (SI 1987 No. 1532).

[37] Nearly one-quarter of structural funding is to accrue to priority 4, namely the development of the primary sectors and related food industries which includes improvement of agricultural structures, development of hill farms and crofts, forestry management, and timber production.

[38] Council Directive 79/409/EEC, OJ 1979 L 103, p. 1.

[39] See DoE Circular 27/87 and SDD Circular 1/1988.

recreational interests may properly give rise to such an overriding general interest.[40]

The point then is not simply that the scope of the principle of 'environmental compatibility', as defined under EC law, is broad, requiring consideration of EC policy as well as law,[41] but that the operation of the planning system is, in itself, no guarantee of compliance even with Community *law* proper. By deferring to decisions of the planning authorities, the monitoring committee fails to acknowledge that planning decisions taken at national level may sanction operations which are incompatible with EC law.

Environmental compatibility and the European Courts

The foregoing analysis has sought to clarify, in the context of the Highlands and Islands 'Objective 1' region, the procedures associated with the implementation of Community structural funding in so far as these pertain to the interface between environment and development. The procedures outlined are as complex as they are opaque. Such an analysis serves in its own right to exemplify the manner in which environmental concerns have infiltrated decision-making in respect of Community structural funding in this region. It serves also to highlight the deficiencies of current operating practices. It would be churlish to deny that, in respect of the Highlands and Islands SPD, environment is very much part of the package. Nonetheless such an overview of the mechanisms introduced to promote, as required by EC law, the integration of environmental and economic concerns illustrates that the 'pathological'—in terms of environmental *in*compatibility (a failure to comply with Community environmental law or policy as required by Article 7(1) of the Framework Regulation) is by no means entirely precluded. The role of the partnership executive in this respect is not sufficiently clearly defined and, in terms of resources, it appears to be ill-equipped to identify the 'pathological'. The advisory groups perform what is essentially a mechanical 'scoring' function which leaves little scope for environmental appraisal. While the composition of the monitoring committee is indicative of an awareness of the sensitive interface between environment and development, environmental organisations which are truly independent from central government do not enjoy representation upon it. The Commission's capacity to ensure the conformity of measures with EC environmental law and policy is similarly undermined by a paucity of resources and the exclusion, in practice, of the directorate with responsibility for environment. While reliance upon domestic planning procedures may, in some cases, serve to diffuse con-

---

[40] Case C-57/89, *Commission* v. *Germany* [1991] I-ECR 883.
[41] See note 3 above.

flict,[42] the broad discretion conferred upon planning authorities may result in a failure to comply with EC environmental law or policy.

Elsewhere in the Community, in regions eligible for Community structural funding during the first programming period, instances of alleged environmental incompatibility have given rise to actions before the European Courts. In two recent cases a number of applicants sought to challenge the legality of alleged Commission 'decisions' adopted in the sphere of Community structural funding.[43] On both occasions the applications for annulment, under Article 173 of the EC Treaty, have been declared inadmissible by the Court of First Instance (CFI). Appeals have subsequently been lodged before the European Court of Justice.[44] These events have led one commentator, not unreasonably, to conclude that ' . . . the safest road to legal protection for private parties in structural fund matters will generally be through national jurisdictions'.[45] It is one thing to state, as Comijs does, that:

[i]t is, after all, a matter of national jurisdiction to ensure legal protection for private parties in order to safeguard the rights that individuals derive from the direct effect of provisions of Community law. If the project was not in accordance with Community environmental law or policy, a national court would have had to defer the implementation measures or declare them void . . .[46]

It is quite another to persuade the national court as to the direct effect of the relevant EC environmental law or the pertinence of EC environmental *policy* before a court of law. Experience in the Scottish courts (and indeed the English courts) has demonstrated the limitations inherent in the concepts of direct and 'indirect' (*Marleasing*)[47] effect in the context of, for example, the Environmental Impact Assessment Directive. Hence remedies at national level may be unavailable or inadequate.[48]

---

[42] For example, in the context of the Cairn Gorm funicular, a management agreement (essentially a contract between the planning authority and the landowner) is currently being drafted which seeks to accommodate both environmental and economic concerns. Essentially this will seek to restrict the movement of those travelling upon the funicular upon their arrival at the Cairn Gorm plateau, through the construction of an enclosed viewing area from which they will be unable to exit. Similarly the agreement would see the introduction of revised parking charges at the entrance to the funicular. This car park currently serves the existing chair lift. Such charges would increase steeply after a short period sufficient merely to ride the funicular. This would be designed to deter those who might wish to undertake 'the long walk in' from the foot of the mountain to the sensitive plateau. The agreement would recognise the possibility of reviewing these arrangements following some years of experimentation. As a result, as was noted, SNH has endorsed the proposal, while a number of environmental NGOs remain firmly opposed. On the subject of planning agreements in Scots law, see Rowan-Robinson and Young, *Planning by Agreement in Scotland* (Edinburgh: W. Green, 1989).

[43] Case T-461/93, *An Taisce & WWF (UK)* v. *Commission* [1994] II-ECR 733; Case T-585/93, *Greenpeace and Others* v. *Commission*, not yet reported, order of 9 August 1995.

[44] Case C-325/94P (*An Taisce*); Case C-321/95P (*Greenpeace*). The appeal in *An Taisce* has been dismissed. See Case C-325/94P, 11 July 1996.

[45] Comijs, 'Individual Legal Protection under the Structural Funds' (1995) 2 MJ 187, at 187.

[46] *Ibid.* at 193–194.

[47] Case C-106/89, *Marleasing* v. *La Comercial Internacional de Alimentación SA* [1990] I-ECR 4135.

[48] See, for example, *Kincardine & Deeside District Council* v. *Forestry Commissioners* 1992 SLT 1180.

However, the above analysis of implementation procedures in the Highlands and Islands may suggest that the futility of pursuing actions before the European Courts is far from settled. Indeed this analysis may be seen (tentatively) as offering sustenance to those who may wish to call upon the European level judiciary to adjudicate at the interface between environment and development. It is to this issue that this chapter will now turn (albeit briefly).

Space precludes a detailed exploration of the findings of the Courts in *An Taisce* and *Greenpeace*.[49] Suffice it to note at this point that though in each of these cases a distinct issue lay at the heart of the Court's findings, in each case a procedural hurdle operated to preclude the admissibility of the applications. On both occasions the Court declined to hear the substance of the complaints submitted. In *An Taisce* the applicants failed in their endeavours to persuade the Courts as to the existence of the alleged Commission 'decision' enjoying legal effect. In *Greenpeace* the *locus standi* of the applicants was denied. It is in the context of a bid to overcome such procedural impediments that a close analysis of implementation practices in any given region may prove to be constructive and illuminating. This can be exemplified by reference to the Highlands and Islands experience.

Turning first to the question of the identity of the Commission 'decision' under review. Implementation procedures in respect of Community structural funding are characterised by opacity and considerable uncertainty regarding the division of decision-making responsibility as between the Commission and the Member States. This stems in part from the wording of the Community level Regulations governing the operation of the structural funds.[50] These do not acknowledge sufficiently the centrality of the role played by monitoring committees in determining the outcome of applications for structural funding. Talk of 'monitoring' implies a task of scrutinising decisions taken elsewhere. Yet, certainly in the context of the Highlands and Islands,[51] the regional monitoring committee, acting on behalf of the implementing authority (SODD), enjoys jurisdiction to approve or reject applications for funding.

This committee, as was seen, comprises multiple layers of government, together with representatives from a number of intermediate associations. The Commission (and in all probability the Scottish Office as implementing authority) claims to enjoy a right to veto project approval, with a view, *inter alia* to securing the conformity of operations part-funded by the structural funds with EC environmental law and policy. On each occasion that the monitoring committee approves a bid for financial assistance the Commission, albeit

---

[49] Note 43 above. See Scott 'Environmental Compatibility and the Community's Structural Fund: A Legal Analysis' (1996) JEL Vol. 8, No. 1, 99; Betlem, 'Being "Directly and Individually Concerned": The *Schutz-norm* Doctrine and *Francovich* Liability', in Reich and Micklitz (eds), *Public Interest Litigation Before the European Courts* (Baden-Baden: Nomos, Verlag, 1996) and Comijs, note 45 above.

[50] See note 1 above.

[51] I am grateful to Diana Comijs for her observations on this matter. She suggests that the same may well be true in the Netherlands and Belgium. The Commission notes, in COM (95) 509 final, at 8, that project selection is the remit of the monitoring communities.

perhaps implicitly, necessarily decides not to exercise its 'non-negotiable right of veto'.[52] The Commission not only 'acts', albeit by way of a 'negative' decision, but in so doing it adopts a decision of profound legal consequence.[53] By refusing to veto the monitoring committee's decision to grant funding, the Commission sanctions the release of an initial tranche of Community structural funding and creates a legitimate expectation that future funding—in the absence of any irregularity—will be forthcoming at regular intervals as agreed. It is important to emphasise that this 'negative' decision, adopted within the framework of the activities of the monitoring committee, is distinct from the alleged 'negative' decision which the applicants sought (unsuccessfully) to challenge in *An Taisce*. In this case the 'negative' decision under attack was an alleged decision not to 'suspend or withdraw' funding from a project which was approved within the framework of a so-called 'operational programme'. Operational programmes are 'packages' of consistent development measures which the Commission approves in outline by way of decision. The Commission Decision approving the relevant operational programme (for tourism in Ireland) was not the subject of review. Indeed it could not be so as it contained a clear and unequivocal statement of the principle of environmental compatibility as well as a declaration that 'where the Commission has evidence that for a given operation or operations Community policies have not been or are not being observed, the Commission will withhold payment of Community funds to the operation or operations in question . . .'. The applicants in this case failed to adduce sufficient evidence before the Court pertaining to the existence of a decision not to withdraw or suspend funding.[54] The CFI and the ECJ emphasised that the Commission was not, at the time of judgment, precluded from taking such a decision in the future as it 'may take such a decision at any time, including after the completion of the work . . . '.[55] The fact that it had not done so at this time should not be taken to imply that it would not conceivably do so in the

---

[52] See note 29 above.

[53] On the subject of 'negative' acts and Article 173 of the EC Treaty see, for example, Case C-313/90, *CIRFS and Others* v. *Commission* [1993] I-ECR 1125, where the European Court of Justice found a Commission Decision not to institute Article 93(2) proceedings in relation to plans to grant or modify state aids to constitute a decision susceptible to review under Article 173.

[54] One of the problems faced by the applicants in this case was the lack of cooperation on the part of the Commission in confirming or denying that any such decision had been reached and an unwillingness to release documents which would allow the applicants to ascertain this fact. On four occasions counsel to the applicants wrote to the Commission requesting access to the relevant documentation. Access was denied by both DGXI (environment) and DGXVI (regional policy) and confirmed by the Secretary General of the Commission. These decisions not to release documentation were the subject of an action before the Court of First Instance (Case T-105/95 *WWF (UK)* v. *Commission*, 5 March, 1997). The applicants argued that the Commission's refusal amounts to a violation of the Code of Conduct on openness and transparency and the Adopting Decision and further that the Code of Conduct and the Adopting Decision establish an obligation for the Commission to grant access to its documents.

[55] See note 43 above, at para. 36. The Court of First Instance referred in para. 36 to Articles 23(2) and 23(3) of the Coordination Regulation 'according to which the Commission may carry out checks with regard to funded operations and is entitled, for a period of three years following the last payment in respect of any operation, to have access to all supporting documents regarding expenditure on that operation'.

future. In this the alleged decision in *An Taisce* is qualitatively different from any decision on the part of the Commission not to exercise its veto within the monitoring committee. A decision not to veto a project application at the outset is a one-off decision which, having been adopted, cannot be undone at some future date, although admittedly its consequences may be mitigated through a later, and legally distinct, decision to suspend or withdraw funding.

It is interesting to observe that the defendants in *An Taisce* argued that the Commission decision to 'contribute funds to the Operational Programme for Tourism merely affords the Irish authorities the opportunity to build certain projects of their choice with Community assistance'.[56] It is my argument that this is not so. It affords this possibility within certain parameters but the purpose of Commission representation within the monitoring committee is precisely to ensure that these parameters are respected at the level of the individual project as well as at the strategic level represented by the operational programme or (since the start of the second programming period in certain Member States)[57] the SPD. Where a decision regarding project finance is adopted by the monitoring committee the Commission, by virtue of its right of veto, is sufficiently implicated to be construed as 'acting' (negatively) in a legal sense and hence its decision might legitimately form the subject of review proceedings before the European Court of Justice.

Turning now to the question of individual *locus standi* before the European Courts. The obstacles confronting non-privileged applicants seeking to institute Article 173 of the EC Treaty proceedings are well known. In the *Greenpeace* case the Court of First Instance emphasised that:

> . . . persons other than the addressees [of a decision] may claim that a decision is of direct concern to them only if that decision affects them by reason of certain attributes which are peculiar to them or by reason of factual circumstances which differentiate them from all other persons and thereby distinguish them individually in the same way as a person addressed . . . whilst the above mentioned line of authority comprises judgments given mostly in cases concerning, in principle, economic interests, it is nonetheless true that the essential criterion applied in those judgments—in substance, a combination of circumstances sufficient for the third-party applicant to be able to claim that he is affected by the contested decision in a manner which differentiates him from all other persons—remains applicable whatever the nature, economic or otherwise, of those of the applicants' interests which are affected'.[58]

More recently this cautious approach has been confirmed by the Court of First Instance in the context of a Commission decision concerning French nuclear

---

[56] Note 43 above, at para. 22.
[57] Member States may choose to submit their regional development plans in the form of a SPD in which case the Commission shall adopt a single decision in a single document. See Articles 5(2) and 10(1) of the coordination regulation (note 1 above). The effect of this is essentially to speed up the development planning process by amalgamating what were previously two separate steps requiring Commission approval (adoption of a strategic Community Support Framework, and decisions approving operational programmes).
[58] Note 43 above, at paras. 48 and 50.

tests in Polynesia.[59] This has led one commentator to bemoan (aptly) that 'the more people are harmed, the fewer can sue!'.[60]

There is, however, one crack in the jurisprudence of the European Courts on the issue of individual standing, through which a number of applicants have been able to squeeze notwithstanding an apparent absence of individual concern as traditionally defined. It is principally in relation to 'quasi-judicial determinations'[61] (in relation, for example, to state aids or anti-dumping) that the Courts have acknowledged the standing of those who, though not the addressee of a decision, or sufficiently differentiated from all other persons to be individually concerned, have participated in the procedures leading to the adoption of the decision (or even regulation) in hand.

In the area of structural policy the case of *Murgia Messapica* v. *Commission*[62] may be cited in support of the proposition that participation in the proceedings leading up to the adoption of a decision is of immense significance in assessing the individual concern of the applicant. In its judgment in this case the Court of First Instance cited the following factors as attesting to the individual concern of the applicant:

The provisional acceptance of its [the applicant's] project by the MAF and the inclusion of the project among those accorded secondary priority and the applicant's repeated participation in the meetings organised by the Commission, and the MAF, and thus in the procedure in conclusion of which the contested decision was adopted.[63]

Although the factor of participation was not solely determinative of the Court's findings on admissibility in this case, this judgment does appear to attest to the willingness of the Court to pay heed to this consideration in the context of decisions adopted in the sphere of Community structural policy. Indeed this may be seen as having been obliquely confirmed in the order of the Court of First Instance in the *Greenpeace* case. Here, the Court of First Instance, in denying the admissibility of the claim, notes that '[n]o specific procedures are provided for whereby individuals may be associated with the adoption, implementation and monitoring of decisions taken in the field of financial assistance granted by the ERDF'.[64]

By denying, in these terms, the standing of the many applicants in this case,[65] the Court appears to have opened the door in the future to those for whose benefit specific procedures are laid down whereby they may be associated with

---

[59] Case T-219/95, *Danielsson and Others* v. *Commission*, not yet reported. For a discussion of this see Betlem, note 49 above.

[60] Betlem, note 49 above.

[61] Hartley, *The Foundations of European Community Law* (Oxford: OUP, 1994) at p. 378 where he provides an excellent analysis of this body of case law.

[62] Case T-465/93, [1994] II-ECR 361. I am most grateful to Nicolas Bernard for drawing this case to my attention.

[63] [1994] II-ECR 361, at para. 26.

[64] Note 43 above, at para. 56.

[65] Included among the 'others' were a local fisherman, farmer, doctor, taxi-driver, teacher, trade unionist, ornithologist and wind-surfer!

the implementation of Community structural funding. The identity of such persons or groups will vary according to the nature of the 'partnership' instituted at regional level. The Commission recognises that partnership will necessarily take many forms and has shown a reluctance to impose a rigid model of partnership conceived at the centre. In the Highlands and Islands one might anticipate that those directly represented upon the 'Objective 1' monitoring committee would be deemed to be adequately involved in implementation tasks and decision-making. Hence it is not inconceivable that SNH or, in the future, the new Scottish Environmental Protection Agency, be accorded standing to commence an action for annulment before the Court of First Instance. However, as was noted, the intensity of their structural links with central government may preclude such a course of action in practice. The monitoring committee may, as was noted, invite non-members to attend and where they do so, they too should participate in the reaching of decisions (by consensus wherever possible). In this event such *ad hoc* players might be thought to enjoy standing in relation only to those decisions considered in their presence.

From a perspective of environmental compatibility it is the advisory groups which comprise the organisations, independent and campaigning in spirit, most inclined to view litigation as a means of placing the spotlight on the environment/development debate and upon the current deficiencies in existing implementation procedures in their region. It is unclear whether such groups (for example, RSPB, which remains categorically opposed to the funicular project even in the wake of the proposed management agreement), operating within an institutional framework which, on the one hand, denies them decision-making authority but, on the other, accords great weight to their recommendations and even invites minority opinions to be heard by the monitoring committee, would enjoy standing under Article 173 of the EC Treaty.

Hence, if, as has been argued, the Commission 'acts' in the context of the monitoring committee by 'deciding' at this stage whether to exercise its veto, its decision may be viewed as susceptible to challenge before the Court of First Instance by a relatively wide range of actors—governmental (including local authorities) and non-governmental (for example, the principal of Thurso College!).

Conclusion

In a region in which it is often claimed that people (with jobs) are the most endangered species the interface between environment and development will inevitably be contested. The Community's regional policy is premised upon a strategy of economic expansion and assumes that environment and development *qua* growth, are not inherently irreconcilable. The principle of 'environmental compatibility' emerges, in the context of Community structural funding, as a concrete expression of the Community's (some would argue, whimsical) quest for 'sustainable growth'.[66] Experience in the Highlands and Islands in implementing the SPD is testimony to the increasing prominence of environmental considerations in development planning. Nonetheless existing structures and operating practices are far from being ideal. This fact, together with the wide variety of implementation practices in place across the Community, highlights the continuing significance (practical and legal) of the Commission's 'non-negotiable right of veto', as well as its power to reduce or suspend assistance. The Commission has indicated its intention to adopt a more active role in the task of upholding the principle of environmental compatibility and its willingness to deploy the strict sanctions which are available to it.[67] Such steps are indispensable if environmental compatibility is to be more than merely eco-friendly icing on a non-biodegradeable cake.

---

[66] Article 2 of the EC Treaty provides that 'the Community shall have as its task . . . to promote throughout the Community . . . sustainable . . . growth respecting the environment . . .'.

[67] COM(95) 509 final, at 10–12.

ADDENDUM TO CHAPTER 3

Since writing this chapter there have been many developments at European level to improve compliance of environmental law. Some of the recommendations made in this chapter have subsequently been suggested by the European Parliament in its report on the implementation and enforcement of Community law.[1] The European Commission also released a communication on implementing Community environmental law, which endorsed many of the suggestions of both the European Parliament and this chapter.[2] The suggested improvements include the introduction of an annual report dedicated solely to the environment, the more effective application of Article 171, and better quality drafting of the legislation.

The main new innovation in securing more effective compliance with Community law is the proposed introduction into the enforcement process of the concept of the regulatory chain. The regulatory chain emphasises that implementation and enforcement issues are not confined solely to the legal stage of the process. The idea is that these issues must be incorporated into stages like the initial design of legislation, institutional structure, and training and education. In the United Kingdom the House of Lords Select Committee on the European Communities have been conducting another major enquiry on this subject and their report is expected in late 1997.[3] The Select Committee is expected to promote the concept of the regulatory chain in its report.

The Commission also endorsed the view that although the main responsibility for enforcing environmental law should remain with them, Member States should assume greater responsibility in the enforcement process. The Commission suggested three new areas for action which would potentially relieve

---

[1] Report of the Committee on the Environment, Public Health and Consumer Protection, on a communication from the Commission on implementing Community environmental law (1997). (PE 221.176)
[2] Communication from the Commission on implementing Community environmental law (COM(96) 500 final, 28.11.1996).
[3] Its first review was in 1992, see footnote 10.

some of its administrative burden: (i) the development of Community-wide minimum criteria for the carrying out of inspection tasks by Member State authorities; (ii) the operation of environmental complaints and investigations procedures within Member States, which will receive and examine complaints from the public about the implementation of Community environmental law; (iii) an increase in the opportunities for environmental cases to be dealt with by national courts, through broader access to justice on Community environmental issues. The European Environment Agency and IMPEL would also assume greater roles in the enforcement process.

Since this chapter was written the European Commission has also published the thirteenth annual report on monitoring the application of Community law.[4] It is presented in a similar fashion to the previous report, with the most obvious difference being the changes in the presentation of the figures in the annex. The directives are no longer listed in chronological order but by subject areas, making analysis far easier. The Commission has again only included a break-down and table for directives which have been notified, and have omitted tables for conformity of implementing measures and incorrect application of directives. The report shows an increase in the number of cases terminated and it appears that a start has been made towards clearing up some of the longest-running cases. However, in 1996 there were still over 600 environmental complaints and infringement cases outstanding against Member States, with 85 of the latter awaiting determination by the Court of Justice. With the recent accession of Austria, Sweden and Finland into what is now a 15 member Community, and the distinct possibility of further expansion of numbers of Member States, the weaknesses in the current mechanisms of implementation and enforcement of Community environmental law will become increasingly apparent.

The recent recommendations made by the European Commission, Parliament, and Council are welcome. However, with the possibility of further enlargements in the membership of the Community and the increasing complexity of environmental policies and standards, it is clear that the whole issue of implementation and enforcement will remain one of high priority.

---

[4] COM(96) 600 of 29.5.1996.

Appendix 1

FAILURE TO NOTIFY

BELGIUM

Waste

Dir 91/157/EEC—*Batteries containing dangerous substances*
Belgium: 92/1005, no measures notified, Article 169 letter in 1992.
Dir 92/112/EEC—*Pollution; titanium dioxide*
Belgium: 93/638, no measures notified, reasoned opinion in 1994.
Dir 93/86/EEC—*Batteries and accumulators containing certain dangerous substances*
Belgium: 94/32, no measures notified, Article 169 letter in 1994.

Air

Dir 92/72/EEC—*Air pollution by ozone*
Belgium: 94/517, no measures notified, Article 169 letter in 1994.
Dir 93/12/EEC—*Sulphur content of liquid fuels*
Belgium: 94/519, no measures notified, Article 169 letter sent in 1994.

Chemicals

Dir 90/517/EEC—*Labelling of dangerous substances*
Belgium: 92/51, no measures notified, reasoned opinion in 1994.
Dir 91/325/EEC—*Labelling of dangerous substances*
Belgium: 92/61, no measures notified, reasoned opinion in 1994.
Belgium: 92/663, no measures notified, Article 169 letter in 1992.
Dir 91/326/EEC—*Labelling of dangerous substances*
Belgium: 92/664, no measures notified, Article 169 letter in 1992.

Dir 91/410/EEC—Labelling of dangerous substances
Belgium: 92/666, no measures notified, Article 169 letter in 1992.
Dir 91/632/EEC—Labelling of dangerous substances
Belgium: 93/624, no measures notified, Article 169 letter in 1993.
Dir 92/32/EEC—Labelling of dangerous substances
Belgium: 93/970, no measures notified, Article 169 letter in 1993.
Dir 92/37/EEC—Labelling of dangerous substances
Belgium: 94/09, no measures notified, Article 169 letter in 1994.
Dir 92/69/EEC—Labelling of dangerous substances
Belgium: 93/973, no measures notified, Article 169 letter in 1993.
Dir 93/21/EEC—Labelling of dangerous substances
Belgium: 94/782, no measures notified, Article 169 letter in 1995.
Dir 93/67/EEC—Principles for assessment of risks
Belgium: 93/978, no measures notified, Article 169 letter in 1993.
Dir 93/72/EEC—Labelling of dangerous substances
Belgium: 94/792, no measures notified, Article 169 letter to be sent in 1995.
Dir 93/90/EEC—Labelling of dangerous substances
Belgium: 94/33, no measures notified, Article 169 letter in 1994.
Dir 93/105/EEC—Information required for technical dossiers
Belgium: 94/35, no measures notified, Article 169 letter in 1994.
Dir 94/15/EC—Genetically modified organisms
Belgium: 94/634, no measures notified, Article 169 letter in 1994.

Radiation protection

Dir 90/641/EEC—Radiation protection; outside workers
Belgium: 94/04, no measures notified, Article 169 letter in 1994.
Dir 92/3/EEC—Shipments of radioactive waste
Belgium: 94/400, no measures notified, Article 169 letter in 1994.

GERMANY

General matters

Dir 90/313/EEC—Freedom of access to information on the environment
Germany: 93/111, no measures notified, Article 169 letter in 1993 (to be terminated in 1995).

Waste

Dir 91/156/EEC—Waste

Germany: 93/668, no measures notified, Article 169 letter in 1993 (to be terminated in 1995).

Dir 91/157/EEC—*Batteries containing dangerous substances*
Germany: 92/1006, no measures notified, reasoned opinion in 1994.

Dir 92/112/EEC—*Pollution; titanium dioxide*
Germany: 93/687, no measures notified, Article 169 letter in 1993, terminated in 1994.

Dir 93/86/EEC—*Batteries and accumulators containing certain dangerous substances*
Germany: 94/94, no measures notified, Article 169 letter in 1994.

Water

Dir 90/415/EEC—*Dangerous substances in the sea*
Germany: 92/118, no measures notified, reasoned opinion in 1993.

Dir 91/271/EEC—*Urban waste-water treatment*
Germany: 93/669, no measures notified, reasoned opinion in 1994.

Air

Dir 93/12/EEC—*Sulphur content of liquid fuels*
Germany: 94/534, no measures notified, Article 169 letter in 1994.

Noise

Dir 92/14/EEC—*Operation of aeroplanes*
Germany: 92/709, no measures notified, reasoned opinion in 1994.

Nature

Dir 92/43/EEC—*Conservation of natural habitats and wild fauna and flora*
Germany: 94/645, no measures notified, Article 169 letter in 1994.

Chemicals

Dir 91/325/EEC—*Labelling of dangerous substances*
Germany: 92/134, no measures notified, reasoned opinion in 1993, terminated in 1994.

Dir 91/326/EEC—*Labelling of dangerous substances*

Germany: 92/704, no measures notified, Article 169 letter in 1992, terminated in 1994.

Dir 91/410/EEC—*Labelling of dangerous substances*
Germany: 92/706, no measures notified, Article 169 letter in 1993, terminated in 1994.

Dir 91/632/EEC—*Labelling of dangerous substances*
Germany: 93/671, no measures notified, Article 169 letter in 1993, terminated in 1994.

Dir 92/69/EEC—*Labelling of dangerous substances*
Germany: 93/991, no measures notified, Article 169 letter in 1993, terminated in 1994.

Dir 93/67/EEC—*Principles for assessment of risks*
Germany: 93/996, no measures notified, Article 169 letter in 1993 (to be terminated in 1995).

Dir 93/90/EEC—*Labelling of dangerous substances*
Germany: 94/95, no measures notified, Article 169 letter in 1994.

Dir 93/105/EEC—*Information required for technical dossiers*
Germany: 94/97, no measures notified, Article 169 letter in 1994.

Dir 94/15/EC—*Genetically modified organisms*
Germany: 94/658, no measures notified, Article 169 letter in 1994.

Radiation protection

Dir 92/3/EEC—*Shipments of radioactive waste*
Germany: 94/413, no measures notified, Article 169 letter in 1994.

DENMARK

Water

Dir 91/271/EEC—*Urban waste-water treatment*
Denmark: 93/646, no measures notified, Article 169 letter in 1993, terminated in 1994.

Nature

Dir 91/244/EEC—*Conservation of wild birds*
Denmark: 93/63, no measures notified, Article 169 letter in 1993 (to be terminated in 1995).

Chemicals

Dir 91/632/EEC—Labelling of dangerous substances
Denmark: 93/648, no measures notified, Article 169 letter in 1993, terminated in 1994.
Dir 93/67/EEC—Principles for assessment of risks
Denmark: 93/987, no measures notified, Article 169 letter in 1993, terminated in 1994.

GREECE

General matters

Dir 90/313/EEC—Freedom of access to information on the environment
Greece: 93/158, no measures notified, reasoned opinion in 1994.

Waste

Dir 91/156/EEC—Waste
Greece: 93/719, no measures notified, reasoned opinion in 1994.
Dir 91/157/EEC—Batteries containing dangerous substances
Greece: 92/1007, no measures notified, reasoned opinion in 1994.
Dir 92/112/EEC—Pollution; titanium dioxide
Greece: 93/698, no measures notified, Article 169 letter in 1993.
Dir 93/86/EEC—Batteries and accumulators containing certain dangerous substances
Greece: 94/100, no measure notified, Article 169 letter in 1994.

Water

Dir 90/415/EEC—Dangerous substances in the sea
Greece: 92/260, no measures notified, reasoned opinion in 1993, referral in 1994. Case 94/180.
Dir 91/271/EEC—Urban waste-water treatment
Greece: 93/718, no measures notified, reasoned opinion in 1994.

Air

Dir 92/72/EEC—Air pollution by ozone
Greece: 94/547, no measures notified, Article 169 letter in 1994.

Nature

Dir 91/244/EEC—*Conservation of wild birds*
Greece: 93/901, no measures notified, Article 169 letter in 1993.
Dir 92/43/EEC—*Conservation of natural habitats and wild fauna and flora*
Greece: 94/703, no measures notified, Article 169 letter in 1994.

Chemicals

Dir 90/219/EEC—*Genetically modified organisms*
Greece: 92/264, no measures notified, reasoned opinion in 1993, referral in 1994. Case 94/170.
Dir 90/220/EEC—*Genetically modified organisms*
Greece: 92/263, no measures notified, reasoned opinion in 1993, referral in 1994. Case 94/170.
Dir 92/32/EEC—*Labelling of Dangerous substances*
Greece: 93/1028, no measures notified, Article 169 letter in 1993.
Dir 92/69/EEC—*Labelling of dangerous substances*
Greece: 93/1025, no measures notified, Article 169 letter in 1993.
Dir 93/21/EEC—*Labelling of dangerous substances*
Greece: 94/989, no measures notified, Article 169 letter in 1995.
Dir 93/67/EEC—*Principles for assessment of risks*
Greece: 93/1020, no measures notified, Article 169 letter in 1993.
Dir 93/72/EEC—*Labelling of dangerous substances*
Greece: 94/978, no measures notified, Article 169 letter to be sent in 1995.
Dir 93/90/EEC—*Labelling of dangerous substances*
Greece: 94/99, no measures notified, Article 169 letter in 1994.
Dir 93/105/EEC—*Information required for technical dossiers*
Greece: 94/98, no measures notified, Article 169 letter in 1994.
Dir 94/15/EC—*Genetically modified organisms*
Greece: 94/687, no measures notified, Article 169 letter in 1994.

Radiation protection

Dir 90/641/EEC—*Radiation protection; outside workers*
Greece: 94/130, no measures notified, Article 169 letter in 1994.
Dir 92/3/EEC—*Shipments of radioactive waste*
Greece: 94/428, no measures notified, Article 169 letter in 1994.

SPAIN

Waste

Dir 91/156/EEC—*Waste*
Spain: 93/720, no measures notified, reasoned opinion in 1994.
Dir 91/157/EEC—*Batteries containing dangerous substances*
Spain: 92/1008, no measures notified, reasoned opinion in 1994.
Dir 93/86/EEC—*Batteries and accumulators containing certain dangerous substances*
Spain: 94/162, no measures notified, Article 169 letter in 1994.

Water

Dir 91/271/EEC—*Urban waste-water treatment*
Spain: 93/721, no measures notified, reasoned opinion in 1994.

Air

Dir 92/72/EEC—*Air pollution by ozone*
Spain: 94/549, no measures notified, Article 169 letter in 1994.
Dir 93/12/EEC—*Sulphur content of liquid fuels*
Spain: 94/552, no measures notified, Article 169 letter in 1994.

Nature

Dir 92/43/EEC—*Conservation of natural habitats and wild fauna and flora*
Spain: 94/659, no measures notified, Article 169 letter in 1994.

Chemicals

Dir 90/219/EEC—*Genetically modified organisms*
Spain: 92/163, no measures notified, reasoned opinion in 1993.
Dir 90/220/EEC—*Genetically modified organisms*
Spain: 92/164, no measures notified, reasoned opinion in 1993.
Dir 92/32/EEC—*Labelling of dangerous substances*
Spain: 93/998, no measures notified, reasoned opinion in 1994.
Dir 92/37/EEC—*Labelling of dangerous substances*
Spain: 94/137, no measures notified, reasoned opinion in 1994.
Dir 92/69/EEC—*Labelling of dangerous substances*

Spain: 93/1000, no measures notified, reasoned opinion in 1994.
Dir 93/21/EEC—*Labelling of dangerous substances*
Spain: 94/826, no measures notified, Article 169 letter in 1995.
Dir 93/67/EEC—*Principles for assessment of risks*
Spain: 93/1005, no measures notified, reasoned opinion in 1994.
Dir 93/72/EEC—*Labelling of dangerous substances*
Spain: 94/831, no measures notified, Article 169 letter to be sent in 1995.
Dir 93/90/EEC—*Labelling of dangerous substances*
Spain: 94/163, no measures notified, reasoned opinion in 1994.
Dir 93/105/EEC—*Information required for technical dossiers*
Spain: 94/164, no measures notified, reasoned opinion in 1994.
Dir 94/15/EC—*Genetically modified organisms*
Spain: 94/672, no measures notified, Article 169 letter in 1994.

Radiation protection

Dir 90/641/EEC—*Radiation protection; outside workers*
Spain: 94/131, no measures notified, Article 169 letter in 1994.
Dir 92/3/EEC—*Shipments of radioactive waste*
Spain: 94/434, no measures notified, Article 169 letter in 1994.

FRANCE

Waste

Dir 91/156/EEC—*Waste*
France: 93/737, no measures notified, Article 169 letter in 1993.
Dir 91/157/EEC—*Batteries containing dangerous substances*
France: 92/1009, no measures notified, reasoned opinion in 1993.
Dir 93/86/EEC—*Batteries and accumulators containing certain dangerous substances*
France: 94/193, no measures notified, reasoned opinion in 1994.

Air

Dir 92/72/EEC—*Air pollution by ozone*
France: 94/555, no measures notified, Article 169 letter in 1994.
Dir 93/12/EEC—*Sulphur content of liquid fuels*
France: 94/558, no measures notified, Article 169 letter in 1994.

Noise

Dir 88/181/EEC—Sound power level of lawnmowers
France: 92/197, no measures notified, reasoned opinion in 1993, terminated in 1994.
Dir 92/14/EEC—Operation of aeroplanes
France: 92/783, no measures notified, reasoned opinion in 1993, terminated in 1994.

Nature

Dir 92/43/EEC—Conservation of natural habitats and wild fauna and flora
France: 94/673, no measures notified, Article 169 letter in 1994.

Chemicals

Dir 92/32/EEC—Labelling of dangerous substances
France: 93/1011, no measures notified, Article 169 letter in 1993, (to be terminated in 1995).
Dir 92/69/EEC—Labelling of dangerous substances
France: 93/1014, no measures notified, Article 169 letter in 1993, terminated in 1994.
Dir 93/67/EEC—Principles for assessment of risks
France: 93/1019, no measures notified, Article 169 letter in 1993 (to be terminated in 1995).
Dir 94/15/EC—Genetically modified organisms
France: 94/686, no measures notified, Article 169 letter in 1994.

ITALY

General matters

Dir 90/313/EEC—Freedom of access to information on the environment
Italy: 93/316, no measures notified, reasoned opinion in 1994.

Waste

Dir 89/369/EEC—Incineration of municipal waste
Italy: 91/417, no measures notified, reasoned opinion in 1993

Dir 91/156/EEC—*Waste*
Italy: 93/785, no measures notified, reasoned opinion in 1994.
Dir 91/157/EEC—*Batteries containing dangerous substances*
Italy: 92/1011, no measures notified, Article 169 letter in 1992.
Dir 92/112/EEC—*Pollution; titanium dioxide*
Italy: 93/801, no measures notified, reasoned opinion in 1994.
Dir 93/86/EEC—*Batteries and accumulators containing certain dangerous substances*
Italy: 94/261, no measures notified, Article 169 letter in 1994.

Water

Dir 91/271/EEC—*Urban waste-water treatment*
Italy: 93/786, no measures notified, reasoned opinion in 1994.

Air

Dir 89/427/EEC—*Sulphur dioxide in the air*
Italy: 91/678, no measures notified, reasoned opinion in 1994.
Dir 89/429/EEC—*Incineration of municipal waste*
Italy: 91/418, no measures notified, reasoned opinion in 1993.
Dir 92/72/EEC—*Air pollution by ozone*
Italy: 94/568, no measures notified, Article 169 letter in 1994.
Dir 93/12/EEC—*Sulphur content of liquid fuels*
Italy: 94/571, no measures notified, Article 169 letter in 1994.

Noise

Dir 89/629/EEC—*Noise emissions from aeroplanes*
Italy: 91/82, no measures notified, reasoned opinion in 1994.
Dir 92/14/EEC—*Operation of aeroplanes*
Italy: 92/837, no measures notified, reasoned opinion in 1994.

Nature

Dir 92/43/EEC—*Conservation of natural habitats and wild fauna and flora*
Italy: 94/718, no measures notified, Article 169 letter in 1994.

Chemicals

Dir 87/217/EEC—*Pollution by asbestos*

Italy: 90/65, no measures notified, reasoned opinion in 1991.
Dir 91/326/EEC—*Labelling of dangerous substances*
Italy: 92/830, no measures notified, Article 169 letter in 1992.
Dir 91/410/EEC—*Labelling of dangerous substances*
Italy: 92/832, no measures notified, reasoned opinion in 1994.
Dir 91/632/EEC—*Labelling of dangerous substances*
Italy: 93/788, no measures notified, reasoned opinion in 1994.
Dir 92/32/EEC—*Labelling of dangerous substances*
Italy: 93/1044, no measures notified, Article 169 letter in 1993.
Dir 92/37/EEC—*Labelling of dangerous substances*
Italy: 94/235, no measures notified, Article 169 letter in 1994.
Dir 92/69/EEC—*Labelling of dangerous substances*
Italy: 93/1047, no measures notified, Article 169 letter in 1993.
Dir 93/21/EEC—*Labelling of dangerous substances*
Italy: 94/876, no measures notified, Article 169 letter in 1995.
Dir 93/67/EEC—*Principles for assessment of risks*
Italy: 93/1054, no measures notified, reasoned opinion in 1994.
Dir 93/72/EEC—*Labelling of dangerous substances*
Italy: 94/885, no measures notified, Article 169 letter to be sent in 1995.
Dir 93/90/EEC—*Labelling of dangerous substances*
Italy: 94/262, no measures notified, reasoned opinion in 1994.
Dir 93/105/EEC—*Information required for technical dossiers*
Italy: 94/263, no measures notified, Article 169 letter in 1994.
Dir 94/15/EC—*Genetically modified organisms*
Italy: 94/731, no measures notified, Article 169 letter in 1994.

Radiation protection

Dir 80/836/EEC—*Health protection; ionizing radiation*
Italy: 87/225, no measures notified, reasoned opinion (171) in 1993.
Dir 84/467/EEC—*Health protection; ionizing radiation*
Italy: 87/233, no measures notified, reasoned opinion (171) in 1993.
Dir 89/618/EEC—*Health protection; radiological emergency*
Italy: 92/334, no measures notified, referral in 1994. Case 94/135
Dir 90/641/EEC—*Radiation protection; outside workers*
Italy: 94/231, no measures notified, Article 169 letter in 1994.
Dir 92/3/EEC—*Shipments of radioactive waste*
Italy: 94/464, no measures notified, Article 169 letter in 1994.

IRELAND

Waste

Dir 91/156/EEC—Waste
Ireland: 93/762, no measures notified, reasoned opinion in 1994.
Dir 91/157/EEC—Batteries containing dangerous substances
Ireland: 92/1010, no measures notified, Article 169 letter in 1992, terminated in 1994.
Dir 92/112/EEC—Pollution; titanium dioxide
Ireland: 93/781, no measures notified, Article 169 letter in 1993 (to be terminated in 1995).

Water

Dir 86/280/EEC—Dangerous substances in the sea
Ireland: 89/254, no measures notified, reasoned opinion in 1992, terminated in 1994.
Dir 90/415/EEC—Dangerous substances in the sea
Ireland: 92/300, no measures notified, reasoned opinion in 1994.
Dir 91/271/EEC—Urban waste-water treatment
Ireland: 93/763, no measures notified, reasoned opinion in 1994.

Chemicals

Dir 90/517/EEC—Labelling of dangerous substances
Ireland: 92/307, no measures notified, Article 169 letter in 1992, terminated in 1994.
Dir 91/325/EEC—Labelling of dangerous substances
Ireland: 92/317, no measures notified, Article 169 letter in 1992, terminated in 1994.
Dir 92/32/EEC—Labelling of dangerous substances
Ireland: 93/1031, no measures notified, Article 169 letter in 1993, terminated in 1994.
Dir 92/69/EEC—Labelling of dangerous substances
Ireland: 93/1034, no measures notified, Article 169 letter in 1993, terminated in 1994.
Dir 93/67/EEC—Principles for assessment of risks
Ireland: 93/1041, no measures notified, Article 169 letter in 1993 (to be terminated in 1995).
Dir 94/15/EC—Genetically modified organisms

Ireland: 94/717, no measures notified, Article 169 letter in 1994.

LUXEMBOURG

General matters

Dir 85/337/EEC—*Assessment of effects of projects on the environment*
Luxembourg: 90/126, no measures notified, referral in 1993. Case 93/313.

Waste

Dir 91/156/EEC—*Waste*
Luxembourg: 93/811, no measures notified, Article 169 letter in 1993 (to be terminated in 1995).

Water

Dir 91/271/EEC—*Urban waste-water treatment*
Luxembourg: 93/812, no measures notified, Article 169 letter in 1993, terminated in 1994.

Noise

Dir 89/629/EEC—*Noise emissions from aeroplanes*
Luxembourg: 91/168, no measures notified, reasoned opinion in 1993, terminated in 1994.
Dir 92/14/EEC—*Operation of aeroplanes*
Luxembourg: 92/865, no measures notified, Article 169 letter in 1992, terminated in 1994.

Nature

Dir 91/244/EEC—*Conservation of wild birds*
Luxembourg: 93/352, no measures notified, reasoned opinion in 1994.

Chemicals

Dir 86/609/EEC—*Protection of animals*

Luxembourg: 90/730, no measures notified, referral in 1993. Case 93/274.
Dir 90/219/EEC—*Genetically modified organisms*
Luxembourg: 92/395, no measures notified, reasoned opinion in 1993.
Dir 90/220/EEC—*Genetically modified organisms*
Luxembourg: 92/396, no measures notified, reasoned opinion in 1993.
Dir 92/32/EEC—*Labelling of dangerous substances*
Luxembourg: 93/1064, no measures notified, Article 169 letter in 1993 (to be terminated in 1995).
Dir 93/21/EEC—*Labelling of dangerous substances*
Luxembourg: 94/900, no measures notified, Article 169 letter in 1995.
Dir 93/67/EEC—*Principles for assessment of risks*
Luxembourg: 93/1072, no measures notified, Article 169 letter in 1993 (to be terminated in 1995).
Dir 93/72/EEC—*Labelling of dangerous substances*
Luxembourg: 94/907, no measures notified, Article 169 letter to be sent in 1995.
Dir 93/90/EEC—*Labelling of dangerous substances*
Luxembourg: 94/296, no measures notified, Article 169 letter in 1994.
Dir 94/15/EC—*Genetically modified organisms*
Luxembourg: 94/742, no measures notified, Article 169 letter in 1994.

Radiation protection

Dir 89/618/EEC—*Health protection; radiological emergency*
Luxembourg: 93/611, no measures notified, reasoned opinion in 1994.
Dir 90/641/EEC—*Radiation protection; outside workers*
Luxembourg: 94/264, no measures notified, Article 169 letter in 1994.

NETHERLANDS

Waste

Dir 91/156/EEC—*Waste*
Netherlands: 93/829, no measures notified, Article 169 letter in 1993, terminated in 1994.
Dir 92/112/EEC—*Pollution; titanium dioxide*
Netherlands: 93/841, no measures notified, Article 169 letter in 1993, terminated in 1994.

Air

Dir 92/72/EEC—*Air pollution by ozone*

Netherlands: 94/583, no measures notified, Article 169 letter in 1994.

Nature

Dir 91/244/EEC—*Conservation of wild birds*
Netherlands: 93/393, no measures notified, Article 169 letter in 1993.

Chemicals

Dir 91/632/EEC—*Labelling of dangerous substances*
Netherlands: 93/832, no measures notified, Article 169 letter in 1993 (to be terminated in 1995).
Dir 92/32/EEC—*Labelling of dangerous substances*
Netherlands: 93/1056, no measures notified, Article 169 letter in 1993 (to be terminated in 1995).
Dir 92/69/EEC—*Labelling of dangerous substances*
Netherlands: 93/1057, no measures notified, Article 169 letter in 1993, terminated in 1994.
Dir 93/67/EEC—*Principles for assessment of risks*
Netherlands: 93/1062, no measures notified, Article 169 letter in 1993 (to be terminated in 1995).

PORTUGAL

Waste

Dir 91/157/EEC—*Batteries containing dangerous substances*
Portugal: 92/1013, no measures notified, reasoned opinion in 1994.
Dir 92/112/EEC—*Pollution; titanium dioxide*
Portugal: 93/865, no measures notified, Article 169 letter in 1993.
Dir 93/86/EEC—*Batteries and accumulators containing certain dangerous substances*
Portugal: 94/360, no measures notified, Article 169 letter in 1994.

Water

Dir 78/176/EEC—*Waste; titanium dioxide*
Portugal: 90/929, no measures notified, reasoned opinion in 1993.
Dir 90/415/EEC—*Dangerous substances in the sea*
Portugal: 92/498, no measures notified, reasoned opinion in 1993.

Air

Dir 92/72/EEC—*Air pollution by ozone*
Portugal: 94/590, no measures notified, Article 169 letter in 1994.
Dir 93/12/EEC—*Sulphur content of liquid fuels*
Portugal: 94/593, no measures notified, Article 169 letter in 1994.

Nature

Dir 92/43/EEC—*Conservation of natural habitats and wild fauna and flora*
Portugal: no measures notified, Article 169 letter in 1994.

Chemicals

Dir 90/517/EEC—*Labelling of dangerous substances*
Portugal: 92/491, no measures notified, reasoned opinion in 1994.
Dir 91/325/EEC—*Labelling of dangerous substances*
Portugal: 92/480, no measures notified, reasoned opinion in 1994.
Portugal: 92/905, no measures notified, reasoned opinion in 1994.
Dir 91/326/EEC—*Labelling of dangerous substances*
Portugal: 92/904, no measures notified, reasoned opinion in 1994.
Dir 91/410/EEC—*Labelling of dangerous substances*
Portugal: 92/902, no measures notified, reasoned opinion in 1994.
Dir 91/632/EEC—*Labelling of dangerous substances*
Portugal: 93/848, no measures notified, reasoned opinion in 1994.
Dir 92/32/EEC—*Labelling of dangerous substances*
Portugal: 93/1075, no measures notified, reasoned opinion in 1994.
Dir 92/37/EEC—*Labelling of dangerous substances*
Portugal: 94/335, no measures notified, reasoned opinion in 1994.
Dir 92/69/EEC—*Labelling of dangerous substances*
Portugal: 93/1077, no measures notified, reasoned opinion in 1994.
Dir 93/21/EEC—*Labelling of dangerous substances*
Portugal: 94/933, no measures notified, Article 169 letter in 1995.
Dir 93/67/EEC—*Principles for assessment of risks*
Portugal: 93/1084, no measures notified, Article 169 letter in 1993.
Dir 93/72/EEC—*Labelling of dangerous substances*
Portugal: 94/943, no measures notified, Article 169 letter to be sent in 1995.
Dir 93/90/EEC—*Labelling of dangerous substances*
Portugal: 94/361, no measures notified, Article 169 letter in 1994.
Dir 93/105/EEC—*Information required for technical dossiers*
Portugal: 94/362, no measures notified, Article 169 letter in 1994.
Dir 94/15/EC—*Genetically modified organisms*

Portugal: 94/764, no measures notified, Article 169 letter in 1994.

Radiation protection

Dir 89/618/EEC—*Health protection; radiological emergency*
Portugal: 92/509, no measures notified, reasoned opinion in 1993.
Dir 90/641/EEC—*Radiation protection; outside workers*
Portugal: 94/332, no measures notified, Article 169 letter in 1994.
Dir 92/3/EEC—*Shipments of radioactive waste*
Portugal: 94/487, no measures notified, Article 169 letter in 1994.

THE UNITED KINGDOM

Waste

Dir 91/156/EEC—*Waste*
United Kingdom: 93/872, no measures notified, Article 169 letter in 1993.
Dir 91/157/EEC—*Batteries containing dangerous substances*
United Kingdom: 92/1014, no measures notified, reasoned opinion in 1994.
Dir 92/112/EEC—*Pollution; titanium dioxide*
United Kingdom: 93/888, no measures notified, Article 169 letter in 1993.
Dir 93/86/EEC—*Batteries and accumulators containing certain dangerous substances*
United Kingdom: 94/392, no measures notified, reasoned opinion in 1994.

Water

Dir 91/271/EEC—*Urban waste-water treatment*
United Kingdom: 93/873, no measures notified, reasoned opinion in 1994.

Air

Dir 92/72/EEC—*Air pollution by ozone*
United Kingdom: 94/599, no measures notified, Article 169 letter in 1994.

Nature

Dir 92/43/EEC—*Conservation of natural habitats and wild fauna and flora*
United Kingdom: no measures notified, Article 169 letter in 1994.

Chemicals

Dir 91/325/EEC—*Labelling of dangerous substances*
United Kingdom: no measures notified, reasoned opinion in 1994.
Dir 91/410/EEC—*Labelling of dangerous substances*
United Kingdom: 92/930, no measures notified, reasoned opinion in 1994.
Dir 91/632/EEC—*Labelling of dangerous substances*
United Kingdom: 93/875, no measures notified, Article 169 letter in 1993.
Dir 92/32/EEC—*Labelling of dangerous substances*
United Kingdom: 93/1086, no measures notified, Article 169 letter in 1993 (to be terminated in 1995).
Dir 92/37/EEC—*Labelling of dangerous substances*
United Kingdom: 94/368, no measures notified, Article 169 letter in 1994.
Dir 92/69/EEC—*Labelling of dangerous substances*
United Kingdom: 93/1089, no measures notified, Article 169 letter in 1993, terminated in 1994.
Dir 93/21/EEC—*Labelling of dangerous substances*
United Kingdom: 94/956, no measures notified, Article 169 letter in 1995.
Dir 93/67/EEC—*Principles for assessment of risks*
United Kingdom: 93/1095, no measures notified, reasoned opinion in 1994.
Dir 93/72/EEC—*Labelling of dangerous substances*
United Kingdom: 94/965, no measures notified, Article 169 letter to be sent in 1995.
Dir 93/90/EEC—*Labelling of dangerous substances*
United Kingdom: 94/393, no measures notified, reasoned opinion in 1994.
Dir 93/105/EEC—*Information required for technical dossiers*
United Kingdom: 94/395, no measures notified, reasoned opinion in 1994.
Dir 94/15/EC—*Genetically modified organisms*
United Kingdom: 94/775, no measures notified, Article 169 letter in 1994.

Appendix 2

CONFORMITY OF NATIONAL IMPLEMENTING MEASURES

BELGIUM

General matters

Dir 85/337/EEC—*Assessment of effects of projects on the environment*
Belgium: 89/652, not properly implemented, referral in 1994. Case 94/133.

Waste

Dir 78/319/EEC—*Toxic and dangerous waste*
Belgium: 90/212, not properly implemented, Article 171 letter in 1990, terminated in 1994.

Water

Dir 75/440/EEC—*Surface water*
Belgium: 87/345 not properly implemented, reasoned opinion 171 to be sent in 1995.
Dir 80/68/EEC—*Protection of groundwater*
Belgium: 88/291, not properly implemented, referral (171) in 1991. Case 91/174, terminated in 1994.

Air

Dir 85/203/EEC—*Air quality; nitrogen dioxide*

Belgium: 88/23, not properly implemented, judgment in 1993. Case 91/186.

Nature

***Dir 79/409/EEC**—Conservation of wild birds*
Belgium: 90/291, not properly implemented, reasoned opinion in 1993, terminated in 1994.

Radiation protection

***Dir 84/466/EEC**—Radiation protection*
Belgium: 90/237, not properly implemented, reasoned opinion in 1992

GERMANY

General matters

***Dir 85/337/EEC**—Assessment of effects of projects on the environment*
Germany: 90/4710, not properly implemented, reasoned opinion in 1994.

Water

***Dir 75/440/EEC**—Surface water*
Germany: 87/372—not properly implemented, reasoned opinion (171) to be sent in 1995.
***Dir 80/68/EEC**—Protection of groundwater*
Germany: 86/121, not properly implemented, referral (171) in 1993, supplementary reasoned opinion to be sent in 1995.
***Dir 86/280/EEC**—Dangerous substances in the sea*
Germany: 89/427, not properly implemented, reasoned opinion in 1993.

Air

***Dir 80/779/EEC**—Air quality*
Germany: 86/119, not properly implemented, judgment in 1991. Case 88/361, terminated in 1994.
***Dir 82/884/EEC**—Lead in the air*

Germany: 88/36, not properly implemented, judgment in 1991. Case 89/59, terminated in 1994.
Dir 85/203/EEC—*Air quality; nitrogen dioxide*
Germany: 88/35, not properly implemented, reasoned opinion in 1990, terminated in 1994.

Nature

Dir 79/409/EEC—*Conservation of wild birds*
Germany: 86/222, not properly implemented, judgment in 1990. Case 88/288.
Germany: 89/48, not properly implemented, judgment in 1993. Case 92/345, terminated in 1994.

Chemicals

Dir 82/501/EEC—*Major-accidents hazards*
Germany: 87/219, not properly implemented, reasoned opinion in 1989.

SPAIN

General matters

Dir 85/337/EEC—*Assessment of effects of projects on the environment*
Spain: 90/129, not properly implemented, reasoned opinion in 1992.

Radiation protection

Dir 84/466/EEC—*Radiation protection*
Spain: 91/723, not properly implemented, reasoned opinion in 1993.

FRANCE

Water

Dir 80/68/EEC—*Protection of groundwater*
France: 90/352, not properly implemented, reasoned opinion in 1993.

Nature

Dir 79/409/EEC—Conservation of wild birds
France: 84/121, not properly implemented, reasoned opinion (171) in 1993. Case 90/355.

ITALY

General matters

Dir 85/337/EEC—Assessment of effects of projects on the environment
Italy: 91/794, not properly implemented, reasoned opinion in 1993.

Water

Dir 75/440/EEC—Surface water
Italy: 89/206—not properly implemented, referral to be sent in 1995.
Dir 76/160/EEC—Bathing water
Italy: 87/356—not properly implemented, referral to be sent in 1995.
Dir 78/659/EEC—Quality of fresh waters
Italy: 90/211, not properly implemented, referral in 1993. Case 93/291, judgment in 1994.
Dir 80/778/EEC—Quality of drinking water
Italy: 87/363, not properly implemented, reasoned opinion in 1988.

Nature

Dir 79/409/EEC—Conservation of wild birds
Italy: 89/573, not properly implemented, reasoned opinion in 1991, terminated in 1994.

Radiation protection

Dir 84/466/EEC—Radiation protection
Italy: 90/240, not properly implemented, judgment in 1993. Case 92/95.

NETHERLANDS

Water

Dir 80/778/EEC—Quality of drinking water
Netherlands: 91/214, not properly implemented, reasoned opinion in 1993.

Noise

Dir 86/662/EEC—Noise emissions from hydraulic excavators
Netherlands: 90/227, not properly implemented, reasoned opinion in 1991, terminated in 1994.

Nature

Dir 79/409/EEC—Conservation of wild birds
Netherlands: 85/400, not properly implemented, reasoned opinion (171) in 1993, terminated in 1994.
Netherlands: 89/60, not properly implemented, judgment (171) in 1992. Case 91/75, terminated in 1994.

Chemicals

Dir 82/501/EEC—Major-accidents hazards
Netherlands: 86/457, not properly implemented, judgment in 1992. Case 90/190, terminated in 1994.
Dir 87/217/EEC—Pollution by asbestos
Netherlands: 90/320, not properly implemented, reasoned opinion in 1993, terminated in 1994.

Radiation protection

Dir 80/836/EEC—Health protection; ionizing radiation
Netherlands: 88/488, not properly implemented, reasoned opinion in 1990.

IRELAND

General matters

Dir 85/337/EEC—Assessment of effects of projects on the environment
Ireland: 89/425, not properly implemented, reasoned opinion in 1993.

Waste

Dir 75/442/EEC—Waste
Ireland: 91/704—not properly implemented, reasoned opinion in 1993.

Water

Dir 80/68/EEC—Protection of groundwater
Ireland: 89/163, not properly implemented, reasoned opinion in 1990.
Dir 86/280/EEC—Dangerous substances in the sea
Ireland: 91/2216, not properly implemented, reasoned opinion in 1993.

Radiation protection

Dir 84/466/EEC—Radiation protection
Ireland: 90/239, not properly implemented, reasoned opinion in 1993.

LUXEMBOURG

Radiation protection

Dir 80/836/EEC—Health protection; ionizing radiation
Luxembourg: 88/487, not properly implemented, reasoned opinion in 1991.

PORTUGAL

Radiation protection

Dir 84/466/EEC—Radiation protection

Portugal: 90/242, not properly implemented, reasoned opinion in 1993.

THE UNITED KINGDOM

General matters

Dir 85/337/EEC—*Assessment of effects of projects on the environment*
United Kingdom: 91/2200, not properly implemented, reasoned opinion in 1993.

Air

Dir 85/203/EEC—*Air quality; nitrogen dioxide*
United Kingdom: 89/5110, not properly implemented, reasoned opinion in 1993.

Nature

Dir 85/411/EEC—*Conservation of wild birds*
United Kingdom: 88/26, not properly implemented, reasoned opinion in 1990, terminated in 1994.

Appendix 3

INCORRECT APPLICATION OF DIRECTIVES

BELGIUM

Waste

***Dir 85/339/EEC**—Containers for liquids for human consumption*
Belgium: 87/330, not properly applied, referral in 1989. Case 89/330.

GERMANY

General matters

***Dir 85/337/EEC**—Assessment of effects of projects on the environment*
Germany: 90/189, not properly applied, referral in 1992. Case 92/431.

Waste

***Dir 78/319/EEC**—Toxic and dangerous waste*
Germany: 90/38, not properly applied, referral in 1992. Case 92/422.

Water

***Dir 76/160/EEC**—Bathing water*
Germany: 89/317, not properly applied, reasoned opinion in 1994.
***Dir 76/464/EEC**—Dangerous substances in the sea*

Germany: 89/2343, not properly applied, reasoned opinion in 1994.
Dir 78/659/EEC—*Quality of fresh waters*
Germany: 90/2203, not properly applied, reasoned opinion in 1994.
Dir 80/778/EEC—*Quality of drinking water*
Germany: 89/650, not properly applied, reasoned opinion in 1993.
Germany: 90/4085, not properly applied, reasoned opinion in 1993.

Nature

Dir 79/409/EEC—*Conservation of wild birds*
Germany: 87/246, not properly applied, referral in 1989. Case 89/57.

GREECE

Waste

Dir 75/442/EEC—*Waste*
Greece: 89/138, not properly applied, judgment 7.4.92. Case 91/45; Article 171 letter to be sent in 1995.

Water

Dir 76/464/EEC—*Dangerous substances in the sea*
Greece: 89/303, not properly applied, reasoned opinion in 1992.
Dir 78/659/EEC—*Quality of fresh waters*
Greece: 90/2204, not properly applied, reasoned opinion in 1993, terminated in 1994.

Nature

Dir 79/409/EEC—*Conservation of wild birds*
Greece: 90/171, not properly applied, reasoned opinion in 1992, terminated in 1994.

SPAIN

Waste

Dir 75/442/EEC—*Waste*
Spain: 90/959—not properly applied, reasoned opinion in 1993.
Dir 78/319/EEC—*Toxic and dangerous waste*
Spain: 89/337, not properly applied, reasoned opinion in 1991.
Dir 85/339/EEC—*Containers for liquids for human consumption*
Spain: 87/337, not properly applied, judgment in 1991. Case 90/192.

Water

Dir 76/160/EEC—*Bathing water*
Spain: 89/418—not properly applied, referral to be sent in 1994.

Nature

Dir 79/409/EEC—*Conservation of wild birds*
Spain: 88/295, not properly applied, judgment in 1993. Case 90/355.

FRANCE

Waste

Dir 85/339/EEC—*Containers for liquids for human consumption*
France: 87/332, not properly applied, referral in 1993. Case 93/255.

Water

Dir 76/464/EEC—*Dangerous substances in the sea*
France: 91/206, not properly applied, reasoned opinion in 1993.
Dir 80/778/EEC—*Quality of drinking water*
France: 91/2316, not properly applied, reasoned opinion in 1993.
Dir 83/513/EEC—*Cadmium discharges*
France: 88/205, not properly applied, reasoned opinion in 1989, terminated in 1994.

ITALY

Waste

Dir 75/439/EEC—Disposal of waste oils
Italy: 86/419—not properly applied, judgment in 1993; Case 89/366.
Dir 75/442/EEC—Waste
Italy: 88/239—not properly applied, judgment in 1991. Case 90/33; Art 171 letter to be sent in 1995.

Water

Dir 76/464/EEC—Dangerous substances in the sea
Italy: 90/416, not properly applied, reasoned opinion in 1994.
Italy: 91/642, not properly applied, reasoned opinion in 1993.
Dir 79/923/EEC—Shellfish waters
Italy: 91/743, not properly applied, reasoned opinion in 1993.
Dir 91/271/EEC—Urban waste-water treatment
Italy: 93/786, no measures notified, reasoned opinion in 1994.

Nature

Dir 79/409/EEC—Conservation of wild birds
Italy: 87/327, not properly applied, reasoned opinion in 1989.
Italy: 91/795, not properly applied, reasoned opinion in 1993.

IRELAND

Waste

Dir 78/319/EEC—Toxic and dangerous waste
Ireland: 90/192, not properly applied, reasoned opinion in 1991.

Water

Dir 79/923/EEC—Shellfish waters
Ireland: 90/957, not properly applied, reasoned opinion in 1993, terminated in 1994.

LUXEMBOURG

Waste

Dir 85/339/EEC—Containers for liquids for human consumption
Luxembourg: 87/334, not properly applied, judgment in 1991. Case 89/252.

Water

Dir 76/464/EEC—Dangerous substances in the sea
Luxembourg: 91/207, not properly applied, reasoned opinion in 1993.
Dir 79/869/EEC—Surface water
Luxembourg: 88/530, not properly applied, reasoned opinion in 1990, terminated in 1994.

THE NETHERLANDS

Water

Dir 76/160/EEC—Bathing water
Netherlands: 89/651, not properly applied, reasoned opinion in 1992, terminated in 1994.

Nature

Dir 85/411/EEC—Conservation of wild birds
Netherlands: 90/461, not properly applied, terminated in 1994.

PORTUGAL

General matters

Dir 85/339/EEC—Containers for liquids for human consumption
Portugal: 87/338, not properly applied, reasoned opinion in 1989, terminated in 1994.

Water

Dir 76/464/EEC—*Dangerous substances in water*
Portugal: 91/556, not properly applied, reasoned opinion in 1993.

THE UNITED KINGDOM

Water

Dir 76/160/EEC—*Bathing water*
United Kingdom: 86/214, not properly applied, judgment in 1993. Case 90/56.
Dir 80/68/EEC—*Protection of groundwater*
United Kingdom: 88/354, not properly applied, reasoned opinion in 1989.
Dir 80/778/EEC—*Quality of drinking water*
United Kingdom: 87/370, not properly applied, judgment in 1992, Case 89/337.
United Kingdom: 91/772, not properly applied, reasoned opinion in 1993.

Appendix 4

ENVIRONMENTAL ASSESSMENT: STATUTORY INSTRUMENTS AND OTHER DOCUMENTS

Council Directive 85/337/EEC of 27 June 1985 on the assessment of the effects of certain public and private projects on the environment (the 'EIA Directive') is at OJ 175, p. 40 dated 5.7.85 and also Appendix 7 of Department of the Environment, 'Guide to the Procedures' (London: HMSO, 1992).

The following regulations implementing the Environmental Impact Assessment Directive in the United Kingdom and Gibraltar have been made:

1. Town and Country Planning (Assessment of Environmental Effects) Regulations 1988 (SI 1988 No. 1199)
2. Environmental Assessment (Scotland) Regulations 1988 (SI 1988 No. 1221)
3. Environmental Assessment (Salmon Farming in Marine Waters) Regulations 1988 (SI 1988 No. 1218)
4. Environmental Assessment (Afforestation) Regulations 1988 (SI 1988 No. 1207)
5. Land Drainage Improvement Works (Assessment of Environmental Effects) Regulations 1988 (SI 1988 No. 1217)
6. Highways (Assessment of Environmental Effects) Regulations 1988 (SI 1988 No. 1241)
7. Harbour Works (Assessment of Environmental Effects) Regulations 1988 (SI 1988 No. 1336)
8. Town and Country Planning General Development (Amendment) Order 1988 (SI 1988 No. 1272). *Note*: revoked by SI 1988 No. 1813 (General Development Order 1988). The 1988 Order has been replaced by the Town and Country Planning (General Permitted Development) Order 1995 (SI 1995 No. 418) and the Town and Country Planning (General Development Procedure) Order 1995 (SI 1995 No. 419)
9. Town and Country Planning (General Development) (Scotland) Amendment Order 1988 (SI 1988 No. 977)
10. Town and Country Planning (General Development) (Scotland) Amend-

ment No. 2 Order 1988 (SI 1988 No. 1249). *Note:* revoked by SI 1992 No. 224 (see item 24 below)

11. Electricity and Pipeline Works (Assessment of Environmental Effects) Regulations 1989 (SI 1989 No. 167). *Note:* revoked by SI 1990 No. 442 (see item 14 below)

12. Harbour Works (Assessment of Environmental Effects) (No. 2) Regulations 1989 (SI 1989 No. 424)

13. Town and Country Planning (Assessment of Environmental Effects) (Amendment) Regulations 1990 (SI 1990 No. 367)

14. Electricity and Pipe-line Works (Assessment of Environmental Effects) Regulations 1990 (SI 1990 No. 442) (*Note:* revoked SI 1989 No. 167)

15. Roads (Assessment of Environmental Effects) Regulations (Northern Ireland) 1988 (SR 1988 No. 344). *Note:* revoked by SR 1988 No. 3160 (NI 15) (see item 25 below)

16. Planning (Assessment of Environmental Effects) Regulations (Northern Ireland) 1989 (SR 1989 No. 20)

17. Environmental Assessment (Afforestation) Regulations (Northern Ireland) 1989 (SR 1989 No. 226)

18. Harbour Works (Assessment of Environmental Effects) Regulations (Northern Ireland) 1990 (SR 1990 No. 181)

19. Drainage (Environmental Assessment) Regulations (Northern Ireland) 1991 (SR 1991 No. 376)

20. Town and Country Planning (Assessment of Environmental Effects) (Amendment) Regulations 1992 (SI 1992 No. 1494)

21. Harbour Works (Assessment of Environmental Effects) Regulations 1992 (SI 1992 No. 1421)

22. Town and Country Planning (Simplified Planning Zones) Regulations 1992 (SI 1992 No. 2414) (reg. 22)

23. Transport and Works (Application and Objections Procedure) Rules 1992 (SI 1992 No. 2902)

24. Town and Country Planning (General Development Procedure) (Scotland) Order 1992 (SI 1992 No. 224) (art. 16)

25. Roads (Northern Ireland) Order 1993 (SR 1993 No. 3160 (NI 15)) (art. 67). *Note:* revokes SR 1988 No. 344 (see item 15 above)

26. Planning (Simplified Planning Zones) (Excluded Development) Order (Northern Ireland) 1994 (SR 1994 No. 426)

27. Town and Country Planning (Assessment of Environmental Effects) (Amendment) Regulations 1994 (SI 1994 No. 677)

28. Town and Country Planning General Development (Amendment) Order 1994 (SI 1994 No. 678)

29. Highways (Assessment of Environmental Effects) Regulations 1994 (SI 1994 No. 1002)

30. Environmental Assessment (Scotland) Amendment Regulations 1994 (SI 1994 No. 2012 (S 91))

31. Roads (Assessment of Environmental Effects) Regulations (Northern Ireland) 1994 (SR 1994 No. 316)

32. Planning (Assessment of Environmental Effects) (Amendment) Regulations (Northern Ireland) 1994 (SR 1994 No. 395)

33. Town and Country Planning (Environmental Assessment and Permitted Development) Regulations 1995 (SI 1995 No. 417)

34. Town and Country Planning (General Permitted Development) Order 1995 (SI 1995 No. 418) (*Note:* art. 3 introduces environmental assessment for otherwise permitted development)

35. Town and Country Planning (General Development Procedure) Order 1995 (SI 1995 No. 419) (*Note:* 1988 Order in respect of art. 14)

36. Town Planning (Applications) (Amendment) Regulations 1993 made pursuant to the Town Planning Ordinance. (Regulations for Gibraltar)

37. Transport and Works (Assessment of Environmental Effects) Regulations 1995 (SI 1995 No. 1541) (amends SI 1992 No. 2902)

38. Land Drainage Improvement Works (Assessment of Environmental Effects) (Amendment) Regulations 1995 (SI 1995 No. 2195)

39. Town and Country Planning (Environmental Assessment and Unauthorised Development) Regulations 1995 (SI 1995 No. 2258)

40. Electricity and Pipeline Works (Assessment of Environmental Effects) (Amendment) Regulations 1996 (SI 1996 No. 442)

SELECT BIBLIOGRAPHY

Adam, T. and Winter, G., 'Framework Element Regulations', in Winter, G. *Sources and Categories of European Law* (Baden-Baden: Nomos Verlagsgesellschaft, 1996).

Alder, J., 'Environmental Impact Assessment—The Inadequacies of English Law' (1993) *Journal of Environmental Law* Vol. 5, No. 2, 203.

Bache, I., *EU Regional Policy: Has the UK Government Succeeded in Playing the Gatekeeper Role over the Domestic Impact of the European Regional Development Fund?*, unpublished PhD thesis, University of Sheffield, 1996.

Ball, S. and Bell, S., *Environmental Law*, 3rd ed. (London: Blackstone Press, 1995).

Batelle Institute, *Rapport Final de L'étude Selection des Projets Destines à Etre Soumis à une Evaluation d'impact sur L'environnement*, ENV/513/78 (Brussels: Commission of the European Communities, 1978).

Bengoetxea, J., *The Legal Reasoning of the European Court of Justice: Towards a European Jurisprudence* (Oxford: Clarendon Press, 1993).

Bennett, G. (ed) *Towards a European Ecological Network* (London: Institute for European Environmental Policy, 1994).

Betlem, D., 'Being "Directly and Individually Concerned": The *Schutz-norm* Doctrine and *Francovich* Liability' in Reich, N. and Micklitz, H.W. (eds) *Public Interest Litigation Before the European Courts* (Baden-Baden: Nomos Verlagsgesellschaft, 1996).

Birtles, W., 'A Right to Know: The Environmental Information Regulations 1992' [1993] *Journal of Planning and Environmental Law* 615.

Birnie, P. and Boyle, A., *International Law and the Environment* (Oxford: Clarendon Press, 1992).

Boehmer-Christiansen, S., 'The Precautionary Principle in Germany—Enabling Government', in O'Riordan, T. and Cameron, J., *Interpreting the Precautionary Principle* (London: Earthscan Publications/Cameron May, 1994).

Böge, S., 'The Well-travelled Yogurt Pot: Lessons for New Freight Transport

Policies and Regional Production' (1995) *World Transport Policy and Practice* Vol. 1, No. 1, 7.

Broom, D.M., 'The Scientific Assessment of Animal Welfare' (1988) *Applied Animal Behaviour Science* 20.

—'Indicators of Poor Welfare' (1986) 142 *British Veterinary Journal* 524.

Broom, D.M. and Fraser, A.F., *Farm Animal Behaviour and Welfare* (London: Baillière, Tindall, 1989).

—'Ethical Dilemmas in Animal Usage' in Paterson, D. and Palmer, M. (eds) *The Status of Animals* (Wallingford: CAB International, 1989).

Brown, L. N. and Kennedy, T. *The Court of Justice of the European Communities* 4th ed. (London: Sweet and Maxwell, 1994).

Bulmer, S., 'Domestic Politics and European Community Policy-Making' (1983) 21 *Journal of Common Market Studies* 349.

Burnett-Hall, R., *Environmental Law* (London: Sweet and Maxwell, 1995).

Carson, R.L., *Silent Spring* (Boston: Houghton Mifflin, 1986).

Charlesworth, A., 'Examining the Applicability of the Environmental Information Regulations 1992: A Strange Case' (1995) *Journal of Environmental Law* Vol. 7, No. 2, 301.

Comijs, D., 'Individual Legal Protection under the Structural Funds' (1995) 2 MJ 187.

Commission of the European Communities (CEC), *Implementing Community Environmental Law*, COM(96) 500 final, 28.11.96. (Brussels: CEC, 1996).

—*Commission Communication to Council and European Parliament on European Community Water Policy*, COM(96) 59 final. (Brussels: CEC, 1996).

—*Highlands and Islands Single Programming Document, 1994–1999* (Luxembourg: CEC, 1995).

—*Proposal for a European Parliament and Council Decision on Community Guidelines for the Development of the Trans-European Transport Network*, COM(94) 106 final, 7.4.1994 (Brussels: CEC, 1994).

—*Report from the Commission of the Implementation of Directive 85/337/EEC* COM(93) 28 final, Vol. 12, 2.4.93 (Brussels: CEC, 1993).

—*Report to the European Council on the Adaption of Community Legislation to the Subsidiarity Principle*, COM(93) 545 final, 24.11.93 (Brussels: CEC, 1993).

Coppel, J. and O'Neill, A., 'The European Court of Justice: Taking Rights Seriously?' (1992) 29 *Common Market Law Review* 669.

Council for the Protection of Rural England (CPRE), *'Mock' EC Directive on Environmental Assessment: Proposals for Amending EC Directive 85/337/EEC* (London: CPRE, 1992).

Curtin, D. and Mortelmans, K., 'The Application and Enforcement of Community Law by the Member States: Actors in Search of a Third Generation Script', in Curtin, D. and Henkels T. (eds) *Institutional Dynamics of European Integration* (Dordrecht: Martinus Nijhoff, 1994).

Davies, P.G., 'The Environment Agency' (1994) 14 *Yearbook of European Law* 313.

Davis, K.C., *Discretionary Justice* (Baton Rouge: Louisiana State University Press, 1969).

De Búrca, G., 'The Principle of Proportionality and its Application in EC Law'
    [1993] *Yearbook of Environmental Law* 105.
Deimann, S. and Dyssli, B. (eds) *Environmental Rights* (London: Cameron May,
    1996).
Department of the Environment/Welsh Office, *Drinking Water 1995: A Report by
    the Chief Inspector, Drinking Water Inspectorate* (London: HMSO, 1996).
—*The Government Response to the Report of the Select Committee on the European
    Communities on COM(94) 612 Final* (London: HMSO, 1996).
—*Biodiversity: The UK Action Plan*, Cmnd. 2428 (London: HMSO, 1994).
—Planning Policy Guidance Note 9, *Nature Conservation* (London: HMSO,
    1994).
—*Environmental Appraisal of Development Plans: A Good Practice Guide* (London:
    HMSO, 1993).
—*Sustainable Development: The UK Strategy*, Cmnd. 2426 (London: HMSO,
    1993).
—The Government's Response to the Second Report of the House of Commons
    Select Committee on the Environment, *Coastal Zone Protection and Planning*
    (London: HMSO, 1992).
—*Policy Appraisal and the Environment: A Guide for Government Departments*
    (London: HMSO, 1991).
—*The Future of Development Plans* (London: HMSO, 1989).
—Circular 15/88 *Environmental Assessment* (London: HMSO, 1988).
Diedrichsen, T., 'The System of Legal Acts in the History of Drafts and Proposals
    of the EC Treaty', in Winter, G., *Sources and Categories of European Law* (Baden-
    Baden: Nomos Verlagsgesellschaft, 1996).
Directorate-General for Fisheries, *The New Common Fisheries Policy* (Luxembourg:
    Commission of the European Communities, 1994).
Dunleavy, P. and Rhodes, R.A., 'Core Executive Studies in Britain' (1990) 68
    Public Administration, 3.
Ehrlich, P.R. and Ehrlich, A.H., *Population, Resources, Environment: Issues in
    Human Ecology* (San Francisco: Freeman and Co., 1972).
Elworthy, S. and Holder, J., 'Blue Babies, Gastric Cancers and Green Ponds:
    The Law's Response to the Nitrate Problem' (1996) *International Journal of
    Biosciences and the Law*, Vol. 1, No. 1, 69.
Elworthy, S., *Farming for Drinking Water: Nitrate Pollution in Water—An Assessment
    of a Regulatory Regime* (Aldershot: Avebury, 1993).
European Economic Community, *Fifth Environmental Action Programme, Towards
    Sustainability—A European Community Programme of Policy and Action in Relation
    to the Environment* OJ C 138, 17.5.93 (Brussels: CEC, 1993).
—*Fourth Environmental Action Programme* OJ C 328, 19.10.87 (Brussels: CEC,
    1987).
—*Third Environmental Action Programme* OJ C 46, 7.2.83. (Brussels: CEC, 1983).
—*Second Environmental Action Programme* OJ C 139, 17.5.77. (Brussels: CEC,
    1977).

—*First Environmental Action Programme* OJ C 112, Vol. 16, 20.12.73. (Brussels: CEC, 1973).

Faure, D.S., 'Protecting Drinking Water Quality Against Contamination by Pesticides: An Alternative Regulatory Framework', (1995) 4(4) RECIEL 321–326.

—'The EC Directive on Drinking Water: Institutional Aspects' in Bergman, L. and Pugh, D.M. (eds), *Environmental Toxicology, Economics and Institutions* (Dordrecht: Kluwer, 1994).

—*International Trade in Endangered Species: A Guide to CITES* (Dordrecht/London: Nijhoff, 1989).

Fitzpatrick, B., 'Redressing the Late Implementation of the Environmental Impact Assessment Directive' (1994) *Journal of Environmental Law* Vol. 6, No. 2, 351.

Freestone, D., 'The Road from Rio: International Environmental Law After the Earth Summit' (1994) *Journal of Environmental Law* Vol. 6, No. 2, 193.

—'The Precautionary Principle', in Churchill, R. and Freestone, D., *International Law and Global Climate Change* (Dordrecht/London: Martinus Nijhoff/Graham and Trotman, 1991).

Freestone, D. and Ijlstra, T. *The North Sea: Basic Legal Documents on Regional Environmental Cooperation* (Dordrecht: Graham and Trolman/Matinus Nijhoff, 1991).

—*The North Sea: Perspectives on Regional Environmental Cooperation* (Dordrecht: Graham and Trolman/Matinus Nijhoff, 1990).

Füredi, F., 'The Dangers of Safety' (1996) *Living Marxism*, 16.

Geddes, A., *Protection of Individual Rights under EC Law* (London: Butterworths, 1995).

—'Unlocking the Doors of Judicial Protection' (1993) *New Law Journal* 98.

—'Locus Standi and EEC Environmental Measures' (1992) *Journal of Environmental Law* Vol. 4, No. 1, 29.

Grant, M., 'Development and the Protection of Birds: the Swale Decision' (1991) *Journal of Environmental Law* Vol. 3, No. 1, 150.

Gray T.S. (ed) *UK Environmental Policy in the 1990s* (London: Macmillan, 1995).

Gundling, L., 'The Status in International Law of the Precautionary Principle' (1990) *International Journal of Estuarine and Coastal Law* Vol. 5, Nos. 1–3, 23.

Habermas, J., *Toward a Rational Society* (London: Heinemann, 1971).

Hadfield, B., *The Constitution of Northern Ireland* (Belfast: SLS Legal Publications, 1989).

Haigh, N., *Manual of Environmental Policy: The EC and Britain*, 3rd release (London: Longman, 1996).

—'Devolved Responsibility and Centralization: Effects of EEC Environmental Policy' (1986) 64 *Public Administration* 197.

Haigh, N. and Lanigan, C., 'Impact of the European Union on UK Environmental Policy Making', in Gray, T.S. (ed) *UK Environmental Policy in the 1990s* (London: Macmillan, 1995).

Hardin, G., 'The Tragedy of the Commons' (1968) *Science* Vol. 162, 1243.

Hartley, T., *The Foundations of European Community Law* (Oxford: Oxford University Press, 1994).

Hession, M. and Macrory, R., 'Maastricht and the Environmental Policy of the Community: Legal Issues of a New Environment Policy', in O'Keeffe, D. and Twomey, P. (eds) *Legal Issues of the Maastricht Treaty* (London: Wiley Chancery, 1994).

—'Balancing Trade Freedom with the Requirements of Sustainable Development', in Emilion, N. and O'Keeffe, D., *The European Union and World Trade Law: After the GATT Uruguay Round* (Chichester: Wiley, 1996).

Hilson, C., 'Ex parte Friends of the Earth: Enforcement of the Drinking Water Directive' (1995) 32 *Common Market Law Review*, 1461.

Hilson, C. and Cram, I. 'Judicial Review and Environmental Law: Is There a Coherent View of Standing?' (1996) 16 (1) *Legal Studies*, 1.

HM Government, *This Common Inheritance*, Cm. 1200 (London: HMSO, 1990).

—*Privatisation of the Water Authorities in England and Wales* Cmnd. 9734 (London: HMSO, 1986).

Hohmann, H., *Precautionary Legal Duties and Principles of Modern International Environmental Law* (Dordrecht/London: Martinus Nijhoff/Graham and Trotman, 1994).

Holder, J., 'A Dead End for Direct Effect? Prospects for Enforcement of European Community Environmental Law by Individuals' (1996) *Journal of Environmental Law* Vol. 8, No. 2, 323.

—'The Sellafield Litigation and Questions of Causation in Environmental Law' (1994) 47(II) *Current Legal Problems* 287.

Holder, J. and Elworthy, S., 'The Drinking Water Directive Cases' (1994) 31 *Common Market Law Review* 123–135.

House of Commons Environment Committee, *Environmental Issues in Northern Ireland*, First Report, Session 1990–92 HC 39 (London: HMSO, 1992).

—*Coastal Zone Protection and Planning*, Second Report, Vol. II, Session 1991–92, HC Paper 17-II (London: HMSO, 1992).

—*Pollution of Beaches*, Fourth Report, Vol. 1, Session 1989–90, HC Paper 12-I (London: HMSO, 1990).

House of Lords Select Committee on the European Communities, *Drinking Water*, Fourth Report, Session 1995–96, HL Paper 31 (London: HMSO, 1996).

—*Bathing Water Revisited*, Seventh Report, Session 1994–5, HL Paper 41 (London: HMSO, 1995).

—*Municipal Waste Water Treatment*, Tenth Report, Vol. 1 Session 1990–91, HL Papers 50-I (London: HMSO, 1991).

—*Implementation and Enforcement of Environmental Legislation*, Ninth Report, Session 1991–92, HL Paper 53 (London: HMSO, 1992).

—*Environmental Assessment of Projects*, Eleventh Report, Session 1980–81, (London: HMSO, 1981).

—*Approximation of Laws under Article 100 of the EEC Treaty*, 22 Report, Session 1977–78, HL Paper 131 (London: HMSO, 1978).

Jans, J., *European Environmental Law* (Deventer: Kluwer, 1995).

Jewkes, P., 'The Principle of Subsidiarity: Its Effect on Existing and Future EC Environmental Regulation' (1994) 6 *Environmental Law and Management* 165.

Jordan, A. and O'Riordan, T., 'The Precautionary Principle in United Kingdom Law and Policy', in Gray, T.S. (ed) *UK Environmental Policy in the 1990s* (London: Macmillan Press, 1995).

Jowell, J. and Lester, A., 'Proportionality: Neither Novel nor Dangerous' in Jowell, J. and Oliver, D. (eds) *New Directions in Judicial Review* (London: Stevens, 1989).

Kapteyn, P.J.G. and VerLoren van Themaat, P., in Gormley, L. (ed) *Introduction to the Law of the European Communities*, 2nd ed. (Deventer: Kluwer, 1989).

Krämer, L. 'The Elaboration of EC Environmental Law', in Winter, G. (ed) *European Environmental Law: A Comparative Perspective* (Aldershot: Dartmouth, 1996).

—'Public Interest Litigation in Environmental Matters Before European Courts' (1996) *Journal of Environmental Law* Vol. 8, No. 1, 1.

—'Rights of Complaint and Access to Information at the Commission of the EC', in Deimann, S. and Dyssli, B. (eds) *Environmental Rights* (London: Cameron May, 1996).

—*The EC Treaty and Environmental Law*, 2nd ed. (London: Sweet and Maxwell, 1995).

—*European Environmental Law Casebook* (London: Sweet and Maxwell, 1993).

—'Environmental Protection and Article 30 EEC Treaty' (1993) 30 CML Rev 111.

—*Focus on European Environmental Law* (London: Sweet and Maxwell, 1992).

—'Community Environmental Law—Towards a Systematic Approach' [1991] 11 *Yearbook of European Law* 151.

—'The Implementation of Community Environmental Directives within Member States: Some Implications of the Direct Effect Doctrine (1991) *Journal of Environmental Law* Vol. 3, No. 1, 39.

Lasok, D. and Bridge, J.W., *Law and Institutions of the European Union*, 6th ed. (London: Butterworths, 1994).

Lee, N. and Wood, C., 'Environmental Impact Assessment Procedures Within the European Community', in Roberts, R. and Roberts, T. (eds) *Planning and Ecology* (London: Chapman and Hall, 1984).

—'Environmental Impact Assessment and the Preparation of Economic Plans and Programmes in the European Communities', ENV/740/79 (Brussels: CEC, 1979).

—'Methods of Environmental Impact Assessment for Major Projects and Physical Plans', ENV/36/78 (Brussels, CEC, 1977).

—'Environmental Impact Assessment of Physical Plans in the European Communities', ENV/37/78 (Brussels, CEC, 1977).

—'The Introduction of Environmental Impact Statements in the European Communities', ENV/197/76 (Brussels: CEC, 1976).

Lister-Kaye, J., *Ill Fares the Land: A Sustainable Land Ethic for the Sporting Estates of the Highlands and Islands of Scotland* (Perth: Scottish Natural Heritage, 1994).

Lomas, O. and McEldowney, J. (eds) *Frontiers of Environmental Law* (London: Chancery, 1991).

Lyster, S., *International Wildlife Law* (Cambridge: Grotius Publications, 1985).

Macrory, R., 'The Enforcement of Community Environmental Law: Some Critical Issues' (1992) 29 *Common Market Law Review* 347.

—'Environmental Law: Shifting Discretions and the New Formalism', in Lomas, O. (ed) *Frontiers of Environmental Law* (London: Chancery, 1991).

Maloney, W. and Richardson, J., *Managing Policy Change in Britain: the Politics of Water* (Edinburgh: Edinburgh University Press, 1995).

Mayda, J., 'Reforming Impact Assessment: Issues, Premises, and Elements' (1996) *Impact Assessment* Vol. 14, No. 1, 87.

Mazey, S.P. and Richardson, J.J., 'British Pressure Groups in the European Community' (1992) 45 *Parliamentary Affairs* 92.

McAleavey, P., *Policy Implementation as Incomplete Contracting: the European Regional Development Fund*, unpublished PhD thesis, European University Institute, Florence, 1995.

McHarg, I., *Design With Nature* (New York: Natural History Press, 1969).

McManus, F., *Public Health Administration in Edinburgh 1833–1879*, unpublished M. Litt. thesis, University of Edinburgh, 1984.

Meadows, D.H., Randers, J. and Behrens, W.W., *The Limits to Growth: A Report for the Club of Rome's Project on the Predicament of Mankind* (London: Earth Island Limited, 1972).

Mertz, S., 'The European Economic Community Directive on Environmental Assessments: How Will it Affect United Kingdom Developers?' [1989] *Journal of Planning and Environmental Law* 483.

Miller, C. 'Environmental Rights: European Fact or English Fiction?' (1995) *Journal of Law and Society* Vol. 22, 374.

Ministry of Agriculture, Fisheries and Food, *Codes of Recommendations for the Welfare of Livestock Cattle* (London: MAFF Publications, 1991).

Moravcsik, A. 'Preferences and Power in the European Community: A Liberal Intergovernmental Approach' (1993) 31 *Journal of Common Market Studies* 473.

Oliver, P., *Free Movement of Goods in the European Community Under Articles 30 to 36 of the Rome Treaty*, 3rd ed. (London: Sweet and Maxwell, 1996).

Paterson, D. and Palmer, M. (eds) *The Status of Animals* (Wallingford: CAB International, 1989).

Pernice, I., 'Kriterien der normativen von Umweltrichtlinien der EG im Lichte der Rechtsprechung des EuGH' [1994] *Europarecht* 325.

Pescatore, P., 'The Doctrine of "Direct Effect": An Infant Disease of Community Law' (1983) 8 *European Environmental Law Review* 155.

Prechal, S., *Directives in European Community Law* (Oxford: Clarendon Press, 1995).

Purdue, M., 'The Possible Will Take A Long While—Enforcing Compliance with the Drinking Water Directive' (1994) *Journal of Environmental Law* Vol. 7, No. 1, 92.

—'The Impact of Section 54A' (1994) *Journal of Planning and Environmental Law* 399.

—'A Harpoon for Greenpeace?: Judicial Review of the Regulation of Radioactive Substances' (1994) *Journal of Environmental Law* Vol. 6, No. 2, 337.

—'Integrated Pollution Control in the Environmental Protection Act 1990: A Coming of Age of Environmental law?' (1991) 54 *Modern Law Review*, 534.

Redman, M., 'European Community Planning Law' (1993) *Journal of Planning and Environmental Law* 999

Rehbinder, E. and Stewart, R., *Environmental Protection Policy* (Berlin: Walter de Gruyter, 1985).

Reid, C., *Nature Conservation Law* (Edinburgh/London: W. Green/Sweet and Maxwell, 1994).

Richardson, G., Ogus, A. and Burrows, P., *Policing Pollution: A Study of Regulation and Enforcement* (Oxford: Clarendon, 1982).

Rodgers, C.P., 'Environmental Gain, Set-aside and the Implementation of EU Agricultural Reform in the United Kingdom' in Rodgers, C.P. (ed) *Nature Conservation and Countryside Law* (Cardiff: University of Wales Press, 1996).

Ross, M. 'Beyond *Francovich*' (1993) 56 *Modern Law Review* 55.

Royal Commission on Environmental Pollution, Tenth Report, *Tackling Pollution: Experience and Prospects*, Cmnd. 9149 (London: HMSO, 1984).

Sandalow, T. and Stein, E., *Courts and Free Markets: Perspectives from the United States and Europe*, Vol. 1 (Oxford: Clarendon Press).

Sands, P., *Principles of International Environmental Law* (Manchester: Manchester University Press, 1995).

Schermers, H. and Waelbroeck, D., *Judicial Protection in the European Communities*, 5th ed. (Deventer: Kluwer, 1992).

Schrecker, T.P., *The Political Economy of Environmental Hazards* (Ottawa: Law Reform Commission of Canada, 1984).

Schwing, R.C. and Albers, W.A., *Societal Risk Assessment: How Safe Is Safe Enough?* (New York: Plenum, 1980).

Scott, C., 'Continuity and Change in British Food Law' (1990) 53 *Modern Law Review*, 785.

Scott, J., 'Environmental Compatibility and the Community's Structural Fund: A Legal Analysis' (1996) *Journal of Environmental Law* Vol. 8, No. 1, 99.

—*Development Dilemmas in the European Community* (Buckingham and Philadelphia: Open University Press, 1995).

Sheate, W., 'The Search for a UK Nuclear Waste Disposal Facility: A Case Study of Disputed 'Project' Definition under the EC Directive 85/337/EEC on EIA' (1996) *Environmental Policy and Practice* Vol. 6, No. 2, 75.

—'Amending the EC Directive 85/337/EEC on Environmental Impact Assessment' (1995) *European Environmental Law Review*, Vol 4, No. 3, 77.

—'Electricity Generation and Transmission: A Case Study of Problematic EIA Implementation in the UK' (1995) *Environmental Policy and Practice* Vol. 5, No. 1, 7.

—*Making an Impact: A Guide to EIA Law and Policy* (London: Cameron May, 1994).

—'Strategic Environmental Assessment in the Transport Sector' (1992) *Project Appraisal* Vol. 7, No. 3, 170.

—*The EEC Draft Directive on the Environmental Assessment of Projects: its History, Development and Implications*, Unpublished MSc thesis, University of London, Imperial College, 1984.

Sheate, W. and Macrory, R., 'Agriculture and the EC Environmental Assessment Directive: Lessons for Community Policy-Making' (1989) *Journal of Common Market Studies* Vol. 28, No. 1, 68.

Snyder, F., 'The Effectiveness of European Community Law: Institutions, Processes, Tools, and Techniques' (1993) 56 *Modern Law Review* 19.

Somsen, H. and Bovis, C., 'Enforcement of EC Environmental Law and the Implications of the Francovich Judgment' [1992] *Water Law* 184.

Somsen, H. and Sprokkereef, A., 'Making Subsidiarity Work for the Environmental Policy of the European Community: the Role of Science' (1996) *International Journal of Biosciences and the Law* Vol. 1, No. 1, 37.

Steiner, J., *Enforcing EC Law* (London: Blackstone Press, 1995).

—*Textbook of EEC Law* (London: Blackstone Press, 1988).

Stuart, G. Combating Non-Compliance with European Community Directives (1994) 6 ELM. 160.

Temple-Lang, J., 'Community Constitutional Law: Article 5 EEC Treaty' (1990) 27 *Common Market Law Review* 645.

Teubner, G., 'The Invisible Cupola: From Causal to Collective Attribution in Ecological Liability', in Teubner, G., Farmer, L. and Murphy, D. (eds) *Environmental Law and Ecological Responsibility: The Concept and Practice of Ecological Self-Organisation* (Chichester: Wiley, 1994).

Toth, A., 'The Legal Status of the Declarations Attached to the Single European Act' (1986) 23 *Common Market Law Review* 802.

Tromans, S., 'Town and Country Planning and Environmental Protection' (1991) *Journal of Planning and Environmental Law: The Planning Balance in the 1990s* 6.

Turner, S. and Morrow, K., *Northern Ireland Environmental Law* (Dublin: Gill and Macmillan, 1996).

Van Gerven, W., 'Bridging the Gap Between Community and National Laws: Towards a Principle of Homogeneity in the Field of Legal Remedies' (1995) 32 *Common Market Law Review*, 679.

Van Kinsbergen, K. and Verbeek, B., 'The Politics of Subsidiarity in the European Union' (1994) 32 *Journal of Common Market Studies* 215.

von Moltke, K. 'The *Vorsorgeprinzip* in West German Environmental Law', in Royal Commission on Environmental Pollution, Twelfth Report, *Best Practicable Environmental Option*, Cm. 310 (London: HMSO, 1988).

—'The Legal Basis for Environmental Policy' (1977) *Environmental Policy and Law* Vol. 3, 136.

Ward, A. 'The Right Environmental Protection: A Case Study of United

Kingdom Judicial Decisions Concerning the Environmental Assessment Directive' (1993) *Journal of Environmental Law* Vol. 5, No. 2, 221.

Warren, L., 'Law and Policy for Marine Protected Areas', in Rodgers, C.P. (ed) *Nature Conservation and Countryside Law* (Cardiff, University of Wales Press, 1996).

Weir, S. and Hall, W., *Democratic Audit: Ego-Trip—Extra-Governmental Organisations and their Accountability* (London: Charter 88 Trust, 1994).

Wilkinson, '*Reay and Hope* v. *British Nuclear Fuels plc*' [1994] *Water Law* 22.

—'Maastricht and the Environment' (1992) *Journal of Environmental Law* Vol. 4, No. 2, 221.

Wils, W., 'The Birds Directive 15 Years Later: A Survey of the Case Law and a Comparison with the Habitats Directive' (1994) *Journal of Environmental Law* Vol. 6, No. 2, 219.

Winter, G., 'The Directive: Problems of Construction and Directions for Reform', in Winter, G., *Sources and Categories of European Law* (Baden Baden: Nomos Verlagsgesellschaft, 1996).

—(ed) *European Environmental Law: A Comparative Perspective* (Aldershot: Dartmouth, 1996).

Wood, C. and Jones, C., 'The Impact of Environmental Assessment on Local Planning Authorities' (1992) *Journal of Environmental Planning and Management* Vol. 35, No 2, 115.

—*Monitoring Environmental Assessment and Planning* (London: HMSO, 1991).

Woolf, H. and Jowell, J., *de Smith's Judicial Review of Administrative Action* (London: Sweet and Maxwell, 1995).

World Health Organisation, *European Standards for Drinking Water* 2nd ed. (Geneva: WHO, 1970).

Wyatt, D. and Dashwood, A., *The Substantive Law of the EEC* (London: Sweet and Maxwell, 1980).

Wynne, B., 'Uncertainty and Environmental Learning: Reconceiving Science and Policy in the Preventive Paradigm' (1992) 2 *Global Environmental Change* 111.

Wynne, B. and Meyer, S., 'How Science Fails the Environment' (1993) *New Scientist* 33.

INDEX